W9-CAF-196

PAUL THE CONVERT

PAUL THE CONVERT

The Apostolate and
Apostasy of
Saul the Pharisee

Alan F. Segal

YALE UNIVERSITY PRESS
New Haven and London

Designed by James J. Johnson
and set in Sabon Roman by
The Composing Room of Michigan.

Library of Congress Cataloging-in-Publication Data

Segal, Alan F., 1945–
    Paul the convert : the apostolate and apostasy of Saul the
Pharisee / Alan F. Segal.
        p.   cm.
    Includes bibliographical references.
    ISBN 0-300-04527-1 (alk. paper)
    1. Paul, the Apostle, Saint—Views on Jews and Judaism.   2. Paul,
the Apostle, Saint—Conversion.   3. Bible. N.T. Epistles of Paul—
Criticism, interpretation, etc.   4. Christianity and other
religions—Judaism.   5. Judaism—Relations—Christianity.
6. Judaism—History—Talmudic period, 10–425.   7. Apostasy—Judaism.
I. Title.
BS2655.J4S44   1990
226'.606—dc20   89–35931
                                                                          CIP

To Meryl, Ethan, and Jordan

CONTENTS

ACKNOWLEDGMENTS

Scholarship, like religion, is both a communal and a solitary enterprise. Scholarship is normally thought of as private research, since the scholar spends innumerable hours of quiet reading and thinking in libraries. But there is also a social dimension to scholarship, when ideas are debated in groups or manuscripts are lent to others for their comments. The scholar relies on the work and opinions of so many colleagues in more ways than can be adequately acknowledged in a personal note.

To write a book on Paul I needed a great deal of help of that kind. I further imposed on my colleagues in New Testament studies in many ways, which I should and can acknowledge publicly. I should like to thank David Balch, Nils Blatz, Thomas Boslooper, James Charlesworth, Adela Yarbro Collins, Celia Deutsch, James Dunn, Jarl Fossum, Paula Fredricksen, John Gager, Henry Green, Joan Hart, Holland Hendrix, Lawrence Hurtado, Don Juel, Lou Martyn, Wayne Meeks, Elaine Pagels, Sally Purvis, Gilles Quispel, Peter Richardson, Harold Remus, Robin Scroggs, David Weiss-Halivni, and Steven Wilson. They agreed to read parts or all of this manuscript, making comments on how to improve it. Many others, not mentioned here, offered suggestions and guidance along the way. The list is too long: I should not have imposed on so many. But all made suggestions for which I am grateful. My need for so much help underlines the difficulty in crossing the boundaries that separate scholars of early Christianity and early rabbinic Judaism. The difficulties in alternating between Semitic studies and Greek studies is but the beginning of the problem. The methodology of New Testament scholarship constrains the novice. These scholars helped me master it.

I should also like to thank Avent Beck, Ted Byfield, Alexandria Kaufman, Jonathan Lupkin, Allan Pantuck, Terry Todd, and Tommy Williams for assisting me with editing, proofreading, and indexing.

Several parts of this book were published previously in slightly different forms. Short segments appeared in a different context in my book *Rebecca's Children*. Parts of chapters 1 and 3 were published in volume 3 of *Anti-Judaism* and in *SBL Seminar Papers of 1988*. Chapter 2 was published in the *SBL Seminar Papers of 1986*. Chapter 7 was published in *Studies in Religion* in 1986 and republished in *The Other Judaisms of Late Antiquity*. All are republished here with the permission of the publishers, though some have been altered substantially.

New Testament quotations are from the Revised Standard Version (RSV), unless otherwise noted.

INTRODUCTION

Jesus left no writing, thereby preventing any direct reconstruction of his self-consciousness. We must suppose his intentions indirectly, from the reports of his disciples, which were often filtered orally through a generation or two of well-meaning and deeply committed reporters. By contrast, Paul wrote directly to his contemporaries, so his thoughts and motivations lie open to analysis. Like Luke (1:2) but earlier chronologically, Paul admits to having never met Jesus in the flesh. He is our earliest witness to the faith in Christ rather than to the life of Jesus. For that reason alone, he has been the subject of innumerable books in Christian history. Paul is also important for Jewish history. He is one of only two Pharisees to have left us any personal writings (e.g., Phil. 3:5).[1] As the only first-century Jew to have left confessional reports of mystical experience (2 Cor. 12:1–10),[2] Paul should be treated as a major source in the study of first-century Judaism.

Yet Paul is hardly ever read seriously by Jewish historians, for he angers Jews of today as much as he angered his contemporaries, both Jewish and Christian. His experience of the postresurrection Christ in visions, though never in the flesh, also made his apostolate suspect to his fellow apostles.[3] But Paul's meditations on the significance of the Christ became the basis of Western understandings of Jesus' purpose, at least as much as those of the disciples did.

Paul's letters are hardly easy to read now, for they are full of ambiguities, complexities, and attacks on half-forgotten adversaries. Yet they reveal the thought and sensibility of one of the most influential persons in the West, as well as glimpses of a continually fascinating personal religious quest. Paul is familiar with Greek rhetoric, as well as Hellenistic Jewish attitudes, Jewish mysticism and apocalypticism, and incipient rabbinism. Scholars now consider these different realms of thought, concentrating their life's work on one or another. Had Paul not evinced them all, few scholars would have thought them to be compatible. Further, these realms of thought are almost impenetrable to modern readers. Without knowing about first-century Judaism, modern readers—even those committed by faith to reading him—are bound to misconstrue Paul's writing. To make matters worse, Paul sometimes outlines different opinions on the same subject without bothering to explain how, why, or if he has changed his mind.

Because Paul's letters are ancient, they challenge modern sensibilities. Paul also challenges any modern sensibility because he is personally relevant to modern faith and to the contemporary predicament of Judaism and Christianity. His thoughts are fiercely personal in a way that still influences people. Behind these letters to his churches are the ruminations of a man who occasionally reveals an intensely personal religious conversion, similar to those reported today. He builds a picture of the relation between his previous life in Pharisaism and his present one in the new Christian sect; that picture has become the basis of Christian understandings of Judaism. In the process, however, Paul's personal and unique perspective has become obscured. As a result, popular Christian notions of Judaism are badly mistaken.

Paul's letters record the thinking of a Pharisee who has converted to a new, apocalyptic, mystical, and—to many of his contemporaries—suspiciously heretical form of Judaism. Even after his conversion, his thinking changes with new events. Though his conversion experience carries him from one variety of Judaism to another, his education in Christianity comes from a gentile community, and his active mission furthers that new enterprise. Although Paul evidently missionized Jews and spent time with Jewish Christians, his writing mostly represents the issues of the gentile Christian community. Paul is a trained Pharisee who became the apostle to the gentiles. His Judaism is Pharisaic and his Christianity is mainly the product of his experience on his gentile mission. I find this combination as novel and explosive as did the ancient world.

Paul's writings are neither systematic nor simple. His writings give evidence of each stage of his life, from Pharisee to fiery young passionate believer, angered by the lack of acceptance his colleagues have shown him, to mature apostle, who gave way on his personal opinions so that the church could progress unhindered. He both challenges and attempts to reconcile his converts to the Jewish Christian community. His letters must be read in the context of his biography, wherever it can be established, and in the context of Jewish life of his day.

Although we have considerable writings from Paul, his biography is incompletely known.[4] To add to this problem, we know little about Judaism or Christianity in the first century; what we do know is refracted through our personal commitments and biases. Paul's letters, though widely read, thus turn out to be among the most difficult and complicated writings in Western literature.

In order fully to appreciate Paul's letters, they need to be read in light of religious experience everywhere, with knowledge of both the atmosphere in which he lived and a modern understanding of human religious behavior. Thus, I will rely on contemporary observations of religious behavior, especially religious conversion.

Paul's letters have been discussed thoroughly by scholars more familiar with them than I am. What, then, could even a concerned Jewish scholar add to the discussion? In this book I write about Paul's Judaism, his Pharisaic education and training before he became a Christian, insofar as this is possible. But I concentrate on the Jewish context of his religious struggle following his conversion. Most scholars assume that once Paul had converted, his writings became irrelevant to Judaism. This is simply not so: Paul wrote to a brand-new Christian community that was still largely Jewish, giving us the only witness to a world of everyday Hellenistic Judaism now vanished. I try to show how these struggles with the Judaism and Jewish Christians of his day informed his Christian commitment. I do not, therefore, systematically portray Paul, but I outline the beginnings of a systematic reappraisal of his work. If I offer what might seem to be an unsystematic, incomplete, and necessarily unfinished reading of Paul, I gain confidence from the fact that Paul's own work is also unsystematic, incomplete, and unfinished.

I am not merely reappraising a first-century heresy. Many of Paul's observations about Christianity mirror contemporary issues within the Jewish community. But I do not engage in a romantic appreciation of Paul's or Jesus' early Jewish life, supposedly available to every Jew naturally through participation in Judaism and impossible for Christians to appreciate.[5] Yet knowing Jewish texts and sensibilities occasionally allows an appreciation for Paul's predicaments and opinions, even if I disagree with Paul's decisions.

However much I may disagree with Paul, my reading accedes to the authenticity of Paul's conversion experience. Religious conflicts of two thousand years ago should not prevent scholars from appreciating genuine religious sentiments, even though they may contradict their own. Paul's religious insights were surely valid ones for him. Religion must take many forms to speak to the different needs of human society. Although Paul met opposition from many Jews of his own day, because they believed Jesus to be neither messiah nor God, his greatest battles were fought against other Christians, especially Jewish Christians. Further, there is little evidence in Paul's letters that he thought of himself as leaving Judaism, though he was aware that his opinions could be construed as transgression. Rather, Paul considered himself as part of a new Jewish sect and hoped to convince both fellow Christians and Jews of his vision of redemption. When Paul perceived the widening gap between Judaism and Christianity, it caused him much pain.

History after Paul has judged Christianity to be different from Judaism. That fact seems undeniable today, but it was hardly evident in the first century. Paul would have objected strenuously against any distinction between his faith and his Judaism, for he continuously preached unity in Christ between Jews and Christians. Yet Paul's inclusion of both gentiles and Jews equally in his community was ironically one great step separating Judaism from Christianity. Paul's Jewish past and the terms of his conversion are the keys to understanding why he advocated inclusion in Christianity. Knowing where he came from and where he was determined to go—what his conversion meant to him—furthers our appreciation of Paul's achievements.

JEWISH HISTORY IN PAUL'S WRITINGS

A Jewish scholar can make a further contribution to the study of Paul: he or she can clarify Jewish history from Paul's writings. Many fundamental rabbinic traditions can no longer be assumed to date from the time of Jesus, though they purport to be even more ancient.[6] Although rabbinic Judaism claims the Pharisees as forebears, the differences between the rabbis and the Pharisees are great. The Pharisaic movement was but one among a variety of sects in the first century, and rabbinic Judaism matured with the publication of the Mishnah around 220 C.E. The Pharisaic traditions described in the Mishnah are of uncertain date. Preserved in oral form, the Pharisaic traditions may have originated in the first two centuries or much earlier, as is often claimed. As in any oral literature, these traditions may have been altered in transmission, especially by rabbinic editors in the late second century. Rabbinic documents transform the

Pharisees' first-century position of shared power into one of comfortable community leadership in the second, third, and fourth centuries.

Rabbinic literature may naturally and unconsciously distort Jewish traditions in the first century, making Paul's contemporary writings an important supplement to rabbinic witness. This is not a matter of concern to scholars alone. A new historical understanding of the development of rabbinic tradition threatens contemporary Jewish assumptions about the divinely inspired continuity of the Jewish legal system. Ironically, the New Testament gives us evidence of Jewish thought and practice in the first century, helping to establish the authenticity of some mishnaic reports. And Paul is almost certainly the only New Testament writer to represent Pharisaic Judaism, though he gives us the view of someone who left it unconditionally.

There is another unanticipated consequence of our new critical perspective on early rabbinism. New understanding of the development of rabbinic tradition has also cast into serious doubt two centuries of Christian scholarship, which too blithely used the Mishnah and Talmud as the main source for understanding the Jewish opposition to Jesus. The converse methodology actually seems more reliable. Study of the New Testament, undeniably a first-century source, has proven to be quite useful for validating mishnaic recollections of first-century Jewish life, but such comparisons are in their infancy. The New Testament is also better evidence for Hellenistic Judaism than is the Mishnah for first-century rabbinism. The famous handbook of Jewish background to the New Testament by Strack-Billerbeck, *Kommentar zu Neuen Testament aus Talmud und Midrasch,*[7] lists important midrashic and mishnaic traditions for each New Testament passage. In spite of the handbook's sometimes unappreciated erudition, its methodology is entirely suspect. Rather, a commentary to the Mishnah should be written, using the New Testament as marginalia that demonstrates antiquity.

Paul clearly gives us important information about first-century Pharisaism and Hellenistic Judaism in general, information that even today has been too easily discounted by an antagonistic Jewish world. Scholars of Jewish studies frequently disparage Paul's writings, as if to say "Nothing serious can be concluded about Judaism from such a person." This is a pretext for ignoring writing with disturbing evaluations of Judaism. It is a pity that few Jewish writers have attempted to understand Paul. Because of the polemical context that forms the basis of Paul's letters, Christianity has been sadly bereft of all but the most daring of Jewish scholars' observations of Paul. Contemporary Jewish scholars, who might be able to read

Paul with new insights for Christians, rarely read Paul at all, and almost never as valid religious experience; instead, they think of him as an apostate. There is some justification for this evaluation, from the perspective of Judaism, as we shall see below. But the term *apostate* must be carefully discussed and nuanced.[8]

To be used effectively, the New Testament should be read with allowance for its anti-Pharisaic and sometimes anti-Jewish tone. Almost every page of the New Testament reveals an intolerance of its Jewish milieu that is borne of an intensely aggravated family conflict. Unfortunately the animosity increases over time. Since Paul's letters are the earliest documents, they are in some ways least affected by dogmatic vituperation. Eloquently describing the lack of acceptance by his peers of his radical interpretation of Torah, Paul's letters turn out to be the easiest to control against the bias of Christian anti-Judaism, although this is not easy.[9] Modern studies of the attitude changes that accompany conversion are helpful in separating fact from opinion in Paul's writing. Paul is, in fact, our best witness to the issues that affected first-century Jews. In spite of his complex feelings about Judaism and his uniquely Christian perspective, Paul is, ironically, one of the most fruitful and reliable sources for first-century Jewish religious life.

¶ PAUL THE JEW

CHAPTER ONE

PAUL AND LUKE

LUKE'S PORTRAIT OF PAUL

In popular Christianity, Paul's name leads the list of converts. Christian history makes him almost the first Christian convert and certainly the most famous one.[1] In the West, Paul typifies conversion, even outside religious contexts. When social scientists offer examples of a sudden emotional conversion, they usually cite Paul first, along with Augustine and Luther. Paul's sudden conversion is, however, neither the only description of his religious experience nor one typical of the first generation of Christians. And Paul's entrance into Christianity is certainly atypical of the apostles, for he never met the man Jesus.[2] Paul is not converted by Jesus' teachings, but rather by an experience, a revelation of Christ, which radically reorients his life. Initially a religious persecutor of Christians, he becomes a principal Christian evangelist.

The stories of Paul's conversion should be carefully evaluated. The description in the Acts of the Apostles of Paul's sudden conversion on the road to Damascus is primarily the creation of Luke, Paul's biographer, for Paul never describes his conversion directly. This presents modern New Testament scholarship with an unexpectedly difficult problem. Although Paul wrote one of the largest portions of the New Testament (second only to Luke's), he left us no straightforward, systematic record of his life. This is not surprising, considering that he also tells us little about Jesus. Like the other first-generation Christians, Paul was intensely interested in the consequences of faith in Christ and less interested in the man Jesus. The earliest followers of Jesus and Paul gave us only fragmentary stories meant to demonstrate a principle. The rabbis wrote no biographies either, often transmitting their teachings anonymously; so too the lack of an auto-biography of Jesus or Paul implies a Jewish religious sensibility, according to which individuals might transmit religious truths but did not claim to innovate.

By contrast, Hellenistic Jewish writers give us biographies of the great figures of Jewish history. Philo writes biographies of each patriarch and concentrates on Moses in several works. Josephus gives us a full account of his own life, clearly meant to justify his radical change of allegiance during the great revolt against Rome. Curiosity for biographical detail and the search for historical significance were no less prevalent in the Hellenistic world than in our own. In Christianity the Hellenistic conventions for discussing religious figures won out over native ones. As important as Paul's concerns were, he did not answer all the questions of the early Christian community. Mark, Matthew, and John realized the need for an account of the life of Christ, and Luke, after writing his gospel of the Christ, also realized the need for a biography of Paul, which he provides in Acts of the Apostles. Luke wrote perhaps fifty years after Paul and in an atmosphere of more confident gentile Christianity. His writing seems to reflect gentile and diaspora sensibilities rather than the sensibilities of the rabbis and the earliest church, though he is concerned with the rift be-tween Jewish and gentile Christians.

The Gospels tell the story of Jesus' life, but they are not what we would call biographical; they exemplify and illustrate the theological beliefs of the evangelists through the events of Jesus' life. Luke's description of Paul is not impartial biography either, for it was intended to dramatize the early church's journey from Judea into the gentile world. In some ways Luke downplays Paul's claims, but he uses Paul's life and mission to illustrate the destiny of Christianity. Luke's biography of Paul brings the story of Christianity to Rome, just as Paul's thought makes the universal church mission possible for Luke. Luke purposely eliminates the disorganization, disunity, and rancor of early Christianity. He portrays the earliest church fathers as united on most important issues, although Paul himself writes angrily about the conflict between the gentile and Jewish factions of the church. The resulting Lukan portrait of Paul lacks the fire and controversy of the Pauline letters. Many New Testament scholars suspect that Luke entirely abandons historical accuracy.[3]

Many of the details of Paul's life come directly from Luke and from nowhere else. The most obvious biographical details are missing from Paul's own letters. Without Luke, we could not suppose that Paul's origins were in Tarsus, that he traveled to Jerusalem, where he studied with the great Pharisaic master Gamaliel, or that he was present at the stoning of Stephen. Coming from Luke, these basic suppositions about Paul's life are disputable. Among the other details missing from Paul's letters but present in his Lukan biography are those of his dramatic conversion. Many readers of Paul deny that he was a convert, because the reports of his conversion come only from Luke. They maintain, instead, that Paul's Christianity was a natural outgrowth of his Judaism, a prophetic call rather than a conversion. Paul himself sometimes uses prophetic language to describe his Christian mission. Paul surely found that his new Christian faith was a fulfillment of his hopes and an outbreak of prophetic spirit, but Paul does not thereafter lose title to the epithet *convert*.

New Testament scholar Krister Stendahl has maintained that Paul was "called, not converted."[4] Many Lutherans had read Paul's writings as an example of the impossibility of justification by the law; other scholars (many of them Jewish) maintained that Paul simply was temperamentally unsuited for Torah. Still others, such as Rudolf Bultmann, had read Paul as if he were an early existentialist philosopher. And the pervasive influence of psychoanalysis in our lives has made Paul an example of deep psychological struggle.

Stendahl rightly attacks these portraits of Paul as a man burdened with guilt. Although Paul does write of his struggles, Stendahl maintains that these struggles are not with a guilty conscience. He cautions against ascribing to Paul the personality characteristics of modern Western Christians and particularly against reading Paul, and especially Romans 7, as evidence of a disturbed mind.[5]

Paul's description of himself as a Pharisee does not allow much room for guilt feelings or lack of self-esteem: "If any man thinks he has reason for confidence, I have more: circumcised on the eighth day, of the people of Israel of the tribe of Benjamin, a Hebrew born of Hebrews; as to the law a Pharisee, as to zeal a persecutor of the church, as to righteousness under the law blameless. But whatever gain I had, I counted as loss for the sake of Christ. Indeed, I count everything as loss because of the surpassing worth of knowing Christ Jesus my Lord" (Phil. 3:4–6).

Paul describes his own conversion but does not claim to be a deeply troubled man. Thus there is much to be said for Stendahl's position. Paul did not repudiate his Jewish background when be came a Christian, and it is inappropriate to psychoanalyze a man who gives us little evidence of his psychological development. Nevertheless, there are problems with Stendahl's view. He gives persuasive evidence of Paul's "robust conscience," or at least shows the inadequacy of evidence to the contrary. But I think

Paul is a convert in the modern sense of the word. He wrote personally of his experience of transformation, as well as of his troubles in being accepted by both Judaism and Christianity, not just before but after his conversion. Paul was both converted and called.

By using the term *conversion* I wish to stress the wrenching and decisive change of Paul's entrance to Christianity, thereby linking Paul with many modern accounts of conversion. Despite considerable differences of opinion in modern scholarship about the definition of a convert, conversion does involve a radical change in a person's experience.[6] No historical prophet came around on his previous experience as Paul did when called to his task. In modern usage and social science the word *conversion* can denote moving from one sect or denomination to another within the same religion, if the change is radical. We may even speak of a conversion when an Anglican espouses evangelical Christianity or an acculturated Jew becomes a Lubavitcher Hasid. We should not however lose track of one connotation of the prophetic commission that Paul clearly intended; namely, his understanding that he had received a new mission to convert the gentiles. This sense of *commission* might be absent in some contemporary understandings of conversion, but it clearly was part of Luke's description and Paul's self-understanding.[7] From the viewpoint of mission Paul is commissioned, but from the viewpoint of religious experience Paul is a convert.

I also emphasize the revelatory character of Paul's conversion, the (too often forgotten) ecstatic aspect of his report, but I do not defend Luke's conception of Paul. My purpose is to show that Paul's writing, thought, and theology are shaped by his personal, religious experience. His religious visions and meditations are not so much the mark of a troubled man as the expression of a deeply committed man beset with adversaries. He was zealous and committed to Torah, both before and after his conversion. As a Christian, he remained a zealot, but the nature of his commitment to Torah changed radically. As a Pharisee, he certainly respected Torah and believed in the resurrection of the dead, and he could easily have framed his religious hopes in messianic, apocalyptic, and prophetic language, although this is not certain. Modern studies of conversion show that there can be many continuities between a convert's life before conversion and after it. But the primary fact of Paul's personal experience as a Christian is his enormous transformation, his conversion from a persecutor of Christianity to a persecuted advocate of it. To read Paul properly, I maintain, one must recognize that Paul was a Pharisaic Jew who converted to a new apocalyptic, Jewish sect and then lived in a Hellenistic, gentile Christian community as a Jew among gentiles. Indeed, conversion is a decisive and deliberate change in religious community, even when the convert nominally affirms the same religion. Therefore, my analysis of Paul relies both on Jewish material of his time and on modern studies of conversion.

Stendahl, however, has made his point well: both Luke and (less often) Paul describe Paul's conversion as a prophetic call, similar to the prophetic calls of the Hebrew Bible.[8] Luke's accounts of Paul's conversion are deliberately patterned on Hebrew prophecy. Much can be made of the discrepancies among Luke's three accounts of Paul's conversion (Acts 9:1–19; 22:1–21; 26:12–23). Like Paul's own accounts in Gal. 1:13 and possibly in 2 Cor. 11:32, Luke's stories of revelatory experience are incomplete narratives, for they do not describe the actual vision. The accounts in Acts say that Paul, then called Saul, was on the road to Damascus when a bright light shone about him and a voice called out: "Saul, Saul, why do you persecute me?" Saul inquires, "Who are you, Lord?" and is answered, "I am Jesus whom you persecute." Luke's Paul begins his career as a Christian by identifying Jesus as Lord. Although Paul uses *Lord* as a term of respect, it is also related to a Hebrew word for God and is a significant divine title for Christ in Christianity.

The similarity of the three versions in Acts ends at this point. In the first account Paul's companions hear the voice but see nothing. In the second, they see the light but hear nothing. In the first two, Paul falls to the ground while his companions stand. In the third account they all fall to the ground. In the first two accounts Jesus tells Paul to go to Damascus to await further orders.[9] But in the third account Paul receives directly from the revelation his commission of apostleship to the gentiles: "I am Jesus whom you are persecuting. But rise and stand upon your feet; for I have appeared to you for this purpose, to appoint you to serve and bear witness to the things in which you have seen me and to those in which I will appear to you, delivering you from the people and from the gentiles—to whom I send you to open their eyes, that they may turn from darkness to light and from the power of Satan to God, that they may receive forgiveness of sins and a place among those who are sanctified by faith in me" (Acts 26:15–18).

Although these differences show that the details of Paul's conversion were not well known and not part of a carefully guarded literary tradition, most of the discrepancies are unimportant for us. But Paul's vocation, the command to proselytize the gentiles, is a fundamental theme of Luke's narrative; discovering how that mission came about is crucial to this book.

In the first two accounts Paul's mission is revealed in Damascus by Ananias immediately after the conversion narrative (Acts 9:15–17; 22:14–16). In the first account Ananias describes Paul's experience as a vision (9:12). In the second, he says that Paul has seen the Just One (22:14). Only in Luke's third version (26:16–17), a shortened narrative, is Paul's commissioning made part of the revelation itself.

We are left with this perplexing problem: Was the commission part of the vision itself (Acts 26:15–18), or did it come later, after Paul had learned more of the Christian message (9:1–19; 22:1–21)? Perhaps the commission was suggested by Paul's teachers of Christianity, symbolized by Ananias. Of course, Luke may be historically accurate on all three occasions, merely recounting what Paul actually said. But this imports to Luke a higher degree of accuracy than was expected of ancient historians. In fact, the conventions of ancient historiography called on historians to invent speeches appropriate for their characters. Possibly, having related the scene twice, Luke intentionally shortens the third narration of the account. But by relating it three times, Luke signals his interest in emphasizing and dramatizing Paul's conversion experience. It thus appears that Luke is trying to place Paul's mission as close to the conversion as possible.

In Paul's own writing, however, the connection is more ambiguous. Although Paul understands his commission to have started in the womb (Gal. 1:15), he concludes more slowly that he was destined to become the apostle to the gentiles. Luke sees that Paul's destiny is to be the apostle to the gentiles, an evaluation that Paul himself shares, but Paul's writing does not unambiguously report that he realized his destiny immediately (e.g., 2 Cor. 11:24–26). Paul's description of himself as the apostle to the gentiles could easily have been the result of his experience of success among gentiles and his rejection among Jews. Evidently there was a period of time when Paul tried less successfully to convince his Jewish brothers. In the hands of Luke, and even occasionally in Paul's own writing, the connection between Paul's vision and the command to proselytize is therefore clear. But the clarity of this connection could have been realized more slowly by Paul, after years of Christian experience. Both the Lukan and Pauline accounts seem to dramatize the effect of the conversion by portraying the outcome as present in the original revelation.

Paul's Vision of the Kavod According to Luke

The importance to Christianity of the divine commissionings in Luke-Acts lies primarily in the thread uniting them, the sudden about-face expressing to the Christian community of Luke's time the significance of Paul's conversion. Although Luke described Paul as a radical convert, he may have intended a fuller description of Paul. When scholars emphasize Paul's description of himself as a prophet in contrast to Luke's description, they ironically are being unduly influenced by Luke's description, for Luke equally intended Paul's conversion to be understood as a prophetic call. Luke's description of Paul's conversion draws on the Hebrew Bible for themes of prophetic calling, paralleling the commissioning of Jeremiah (Jer. 1:5–11) and Isaiah (Isa. 6:1–9). These themes include an encounter with God, a divine commissioning, demur and resistance by the prophet, divine assurance, and preparation for the task by signs and wonders.

The most provocative parallel to Luke's account of Paul's conversion is the commissioning of the prophet Ezekiel, whose call was special in several respects. Ezekiel was granted a vision of a figure shaped like a man, which is called "the likeness of the image of the Glory of God."[10] When Ezekiel beheld the Glory of God, he reported, "I fell upon my face, and I heard the voice of one that spoke" (Ezek. 1:28). The Lord then ordered Ezekiel to stand, saying: "Stand upon your feet, and I will speak with you. . . . I send you to the people of Israel, to a nation of rebels, who have rebelled against me" (2:1–3). According to Luke, Paul also has a revelation of the Glory of God. Paul hears a voice speaking,[11] and it is clearly a revelatory voice because Paul reacts as Ezekiel did: he falls to the ground. Luke's Paul then rises, but with a significant modification: He receives the charge to go to foreign lands to proselytize a nation of rebels, gentiles rather than Jews as in Ezekiel. Moreover, claims of prophetic appointment were not commonplace in first-century Judaism. The Jewish authorities had promulgated the idea that prophecy had ceased. A self-proclaimed prophet would therefore attract powerful enemies in the Jewish community.

Luke's reference to Ezekiel illustrates his contention that Paul's mission to the gentiles was contained by his conversion experience itself. Western religious notions of the connection between conversion and vocation are based on Luke's story of Paul, but this story shows that the emotional and religious phenomenon of conversion was understood by Paul's contemporary generation of Jews and Christians as a prophetic commissioning to spread God's word to a special audience. The scholarly distinction between Paul's description of himself as commissioned prophetically and Luke's evaluation of Paul as a convert is thus too sharply drawn. It preserves modern scholarly suspicion of Luke's account of Paul, the recognition that Luke's description of Paul contains a number of judgments about Paul's significance, but it does not reflect the similarity of commission and conversion in Luke and Paul; therefore, it does not do justice to the religious categories of the first century, where conversion could be continuous with prophetic commissioning.

One of the unique aspects of Ezekiel's prophecy was that he envisioned what seemed to be a human figure, "the likeness of a man," on God's heavenly conveyance, pulled by heavenly beasts (Ezek. 1:26). Ezekiel calls this figure *Kavod*, the Glory of God (1:29).[12] By using this direct parallel, Luke implies to his original audience that the Glory of God was revealed to Paul. Such a claim is not merely a stylistic convention, for the idea has a deep mystical meaning in Judaism. Further, this identification is rare in exoteric Jewish literature, but it is characteristic of some kinds of Christianity, especially the type espoused by Justin Martyr (see Alan F. Segal, *Two Powers in Heaven*, 220–34).

Christ is not explicitly given the title *Glory of God* in the New Testament.[13] But there are several New Testament passages in which *doxa* (glory) and, more relevantly, *the* Glory are attributed to Christ or the Son. It is possible to translate James 2:1 as "our Lord Jesus Christ, the Glory." Paul himself repeatedly uses the term *Glory* to refer to Christ. In Phil. 3:21 Paul speaks of Christ's "Body of Glory" (*sōma tēs doxēs*) to which the believer's body is to be conformed.[14] He thinks of Christ as the Lord of Glory (1 Cor. 2:8). Through the Glory of the Father, Christ was raised from the dead (Rom. 6:4). God makes known the riches of Glory in or through the exalted Christ (Rom. 9:23; Phil. 4:19. See also Eph. 1:18; 3:16; Col. 1:27). The gospel that Paul preaches, which features the death, resurrection, and return of the Christ, is called the Gospel of Glory (2 Cor. 4:4; Tim. 1:11. See also Col. 1:27). Other passages bearing on this theme would include 1 Cor. 2:8, describing Christ as the "Lord of Glory," and the doubtfully Pauline Heb. 1:3: "He reflects the Glory of God and bears the very stamp of his nature, upholding the universe by his word of power." In Eph. 1:17 "the God of our Lord Jesus Christ, the Father of the Glory" appears.

Paul describes the "Glory of the Lord" (2 Cor. 3:16–4:6) in the places where he describes his own conversion, which he also uses as a pattern for experience by which other believers come to be in Christ, as Paul expresses it. As an heir of Christ, the believer shares the Glory of Christ (Rom. 8:17), which eclipses any suffering that may have been experienced in the believer's life (Rom. 8:18; 2 Cor. 4:15–17). This exchange of suffering for Glory will occur at Christ's coming, according to Col. 3:4. Paul himself talks of the faithful being changed or transformed into the "image of

Christ" (Rom. 8:29; 1 Cor. 15:49), which again resembles Ezekiel's language of "the appearance of the likeness of the Glory of the Lord" (Ezek. 1:28, cf. LXX). Central to Paul's Christian experience is the transformation of believers at the apocalypse. More important, Paul anticipates the technical terminology of the transformation of believers into angels in Jewish mysticism.

Luke ascribes Paul's blindness to the "glory of that light" (22:11) and describes Paul as seeing the "Just One" (22:14). Although the importance of these phrases is debatable, Luke did not fabricate a relationship between Paul and Ezekiel; he is not alone in seeing the identification between Christ and the Glory of the Lord. This unusual feature of identification between the believer and Christ, closely related to Paul's own conversion, is a fascinating unexplored aspect of Paul's thought. It is the mystery that can be most clearly addressed by the serious study of Jewish apocalypticism and mysticism. To comprehend Paul's experience, we must therefore inquire into the secret and imperfectly understood Jewish mysticism of the first century—later called *Merkabah* mysticism, after the Mishnaic term for the chariot that Ezekiel saw—which sought this same vision. In doing so, we find that Paul is indeed one of our best witnesses to the existence and content of these traditions in the first century (see chapter 2 below).

The connection made by Luke between Paul and the call of Ezekiel can be seen clearly in Paul's own writing. The theological implications of this hypothetical identification are staggering. Is Paul's Christianity rooted in the identification of Jesus with the Glory of God (the Hebrew *Kavod*), God's sometimes human appearance in the visions of the Hebrew Bible? Luke provides the first interpretation of Paul's conversion by figuring it in terms of Ezekiel's prophetic commissioning: as a conversion, commission, or vocation, Paul's movement to Christianity is interpreted as the result of a revelation of the image of God's Glory.

Luke describes Paul explicitly as a new prophet, but he also portrays Paul's experience as a radical conversion. A deeply disturbing and emotional experience, which turns Paul's life completely around, is offered as the model experience for other believers. To call Paul's experience a conversion not only has the effect of authenticating it with great emotional power and mystery, but it also clarifies Paul's call to Christianity as a call to join and later define a new community. Paul's conversion is best defined in terms of the Pharisaic Jewish community he left behind and the gentile Christian community he joined.

PAUL'S ACCOUNT OF HIMSELF

New Testament scholarship has tended to downplay Paul's conversion because Paul does not talk of it with Luke's clarity.[15] A large number of Pauline texts, however, do betray the crucial importance of visions and spiritual experience. These include the generally recognized passages such as 1 Cor. 9:1, 15:8–10, Gal. 1:13–17, and Phil. 3:4–11, and as Seyoun Kim has shown,[16] Rom. 10:2–4 and especially 2 Corinthians 3–5 are important passages in which Paul's spiritual experience is certainly a source.[17] The scholarly reticence to ascribe spiritual experience to Paul may be rooted in theological embarrassment with the nonrational aspects of the human soul; but it is fueled by an important historiographical issue. Methodologically, we can be sure of Luke's portrayal of Paul only when Paul's own letters confirm them. Even when the facts of Luke's account are acceptable, Luke has an obvious interest in coloring them to fit his conception of Christian destiny. Paul's conversion is one such episode. Paul is surely the apostle to the gentiles as Luke has portrayed him. Succeeding generations of critics can find no dispute with Luke over this basic contention about Paul. But Paul's fragmentary accounts of the import of his mission differ significantly from and even contradict the Lukan description. Further, no one can write dispassionately about himself or herself; Paul also has axes to grind. Because Luke is suspect, Paul himself is not necessarily accurate. The Bible offers no easy escape from historical methodology.[18]

Paul is not simply a newly formed gentile convert to Christianity; rather, he remains a knowledgeable Jew representing, endorsing, and furthering the gentile mission. In Rom. 1:16 he speaks of salvation coming to the Jew first and then to the gentile. Paul's own account of his call and purpose is less detailed than Luke's, but it does not entirely contradict Luke's portrait. From his authentic letters we know only a few details of Paul's life. In Phil. 3:4–8 he tells us that he was circumcised properly, that he was from the tribe of Benjamin, that he became a Pharisee, that he persecuted the church, and that he was blameless under the law. When Paul talks about his conversion to Christianity, it is with more muted tones than Luke; but it is no less a conversion.

The central theme of Paul's autobiographical sections is the contrast between his previous life and his present one. Paul says in Gal. 1:23–24: "He who once persecuted us is now preaching the faith he once tried to destroy. And they glorified God because of me." Paul's life is already proverbial in the community as a miraculous proof of the power of the spirit. The experience of Paul is significant for the early church in that it is a mighty and unexpected conversion. Paul agrees with the characterization; indeed, he uses himself as the best example of the power of the spirit.

Whenever Paul relates his conversion he also reveals a central aspect of its meaning for him. Not only is his new self entirely dependent on his conversion, his mission comes directly from his conversion as well: "But when he who had set me apart before I was born, and had called me through his grace, was pleased to reveal his Son to me, in order that I might preach him among the gentiles" (Gal. 1:15–16). Paul's conversion prompts his mission and derives its authority directly from God's revelation (*apokalypsis*) of his son to him. The Greek version is even more compelling than the English, for the mission follows as a purpose clause (*hina*) on the revelation: "for the exact purpose that I might preach him among the gentiles." But Paul does not say explicitly that his gentile mission came immediately after his conversion.

As in Acts, Paul's conversion is a revelation. Unlike Acts, however, Paul more explicitly interprets the revelation as the source of his salvation through his death in Christ (Romans 6; Rom. 7:9; 8:14; 2 Cor. 4:11–12) and thereafter through being made like Christ. It is also the source of his mission to the gentiles. This is Paul's destiny, although he may not have realized it immediately. This radical evaluation of the two aspects of his life, even when there are grounds for moderation, is the hallmark of a convert, and it is paralleled by social science research today. Although conversion is often thought of as a sudden change that alters one's life immediately, the study of modern conversions shows that Paul's own description is more characteristic. Such a turnabout might be called a conversion today, depending on the group that describes it.[19] That Paul claims the conversion took place without the help of flesh and blood underlines the extraordinary circumstances of the religious decision, but it does not mean that he immediately realized all the implications of his conversion experience. Only time could have disclosed these to him.

There is also a less overt agenda in Galatians 1. Paul is displaying his credentials because the other apostles do not recognize a person as an apostle who did not know Jesus. His counterclaim is that his understanding of Christianity comes directly from a vision of the resurrected Christ, not through the preaching of any human disciple—yet another example of the prophetic nature of the calling.[20] Like Jeremiah's predestined mission from the womb of his mother (Jer. 1:5), Paul claims to have received his

mission before birth. Before his conversion, all is equally irrelevant for
Paul. His training in Pharisaism, however, does frequently affect his perception and analysis.

Although predestined for his task, Paul maintains that the radical
change in his life is still a sign of the spirit's activity. The vivid contrast
between his former life as a persecutor of Christianity and his present one
as an apostle starts as a personal reflection on his conversion experience,
which Paul sees both in terms of the commission of a prophet and a radical
reversal of his previous life. Its personal meaning for Paul lies not only in
his Christian commitment but in his personal knowledge of Christ as well.
Paul believes that he himself has met the Christ, though he never met the
man Jesus. Paul may cast his mission to the gentiles in terms of a prophetic
commission, but his explicit use of prophetic forms of speech is restricted.
He never explicitly calls himself a prophet either, preferring instead the
term *apostle*.[21] There is some relationship between the terms *apostle* and
prophet in Christianity, but the two are not identical. Paul's great change
of direction is better understood as a conversion.

PAUL AND LUKE COMPARED

There are important differences between Paul and Luke, rooted in their different purposes. Paul wants to vindicate his position as an
apostle, while Luke wants to portray the progress of the church from the
Jewish community to the gentile one. The chronology of Luke's history of
the church is unemphasized in Paul's own writing. Paul tries to express the
content of his revelation, and Luke uses Paul's ecstatic experience as a
model for gentile conversions. Most important, although Paul calls his
conversion a revelation, Luke substitutes a revelatory audition unknown
in Paul's writing.

Luke wrote with more historical perspective than Paul and, of course,
less personal knowledge of the experience, but he understood the importance of Paul's conversion in ways that Paul himself perhaps did not fully
realize. Luke's description of Paul's conversion contains a radical distinction between resurrection appearances of Christ and experiences of the
spirit.[22] Neither Paul himself nor John distinguishes so clearly between
spiritual and "resurrection" appearances. In 1 Cor. 15:45, for instance,
Paul shows no sensitivity to Luke's interpretive categories when he con-
flates the appearance of the risen Jesus with "a life-giving spirit." Luke,
however, distinguishes Paul's experience from that of the original twelve
apostles. For Luke, the authentic resurrection appearances of Jesus in the

gospel and Acts are far more mundane and "realistic." Jesus walks and talks with wayfarers, blesses them, eats, and is sometimes unrecognized at first. These are not visionary appearances but descriptions of ordinary consciousness to Luke. He understands the first sightings of Jesus as actual physical manifestations. The resurrection appearances are then brought to an end by the ascension (Acts 1:9ff).[23] Conversely, for Luke, Paul's conversion is a visionary audition, with no specific image described. Although Paul's experience may have been visionary, it falls into a second category of sightings, an expression of the spirit after Jesus' ascension.[24] Luke identifies the original twelve disciples as apostles, limiting apostolic status to those who had accompanied Jesus during his ministry (Acts 1:21–26); by implication, Paul falls into the secondary category of converts to Christ by means of the holy spirit.

Paul may accept the status of the twelve as special disciples, but he argues that the appearance of Christ to him vindicates his equal status as apostle, even though it occurred in a revelation and vision. Indeed, he includes himself in the list of those to whom Jesus' resurrection was made manifest (Galatians 1; 1 Cor. 9:1; 15:8f). Paul may recognize that he is "last of all" and "untimely born," but he will not give up his claim to the apostolate because Christ appeared to him. He uses the same simple word (*see*) to describe his and the other apostles' experience of Christ. Paul therefore does not distinguish between the kind of appearance made known to him and those made known to his forebears.

I. M. Lewis's sociological distinction between peripheral and central possession offers another way to express the difference between Luke and Paul's conception of conversion.[25] When claims for ecstasy occur in groups peripheral to power, they tend to function as bids to short-circuit the legitimate organization of power. In contrast, when spirit possession or ecstasy occurs close to the center of a political movement, it is carefully controlled, usually by an established religious authority. Ecstatic religion represents a peripheral strategy in first-century Judaism; it was an oblique attack against established order, as when the Qumran sectarians practiced ecstatic ascent. They were priestly functionaries, locked out of their hereditary temple functions, so they sought contact with the divine in the desert.

Within the Christian movement ecstasy carried different social distinctions. Positing only two social strategies leaves out many intermediate, ambiguous cases in early Christianity, but one difference between Paul and Luke emerges from the function of ecstatic experience in their writings. For Luke, Paul's ecstatic experience was the model for the conversion of gentiles. But this experience is not the model for resurrection appearances, which are treated literally and give a special status to the first apostles. For Paul, in contrast, the revelatory vision of Christ functions as a bid for power, since he was a peripheral figure in Christianity, as his battle for apostolic acceptance shows.[26] The motif of realistic appearances in Luke is similar to a Graeco-Roman apologetic designed to impress critics and friends with the power of Jesus' resurrection, whereas the ecstatic visions of Paul are more in line with the original Jewish apocalypticism out of which Christianity arose.

Luke and Paul's description of the risen Christ is socially significant as well. The contrast between the descriptions points to an incipient crisis in the church—between the (mostly Jewish) Christians who based their new faith on an experience of Jesus in the flesh and the (mostly gentile) Christians championed by the ex-Pharisee Paul, who based their faith on a spiritual interpretation of Christ, seen primarily in his resurrection or spiritual body. The theology, then, parallels the social distinction in early Christianity between those who knew Christ in a fleshly way and those who knew him in his spiritual body. This vision and the subsequent success of the gentile mission convinced Paul that the new age was not only imminent but that it had already begun. It also convinced him that his Jewish opponents saw the Christ in a fleshly rather than a spiritual way.

ELIMINATING SOME FALSE DICHOTOMIES

An enormous shift in emphasis in the study of conversion has taken place in the past twenty years: scholars have begun to rely on sociology more than psychology to understand the phenomenon of conversion, partly because sociological research is more easily quantifiable than psychological research.[27] In L. R. Rambo's "Current Research in Religious Conversion," only twenty-five psychological studies are listed since 1970, while there are over one hundred sociologically oriented studies.[28]

One major point of contemporary sociological research, as opposed to the psychological approach, is that there is no universal psychological definition of conversion. Each community defines what it means by conversion. Psychological studies of conversion have merely accepted Western religion's definitions of conversion. Some researchers stressed the emotional nature of conversion over rational decision. Others stressed the speed of some conversions over a long period of education in a new movement or one of many other concepts: transformation, transcendence, typology, tradition, institution, affiliation, intensification, apostasy, context, crisis, or religious quest. Conversion, however, is not a cultural universal. Each community evolves a definition of conversion that makes sense to it. But if a universal definition of conversion is lacking, community definitions of the phenomenon are never absent.

Many descriptive studies of conversion in special communities note a stereotypic character of the narration.[29] A conversion report idealizes and conventionalizes the conversion experience from the group that values it, guiding potential converts. Following the expected pattern developed from modern data, Paul himself uses his conversion story to advance his gospel. When the reports are written down and collected, conventionalization becomes even more evident.[30] The stereotypes are often formed by the narration of a founder figure's conversion, as in Luke's stories about Paul and equally so in the pastoral Epistles. Paul's own experience stands squarely within Jewish mysticism, and Luke's description of Paul's conversion is cognizant of that connection, but Luke is more taken with the issue of spirit possession in the later church. Luke's model reflects an evolved definition of conversion within the Church, a model for many converts to follow. For Luke, Paul's ecstatic conversion on the road to Damascus is the first of a large number of ecstatic conversions.

Another example of the newly developing definition of Christian conversion comes toward the end of Luke's narration of Paul's life. When Paul is interrogated by King Agrippa and the Roman procurator Festus, the following dialogue takes place:

> And as he thus made his defense, Festus said with a loud voice, "Paul, you are mad; your great learning is turning you mad." But Paul said, "I am not mad, most excellent Festus, but I am speaking the sober truth. For the king knows about these things, and to him I speak freely; for I am persuaded that none of these things has escaped his notice, for this was not done in a corner. King Agrippa, do you believe the prophets? I know that you believe." And Agrippa said to Paul, "In a short time you think to make me a Christian!" And Paul said, "Whether short or long, I would to God that not only you but also all who hear me this day might become such as I am—except for these chains." (Acts 26:24–29)

Luke has fashioned this encounter into a conventional confrontation between the wise man and the ruler. But it is not thereby devoid of historical meaning. As Abraham Malherbe has pointed out, the wit, irony and sarcasm in this passage depends on understanding differing communities' definitions of conversion.[31] Philosophical (and most Jewish) definitions of conversion are characterized by long training; they depend on this trait for their credibility. Therefore Paul is being criticized for thinking to make converts too quickly. Luke's Paul answers that he does not care whether it be a quick or slow conversion, provided that the king is converted. Luke thus certifies that his contemporary Christian missionaries could hope for quick conversions, as well as slower, more conventional ones. By the time of Justin Martyr, who keeps to a more philosophical definition of Christianity, such a conversion would have been viewed with suspicion among some Christians as well. But in Luke's time the quickness of the conversion apparently emphasizes the miraculous power of the spirit. So Luke also portrays Paul's conversion as a sudden Damascus Road experience. Luke uses Paul's example doubly, both as a paradigm of a convert and as the model for Christian missionaries.

This Christian use of Paul as the role model for a convert is clear in the pastoral Epistles. First Tim. 1:12–17 purports to be Paul's own description of his conversion, but it has more in common with Luke's ideas about Paul:[32]

> I thank him who has given me strength for this, Christ Jesus our Lord because he judged me faithful by appointing me to his service, though I formerly blasphemed and persecuted and insulted him; but I received mercy because I had acted ignorantly in unbelief, and the grace of our Lord overflowed for me with the faith and love that are in Christ Jesus. The saying is sure and worthy of full acceptance, that Christ Jesus came into the world to save sinners. And I am the foremost of sinners; but I received mercy for this reason, that in me, as the foremost, Jesus Christ might display his perfect patience for an example to those who were to believe in him for eternal life. To the King of Ages, immortal, invisible, the only God, be honor and glory for ever and ever. Amen.

This pastoral letter stresses the contrast between Paul's life before conversion and after it. But before conversion Paul is portrayed as the foremost of sinners (1 Tim. 1:16), while Paul himself asserts that he is blameless according to the law (Phil. 3:6). Although Paul emphasizes his conversion and may even regret his former life as a persecutor of Christianity, he never considers himself to be the foremost sinner. This passage in Timothy, then, has a distinctly post-Pauline character. At least as much as in Paul's version, his conversion is depicted as a model (hypotypōsin) for the conversion of all non-believers (1 Tim. 1:16). The theme of repentant sinners, however, is appropriate to the gentile mission, where repentance from a sinful life was a prominent theme. Although the message is mostly Pauline, the narrative comes from the historical distance, closer to Luke than to Paul's authentic voice. And the Timothy passage points out how, by means of Luke's narrative, Paul's life came to be a model for Christian conversion. Thus we have at least three distinct stages of development in the early church's understanding of ecstatic conversion: (1) Paul's own ecstatic, emotional experience, which is intensely personal, special, and visionary and which he uses to establish his apostolate, as well as to exemplify the power of the spirit; (2) Luke's contention that Paul's experience is typical of gentile conversions (but not equivalent to the experience of the disciples); and (3) the deliberate attempt to make Paul into a paradigm for gentile conversion experiences. Stages 2 and 3 are typical of Luke, and stage 3 continues into the pastoral Epistles.

If prophetic commissioning and conversion were analogous to first-century Jewish experience, why did Paul not use Jewish terms for conversion to discuss his own experience? Any description of Paul's conversion must begin with the seeming lack of conversion language in Paul's letters. In Galatians, Paul describes his entrance into the Christian community in ways reminiscent of a prophetic call. He does not often use the Greek words *epistrephō* or *metanoia,* which normally imply conversion, to describe entrance into Christianity, and he never uses them to describe his own experience. In fact, these Greek terms do not actually mean conversion; they signify repentance. Paul uses these terms consistently with the Septuagint's translation of the Hebrew terms: "For they themselves report concerning us what a welcome we had among you, and how you turned [*epestrepsate*] to God from idols, to serve a living and true God, and to wait for his Son from heaven, whom he raised from the dead, Jesus who delivers us from the wrath to come" (1 Thess. 1:9–10). Paul is describing the conversion of gentiles to Christianity, an important clue to his usage of the term. Paul is actually talking about their repentance from sinful ways. His other uses of the term clarify its meaning as gentile conversion: "Formerly, when you did not know God, you were in bondage to beings that by nature are not gods, but now that you have come to know God, or rather to be known by God, how can you turn back [*epistrephete*] again to the weak and beggarly elemental spirits, whose slaves you want to be once more?" (Gal. 4:8–9).

Epistrephō implies repentance or backsliding, as the context demands. Paul even makes the point that this gentile conversion is better than Jewish piety: "Yes, to this day whenever Moses is read a veil lies over their minds, but when a man turns [*epistrepsei*] to the Lord, the veil is removed" (2 Cor. 3:15–16).

Paul's does use the term *metanoia* to refer to the change in status of both Jews and Christians. *Metanoia* indicates Jewish as well as gentile conversions to Christianity (2 Cor. 7:9–10; 2 Cor. 12:21; Rom. 2:4).[33] But not all Jews could boast of Paul's Pharisaic blamelessness. The sense of *metanoia*, as of *epistrephō*, is that of repentance, which is in keeping with the Jewish use of the term.

Paul's reticence to apply these terms to himself—indeed, his sparing use of the terms entirely—can be explained by the nature of Paul's own conversion. The two relevant terms for conversion are rare in Greek and just as rare in Paul. Their standard usage derives from the translation of *shuv* (turn or return) from the Hebrew into Septuagint Greek. In Hebrew the noun construction *teshuvah* is the most common biblical and rabbinic idiom for repentance and return to righteousness. Paul thus does not use them for his own experience. He obviously thought himself to be guilty of no infraction of Torah before he became a Christian, as Galatians 1 and Philippians 3 tell us and as Stendahl has emphasized. Nor could Paul use the Hebrew term *gayyar* to describe his conversion because it refers only to gentile adoption of Jewish ways. Since Paul uses the verb *epistrephō* to describe conversion from paganism to Judaism, it could not be applied to him. But converting from one variety of Judaism to another is a conversion as well. Unfortunately there is no term in ordinary Judaism besides *repentance* to discuss the transformation that Paul undergoes, and that term, as we have seen, is not relevant to Paul.

PAUL AND THE MODERN STUDY OF CONVERSION

Methodologically, in the study of Paul, are we limited only to terms that Paul himself would have used? For generations anthropologists have distinguished between vocabularies used by their subjects and those used for analysis. By analogy from linguistics, *emic* vocabulary is the terminology that a culture itself uses to describe a cultural artifact; it corresponds to Paul's self-description. Emic vocabulary is well suited to a complete and thorough ethnography, because it relies on the terms that the society or culture itself uses. An anthropologist's first responsibility is to describe the emic statements of a culture. New Testament scholarship itself, at least in its most reliable moments, has concentrated on an accurate emic analysis of Paul.

Etic vocabulary is modern analytic vocabulary. It is or should be imposed self-consciously on a culture by an analyst as a comparative, analytic tool. To call Paul a convert is to use etic vocabulary. Emic statements are falsifiable by a truthful informant, and etic statements are never true in the same way that emic ones are. While emic statements may be worthless for comparison because they reproduce local distinctions, a carefully drawn etic statement has worth for some kinds of crosscultural study. Etic analyses may be valid even if the informant denies them.[34] In the study of the New Testament itself, Paul's description of Christ is etic, as is Luke's description of Paul. Pure emic description is not possible about the beginning of Christianity because a standard vocabulary had not yet evolved.

Anthropologists themselves argue over the merits of the two styles of description. Bible scholarship obviously needs both. Good exegesis demands an attempt to approximate the emic vocabulary and the meanings that the informant would have invested in it. But analysis of religious experience demands broader categories as well. Most New Testament scholars who claim not to impose categories on the text are merely not conscious of their own biases. Scholars should try to be self-conscious in the use of analytic terms.

Paul's resemblance to contemporary converts is too important to be ignored, even though Paul himself avoided the vocabulary. It is necessary to understand and use both emic and etic systems of description to do justice to the complex religious position that Paul represents. It is important not to confuse the two systems of description, to be aware of when a vocabulary is imposed by outside analysis on the phenomenon and when it is being used by the informants. The confusion here is that both the ancients and moderns use the term convert. But the Jews used it with the implication of repentance, which Paul found inappropriate to his own circumstances. With these reservations, I maintain that Paul is indeed a convert in the modern sense of the term.[35]

Although Luke described Paul's conversion as a prophetic mission and Paul uses prophetic language to describe his task, prophecy clearly does not apply to the conversions of all those whom he evangelized. Paul never directly calls himself a prophet and the language of prophecy does not become a standard vocabulary for conversion in Christianity. In describing a believer's change in status, Paul uses a variety of terms.[36] The terms for rebirth, which so often are applied by today's "born-again" Christians, are rarely used by Paul, though John uses this vocabulary sparingly. As the title of Beverly Gaventa's book implies, *From Darkness to Light* shows that the vocabulary of light and darkness is more often used.

Paul sometimes uses a term that suggests conversions in contemporary life as well—the transformation from one state to another. These terms, used in Rom. 12:2 for instance, imply not just a renewal, as Koenig argues, but something much more. Paul himself says: "Do not be conformed to this world, but be transformed [*metamorphousthe*] by the renewal of your mind" (Rom. 12:2). They suggest a mystical reformulation and immortalization process, which was discussed in contemporary Jewish apocalypticism and pagan spirituality. This process is the transformation meant by Paul when he discusses his own conversion. This important metaphor is both part of Paul's description of his own experience and, at the end of time, part of the experience of his converts. Since his converts have not had the same visionary experience as Paul himself, they might not be aware of the meaning. But Paul implies that transformation is what every believer can expect at the end of time. To understand what Paul means by conversion, Paul must be seen as one of the early mystical-apocalyptic adepts of divine transformation.

In Jewish mysticism and pagan spirituality transformation is a term that suggests what may happen when a human encounters a gracious divinity. In this respect, Paul gives us wonderful and until now nearly unnoted evidence of the experience of Jewish mysticism in the first few centuries C.E. His language for Christian conversion comes from his experience of the divine and is reapplied to what we now call conversion. The same is true in Phil. 3:7–11: "But whatever gain I had, I counted as loss because of the surpassing worth of knowing Christ Jesus my Lord. For his sake, I have suffered the loss of all things, and count them as refuse, in order that I may gain Christ and be found in him, not having a righteousness of my own, based on law, but that which is through faith *in* Christ, the righteousness from God that depends on faith; that I may know him and the power of his resurrection, and may share his sufferings, becoming like him in his death, that if possible I may attain the resurrection from the dead." The contrast between Paul's former life and present one implies a contrast between law and faith, and the attainment of resurrection from the dead, becoming like Christ in his death (*symmorphizomenos tō thanatō autou*). The language Paul uses is not merely that of analogy or imitation; it is that of transformation (*metamorphosis*) from one state of being to another, in which he has become the same substance as Christ through his death (*symmorphosis*). Metamorphosis is the same word that we use to describe a caterpillar's change into a butterfly after its seeming death in its chrysalis. It is also the term that the ancient world would use to describe the seeming decay of a seed underground before it begins new growth. By using the prefix *sym-,* meaning "in, together with," Paul means to imply that faith in Christ brings about a change of equal miraculousness and magnitude: "Brethren, join in imitating me, and mark those who so live as you have an example in us. . . . But our commonwealth is in heaven, and from it we await a Savior, the Lord Jesus Christ, who will change our lowly body to be like his glorious body, by the power which enables him even to subject all things to himself" (Phil. 3:17–21). This process of transformation will end in a glorious new body, spiritual rather than material, which corresponds with the body Christ has already revealed to him.

In 1 Cor. 15:37–42 Paul uses the metaphor of a planted and growing seed to describe resurrection, possibly interpreting Jesus' parables of growth in a new way: "What you sow does not come to life unless it dies. And what you sow is not the body which is to be, but a bare kernel, perhaps of wheat or of some other grain. But God gives it a body as he has chosen. . . . So it is with the resurrection of the dead. What is sown is perishable, what is raised is imperishable." In 1 Cor. 15:51 Paul explicitly says that the dead shall be changed (*allagēsometha*), putting on a new body as if it were new clothes (*endysasthai* [15:53]), words normally associated with baptism but clearly associated with spiritual transformation as well.

Outside of Jewish apocalypticism and mysticism the closest analogy to Paul's experience phenomenologically is also termed a metamorphosis by the ancient world. Although separated from Paul by culture and by a century, and ostensibly a fictional account of a transformation, the *Golden Ass* of Apuleius describes the explicit metamorphosis of the novelistic hero Lucius from an ass back to his natural form as a young man. While the entire romance seems like fantasy, the moral is real and religious. Scholars have pointed out that the story actually discusses a religious conversion to the mystery religion of Isis, albeit in a fictionalized form.[37]

The analogy of the transformation in the *Golden Ass* with religious conversion must be seen in context. The main character of the novel, Lucius, is led by his reprobate lifestyle into a careless dabbling with magic, and as a result he finds himself accidentally transformed into an ass. Each of his adventures surpasses the previous ones in depravity (and at the same time seduces the reader's attention with blatant sex and violence). While seeking escape on the beach at Cenchreae, the same place where Paul stopped on his way to Jerusalem, Lucius prays to the moon for deliverance. In response to the prayer, the goddess Isis intervenes and tells him how to regain his human form. He then becomes an initiate into more and more secret rites of the goddess, who gives him not just deliverance from his earthly predicaments but, through the ever more demanding rites of the mysteries, heavenly journeys and eventual postmortem salvation: "You will as a dweller in the Elysian fields constantly adore me whom you now see, shining in the darkness of Acheron, reigning in the recesses of Styx, and you will find me gracious toward you" (11.6).[38] The reader, at first seduced by the sex and violence of the narrative, as Lucius himself is seduced into magically altered form, also undergoes salvation with Lucius, though some of the rites are too secret to describe openly. This parallels Christian experience. But unlike Isiac initiations, Christian salvation was not a carefully guarded secret. Christianity's public mission explains its success in competing against the mystery cults. Yet when Paul speaks of the person who has heard unutterable things (2 Corinthians 12), he may equally be admitting to the existence of secret traditions in Christianity. Although the process of salvation may be public, some aspects of the experience may be private and reserved for the lucky few who have undergone visions.

Lucius's metamorphosis is symbolic of his leaving behind his previous life of vanity, enslaved by sex, magic, and chance, for a new, pure, moral life destined for divine purposes and guided by the goddess Isis. The Latin verb is most often *reformare,* employed as a passive *reformari,* "to be reformed" bodily as well as morally, as the context makes clear. Lucius's reformation involves many experiences of unclothing and reclothing, both literal and symbolic, a celestial journey within the ritual of the mystery rites, and the overcoming of mortality with the assurance of semidivine status, together with a significant advancement in his moral development. This imagery is characteristic of Christian conversion as well, where the rite of baptism formalizes the change of status.

Although Apuleius wrote a century after Paul, they share a vocabulary. Ovid wrote the pagan *Metamorphoses* around the time of Paul. The *Metamorphoses* begins with an invocation to the gods and ends with Caesar's transformation into a star, assuring his celestial immortality. But the body of Ovid's text describes metamorphoses that seem more like the disease that afflicted Lucius rather than the cure provided by Isis. Although Ovid's text presents a much less spiritual description of transformation than the *Golden Ass,* it highlights contemporary uses of the term.

The Roman world of course knew how to satirize religious emotions, as Lucian did in his *Death of Peregrinus.* Nevertheless, we miss something important about the ancient world if we do not take these transformations and heavenly meetings with divinities seriously as religious experience.

Among Ovid's many examples are a few of moral edification, such as Caesar's transformation. In the Jewish world, we find a similar respect for the experience of ascent and astral immortality. So the language of transformation was clearly available to the religious world in Paul's own day.

No one knows what Paul's state of mind was or what his early development was like. So it is fruitless to attempt to psychoanalyze Paul. Luckily, the modern study of conversion is not limited to psychoanalysis. Anthropology, social psychology, and sociology represent three alternatives in the rational study of conversion, defusing the polemic about Paul's guilty conscience or sanity. Nor does it matter whether or not ancient or modern observers approve of Paul's behavior. In fact, any observer valuing Pharisaic Judaism would naturally view the conversion with hostility. Conversion, however, is a valid religious phenomenon, though it always distresses the believers of the religion abandoned. The historian of religion, then, should understand Paul's experience, not justify or attack it.

When we look at both Luke and Paul's accounts of Paul's conversion, we find that the social setting of the conversion has been ignored, largely because of the revelatory language describing the act of conversion. Paul explicitly says in Galatians that his knowledge of Christ comes from God and not from man (Gal. 1:1). Though the context of this statement also allows that he spent time in Christian communities, Paul asserts that his Christianity came from his revelation. When one looks carefully at what Paul says and his reasons for saying it, however, his conversion is not likely to have been as sudden as Luke says and certainly not as isolated from human contact.

A good deal of Paul's early life has been open to speculation. Because Luke says that he came from the Diaspora, he may have come from a relatively acculturated Jewish family that did not practice Torah with the same thoroughness as the Judean Pharisees.[39] However, Acts implies that Paul came from a believing Pharisaic family, which would have kept itself aloof from the more Hellenized community and would have continued to speak a Semitic language. We know that converts to new religions both identify themselves as religious questers after the fact and come disproportionally from the more acculturated and secular classes of society.[40] It is almost as if the secularization brings with it a desire to find religious meaning.[41]

In Paul's description of his Judaism prior to conversion, he states that he excelled beyond many his own age (Gal. 1:14). This statement is verified throughout his letters by the considerable skill Paul shows in exegetical dialectics. It is also significant evidence for Paul's predisposition toward conversion, since it implies either that Paul was a religious quester or that his parents instilled an unusually strict training in him. Both factors have been identified as predictors of future conversion experiences. If one adds Luke's contention that Paul or his family came from Tarsus, a Hellenistic environment, there would be even more evidence for Paul's religious questing: though Acts claims he came from a Pharisaic family (23:6), he would still have had to make a long journey from the Hellenistic environment of the Diaspora to the Pharisaic heartland in Judea. Acts suggests that Paul spent long years in strict training (22:3), but this is a conventional detail in religious biographies. According to Acts, Paul could have shown characteristics of both an acculturated Jew and a religious quester. But the details are far too questionable to be of specific help in understanding Paul's writings.

The lack of information about Paul's upbringing is partly due to our sparse knowledge of Pharisaism. We have little information about Pharisaism in the first century, let alone what form the Pharisees could have assumed in Diaspora, if Luke is correct. Consequently, all discussion of Paul's early life, especially with details gleaned from Luke, is bound to end in pure speculation. Although a sympathetic reading of Luke gives us some characteristics that might show Paul as predisposed toward conversion experiences, there is but slim evidence for a psychological understanding of Paul's life based on the past that he and Luke supply to us.

As in the history of conversion scholarship in general, a better tack for understanding Paul's conversion is to be found in the examination of his social world. Paul came from a Pharisaic community and entered a gentile one. This is clear from his writing. We can investigate what that means and, in the process, discover something new about Paul. When we look at Paul's experience after conversion, we discover that his social context can be located. From his description in Galatians we know that Paul went off to Arabia and back to Damascus. Arabia of the time probably included the area around Damascus itself, so Paul's first Christian atmosphere was Syrian (Arabian) and Hellenistic. Paul was apparently involved in the leadership of the Damascus and Antiochene churches but not in intimate contact with Jerusalem during these years. Yet during that time he obviously lived with and learned from other Christians. As he states, these Christians were not heavily influenced by the Jerusalem church. Paul lived in a gentile community during his formative years as a convert. That community helped him understand the meaning of his revelation.

Paul's disclaimer that his insight into Christianity came not from men is not contradicted by his having entered a Christian community after conversion. In fact, he states several times that he has received from his Christian brethren authentic traditions about the Eucharist, baptismal ritual, and the order of Christ's postresurrection appearance, as well as other teachings, that he then passed on to his congregations. His claim of divine guidance refers to his conversion and call to his apostolate. But he also learned the content of the revelation from his community:

> Now I would remind you, brethren, in what terms I preached to you the gospel, which you received, in which you stand, by which you are saved, if you hold it fast—unless you believed in vain. For I delivered to you as of first importance what I also received, that Christ died for our sins in accordance with the scriptures, that he was buried, and that he was raised on the third day in accordance with the scriptures, and that he appeared to Cephas, then to the twelve. Then he appeared to more than five hundred brethren at one time, most of whom are still alive, though some have fallen asleep. Then he appeared to James, then to all the apostles. Last of all, as to one untimely born, he appeared also to me. For I am the least of the apostles, unfit to be called an apostle, because I persecuted the church of God. But by the grace of God, I am what I am, and his grace toward me was not in vain. On the contrary, I worked harder than any of them, though it was not I, but the grace of God which is with me. Whether then it was I or they, so we preach and so you believed. (1 Cor. 15:1–11; see also 11:2, 23–26)

Paul considers himself the last apostle. Paul's apostolate came later than those who met Jesus in the flesh. But he does not fail to point out how much more energetic he has been than other apostles, maintaining that the success of his mission is a proof of his election as apostle. He also discloses that the doctrines of Christianity were *received* by him and *passed on*— likely to be Greek translations of the two technical terms for the transmission of oral tradition within Pharisaism: *kibel* and *masar*.[42] If his claim to the apostolate has a function within his political battles in the church, the disclaimer of his righteousness under the law has one as well. It shows he was a success as a Jew, not a failure. Therefore, it is the very unlikeliness of his conversion, the persecutor who became the latest apostle, that proves the power of the Holy Spirit. His gentile hearers also participate in this marvelous process, since they too (like him) have been converted.

Paul might have been a radical convert, as Luke suggests, but he does not evince all the qualities of the pure type. Although Paul's conversion possibly came in his adolescence, from his own chronology it is unlikely that it came at the beginning of his adolescence. While it is possible to think that he grew up in an authoritarian environment since we know nothing of his parents, the Pharisees were more lenient in punishments and other legal interpretations than the Sadducees, and, although they were caricatured by Matthew for ritual observances, the Pharisees were not uniquely ritualistic in this traditional society.

But not all psychological descriptions of conversion need to be carried out with analytic assumptions. Cognitive and social psychology provide insights about the thoughts and behavior of converts. Recent research in this direction has been carried on as part of the test of attribution theory. Snow and Machalek[43] tried to isolate "rhetorical indicators" characteristic of conversion accounts. They studied Nichiren Shoshu, and found that a master attribution scheme, biographical reconstruction, the suspension of analogical reasoning, and the embrace of a master role were indicative of conversion. In a more recent study by Staples and Mauss,[44] all four indicators turned up in a study of "Jesus Freaks." However, only biographical reconstruction seemed to be unique for converts, the other indicators also being characteristic of lifelong, highly committed Christians. This is extremely important for the study of Paul. One of the most characteristic aspects of Paul's autobiographical statements, as we have seen, is his insistence on indulging in what these researchers have called biographical reconstruction. Indeed, modern scholars use terms that closely parallel Paul's own usage. They point out that the language of converts is a language of *self-transformation:* "To distinguish the self-concept change involved in conversion from other, more routine changes in the self-concept . . . we use the term *self-transformation.* Self-transformation, as we define it here, refers to a change in, or the creation of . . . the 'real self.' "[45] As attributionists, they focus on the language and rhetoric of the converts as a useful direction for finding a definition of their experience.

There is more than a fortuitous similarity in terminology between Paul's use of a language of transformation and these social-science researchers' use of the humanistic term *self-transformation.* Paul's use of an established ancient language of transformation to speak of the differences between his former self and his present self, though specific to the first century, contains some connotations similar to those that Snow and Machalek describe among their subjects. Paul's language comes from very different sources than the present day converts'—namely, first-century Jewish mystical piety. But his emphasis on transformation, renamed biographical reconstruction in modern parlance, is one significant clue in both the ancient and modern world that a conversion has taken place. The differing natures of the transformation in our society and in Paul's must be acknowledged; the ancient definition of transformation assumed a metaphysical realm ours does not. Whether transformation is seen as a personality reconstruction, as do modern researchers, or as a transformation in status from fleshly to immortal body, as did Paul, the language of transformation itself is one continuous metaphor from ancient times to the present. Modern researchers might have an impoverished sense of causation; however, Paul's transformation could have been active questing in ways he could not recognize or acknowledge.

The basic metaphor is one of radical disjunction between past and present, punctuated by a remaking of a person's sense of meaning. This is a common trait unifying Paul's life with modern subjects. A strict contrast between present life and past life is a significant aspect of the way converts describe their lives before and after conversion. This appears to be true in Eastern and Western cults today and also in Western conversions in the first century. Whatever may separate us from Paul or separate our understandings of personality from ancient ones, these attributions argue that there are some simple continuities in the phenomenon of conversion throughout Western history.

This continuity does not lead to facile generalization. Because community traditions are so strong in evaluating conversion narrative, Brian Taylor suggests that nothing that a convert relates of his or her life previous to conversion can be taken at face value. It is always mediated through the values of the convert's new community, which defines what a conversion is and actually teaches the convert how to think of it. This emphasizes that the community has an enormous influence on the interpretation of the emotional life of a believer, not only in the case of gradual conversions, where such control would be expected, but also in sudden conversions, where the social messages must be both more subtle and more quickly transmitted. But after the convert settles into the new life, the community teaches how that life is to be understood, and the past is revalued accordingly, often erasing previous understandings of the experience. Of course, the more time that elapses after the conversion, the more time there is for the convert to learn the social significance of the emotional experience he or she has undergone. Thus, the accounts of Paul's and other ancient conversions, even the first-person accounts, are retrospective retellings of events, greatly enhanced by group norms learned and appropriated in the years prior to the writing.[46]

Paul's statements about his past are therefore greatly influenced by his present commitments. And Luke is obviously even less reliable. Luke's model of conversion, we have seen, was that of Hebrew prophecy. The resulting portrait of Paul, in turn, formed the basis of a convention of conversion in the West that deeply affects even scientific research. So we should expect that Paul's own story, written many years after his conversion, would exhibit conventional aspects of conversion.

The history of research of the phenomenon of conversion has been changing from psychological to sociological orientation. In place of a passive subject, converted by external powers over which he or she has no control, as in Luke's description of Paul's conversion, current research stresses the social dimension of the conversion experience and an active subject who develops a new world of meaning by conversion and entrance into a new community. It also sees that the community itself has an enormous effect over the meaning of the conversion.[47] This perception of the active role of the convert in reforming the world is key to understanding Paul's writing. Paul is an example of such an active convert, remaking his world. More important is the effect that Paul's social context has in evaluating the meaning of his letters.

IMPERIALISM AND CONVERSION

Conversion can only take place where religious decisions are possible and necessary, which means that most ancient societies had no mechanism for conversion, though individuals may have felt called to a special vocation. Hellenistic society, as opposed to traditional first-temple Israelite society, contained multiple possibilities for religious choice. Indeed, this difference between Hellenistic society and ancient Israelite society is one reason why it is more appropriate to call Paul a convert than a prophet.

Israelite society, however, even during first-temple times, necessarily prescribed a certain number of conversion possibilities, because the religion of the God of Israel was itself a newcomer on the land, and it was in close competition with the earlier religions of the Canaanite population. The prophets constantly exhorted the people to remain true to the LORD, Israel's God, and not to choose the religion of the Canaanites. Deuteronomy explicitly outlined a religious choice:

> See I have set before you this day life and good, death and evil. If you obey the commandments of the Lord your God which I command you this day, by loving the Lord your God, by walking in his ways, and by keeping his commandments and his statutes and his ordinances, then you shall live and multiply, and the Lord your God will bless you in the

land which you are entering to take possession of it. . . . I call heaven and earth to witness against you this day, that I have set before you life and death, blessing and curse; therefore choose life, that you and your descendants may live, loving the Lord your God, obeying his voice, and cleaving to him; for that means life to you and length of days, that you may dwell in the land which the Lord swore to your fathers, to Abraham, to Isaac and to Jacob, to give them. (30:15–16, 19–20)

The passage presupposes that the Israelites have been given a rational choice for religious life and death. But the choice did not come from any sense of human free will. Instead it was part of the Hebrew mythological scheme known as the covenant. Making a covenant or agreement demanded a decisive choice. The ancient Israelite custom of covenanting, which became the model for the relationship between God and his people, guaranteed a certain amount of religious choice. Theoretically, one could always refuse; therefore, it was hoped, every worshiper of the LORD, the God of the Hebrews, had chosen to be his worshiper. For excellent reasons, this passage in Deuteronomy forms the basis for Paul's most extended analysis of the plan for Israel: the Hellenistic world only accelerated the possibilities for religious choice. But Deuteronomy 30 pointed out that the Israelites had always lived in an atmosphere of religious competition, which necessarily demanded religious choice as one paradigm of belonging to Israel.

The atmosphere of religious competition intensified after the destruction of the first temple by the Babylonians in 587–86 B.C.E. and its eventual rebuilding by Nehemiah and Ezra under Persian hegemony after 534 B.C.E. During this period foreign influences were strongly evidenced in Judah because of foreign military domination. After Persian rule gave way to the armies of Alexander the Great (333 B.C.E.), social conditions favored the development of competing religions and ideologies within Judah.[48] With Alexander's conquest came not only Greek domination, but the Greek language and culture. Because virtually the entire city population of the ancient Near East was forced into contact with the Greek language, for trade as well as political necessities, cultural interaction with foreign ideas quickened in an unprecedented way.

Yet the common culture that evolved out of Greek order and communication had little to do with the values of ancient Greece. It was an amalgamation of the religious ideas of all the lands that Alexander conquered, most of which were oriental in religion and political order. The Jews shared in this cultural pluralism both because exile had dispersed them throughout the Persian and Greek empires and because tiny Judah had to face the reality of foreign domination more squarely than the larger countries.

These developments tended to decrease the political importance of the agricultural interests and the traditional national agricultural divinities and their priesthoods. Greater world organization and communication increased the importance of individual, personal identity over the traditional corporate concepts of the identity of the ancient state.[49] Instead of defining themselves merely as children of Israel, individual Jews among the developing cosmopolitan culture of Hellenistic cities, like all other peoples throughout the ancient Near East, began to look at themselves as individuals with unique personal histories. As the educated classes became aware of their unique histories among the varieties of cultures in the Hellenistic world, they exercised a new, broader choice in their religion and life-style. As in trade, the freer atmosphere brought new competition between religious establishments, which could no longer take for granted the allegiance of their populations. As a result, the religious tradition, which had been an almost unconscious, self-evident assumption about the world, became a set of beliefs to be marketed.[50]

Ancient Israel reacted to the influx of Hellenistic culture as colonized nations have always reacted to imperialism. Colonialism bred both personal choice undreamed of in traditional society and strong resentment of the imperial order, which oppressed the native population. New politico-religious movements sprang up to explain God's ultimate plan against domination by foreign powers and sometimes to foment revolution against those powers. Meanwhile, other classes of people acculturated to the new powers and learned to share in the government of the country.[51] During the Hellenistic period, Israelite society divided into different sects, which differed over such religious issues as the existence of an afterlife and such political, social, and economic issues as the role of priests and scribes in national life. These sects competed with each other fiercely, but their interaction was absolutely essential to national unity in the cosmopolitan and individualistic Hellenistic world, for no one interpretation of Israel's traditional religious life could have satisfied the enormous spectrum of personal opinion that had developed. The sectarian rivalry, like the party system in the United States, allowed for an orderly expression of conflict.

In this atmosphere religious conversion was as common as it is today. The two other Jewish writers of the period who left us confessional literature, Josephus and Philo, also outline their personal religious quests, including their experimentation with the sects of the day. Underscoring the importance of individualism in the first century, their experiences differ radically from Paul's and from each other's. Paul, by his own admission, qualifies as a convert from one Jewish sect to another. But, when compared with Luke's account, Paul's writing shows other characteristics of modern conversion as well. Paul's own account of ecstatic experience must then be read to try to understand how his experience compares with contemporary views of conversion and with Jewish and Graeco-Roman religious phenomena.

CHAPTER TWO

℘PAUL'S ECSTASY

PAUL'S MYSTICAL REPORTS

Paul is a mystic. Like conversion, mysticism is a modern, analytic category, which cannot be applied to Paul without qualification. Mysticism has seemed more congenial than conversion to New Testament scholars, and the term has been employed extensively since the publication of Albert Schweitzer's influential *Mysticism of Paul the Apostle*.[1] Mysticism, however, is no more a part of Paul's vocabulary of self-understanding than conversion, though he uses the term *mystery* at several crucial points.[2] Mysticism has an esoteric, particular meaning in first-century Judaism; it is not merely a style of doing theology, as modern students of Paul have viewed it, or quiet contemplation. Rather, mysticism in first-century Judea was apocalyptic, revealing not meditative truths of the universe but the disturbing news that God was about to bring judgment. So scholarly use of mysticism has been etic, whereas the term retains its analytic power only when its first-century context has been adequately explored.

Paul is both a mystic and a convert. Perhaps because of modern reticence in the face of subjective and extraordinary aspects of experience, Paul's mysticism is no better understood by scholars than his conversion. Paul is a first-century Jewish apocalypticist, and as such, he was also a mystic. In fact, he is the only early Jewish mystic and apocalypticist whose personal, confessional writing has come down to us. To understand Paul's Judaism and his conversion, his mysticism must be investigated. In the process a great deal can be discovered about the religious life of early Christians and about Jewish mysticism in the first century.

Paul describes his own spiritual experiences in terms appropriate to a Jewish apocalyptic-mystagogue of the first century. He, like Enoch, relates his experiences of heavenly travel, in which he sees the secrets of the universe revealed. He believes his salvation to lie in a body-to-body identification with his heavenly savior, who sits on the divine throne and functions as God's glorious manifestation. He identifies this experience with his conversion, although it apparently characterizes a lifetime of spiritual discipline rather than a single event. As we have seen, the significance of this experience is later reworked by the church when Paul's life is made into the model for gentile conversion. In the later context, the mystical aspects of Paul's experiences are downplayed, and his new understanding of law becomes the primary value of his conversion.

Although the account of Paul's ecstatic conversion in Acts is a product of Luke's literary genius, Paul gives his own evidence for ecstatic experience. In Galatians 1, Paul claims that he did not receive the gospel from a human source. In 2 Cor. 12:1–9, he describes an experience that transcends human ken[3]:

> I must boast; there is nothing to be gained by it, but I will go on to visions and revelations of the Lord. I know a man in Christ who fourteen years ago was caught up to the third heaven—whether in the body or out of the body, I do not know, God knows. And I know that this man was caught up into Paradise—whether in the body or out of the body, I do not know, God knows—and he heard things that cannot be told, which man may not utter. On behalf of this man, I will boast, but on my own behalf I will not boast, except of my weaknesses. Though if I wish to boast, I shall not be a fool, for I shall be speaking the truth. But I refrain from it, so that no one may think more of me than he sees in me or hears from me. And to keep me from being too elated by the abundance of revelations, a thorn was given me in the flesh, a messenger of Satan, to harass me, to keep me from being too elated. Three times I besought the Lord about this, that it should leave me; but he said to me, "My grace is sufficient for you, for my power is made perfect in weakness."

As in Galatians 1, Paul calls this experience an *apokalypsis,* an apocalypse, a revelation. As in Acts and Galatians 1, the actual vision is not described. Unlike Acts and Galatians 1, however, this passage is a confessional description of a vision, or possibly two different ones, depending on whether the paradise visited in the ascension can be located in the third heaven.[4] Thus, the vision is both mystical and apocalyptic.[5]

The vision should be examined in the context of first-century Jewish apocalypticism. Second Corinthians 12 is so abstruse and esoteric that it must be teased from context and combined with our meager knowledge of apocalypticism and Jewish mysticism. Techniques of theurgy and heavenly ascent were secret lore in rabbinic literature (see b. Hagiga 13a–15b), which dates from the third century. Paul alone demonstrates that such traditions existed as early as the first century.[6]

Most people believe that 2 Corinthians 12 refers to Paul himself.[7] Paul says that he is boasting, yet he does not explicitly identify himself as the ecstatic voyager, since rhetoric demands his modesty and he says that nothing will be gained by his boasting. This follows from his statement that charismatic gifts cannot themselves prove faith (1 Corinthians 12–13). Paul may actually be revealing secret information in this passage.

By the end of the passage, Paul undoubtedly speaks about himself without specifying that he has changed the subject. He says that he has spoken three times with the Lord about "a thorn in the flesh" (2 Cor. 12:7–10), probably an infirmity; but the Lord had decided that it perfected his power. As a sudden change in subject would be clumsy, most scholars affirm that Paul is speaking about himself throughout. Further, Paul's admission that he has spoken to Christ about his infirmity three times in itself implies a communication greater than petitionary prayer.[8] Although the passage can be understood in other ways, Paul reveals modestly that he has had several ecstatic meetings with Christ over the previous fourteen years. One important meeting, possibly but not necessarily the first one, took place in a heavenly ascent to the enthroned presence of Christ. Paul's claim is not strange or ridiculous for a first-century Jew, since this experience parallels ecstatic ascents to the divine throne in other apocalyptic and merkabah mystical traditions in Jewish Hellenism. Paul's identity as the mystic seems assured, though his reputation has never featured ecstasy, perhaps because he opposed the excessive claims made by his opponents on the basis of his own ecstatic experiences described in this passage.

It is possible, if unlikely, that 2 Corinthians 12 records Paul's original conversion experience. In Galatians Paul speaks of his conversion as a revelation (apocalypse [1:12]), and in 2 Corinthians 12 he also speaks of revelations (apokalypseis). Acts 26:19 and 2 Cor. 12:1 describe (heavenly) visions (optasias). Yet in Galatians, Paul mentions a three-year hiatus between his conversion and his first visit to Jerusalem. Paul mentions that fourteen years passed before his second visit to Jerusalem, which was made at the direction of another revelation (Gal. 2:2). But ancient writers did not count years as we do; they could count initial and final fractions of a year as an entire year. Therefore, Paul's ministry must begin fourteen to seventeen years before the writing of Galatians, depending on whether the fourteen years includes the three years between his conversion and his first visit to Jerusalem. If 2 Corinthians was written subsequently, as many scholars believe, it may not be referring to his conversion, but arithmetical conventions prevent surety. Second Corinthians, however, is certainly a composite work, and since Paul's life is largely a mystery, it cannot be dated precisely. It would be unwise to proclaim that 2 Corinthians 12 was definitely Paul's conversion. It remains one of innumerable historical problems that cannot be resolved without further evidence or insight.

It is just as likely that Paul is describing a revelation both similar and subsequent to his conversion. We know that Paul necessarily had several ecstatic experiences. This is Luke's opinion as well, for Luke describes ecstatic revelations in the three narrations of Paul's conversion (9:3f; 22:6f; 26:12f). But Acts 16:9f, 18:9f, and especially 22:17f describe other ecstatic visions (*en ekstasei* [22:17]).[9] Even allowing for Acts' repetition, Paul's earliest biographer claimed that he had several ecstatic experiences. This is not surprising, given Paul's cultural environment. Jewish mysticism, and perhaps apocalypticism as well, sought out visions and developed special practices to achieve them.[10] Thus, we can assume that Paul had a number of ecstatic experiences in his life, that his conversion may have been one such experience—though it need not have been one—and that the meaning of these experiences was mediated by the gentile Christian community in which he lived.

We know that converts learn the meanings of their experience in their new community. This appears to be true of Paul's mysticism as well. He may have learned about ecstatic experience as a Pharisee or merely known about them generally from his Jewish background. He may also have learned about them in Christianity, but this merely begs the question; ultimately, someone Jewish must have brought them into Christianity, and there is not much time between the end of Jesus' ministry and the beginning of Paul's.

The Christian interpretation by Paul of his visions does mark his long association with the Christian community. The divine nature of Paul's revelation does not preclude the influence of his supporting Christian community. Converts naturally find the meaning of their conversions and their visions in the community that values them. Thus, we can ask but we need not answer why a Pharisee would have a vision of Christ. Any convert and especially a converted Pharisee who knew of mystical and apocalyptic traditions would give these experiences Christian interpretations if that person had chosen to join a Christian community. Instead of trying to pin these ecstatic visions to Paul's conversion, as evangelical and Pentecostal Christians try to do, the modern data about conversions suggests that the interpretation of the visions is mediated by an education in Christian community. Paul may have decided to become a Christian for the reasons that Luke suggests, or the experience itself may be lost forever since Paul himself does not tell us how it took place. It may be either rational or mystical. But it is clear that Paul had visions. He used these visions to interpret the consequences of his faith and to express the meaning of his conversion. To understand Paul's interpretation we must first try to understand the features of Jewish apocalypticism and mysticism. Indeed, we can understand a good deal more about first-century Jewish mysticism if we take Paul seriously as a Jewish mystic, with a special Christian cast.

APOCALYPTICISM AND MYSTICISM

Apocalypticism and mysticism have remained separate scholarly categories because they refer to two different, easily distinguishable types of literature. But they are not unrelated experiences. Jewish mystical texts are full of apocalypses; early apocalyptic literature is based on ecstatic visions with profound mystical implications. This suggests that scholars have carried a distinction in literary genre into the realm of experience without sufficient warrant. It is likewise misleading to distinguish strictly between ecstatic, out-of-body visions as found in mysticism and literal bodily ascensions to heaven as are more frequently found in apocalypticism.[11] In merkabah mysticism the voyager often speaks as though he is actually going from place to place in heaven, yet we know from the frame narratives that the adept's body is on earth, where his utterances are being questioned and written down by a group of disciples.[12] Paul speaks at a time before these distinctions were clear or accepted by his community. He is not sure whether the ascent took place in the body or out of it. We should also note that Paul does not utilize the concept of a soul (*psyché*) to effect this heavenly travel. Paul's concept of the soul is quite limited, undisturbed by Platonic ideas of the soul's immortality. Rather, Paul refers to spirit (*pneuma*) more frequently. This suggests that Paul understood being *in Christ* as a literal exchange of earthly body for a new, pneumatic one to be shared with the resurrected Jesus at the eschaton.

Under what terms could a credible journey to heaven take place?

Modern sensibilities balk at the notion of physical transport to heaven, whereas a heavenly journey in vision or trance is credible. When a heavenly journey is described literally, the cause may be literary convention or the belief of the voyager; when reconstructing the actual experience, only one type can pass modern standards of credibility. Paul's confusion over the nature of his ecstatic journey to heaven provides a rare insight into first-century thinking, since it demonstrates either a disagreement in the community or more likely a first-century mystic's inability to distinguish between bodily and spiritual journeys. Our world no longer supports his quandary; nor did the ancient world shortly after Paul's time. They adopted the Platonic notion of the soul, which answered the question sufficiently for them and which still informs religious life today. Paul, however, conceived his journey without a developed concept of the soul. Thus, he is apparently describing a mystical notion of a spiritual body that is received by and finds residence in Christ.

Based on Paul's report, it is not possible to know whether any liturgical rites accompanying or even stimulating the astral journey existed in first-century Judaism. Since the apocalyptic and pseudepigrapical literature is vast, with an enormous variety of ascension accounts, many different concepts (and perhaps techniques) of spiritual journeys were available to mystics and apocalypticists.[13] Because Paul's experience was a journey by means of a spiritual body, it seems warranted to call it an ecstatic or paranormal experience, rather than physical transport, though Paul himself would caution against claims of authority based on ecstasy.

PAUL'S CONVERSION IN LIGHT OF APOCALYPTICISM AND MYSTICISM

With only the most general hints about Paul's conversion in his own writing, we must fill in the Jewish cultural context informing his experience. Ezekiel 1 was one of the central scriptures that Luke, and Paul, used to understand Paul's conversion. The vision of the throne-chariot of God in Ezekiel 1, with its attendant description of Glory (*Kavod*), God's Glory or form, for the human figure, is a central image of Jewish mysticism, which is closely related to the apocalyptic tradition.[14] The name *merkabah*—that is, throne-chariot mysticism, which is the usual Jewish designation for these mystical traditions as early as the mishnaic period (ca. 220 C.E.; see Mishnah Hagiga 2.1)—is the rabbinic term for the heavenly conveyance described in Ezekiel 1.[15] (The ground-breaking work of Hugo Odeberg, Gershom Scholem, Morton Smith, and Alexander

Altmann[16] showing the Graeco-Roman context for these texts in Jewish mysticism has been followed up by a few scholars who have shown the relevance of these passages to the study of early rabbinic literature,[17] as well as apocalypticism and Samaritanism and Christianity.[18] The entire collection of Hekhaloth texts has been published recently by Peter Schaefer[19] and translations of several of the works have already appeared.[20] Nevertheless, the results of this research have not yet been broadly discussed, nor are they well known. The ten-volume compendium known in English as *The Theological Dictionary of the New Testament,* edited by G. Kittel, has scarcely a dozen references to Ezekiel 1, although it is a crucial passage informing the christology of the New Testament, as Gilles Quispel has so cogently pointed out.[21])

Those of us who have championed the importance of this material had been waiting for the publication of the full text of the Angelic Liturgy from Qumran, for the existence of speculation on the heavenly hierarchy has been strongly suggested in the initial reports of the finds in cave 4 (4QShir-Shab).[22] Recently, the long-awaited text has been published. The new critical edition confirms the same themes of Jewish mysticism that we can only date to the third century from mystical sources. The Angelic Liturgy is pre-Christian and could not have appeared later than the first century C.E. It contains many oblique references to the divine hierarchies, the seven heavens inside one another, and the appearance and movements of God's throne-chariot, familiar to scholars of merkabah mysticism. First Enoch and Ezekiel 1 seem to be the informing scriptural passages, but the hierarchy of heavens is best known from such merkabah documents as the *Reuyoth Yehezkel* (The visions of Ezekiel).[23] The Angelic Liturgy evinces some of the most characteristic aspects of Jewish mysticism in an apocalyptic community of the first century. Exactly which parts of merkabah speculation were understood this early, however, is unclear. In this general atmosphere, Paul is an important witness to the kind of experience that apocalyptic Jews were reporting and an important predecessor to merkabah mysticism.

MERKABAH AND ITS PREDECESSORS

Though it would be impractical to review all work currently underway on apocalyptic and merkabah mysticism, its relationship to Christianity and Paul's writings can be briefly summarized. In the Hebrew Bible, God is sometimes described in human form. Exod. 23:21 mentions an angel who has the form of a man and who carries within him or represents "the name of God." A human figure on the divine throne is described in Ezekiel 1, Daniel 7, and Exodus 24, among other places, and was blended into a consistent picture of a principal mediator figure who, like the angel of the Lord in Exodus 23, embodied, personified, or carried the name of God, YHWH, the tetragrammaton. This figure, elaborated on by Jewish tradition, would become a central metaphor for Christ in Christianity.

Several Jewish traditions discuss the *eikōn* or image of God as Adam's prelapsarian appearance, an especially glorious and splendid form that humanity lost when Adam sinned. The lost "image and form of God" (Gen. 1:26) is thereafter associated with God's human appearance in the Bible or with the description of the principal angel of God who carries God's name. The human figure on the merkabah described by Ezekiel is called "the appearance of the likeness of the Glory of the Lord." Thus, God's Glory or *Kavod* can be a technical term for God's human appearances.[24]

This enigmatic human appearance of God, discussed with appropriate self-consciousness in the Bible, is probably related to the so-called son of man, which is not a proper name. The heavenly son of man appears in the vision in Dan. 7:13 in which an "ancient of days" appoints a human figure ("one like a son of man") to execute justice in the destruction of the evil ones. This human figure is best understood as an angel.[25] In Dan. 12:3 resurrection is promised both for the faithful dead and for the most heinous villains, who will be resurrected so that they may be sentenced to eternal perdition. *Hamaskilim,* or "those who are wise," the elite of the apocalyptic group, will then shine as the stars in heaven. This scripture implies that the leaders will be transformed into angels, since the stars were identified with angels in biblical tradition (e.g., Job 38:7).

The preeminence of the enigmatic human figure is due primarily to the description of the angel of the Lord in Exodus. Exod. 23:20–21 states: "Behold, I send an angel before you, to guard you on the way and to bring you to the place which I have prepared. Give heed to him and hearken to his voice, do not rebel against him, for he will not pardon your transgression; for my name is in him." The Bible expresses the unique status of this angel by means of its participation in the divine name.[26] In Exod. 33:18–23, Moses asks to see the Glory of God. In answer, God makes "his goodness" pass in front of him but he cautions, "You cannot see my face; for man shall not see me and live. . . . Behold, there is a place by me where you shall stand upon the rock; and while my Glory passes by I will put you in a cleft of the rock, and I will cover you with my hand until I have passed by; then I will take away my hand and you shall see my back; but my face shall not be seen." Yahweh himself, the angel of God, and his Glory are peculiarly melded together, suggesting a deep secret about the ways God manifested himself to humanity.

The Septuagint, the second-century B.C.E. translation of the Hebrew Bible into Greek, identifies the figure on the throne in Ezek. 1:26 with the form (*eidos*) of man. This term has a philosophical history dating from Plato's *Parmenides* 130c, where *eidos* means the *idea* of man. For Platonists, *eidos* meant the unchanging immortal idea of man that survives death. Because of Plato's fortunate use of language, Hellenistic Jews could reinterpret the phrase "form of man" to mean *eidos*. So for Hellenistic Jewish mystics like Philo, the figure of man on the divine throne described in Genesis, Exodus, Ezekiel, Daniel, and the Psalms (forming the basis of the son of man speculation) was also understood as the ideal and immortal man. His immortality and glorious appearance were things Adam possessed in the Garden of Eden and lost when he sinned.[27] In this form, the traditions concerning the son of man are centuries older than Christianity, and Paul, as we shall see, uses them to good advantage.

In the Hellenistic period many new interpretations of Ezek. 1:26 grew up. In various Jewish sects and conventicles the foremost name given to the figure on the throne is Yahoel. The first-century *Apocalypse of Abraham* presents Yahoel as a version of the divine name, since it is a combination of the tetragrammaton and a suffix denoting angelic stature. Yahoel appears in chapters 10 and 11, where he is described as the one "in whom God's ineffable name dwells." Other titles for this figure included Melchizedek, Metatron, Adoil, Eremiel, and preeminently the son of man. Melchizedek appears at Qumran, in the document called 11QMelch, where he is identified with the *Elohim* of Ps. 82:1, thus giving us yet another variation on the theme of carrying the name of God. Metatron is called YHWH *hakaton*, or YHWH, Jr., and sits on a throne equal to God's in 3 Enoch 10.1.[28] The name of the angel varies from tradition to tradition. Michael is God's "mediator" and general (*archistrategos* [2 Enoch 33.10; T. Dan. 6.1–5; T. Abr. 1.4; cf. Life of Adam and Eve 14.1–2]). Eremiel appears in the *Apocalypse of Zephaniah* 6.1–15, where he is mistaken for God. In the *Ascension of Isaiah* 7.2–4, an angel whose name cannot be given appears.

Chief angelic mediators appear in Jewish literature of the first several centuries.[29] The chief angelic mediator, whom we can call by a number of terms—God's vice-regent, his Wazir, his gerent—is easily distinguished from the plethora of divine creatures, for the principal angel is not only head of the heavenly hosts but sometimes participates in God's own being or divinity. The rabbis most often call God's principal angel Metatron. In rabbinic literature and Jewish mysticism Metatron is probably not a proper name but a title adapted from the Greek word *Metathronos*, meaning "one who stands after or behind the throne." This represents a rabbinic softening of the Hellenistic term *synthronos*, or "one who is with the throne," that is, sharing enthronement or acting for the properly enthroned authority. The rabbis would have changed the preposition from one connoting equality (*syn-*, "with") to one connoting inferiority (*meta-*, "after or behind") in order to reduce the heretical implications of calling God's principal helping angel *synthronos*.[30]

Alongside these traditions lies the notion more relevant to Christianity that certain heroes can be transformed into angels as part of their ascension. This may be the most puzzling part of the mystic traditions but it is important in view of Paul's mysticism.[31] In the *Testament of Abraham* 11 (Recension A), some patriarchs are exalted as angels. Adam is pictured on a golden throne with a terrifying appearance and adorned with Glory. Abel is similarly glorified, acting as judge over creation until the final judgment (chaps. 12–13). 2 Enoch 30.8–11 also states that Adam was an angel: "And on earth I assigned him to be a second angel, honored and great and glorious."[32] In the Prayer of Joseph, found in Origen's Commentary on John 2.31 and with a further fragment in Philocalia 23.15, Jacob describes himself as "an angel of God and a ruling spirit," and he claims to be the "first-born of every living thing," "the first minister before the face of God," "the archangel of the power of the Lord, and "the chief captain among the sons of God."[33]

Enoch and Moses are the most important non-Christian figures of divinization or angelic transformation. Philo describes Moses as divine, based on the word *God* used of him in Exod. 4:16 and 7:1. In Sir. 45:1–5 Moses is compared to God ("equal in glory to the holy ones," in the Greek version of the text). Philo and the Samaritans also expressed Moses' preeminence in Jewish tradition by granting him a kind of deification.[34] In the *Testament of Moses,* Moses is described as the mediator or "arbiter of his covenant" (1:14) and celebrated as "that sacred spirit, worthy of the Lord . . . the Lord of the Word . . . the divine prophet throughout the earth, the most perfect teacher in the world," the "advocate," and "the great messenger" (11:16–19). Wayne Meeks concluded that "Moses was the most important figure in all Hellenistic Jewish apologetic."[35]

Evidence of the antiquity of mystical speculation about *Kavod* is found in the fragment of the tragedy *Moses* written by Ezekiel the Tragedian in the second century B.C.E. or earlier.[36] Moses is depicted as seeing a vision of the throne of God with a figure seated on it. The figure on the throne is called *phōs gennaios,* "a venerable man," which is a double entendre in Greek, since *phos* can mean either light or man depending on the gender of the noun.[37] The surviving text of *Moses* also hints at a transformation of an earthly hero into a divine figure. Ezekiel the Tragedian relates that the venerable man handed Moses his scepter and summoned him to sit on the throne, placing a diadem on his head. Thereafter the stars bow to him and parade for his inspection. Since throughout the biblical period the stars were thought to be angels (Job 38:7), Moses is being depicted as leader of the angels and hence above the angels. Moses' enthronement as a monarch or divinity in heaven resembles the enthronement of the son of man. This scene illustrates some of the traditions that later appear in Jewish mysticism and may have informed Paul's ecstatic ascent. The identification of Jesus with the manlike appearance of God is both the central characteristic of Christianity and understandable within the context of Jewish mysticism and apocalypticism.[38]

Philo often speaks of Moses as being made into a divinity (*'eis theon* [e.g., *Sacrifices* 1–10; *Moses* 1.155–58]). In exegeting Moses' receiving the Ten Commandments, Philo envisions an ascent, not merely up the mountain but to the heavens. This possibly describes a mystical identification between God and Moses, suggesting that Moses attained a divine nature through contact with the *logos.* In *Questions and Answers on Exodus* 1.29, 40, Philo writes that Moses was changed into a divinity on Mount Sinai. In *Moses* 1.155–58, he says that God placed the entire universe into Moses' hands and that the elements obeyed him as their master; then God rewarded Moses by appointing him a "partner" (*koinonon*) of God's own possessions and by giving into his hand the world as a portion well-fitted for God's heir (155). In the *Sacrifices of Cain and Abel* 8–10, Philo refers to Deut. 5:31 as proof that certain people are distinguished by God to be stationed "beside himself." Moses is preeminent among these people as his grave is not known, which for Philo apparently means that Moses was transported to heaven.

The Hebrew term *shutaf* (partner), describing any of God's helpers, became a heresy to the rabbis in first- and second-century Judaism. Thus, the stage was set for a great conflict over the existence, nature, status, and meaning of God's primary angelic mediator. Merkabah themes of viewing God can be seen in Philo's allegory. In light of the subsequent battle, it is amazing that such a prominent Jew of the first century as Philo could suggest so clearly a mystical merging of humans with a divine manifestation.[39] Philo himself cannot possibly be the author of these traditions. He relied on the Hebrew Bible, but he must also have had access to traditions that amplified these texts in a mystical direction, as did the other Hellenistic Jewish writers.

Philo also made use of biblical traditions of intermediation in his description of the *logos,* his name for God's demiurge in creation and for the pattern of the world. Philo claimed Gen. 1:26 described the creation of the heavenly man, and he took Gen. 2:7 to refer to the creation of the earthly man (*On the Creation* 134; *Allegory* 1.31, 53ff, 88f; *Questions on Gen.* 1.4; 2.56). He calls the heavenly man the image of man (*ho kat' eikona anthrōpos*) and the *logos* a second God (*deuteros theos*): "Why does he say, as if of another god: 'in the image of God he made man' and not 'in His own image'? . . . It is because nothing can be made in the likeness of God but only in that of the second God *deuteros theos,* who is His *logos*" (*Questions on Gen.* 2.62). On the basis of the divine likeness, Philo calls the visible embodiment of God a *second God.* The heavenly man shares his image with mankind as well, since he is the Platonic form of man.

Philo allegorizes any reference to God's human features in the Hebrew Bible as the *logos.* Moses and the elders see the Lord, who is the logos (*Of Flight and Finding* 164f). The Lord whom Jacob saw on the heavenly ladder (Gen. 28:13) was the archangel, that is, the logos, in whose form God reveals himself (*On Dreams* 1.157; *On the Change of Names* 87, 126; *On the Migration of Abraham* 168; *Allegory* 3.177; *Who is Heir* 205). These references anthropomorphize God, because they symbolize the likenesses he shares with humanity.

Enoch is similarly esteemed as a heavenly voyager. His exploits form an enormous body of material, second only to Moses. According to the sectarian book of *Jubilees,* Enoch receives a night vision in which he sees the entire future until the judgment day (4:18–19). He spends six jubilees of years with the angels of God, learning everything about the earth and heavens, from their composition and motion and to the locations of hell and heaven (4:21). When he finally ascends, he takes up residence in the Garden of Eden "in majesty and honor," recording the deeds of humanity and serving in the sanctuary as priest (4:23–26); he writes many books (21:20), and there are indeed references to his writings in many other pseudepigrapha.[40]

The various incarnations of God's principal angel carry or personify his name, which can be identifical to the form of man.[41] Exemplary men can also ascend to divinity by identification with or transformation into the enthroned figure. The rabbis polemicized against the idea that God has a partner or that there are "two powers in heaven" (*shtei reshuyot b'sham-*

ayim).[42] Because no early Jewish mediator figure helps in creation, and because the Gnostic mediators primarily do so, a creative function for the mediator would signal an important intermediary role in transmitting and possibly transforming these traditions into Gnosticism—which J. Fossum finds in Samaritanism.[43]

One apocalyptic mediator, Enoch, predates Paul. He is portrayed in the Enochic literature, which was widespread in Judaism, as we have learned from the Dead Sea Scrolls.[44] Enoch is a primeval hero of the Bible whose death is not mentioned. Gen. 5:18–24 twice relates that Enoch walked with God and then disappeared, for "God took him."

First Enoch is the first of many books based on the terse biblical report. Enoch begins his journey to heaven to intercede for the fallen angels (14). In Enoch's vision,[45] believers are mystically transformed into white cows, which appear to symbolize the messiah: "And I [Enoch] saw that a snow-white cow was born, with huge horns; all the beasts of the field and all the birds of the sky feared him and made petition to him all the time. I went on seeing until all their kindred were transformed, and became snow-white cows; and the first among them became something, and that something became a great beast with huge horns on its head" (90:37–39). The believers symbolically share the being of the messiah. The messiah not only saves but serves as the model for transformation of believers.

In *The Parables of Enoch* (1 Enoch 37–71), Enoch performs various messianic functions. He is righteous and knows divine secrets (46.3). He is victorious over the mighty of the earth and judges the wicked (46.4–8; 62.9; 63.11; 69.27–29). He is probably the figure described as the "Chosen One" or the "Elect One" or the "messiah," since virtually identical functions are attributed to these three figures (49.2–4; 51.3–5; 52.4–9; 55.4; 61.4–9; 62.2–16).[46] He judges "in the name of the Lord of Spirits" (55.4), sitting on the throne (51.3; 55.4; 61.8; 62.2–6; 70.27), and at the end of his life he ascends to his enthroned status.

The Parables of Enoch contain several references to angelic transformation. Enoch ascends to heaven while reciting hymns and blessings, as do the merkabah mystics, where he is overcome with the splendor and glory of the throne rooms (39). His face changes on account of the vision, which evidently reflects the prophecy that "those who are wise shall shine as the stars" (Dan. 11:2). First Enoch 62.15 states that the elect shall shine as stars and be clothed with garments of glory. Most important, at the end of *The Parables of Enoch* (70–71), Enoch is mystically transformed on the throne into the figure of the son of man: "My whole body mollified and my spirit transformed" (1 Enoch 71:1).[47] This event underlines the importance of mystic transformation between the adept and the angelic vice-regent of God, giving a plausible explanation of how the sectarians that produced the visions in Daniel expected to be transformed into stars. It is possible to say that 1 Enoch 71 gives us the experience of an adept undergoing the astral transformation prophesied in Dan. 12:2, albeit in the name of a pseudepigraphical hero. If this is true, then Paul gives us the actual, confessional experience of the same spiritual event, with Christ substituting for the son of man. In both cases, the believer is subsumed into the body of heavenly savior and becomes a kind of star or celestial immortal.

Because the ascent of the living is supposed to parallel exactly the ascent of the dead after death, 1 Enoch 70–71 either retells Enoch's earthly ascent or refers to the ascent at the end of his life. The puzzling superscription to chapter 70, the composite nature of the text, and some possible imprecision in chronology prevent complete surety on this issue: "And it happened after this that his living name was raised up before that son of man and to the Lord from among those who dwell upon the earth" (70.1). The journey is taken by Enoch's name, not precisely his soul, again reflecting a level of mystical speculation that predates the importation of the platonic notion of a soul. It may be that the transformation motif is particularly important because the notion of the soul had not deeply penetrated this level of Jewish society. This transformation motif is, of course, amenable to the explicit concept of the immortal soul as it develops within Judaism and Christianity.

Whatever the intention of the author of 1 Enoch, the relationship to Paul's experience is important.[48] Like Enoch, Paul claims to have gazed on the Glory, whom Paul identifies as Christ; Paul understands that he has been transformed into a divine state, which will be fully realized after his death; Paul claims that his vision and transformation is somehow a mystical identification; and Paul claims to have received a calling, his special status as intermediary. Paul specifies the meaning of this calling for all believers, a concept absent in the Enochic texts, although it may have been assumed within the original community.

Complete surety about the history of this tradition is elusive. Paul does not explicitly call Christ the Glory of God.[49] And because 1 Enoch 37–71 are missing from the Dead Sea Scrolls, we cannot date them accurately. They might date from the first century or later and be influenced by Christianity, since they are extant only in the Ethiopic Version of Enoch, the official canon of the Ethiopian Christian Church. Whatever the date of 1 Enoch 70–71, the stories of Enoch's ascensions in 1 Enoch 14 antedated

Paul and would have influenced his conceptions about heavenly journey.[50] Further, as long as the date of 1 Enoch 70–71 cannot be fixed
exactly and the evidence from the Dead Sea Scrolls remains ambiguous,
Paul himself remains the earliest author explicitly expressing transformation in Judaism. If his discussion of transformation can be related to
apocalyptic mysticism in Judaism, he also becomes the only Jewish mystic
of this period to relate this experience confessionally.

The theme of angelic transformation usually appears in a story of a
heavenly journey. It becomes especially important in Kabbalah, but it is
sparsely attested in first-century Judaism. Since we have no rabbinic works
that can be firmly dated to the first century, Paul's confessional reports are
important as evidence for dating merkabah mysticism.[51] Paul's texts provide information about first-century Judaism and Jewish mysticism, as
important as the Jewish texts that have been found to establish the meaning of Christian texts. Indeed, Paul's letters may be more important to the
history of Judaism than the rabbinic texts are to the interpretation of
Christian Scriptures.

Second Enoch, extant only in two Slavonic versions, is an extension of
the Enoch legend, most probably through a Christian recension, since
Torah does not figure in the story. Yet, the possibility of a Semitic, possibly
even a Jewish *Vorlage,* especially in the shorter version, cannot be ruled
out. In 2 Enoch 22.7, Enoch is transformed into "one of his glorious
ones," an angel, during a face-to-face encounter with the Lord. But note
the use of glorification language to characterize angelic status: God decrees, "Let Enoch join in and stand in front of my face forever," explaining
the rabbinic term *Prince of the Presence,* which is normally applied to
Metatron. Then Enoch is transformed: "And the LORD said to Michael,
'Go, and extract Enoch from [his] earthly clothing. And anoint him with
my delightful oil, and put him into the clothes of my glory.' And so
Michael did, just as the Lord had said to him. He anointed me and he
clothed me. And the appearance of that oil is greater than the greatest
light, and its ointment is like sweet dew, and its fragrance myrrh; and it is
like the rays of the glittering sun. And I looked at myself, and I had become
like one of his glorious ones, and there was no observable difference"
(2 *Enoch* 22.8–10, recension A).

This transformation is effected through a change of clothing. The
clothing functions as or symbolizes Enoch's new, immortal flesh, as they
are immortal clothes emanating from the throne room, not from earth.
This parallels Paul's future glorification of the mortal body in 2 Cor. 5:1–
10.[52] Enoch has been put *in* the body of an angel, or he is *in* the manlike

figure in 1 Enoch 71. This could explain Paul's use of the peculiar terminology *in Christ*.

The *Ascension of Isaiah* also focuses on ascent and heavenly transformation. In chapters 6–11, usually attributed to a Christian hand, the theophany of Isaiah 6 is described as a heavenly journey in which the prophet sees God. The prophet is taken through each of the seven heavens, stopping to view the glorious figure seated on the throne of each heaven. When he worships the figure in the fifth heaven, he is explicitly warned not to worship any angel, as the rabbis warn against the crime of assuming that there are two powers in heaven. Isaiah is told that his throne, garments, and crown await him in heaven (7.22). All those who love the Most High will at their end ascend by the angel of the Holy Spirit (7.23). At each heaven, Isaiah is glorified the more, emphasizing the transformation that occurs as a human travels closer to God (7.24); he effectively becomes one of the angels. According to the other angels, Isaiah's vision is unprecedented; no one else has been vouchsafed such a complete vision of the reward awaiting the good (8.11–13). But Isaiah must return to earth to complete his prophetic commission before he can enjoy the rest that awaits him in heaven.[53]

The climax of the story is angelic transformation, but the stated purpose of the journey is theodicy—to understand God's justice. The journeys in these early apocalyptic texts usually begin after a crisis of human confidence about God's intention to bring justice to the world, and they result in the discovery that the universe is indeed following God's moral plan. The ancient scriptures about God's providence are proved true, and it is foretold that the evil ones who predominate on earth, oppressing God's saints, are to receive the punishment that they richly deserve. The ascension story, especially if performed by an earthly hero before his death, functions as a justification for the suffering of the righteous because it verifies what the community would like to believe—namely, that injustices will be recompensed by their ascension to heavenly immortality after death and that the evil ones will be condemned to hell. Although its narration describes exotic and amazing events, the purpose is pragmatic, explaining the structure of heaven and providing an eschatological verification that God's plan will come to fruition. Immortalization is the explicit purpose of the pagan ascension texts. In some of the Jewish material, where immortality is automatically guaranteed by moral living, more complex purposes are promulgated. Besides confirming God's plan in the face of the earthly victory of the ungodly or the slaughter of the righteous, the stories describe the mechanism by which immortality is achieved.

Transformation to one's immortal state is pictured as becoming one with an angelic figure, perhaps illustrating the person's identification with a preexistent guardian angel.

In 2 Baruch (Syr.) the theme of angelic transformation sounds loud and strong. This book is widely believed to have been influenced by Christianity, but it is variously dated from the first century to the third. Second Baruch 51.3ff portrays a gradual transformation of all believers into angelic creatures, as the process of redemption is fulfilled:

> Also, as for the glory of those who proved to be righteous on account of my law, those who possessed intelligence in their life, and those who planted the root of wisdom in their heart—their splendor will then be glorified by transformations, and the shape of their face will be changed into the light of their beauty so that they may acquire and receive the undying world which is promised to them. . . . When they therefore will see that those over whom they are exalted now will then be more exalted and glorified than they, then both these and those will be changed, these into the splendor of angels and those into startling visions and horrible shapes; . . . For they will live in the heights of that world and they will be like the angels and be equal to the stars. And they will be changed into any shape which they wished, for beauty to loveliness, and from light to the splendor of glory. . . . And the excellence of the righteous will then be greater than that of the angels.[54]

This is a true fleshing out of the visions of Daniel. The evil ones are transformed into the terrible beasts of the Daniel vision, and the righteous are explicitly transformed into stars.

Another aspect of this tradition is the enormous size of the principal angelic vice-regent of God; an analogy with Indo-European mythology may have influenced the development of the Judeo-Christian tradition. A correspondence between a cosmic man and the features of the cosmos is an ancient aspect of Indo-European thought.[55] Such conceptions probably enter Greek literature through Orphism. Representations of a giant man, the Macranthropos, with a head composed of the heaven, a belly or body composed of the sea or the ether, feet composed of earth, eyes of the sun and moon, are found in the Derveni papyrus, the Sarapis Oracle in Macrobius, the Greek Magical Papyri, and the Hermetic literature.[56]

In merkabah mysticism, the mediator figure is apparently not God himself, though he is often described in divine terms, as when he is given the name Zoharariel YHWH. In this case, it is not possible to distinguish between the angel and God. In other references, the awe and reverence of the supreme deity is protected by giving the figure on the throne a clear angelic identity, like Metatron. Divinizing Metatron is explicitly labeled heresy both in rabbinic writings and the hekhaloth texts. These traditions no doubt reflect different rabbinic understandings of the contradiction between biblical passages describing God's self-revelation (e.g., Exod. 24:10) and the statements that no one may see God and live (Exod. 33).[57]

In writings of the church fathers and in Gnostic sources, similar ideas of ascent and mediation are found. Gnostic sources often depict an opposition between two heavenly hypostases, one a savior and other an ignorant demiurge.[58] The difference between the high God and the intermediary forms can be described in the relationship between an object and its image. God's image is often the intermediary and can also be described as the perfect man, as is Adamas in Irenaeus's account of the Barbelognostics (*Against the Heresies* 1.29.33).[59]

In the Merkabah tract now called 3 Enoch (*Sefer Hekhaloth*), the man Enoch is transformed into Metatron (3–15). Metatron bears a striking resemblance to Moses in Ezekiel the Tragedian's play. God makes a throne for Enoch-Metatron in 3 Enoch (10.1); he gives him a special garment of Glory and a royal gown (12.1–3); God makes him ruler over all kingdoms and all heavenly beings (10.3); all the angels of every rank, and the angels of the sun, moon, stars, and planets, fall prostrate when Enoch sits on his throne (14.1–5); he knows the names of all the stars (46.1–2; see Ps. 147:40)[60]; God reveals to him all the secrets of heaven and earth so that Enoch knows past, present, and future (10.5; 11.1; cf. 45.1; 48 (D).7); God calls him YHWH hakaton, another interpretation of Exod. 23:21 (12.5).[61] The date of these documents is far too late to be of specific guidance for Paul.[62] Whatever the date of Daniel or the earliest son of man traditions, this angelic figure, the figure that the Bible sometimes calls the *Kavod* or the principal angel of God, is pre-Christian and is a factor in Paul's description of Christ.[63]

There is adequate evidence that many Jewish mystics and apocalypticists sensed a relationship between the heavenly figure on the throne and important figures in the life of their community. The roots of this tradition are pre-Christian. Further, Jewish scholars have overlooked Christianity as evidence for the existence of these traditions in first-century Judaism. Paul did not have to be a religious innovator to posit an identification between a vindicated hero and the image of the *Kavod*, the manlike figure in heaven, although the identification of the figure with the risen Christ is obviously a uniquely Christian development.[64] Paul is the only Jewish mystic to report his own personal, identifiably confessional mystical experiences in the fifteen hundred years that separate Ezekiel from the rise of Kabbalah.

THE ECSTATIC DIMENSION OF VISIONS AND TRANSFORMATIONS

Because Paul's experiences are manifestly ecstatic, there has been no need to question the existence of ecstasy within the Jewish mystical tradition. But biblical tradition and early Judaism also hint that visions normally took place in religiously altered states of consciousness. Besides the exegesis of Ezekiel and related passages, a tradition of ecstatic vision was well established in Hebrew society and was interpreted as ecstatic from its biblical precedents.[65] The vocabulary of biblical theophanies and the visions of God in the Hebrew Bible imply ecstasy or paranormal consciousness—not only with the preposition *like* (*k*), but also of other terms suggesting likeness and comparison, such as *mar'eh*, *demuth*, *tavnith*, and *ṣelem*. The terms in Hebrew originally signified the paranormal quality of the experience of these theophanies, safeguarding the sight of God from ordinary human vision. Thus, they are also closely associated with the revelation of the appearance of God's manlike form and with the creation of man throughout scripture: "Let us create man in our *likeness* and *form*" (Gen. 1:26).

In Ezek. 1:2, the prophet receives his call through a theophany at the river Chebar. In his "visions of God" (Ezek. 1:1) he sees the likeness (*demuth*) of living creatures who had the likeness (*demuth*) of men in the front but animal faces on the other sides. Above the firmament he sees the likeness (*demuth*) of a throne with a figure with the likeness of a man (*demuth kmar'eh adam*) seated thereon (Ezek. 1:26 LXX: "kai epi tou homoiōmatos tou thronou homoiōma hōs eidos anthrōpou anōthen"). Ezekiel understands this vision as a description of God's Glory: "Such was the appearance of the likeness of the Glory of the Lord" (1:28; in Hebrew, "Mareh demuth kavod YHWH"). That the Glory of God refers to the manlike figure and not the whole vision is manifest from the rest of Ezekiel where *Kavod* YHWH or the God of Israel is described as sitting on the throne or otherwise personified (3:12, 23; 8:4; 9:3; 10:4, 18–22; 11:22–25; 43:2–5; 44:4). In this particular place, the vision means that the presence of God has left Jerusalem before the destruction of the temple and remains with the exiles in Babylonia.[66]

The term *Glory* is itself a way of safeguarding the actual appearance of God. We do not know God himself, who is beyond our figuration. We only know his Glory, the form in which he chooses to reveal himself. The terms for likeness, then, suggest two things: first, that the experience is visionary, not normal; second, that Ezekiel saw an appearance or an image of the Glory, not the Glory itself, which further safeguards the majesty of God. No one can see God and live (Exod. 33:20), nor apparently can one see his Glory directly as Moses did, but people do see images of his Glory in religiously altered states of consciousness. Once the dignity of the divinity is protected, the human features of his appearance are described with no sensitivity to anthropomorphism.

Both terms, *appearance* and *image,* later become technical terms for the Glory of God, but in their original context they function to indicate paranormal experience. In Daniel 7, likeness (*demuth* is not used, but the scene is a dream vision [Dan. 7:2]) and the Hebrew preposition *k* make it clear that the experience is paranormal. The adept is not seeing these things in the way one normally sees, but he sees them in a religiously altered state of consciousness. Hence, the visions look like normal sights but are not. The scene is a heavenly throne room with two manlike figures, one an ancient of days and the second a son of man. Son of man is not a title and can only mean that the divine figure has a manlike form because the phrase usually means simply *a human being.* The exact phrase in Daniel is "one like a son of man" (*kbar 'enash*), signifying that the next visionary figure was shaped like a man.[67]

The best guess as to the identity of the figure shaped like a man is that he is simply one of the principal angels, in whose form God deigns to appear, for some angels were envisioned in human form. At his second appearance, Gabriel is described as "the man Gabriel whom I had seen in the vision at first" (9:21). Then in Daniel 10:5 "a man clothed in linen," probably an angel, is described in a way reminiscent of Ezekiel's description of God's Glory. Again, in Daniel 10:16, Daniel sees a human figure, probably, as before, an angel shaped as a man (*kdemuth bnei adam*).

Because merkabah mysticism is esoteric and the rabbis comment on it only within works that are fundamentally exegetical in nature, some scholars have maintained that there is no mystical content to the stories at all.[68] This is a hasty conclusion, however, based only on the exegetical hints one finds in talmudic literature. There is no firm evidence of ecstasy or mystical rites among the rabbinic writers because they are exegetes interested in the legal consequences of these experiences, not the experiences themselves.[69] The first century, like all preceding and succeeding centuries, took experience gained in visions and dreams seriously.[70] It also valued ecstasy or trance as a medium for revelation and developed tech-

niques for achieving the ecstasy or trance in which these visions occurred.[71] These beliefs pervaded Jewish culture as well and enriched Jewish spirituality. In the Hellenistic period, these terms become associated
with the language of ascension or theurgy, the magic use of shamanic
techniques to stimulate these out-of-body experiences. This vocabulary, as
we shall see, was known to Paul and became a central aspect of Paul's
explanation of the Christian message.[72]

In the *Poimandres*, usually considered a later document but which
might date from as early as the first century, many of these themes come
together in a mélange of Hellenistic Jewish exegesis of Genesis and
gnosticizing spirituality. The *Nous* is the highest God. His son, the Pri-
mordial Man, is described as the image or form of the father. The vision
starts with an ecstatic reverie. The purpose of the mystical contemplation
of the *Nous* is both cosmological in that it gives a coherent view of the
universe and soteriological because that view forms the basis of salvation.[73] The tractate echoes Genesis, using Greek philosophy to reformu-
late the biblical creation. Poimandres, who is a figure of gigantic size,
identifies himself with the light and embodies the highest god, Nous (1.6).
After revealing the secrets of cosmology, he outlines how a person can
enter into the Good. The person mounts upward through the heavens
until, stripped of all materiality, he or she begins to sing hymns to the
father, accompanied by those who have preceded him or her. All who are
in the eighth sphere give themselves to the powers, and becoming powers
themselves, they enter into God (*en theō ginontai* [1.25]). A similar pattern
is revealed in tractate 13, though this is usually regarded as a later document.[74]

In the *Poimandres*, the ecstatic nature of the vision is clear and appears
to be sought after by a special technique resembling meditation or contemplation. Philo also mentions meditation as his method for speculating
on cosmological problems in his youth (*Special Laws* 3.1–6), though he
was forced to abandon these experiences due to his mature responsibilities. Philo's account of revelation occasionally uses mystical terminology—for example, he mentions ecstasy and korybantic frenzy, described as the root of humanity's most cherished perceptions.[75] For Philo,
Moses' visions of the angel of the Lord were also meant to be ecstatic
visions of the *logos*, the form of man, the sum of the perceptible world that
God makes available to his prophets. Since Philo only alludes to the experiences and prophetic literature contains few explicit instructions about
obtaining visions, it is impossible to define exactly what kind of experience

is meant in these visions. But it would be loosely understood as ecstasy or trance in contemporary parlance. Ecstatic trance has a long history in the ancient Near East as a way in which God spoke to humanity, and it was closely associated with prophecy. But in the Hellenistic and Graeco-Roman period, these experiences were widely popular because of growing respect for altered consciousness. The so-called *interpretatio Graeca* allowed disparate cults of the ancient Near East and Hellenic world—cults as separate in their origins as Eleusis, Isis, Cybele, Mithras, and others—to seek a similar ritual form involving secret initiations by means of carefully controlled religious rituals that often involved ecstasy and stressed Platonic anthropology, or the myth of the soul's proper journey heavenward.

The Paris Magical Papyrus contains a rather detailed example of the rites that might accompany the mystic's journey upward. The ascent is stimulated by various magical preparations and by inhalation of vapors and the sun's rays. Of course, the setting in the magical papyrus is pagan, and it is a crude magical rendering at that, but the purpose of this face-to-face encounter with the great god Helios Mithras is immortalization. Something like the same assurances given to this magical practitioner can be found in Apuleius's *Golden Ass,* where Lucius is initiated into the mysteries of Isis. In this case, secrecy prevented any exact description of the mystic experience, though the rituals were figured in general terms. Lucius's initiation into the Isis cult is meant to be profoundly religious, but it is similar in content and structure to the journey described in the magical papyri. Both were considered significant religious experiences in their day.

In Jewish mysticism, the so-called *Shiur Koma* gives the exact measurements of the image and reflection of the divinity in figures meant to promote contemplation and trance—like the songs, spells, and charms of the hekhaloth literature. One stated purpose of merkabah mysticism, as outlined in the hekhaloth texts, is to "see the king in his glory."[76] In the ninth century, Hai Gaon recounts that the journey to view this divine figure was undertaken by mystics who put their heads between their knees (the posture Elijah assumed when praying for rain in 1 Kings 18:42),[77] reciting repetitive psalms, glossolalic incantations, and mantra-like prayers, which are recorded in abundance in the hekhaloth literature[78]: "When he seeks to behold the merkabah and the palaces of the angels on high, he must follow a certain procedure. He must fast a number of days and place his head between his knees and whisper many hymns and songs whose texts are known from tradition. Then he perceives the chambers as if he saw the seven palaces with his own eyes, and it is as though he entered one palace after another and saw what is there. And there are two *mish-nayoth* which the tannaim taught regarding this topic, called *Hekhaloth Rabbati* and *Hekhaloth Zutreti*."

Hai Gaon is aware of the mystical techniques for heavenly ascent and describes them as out-of-body experiences where the adept ascends to heaven while his body stays on earth. It is even possible that he understands the entire journey as an internal, intrapsychic one, but this is not entirely clear.[79] The hekhaloth texts themselves mention the transformation of the adept into a heavenly being, whose body becomes fire and whose eyes flash lightning, a theme repeated in the *Paris Magical Papyrus*.[80]

THE MANLIKE FIGURE AND EARLY CHRISTIANITY

Heavenly man traditions are crucial to the development of the Christian meaning of Jesus' earthly mission.[81] They inform the New Testament discussions of the son of man in ways that have been infrequently discussed.[82] It is quite likely that some of Jesus' followers thought of him as a messiah during his own lifetime, though they were disabused of that idea by his arrest, trial, and death on the cross as the King of the Jews, for no pre-Christian view of the messiah conceived of the possibility of his demise at the hands of the Romans.[83] Instead, the disciples' experience of Jesus' resurrection and ascension to the right hand of God confirmed the originally discarded messianic title retrospectively in a new, dynamic, and ironic way. Resurrection and ascension had entered Jewish thought in the century before Jesus as a reward for the righteous martyrs of the Maccabean wars. Thus, although Christianity represents a pure Jewish reaction to a tragic series of events, the reaction was at the same time absolutely novel. The process should be of special interest to Jewish scholars as well as students of Christology, because it is the clearest evidence we have on the intersection of the historical founding of new religious groups and Jewish expectations derived from biblical texts. The events were given meaning by creative interplay between the facts and the hermeneutic process.

Since Jesus died as a martyr, expectations of his resurrection would have been normal in sectarian Judaism.[84] But the idea of a crucified messiah was unique. In such a situation, the Christians only did what other believing Jews did in similar circumstances; they turned to biblical prophecy for elucidation. No messianic text suggested itself as appropriate to the situation. But Ps. 110:1 was exactly apposite: "The Lord says to my lord: 'Sit at my right hand, 'til I make your enemies your footstool.'" This description of the enthronement of a Davidic descendant was now understood as a heavenly enthronement after death and resurrection. Yet nothing in the text makes the death or resurrection part of the narrative inevitable. It must have come from the historical experience of the early Christian community, after they experienced these events. Thereafter, Ps. 110:1 could be combined easily with Dan. 7:9–13, the description of the enthronement of the son of man. Dan. 7:9–13 seemed to describe the scene of Christ's exaltation and ascension, because Jesus could be identified with the son of man, the angelic figure. Further, Dan. 12:2 had promised astral immortality to those who taught wisdom, making plausible while it confirmed the entire set of expectations.

Jesus apparently used the term *son of man* while alive, though deciding what he meant by the phrase remains problematic. He may have predicted the future coming of a human figure, or he may not have referred to the Daniel passage at all.[85] After his crucifixion and the experience of his resurrection, the son-of-man phrases Jesus used were put in the context of the statement in Dan. 7:13 about the enthronement of the son of man, and Jesus' disciples believed that Jesus' victory over death was followed by his ascension and enthronement in heaven as the gigantic angelic or divine figure who was to bring God's coming justice. Through the imagery of the son of man, the man Jesus was associated with the figure on the throne in Dan. 7:13 while the traditions of Jesus' messianic function were associated with traditions about the son of man, taking on a uniquely Christian interpretation. Like the description of the venerable, fatherly figure in Ezekiel the Tragedian's writing, the scene in Daniel involves the enthronement of an ancient of days with the son of man coming to sit next to the ancient of days. The traditions themselves were present in Judaism before Christianity, but it was Jesus' life and mission itself, along with the post-Easter expectations of his followers, that brought messianism, judgment, and heavenly ascent together in this particular way.[86]

The Christians identified the son of man, the human or angelic representation of God, with the risen Christ.[87] Christians took the second lord of Ps. 110:1 to refer to Jesus and to signify the divine name Lord. Thereafter, the risen Christ was understood as an aspect of the divinity.[88] Since the angel with the human figure was also divine itself, carrying the name YHWH (Exod. 23:21), Jesus can be said to have attained to divinity. In the Gospel of John, Christ also became logos, God's intermediary form, and *light,* which was Philo's term for God's principal hypostasis as well. Christ as Son is said to be above the angels, just as Moses is enthroned and worshiped by the stars in Ezekiel the Tragedian's work. This is made explicit in the later document, Heb. 1:8, where the Son is identified with the Elohim in Ps. 45:7.

There were other conceptions of Jesus as prophet and as Son, but they were summed up in the earliest Christian designation of Jesus as Lord, the name of God. This identification of Christ as the human figure of God enthroned in heaven, the vision that Ezekiel saw, was vouchsafed to Paul. Paul's experience differs from other Jewish mystics in that he identified the figure as Christ, but Paul himself cannot be a good witness to how these elements originally came together in his mind. In his writing, many years after the vision, he has completely subsumed the content of the vision into an acceptable Christian theophany. Leaving aside the special Christian polemic that the man on the throne is the messiah Jesus and is also greater than an angel, Paul's statements are important evidence for the existence of first-century Jewish mysticism.

PAUL'S USE OF MYSTICAL VOCABULARY

Paul himself gives the best evidence for the existence of ecstatic journeys to heaven in first-century Judaism with his report in 2 Corinthians.[89] His inability to decide whether the voyage took place in the body or out of the body is firm evidence of a mystical ascent and shows that the voyage has not been interiorized as a journey into the self, which becomes common in Kabbalah. Further, since the rabbis proscribed the discussion of these topics except singly, to mature disciples, and only then provided that they had experienced it on their own (*mevin meda'ato* [M. Hag. 2.1]), the rabbinic stories interpreting the merkabah experience often take place while traveling through the wilderness from city to city, when such doctrines could be discussed privately. This is the scene that Luke picks for Paul's conversion.[90]

In 2 Corinthians 12, when Paul talks about mystical journeys directly, he too adopts a pseudepigraphical stance. He does not admit to the ascent personally. Apart from the needs of his rhetoric, rabbinic rules also forbid public discussion of mystic phenomena. A first-century date for this rule would explain why Paul could not divulge his experience *in his own name* at that place. It also suggests why Jewish mystics consistently picked pseudepigraphical literary conventions to discuss their religious experience, unlocking the mystery behind the entire phenomenon of pseudepigraphical writing. None of the standard discussions of this incompletely understood phenomenon mentions Paul's confession or the Mishnah.[91] Again, Paul may be giving us hitherto unrecognized information about Jewish culture in the first century that is unavailable from any other source.

When Paul is not faced with a direct declaration of personal mystical experience, he reveals much about the mystical religion as it was experienced in the first century. Paul himself designates Christ as the image of the Lord in a few places (2 Cor. 4:4; Col. 1:15 [if it is Pauline]), and he mentions the *morphē* of God in Phil. 2:6.[92] More often he talks of transforming believers into the image of God's son in various ways (Rom. 8:29; 2 Cor. 3:18; Phil. 3:21; 1 Cor. 15:49; see also Col. 3:9). These passages are critical to understanding Paul's experience of conversion. They must be examined in close detail to understand their relationship to Jewish apocalypticism and mysticism, from which they derive their most complete significance for Paul. Paul's longest discussion of these themes occurs in an unlikely place (2 Cor. 3:18–4:6), where he assumes the context rather than explaining it completely:

> And we all, with unveiled face, beholding the glory of the Lord, are being changed into his likeness from one degree of glory to another; for this comes from the Lord who is the Spirit. Therefore, having his ministry by the mercy of God, we do not lose heart. We have renounced disgraceful, underhanded ways; we refuse to practice cunning or to tamper with God's word, but by the open statement of the truth we would commend ourselves to every man's conscience in the sight of God. And even if our gospel is veiled it is veiled only to those who are perishing. In their case, the god of this world has blinded the minds of the unbelievers to keep them from seeing the light of the gospel of the glory of Christ, who is the likeness of God. For what we preach is not ourselves, but Jesus Christ as Lord, with ourselves as your servants for Jesus' sake. For it is the God who said, "Let light shine out of darkness," who has shone in our hearts to give the light of the knowledge of the glory of the Lord in the face of Christ. (2 Cor. 3:18–4:6)

Paul again used the imagery of darkness and light, which Gaventa notes is important to his conversion vocabulary.[93] The social aspect of this mysticism-apocalypticism is equally important to Paul. In calling him a mystical Jew, we discover a whole social and ethical side to first-century mystical writings normally missed in the modern separation of ethics, apocalypticism, and mysticism. Paul's writings are social and ethical; yet behind them lies a mystical experience that he calls ineffable and that is always confirmed in community.

Paul's use of the language of transformation often goes unappreciated. In 2 Cor. 3:18, Paul says that believers will be changed into Christ's likeness from one degree of glory to another. He refers to Moses' encounter with the angel of the Lord in Exodus 33–34. Earlier in the Exodus passage, the angel of the Lord is described as carrying the name of God (23:21). Moses sees the Glory of the Lord, makes a covenant, receives the commandments on the two tables of the law, and when he comes down from the mount, the skin of his face shines with light (Exod. 34:29–35). Moses thereafter must wear a veil except when he is in the presence of the Lord. Paul assumes that Moses made an ascension to the presence of the Lord, was transformed by that encounter and that his shining face is a reflection of the encounter.

Paul uses strange and significant mystical language in 2 Cor. 3:18–4:6. What is immediately striking is that he uses that language to discuss his own and other Christians' experience in Christ. Paul explicitly compares Moses' experience with his own and that of Christian believers. The experiences are similar, but the Christian transformation is greater and more permanent. Once the background of Paul's vocabulary is known, his daring claims for Christian experience become clear. His point is that some Christian believers also make such an ascent and that its effects are more permanent than the vision that Moses received. The church has witnessed a theophany as important as the one vouchsafed to Moses, but the Christian theophany is greater still, as Paul himself has experienced. The Corinthians are said to be a message from Christ (3:2), who is equated with the Glory of God. The new community of gentiles is not a letter written on stone (Jer. 31:33), but it is delivered by Paul as Moses delivered the Torah to Israel. The new dispensation is more splendid than the last, not needing the veil with which Moses hid his face. Paul's own experience proved to him and for Christianity that all will be transformed.

Paul's phrase the Glory of the Lord must be taken both as a reference to Christ and as a technical term for the *Kavod,* the human form of God appearing in biblical visions. In 2 Cor. 3:18, Paul says that Christians behold the Glory of the Lord (*tēn doxan kyriou*) as in a mirror and are transformed into his image (*tēn autēn eikona*).[94] For Paul, as for the earliest Jewish mystics, to be privileged to see the *Kavod* or Glory (*doxa*) of God is a prologue to transformation into his image (*eikōn*). Paul does not say that all Christians have made the journey literally but compares the experience of knowing Christ to being allowed into the intimate presence of the Lord. We do know that he himself has made that journey.

The result of the journey is the identification of Christ as the Glory of God. When Paul says that he preaches that Jesus is Lord and that God "has let this light shine out of darkness into our hearts to give the light of knowledge of the glory of God in the face of Christ" (4:6), he is describing his own conversion and ministry, as he described it in Galatians 1, and as he explains the experience for the purpose of furthering conversion. His apostolate, which he expresses as a prophetic calling, is to proclaim that the face of *Christ* is the Glory of God. When reading this passage in terms of Paul's later description of the ascension of the man to the third heaven, one could conclude that Paul's conversion experience involved his identification of Jesus as the image and Glory of God, as the human figure in heaven, and thereafter as Christ, son, and savior. At least this is how Paul construes it when he recalls it.

Ecstatic ascensions like the one described in 2 Corinthians 12, and spiritual metamorphoses like 2 Corinthians 3, are strangely unfamiliar to modern Jewish and Christian religious sentiments. Neither Christianity nor rabbinic Judaism openly transmitted these lively mystical Jewish traditions of the first century. But in the context of the first few centuries, the combination of the themes of ascension and transformation, both inside and outside Judaism, suggested the attainment of immortality. The context of Jewish mysticism also connects these themes with theodicy. Daniel 12 suggests that the enlighteners who lead others to wisdom (*hamaskilim*) will shine as the brightness of the heavens (the stars), and that they will be among those resurrected for eternal reward. First Enoch 37–71 contains the interesting narration of the transformation of Enoch into the son of man, but this might be a Christian addition to the text, since it agrees so completely with the transformation that Paul outlines.[95] Without Paul we could not suppose that this experience is evidenced in the first century because the date of 1 Enoch is uncertain. Nor would we know that the mystic experience was even possible within Judaism.

In apocalypticism and Jewish mysticism ascensions to God were the prerogative only of the most pure, made after the adept went through several ritual preparations, including fasting and cleansings but preeminently through ritual immersion (*tevilah*). Qumran is an important location for purity rites. The Angelic Liturgy found at Qumran, which specifies the Psalms for human and angelic Sabbath singing, assumes that the purity rules of the community have been observed.[96] It is not surprising therefore that many scholars have felt echoes of a baptismal liturgy in 2 Corinthians

3 and especially in 2 Cor. 4:4–6.[97] The word *phōtismos* (4:4; 4:6) and the phrase *kainē ktisis* (5:17) are reminiscent of baptismal liturgy. Since the words *lampō, augazō,* and *phōtismos,* which are commonly used in baptismal liturgy, are used by Paul here only, it is quite possible that Paul is paraphrasing a baptismal liturgy to express this mystic identification. Paul's quotation might then indicate that it was specifically during baptism that the identification between the image of the savior and the believer was made.

Paul's famous description of Christ's experience of humility and obedience in Phil. 2:5–11 also hints that the identification of Jesus with the image of God was reenacted in the church in a liturgical mode: "Have this mind among yourselves, which is yours in Christ Jesus, who though he was in the form of God, did not count equality with God a thing to be grasped, but emptied himself, taking the form of a servant, being born in the likeness of men. And being found in human form he humbled himself and became obedient unto death, even death on a cross. Therefore God has highly exalted him and bestowed on him the name which is above every name that at the name of Jesus every knee should bow, in heaven and on earth and under the earth, and every tongue confess that Jesus Christ is Lord, to the glory of God the Father."

This passage has several hymnic features, indicating that Paul is quoting a fragment of primitive liturgy or referring to a liturgical setting.[98] Thus Philippians 2 is probably the earliest writing in the Pauline corpus, as well as the earliest Christology of the New Testament; it is not surprising that it is the most exalted Christology.[99]

In Phil. 2:6, the identification of Jesus with the form of God implies his preexistence. Christ is depicted as an eternal aspect of divinity, which was not proud of its high station but consented to take on the shape of a man and suffer the fate of men, even death on a cross (though many scholars see this phrase as a Pauline addition to the original hymn). This transformation of form from the divine to the human is followed by the converse, the transformation back into God. Because of this obedience God exalted Jesus and bestowed on him the "name which is above every name" (Phil. 2:9). For a Jew this phrase can only mean that Jesus received the divine name Yahweh, the tetragrammaton YHWH, translated as the Greek name *kyrios,* or Lord. We have seen that sharing in the divine name is a recurring motif of early Jewish apocalypticism, where the principal angelic mediator of God is or carries the name Yahweh, as Exodus 23 describes the angel of God. The implication of the Greek term *morphē,* "form," in Philippians 2 is that Christ has the form of a divine body identical with *Kavod* and equivalent also with the *eikōn*, for man is made after the *eikōn* of God and thus has the divine *morphē* (in Hebrew: *demuth*). The climax of Paul's confession is that "Jesus Christ is Lord to the glory of God the Father" (Phil. 2:11), meaning that Jesus, the messiah, has received the name Lord in his glorification, and that this name, not Jesus' private earthly name, is the one that will cause every knee to bend and every tongue to confess.[100]

In paraphrasing this fragment from liturgy, Paul witnesses that the early Christian community directed its prayers to this human figure of divinity along with God (1 Cor. 16:22; Rom. 10:9–12; 1 Cor. 12:3)—all the more striking since the Christians, like the Jews, refuse to venerate any other god or hero. When the rabbis gained control of the Jewish community they vociferously argued against the worship of any angel and specifically polemicized against the belief that a heavenly figure other than God can forgive sins (b. Sanhedrin 38b), quoting Exod. 23:21 prominently among other Scriptures to prove their point. The heresy itself they called believing that there are two powers in heaven. This heresy mainly (but not exclusively) referred to Christians, who, as Paul says, do exactly what the rabbis warn against—worship the second power.[101]

Concomitant with Paul's worship of the divine Christ is transformation. Paul says in Phil. 3:10 "that I may know him and the power of his resurrection and may share his sufferings, becoming like him [*symmorphizomenos*] in his death." Later he says: "But our commonwealth is in heaven, and from it we await a Savior, the Lord Jesus Christ, who will change [*metaschēmatisei*] our lowly body to be like [*symmorphon*] his glorious body, by the power which enables him even to subject all things to himself" (3:20–21). The body of the believer eventually is to be transformed into the body of Christ.

Paul's depiction of salvation is based on his understanding of Christ's glorification, partaking of early Jewish apocalyptic mysticism for its expression.[102] In Rom. 12:2 Paul's listeners are exhorted to "be transformed [*metamorphousthe*] by renewing of your minds." In Gal. 4:19 Paul expresses another transformation: "My little children, with whom I am again in travail until Christ be formed [*morphōthē*] in you!" This transformation is to be effected by becoming like him in his death *(symmorphizomenos tō thanatō autou* [Phil. 3:10]). Paul's central proclamation is: Jesus is Lord and all who have faith have already undergone a death like his and so will share in his resurrection. As we have seen, this proclamation reflects a baptismal liturgy, implying that baptism provides the moment whereby the believer comes to be in Christ. Christianity is a unique Jewish sect in that it makes baptism a central rather than a preparatory ritual, but some of the mystical imagery comes from its Jewish past.

Alternatively, Paul can say, as he does in Gal. 1:16 that "God was pleased to reveal His Son in me [*en emoi*]." This is not a simple dative but refers to his having received in him the Spirit, in his case through his conversion. Being in Christ in fact appears to mean being united with Christ's heavenly image. The same, however, is available to all Christians through baptism. This is not strange since apocalyptic and mystical Judaism also promoted *tevilah,* ritual immersion or baptism, as the central purification ritual preparing for the ascent into God's presence. The Jewish ritual of purification for coming into the divine presence and proselyte baptism has been transformed by Paul's community into a *single* rite of passage, though it does not thereby lose its relationship to its source. Dying and being resurrected along with Christ in baptism is the beginning of the process by which the believer gains the same image of God, his *eikōn,* which was made known to humanity when Jesus became the son of man—the human figure in heaven who brings judgment in the apocalypse described by Daniel. Paul's conception of the risen body of Christ as the spiritual body (1 Cor. 15:43) at the end of time and as the body of Glory (Phil. 3:21) thus originates in Jewish apocalypticism and mysticism, modified by the unique events of early Christianity. The meaning of Rom. 8:29 can be likewise clarified by Jewish esoteric tradition: Paul speaks of God as having "foreordained his elect to be conformed to the image of his Son" ("proōrisen symmorphous tēs eikonos tou huiou autou"). Paul uses the genitive here rather than the dative as in Phil. 3:21, softening the identification between believer and savior. But when Paul states that believers conform to the image of God's son, he is not speaking of an agreement of mind or ideas between Jesus and the believers. The word *symmorphē* itself suggests a spiritual reformation of the believer's body into the form of the divine image. Paul's language for conversion—*being in Christ*—develops out of mystical Judaism.

Paul speaks of the transformation being partly experienced by believers in their preparousia existence. His use of present tense in Rom. 12:2 and 2 Cor. 3:18 underscores the idea that transformation is an ongoing event. In 1 Cor. 15:49 and Romans 8, however, it culminates at Christ's return, the parousia. This suggests that for Paul transformation is both a single, definitive event and a process that continues until the second coming. The redemptive and transformative process appears to correspond exactly with the turning of the ages. This age is passing away, though it certainly remains a present evil reality (1 Cor. 3:19; 5:9; 2 Cor. 4:4; Gal.

1:4; Rom. 12:2). The gospel, which is the power of God for salvation (Rom. 1:16), is progressing through the world (Phil. 1:12; Romans 9–11).

First Cor. 15:42–51 is one of the most systematic uses of this apocalyptic and mystical tradition, which is central to Paul's message of the meaning of Christ:

> So is it with the resurrection of the dead. What is sown is perishable, what is raised is imperishable. It is sown in dishonor, it is raised in glory. It is sown in weakness, it is raised in power. It is sown a physical body, it is raised a spiritual body. If there is a physical body, there is also a spiritual body. Thus it is written. "The first man Adam became a living being"; the last Adam became a life-giving spirit. But it is not the spiritual which is first but the physical, and then the spiritual. The first man was from the earth, a man of dust; the second man is from heaven. As was the man of dust, so are those who are of the dust; and as is the man of heaven, so are those who are of heaven. Just as we have borne the image of the man of dust, we shall also bear the image of the man of heaven. I tell you this, brethren; flesh and blood cannot inherit the kingdom of God, nor does the perishable inherit the imperishable.

As Paul connects his own conversion with his resurrection in Christ, it is resurrection that brings the salvation of God and a return to the pristine state of humanity's glory before Adam's fall. He says this explicitly in 1 Cor. 15:21: "For as by a man came death; so by a man has also come resurrection of the dead." Paul makes Adam and Christ contrasting images of fall and salvation respectively. But Paul seems to have more than Jesus' earthly existence in mind, since he uses the term *anthrōpos,* which can also refer to his resurrected nature: "Just as we have borne the image of the man of dust, we shall also bear the image of the man of heaven."[103] The agent that begins and is responsible for this change on earth is the spirit. The spirit not only creates the Christ that is within believers, but itself takes on the character of Christ. The risen Jesus is to be experienced as a life-giving spirit, explaining how the transformation starts, and culminates in the mystic process in the apocalyptic end.[104]

When speaking of the resurrection, Paul describes a reciprocal relationship between Adam and Christ: as Adam brought death into the world, Christ, the second Adam, will bring resurrection. This depends on interpreting Adam's divine likeness as being identical to the Glory that the Christ had or received. Because of the first human, all humanity is brought to death; but because of Christ's divine image all will be brought to life (15:21–22). The first man, Adam, became only a living soul, whereas the last Adam became a life-giving spirit (15:45). The first man was of the earth and therefore earthly; the last man is from heaven, therefore divine. Just as humanity has borne the outward image of the old Adam, those who inherit the kingdom will also bear the inward spiritual *eikōn* of the heavenly man (15:47–49). Paul, however, is not so much talking about the man Jesus as he is talking about Christ's exalted nature as *anthrōpos*. Since the imagery depends on the contrast between fallen and raised states, this passage also implies a baptismal setting. It is interesting that the alternation is conceived in bodily terms, not as a transmigration of souls.

The antonymous pairs, natural/spiritual, earthly/heavenly, corruptible/incorruptible, point to the contrast between the nature of Christ's resurrected body and ordinary human life. All these contrasts are characteristic of a man who underwent a radical conversion. One cannot ignore the close relationship between Paul's view of the future immortality of believers and his description of the risen Christ from his own conversion, as his conversion experience may have been a process involving several visions and the search for their meaning. When Paul says that Christians shall be raised imperishable, as he does in 1 Cor. 15:51–58, the background for this conception is his other descriptions of transformation into the raised Christ, Paul's own context. His view of the coming end is merely the culmination of the process that has started with conversion and baptism:

> Lo! I will tell you a mystery. We shall not all sleep, but we shall all be *changed*, in a moment, in the twinkling of an eye, at the last trumpet. For the trumpet will sound, and the dead will be raised imperishable and we shall be changed. For this perishable nature must put on the imperishable, and this mortal nature must put on immortality. When the perishable puts on the imperishable, and the mortal puts on immortality, then shall come to pass the saying that is written:

> > "Death is swallowed up in victory."
> > "O death, where is thy victory?
> > O death, where is thy sting?"
> > > [Isa. 25:8; Hos. 13:14]

> The sting of death is sin, and the power of sin is the law. But thanks be to God, who gives us the victory through our Lord Jesus Christ.

Paul's view of the immortality of believers is parallel to and depends on his description of the raised Christ in heaven. Paul's imagery for the description of the coming resurrection in 1 Corinthians 15 fulfills the vocabulary of spiritual body and Glory of God that ultimately derives from his conversion. Because believers on earth, by virtue of their conversion, have been transformed into the body of Christ, who is the image of God, the destiny of believers will be the same as the destiny of Christ. The believer is to share in Christ's immortality at the last trumpet, as Paul himself experienced transformation by Christ. It appears that Paul considers himself special in that the whole process of salvation has been revealed to him. Others have not had his visions, so his visions give him special powers to speak on the meaning of Christian life. But the process has started within the Christian community, continuing there, whether those who have acknowledged Christ recognize it or not. Although Jesus' humanity is mentioned here and in Romans 5, it is not the human life that is the point of the exegesis. Christ's resurrection and metamorphosis into the true man power the analogy. Christ is the man from heaven. His power on earth is the spirit.

The relationship between transformation and justification can be seen in a later part of the Corinthian correspondence, where Paul discusses the effect of the spiritual transformation. Transformation and community are clarified there, making the differing social contexts of the two letters besides the point. In 2 Cor. 5:15–6:1, Paul speaks of the Christian as a new creation:

> From now on, therefore, we regard no one from a human point of view; even though we once regarded Christ from a human point of view, we regard him thus no longer. Therefore, if any one is in Christ, he is a new creation; the old has passed away, behold, the new has come. All this is from God, who through Christ reconciled us to himself and gave us the ministry of reconciliation; that is, in Christ God was reconciling the world to himself, not counting their trespasses against them, and entrusting to us the message of reconciliation. So we are ambassadors for Christ, God making his appeal through us. We beseech you on behalf of Christ, be reconciled to God. For our sake he made him to be sin who knew no sin, so that in him we might become the righteousness of God. Working together with him, then, we entreat you not to accept the grace of God in vain.

The "human point of view" is literally "according to the flesh" (*kata sarka*), whereas the believer is a new creation of spirit. The reformulation experience changes the believer from a physical body to a new spiritual creation. It turns the believer into the righteousness of God, although the final consummation has not yet occurred. Paul can refer to himself even as an ambassador and fellow worker with Christ before the final transformation, participating in his body with him as he works. Because the verb is implied, the passage can also mean that "there is a new creation," giving the event a cosmic as well as an individual significance.[105] It is also clear that the experience of being made righteous is coterminous with this transformation. Thus, conversion for Paul means both a transformation and a parallel process of being made righteous. This process takes place in community. Like many visionaries, Paul suggests not just a personal transformation but a transformation of community and of the cosmos as well.

The mystical experience of conversion is not only with the risen Christ but with the crucified Christ. The most obvious relationship between the believer and Christ is suffering and death (Rom. 7:24; 8:10, 13). By being transformed by Christ, one is not simply made immortal, given the power to remain deathless. Rather, one still experiences death as Christ did and like him survives death for heavenly enthronement. This is a consequence of the Christian's divided state. Although part of the last Adam, living through spirit, the Christian also belongs to the world of the flesh. As James Dunn has noted, "Suffering was something *all* believers experienced—an unavoidable part of the believer's lot—an aspect of experience as Christians which his converts shared with Paul: Rom. 5:3 ('we'); 8:17f ('we'); 2 Cor. 1:16 ('you endure the same sufferings that we suffer'); 8:2; Phil. 1:29f ('the same conflict which you saw and now hear to be mine'); 1 Thess. 1:6 ('imitators of us and of the Lord'); 2:14 ('imitators of the churches of God in Judea: for you suffered the same things'); 3:3f ('our lot'); 2 Thess. 1:4ff."[106]

Thus, the persecution and suffering of the believers is a sign that the transformation process has begun; it is the way to come to be *in* Christ. Paul is convinced that being united with Christ's crucifixion means not immediate glorification but suffering for the believers in this interim period. The glorification follows on the final consummation. The connection between suffering and resurrection is clear in Jewish martyrology; indeed, the connection between death and rebirth was a prominent part of the mystery religions as well. The language of transformation is not solely a Jewish vocabulary. It is also part of Hellenistic religious piety throughout the period. The identification of the adept with the divinity through a vision is characteristic of later Hellenistic mysticism, where the mystic adept may seek a vision of the divinity face to face, intuit the saving *gnosis* as in the *Poimandres*,[107] or end by breathing in the divine to become divine himself or herself.[108] But understanding suffering as the uniting experience is a special Christian interpretation of the martyrdom theme underlying the ascension story from Daniel. The genesis of the doctrine points both to the passion of Jesus and to the persecution of the community.

In the letters of the Pauline school, some of these themes receive even fuller development. Colossians is a veritable summary of the whole constellation of language describing transformation into the heavenly *Kavod*, understood as Christ. Christ is called, "the image of the invisible God" (1:15–20) and the "firstborn of all creation" (1:16). He is the author of creation and the captain of the heavenly hosts and is coeternal with God. As Christ, he is also "firstborn from the dead." He is the head of the body, the church, a remark that hints at possible relationships with Jewish *Shiur Koma* speculation as well as pagan concepts of the Macranthropos.

In Colossae, important baptismal practices, similar to Jewish mysticism and Qumran, developed.[109] Col. 3:10 speaks of Christians as having taken off an old nature and put on a new nature in baptism, "which is being renewed in knowledge after the image of its creator." Eph. 4:24 speaks also of putting on a new nature created after the likeness of God. This language of transformation comes from Jewish apocalyptic mysticism, yet it implies a specifically Christian theology and a baptismal setting. If contemporary scholars were not convinced of the Pauline authorship of these letters, one can nonetheless say that they give irrefutable evidence about the popularity of Paul's mystical teaching among his earliest disciples and the direction in which these teachings were interpreted.

Paul's conversion experience and his mystical ascension form the basis of his theology. His language shows the marks of a man who has learned the contemporary vocabulary for expressing a theophany and then has received one. This language of vision has informed his thought in a number of crucial respects. First, it has allowed him to develop a concept of the divinity of Christ or the messiah both as a unique development within the Jewish mystical tradition and as characteristically Christian. Second, he uses this Jewish mystical vocabulary to express the transformation experienced by believers. Believers warrant immortality because they have been transformed by becoming formed (*symmorphous*) like the savior. Third, he uses the language of transformation, gained through contact with Jewish mystical-apocalypticism and presumably through ecstatic conversion, to discuss the ultimate salvation and fulfillment of the apocalypse, raising believers to immortality. Fourth, he uses the terms of fleshly and spiritual existence to distinguish between true faith, independent of fleshly rules, and false faith, depending on the flesh.

Though Paul's language constantly invokes the concept of prophetic commissioning (*kletos* [see Galatians 1 and Romans 1]), his commissioning also clearly represents a religious conversion. In fact, his conversion experience and other experiences like it allow Paul to argue for something controversial to early Christianity: his commission as an *apostle* to proclaim the gospel to the gentiles (Rom. 1:1; 11:13;, 15:16; Gal. 1:16; 2:6–8; etc.).[110] Paul's credentials as apostle for this mission were widely disputed in both Judaism and Christianity, forcing Paul continually to answer his detractors with the defense that his mission comes not from men, who largely opposed it, but solely from the command of Christ and God himself (Gal. 1:16). In contrast to the Jerusalem church's conception of apostolate as deriving from Jesus' personal appointment, Paul develops a charismatic idea of apostleship dependent on a vision of the risen Christ. This is exactly what modern psychology and sociology would call a conversion. Because of his vision, he can claim that his apostolate is an agency of the Holy Spirit (1 Cor. 12:4), unlike the previous apostles who were tutored directly by Jesus, and, like his detractors, he can call himself a *miscarriage,* an apostle born out of time (*ektrōma* [1 Cor. 15:8]), perhaps relying on Isaiah 49.[111] His vision allows him to describe his teaching as an *apocalypse*—a revelation of hidden knowledge—through the Holy Spirit (1 Cor. 2:10), though it is mediated through the mind, not through the speaking of tongues (1 Cor. 14:19). Acts 22:17 also describes Paul as receiving his commission in ecstasy (*en ekstasei*). The implication of these statements for the church cannot be missed. Ordinary apostles link their apostolate to traditions derived directly from Jesus, legitimating their authority through the apostolic succession. In a ploy that has been repeated throughout the history of religion, Paul opposed the apostolic claim by a claim of direct revelation. He also includes in his claim of legitimacy his gentile converts, for they are his letter from Christ. There is ample evidence that this is one of the basic sociological conflicts that has been played out time and time again in world religion: the opposition of traditional authority to claims of direct, ecstatic revelation, though the conflict can take several forms, depending on the opinion of central authority about ecstatic knowledge of God.[112]

We shall never know Paul's experience. But we can see how Paul reconstructs it. In retrospect, Paul construes his first Christian experience as (ecstatic) conversion. Nor should we dispute Paul's own opinion. The clearest demonstration of Paul's conversion is merely to compare him with other Christians who, like Paul, came from Judaism but whose entrance into Christianity changed none of their disposition about Torah (see Acts 15:5) and so opposed Paul. It was possible to go from Pharisaic Judaism to Christianity without having a conversion experience such as Paul's. There are Christians whose faith in Christ only completed their previous belief in Judaism. But Paul is not one of these Jews. He is no Pharisee whose faith in Christ confirms his Judaism; rather, his conversion makes a palpable difference in his Christianity. His conversion caused him to revalue his Judaism, in turn creating a new understanding of Jesus' mission. This metamorphosis seems always to underlie Paul's understanding of the difference between flesh and spirit.

CHAPTER THREE

ℭCONVERSION IN PAUL'S SOCIETY

Conversion is an appropriate term for discussing Paul's religious experience, although Paul did not himself use it. The modern study of conversion shows how conversion can be employed as a technical term, within specific limits. It also illustrates the contention that every community develops its own definition of conversion. This contention is illustrated in the change of the definition of conversion from Paul to Luke to the pastoral Epistles. Paul, as well as other first century Jews, spoke of internal states in prophetic, ecstatic, or mystical vocabularies, developing several words that approximate modern terms of conversion. The one expression that Paul uses most comprehensively in his own writing to describe this experience is *transformation*. This links Paul's religious experience with both conversion and ancient mystical appearances of the deity. Once the different boundaries of the ancient and modern vocabularies are recognized, there are adequate grounds for continuing the study of conversion in the ancient world and applying our results to Paul.

There were many consequences in changing commitment from one social group in Judea to another, whether from a gentile to a Jewish group, Jewish to gentile, or from one group within the Jewish community to another. Arthur Darby Nock defined the study of conversion in the ancient world by showing that conversion was a distinctly specialized and rare religious experience.[1] Most religious rites of the time helped maintain the political order because they were civic ceremonies. Participation involved adherence, a low level of involvement, as an act of civic piety. But prophetic religions such as Judaism and Christianity stimulated conversion, raising commitment far above simple adherence. Conversion necessarily involved a radical change of life-style, often a move to a socially stigmatized group. Nock showed that the strong personal commitment of conversion was characteristic of Judaism, of some of the philosophical sects and mystery religions, and preeminently of Christianity. He maintained that conversion uniquely enabled Christianity to gain in popularity while conquering opposition. Further, highly personal piety, an effect of the conversion experience, was characteristic of Christianity and a small number of other cohesive religions in the Roman Empire. Conversion provided the dynamic for a true religious revolution in the late Roman Empire and a startling innovation in religious patterns. According to Nock, the phenomenon of conversion was remarkably important for understanding the popularity and attractiveness of Christianity even before Paul. Christian communities organized all their resources for the dissemination of the gospel and quickly spread throughout the Roman world.

Nock recognized and emphasized an important dynamic in the spread of early Christianity. Time has not disproven his insight, but has deepened and broadened it. Nock, however, overstressed internal factors in the later empire, dismissing the importance of Constantine and the Christian emperors' patronage for the success of Christianity.[2] His understanding of conversion was stereotypic, following William James in limiting the experience of conversion to a radical emotional experience or a quick turning to a new way of life and a complete reorientation in attitude, thought, and practice. Nock's understanding of conversion was also traditionally Christian, hence strongly influenced by Luke's description of Paul. Further, Nock probably underestimated the level of commitment that adherence to a civic form could generate among the local pagan aristocrats, who vied with each other for social prominence through public benefaction—a process in which Judaism and later Christianity participated in the late Hellenistic era, when a church or synagogue achieved regional importance. Since both internal and external factors are important to the history of any group, Nock's work remains significant.

The relationship between conversion, high personal commitment, and group cohesion is crucial for understanding the spread and success of early Christianity. Many questions were left unanswered by Nock's intuition: Why did conversion become important in Judaism and Christianity? How did conversion continue to play an important role in Christianity in the second and succeeding generations of family membership? Nock saw conversion as a continuous process typical of the way in which all Christians entered their movement, but this cannot be entirely true. Common sense dictates that only in the first generation of Christianity in a family did all enter necessarily by conversion. Thereafter, the progeny of the converts would be socialized into Christianity. The child needs no conversion, for social mores, values, and institutions present themselves as self-evidently true in a family that provides instruction into its religious rites. Primary socialization of the child, the process by which the family's accepted truths become internalized and recognized as objective reality, can therefore be an important analogy to the way in which conversion works in developing commitment. We must therefore differentiate between conversion and other factors that raised group commitment. We must also account for communities in the most ascetic and monastic varieties of Christianity, which eschewed family life, but nevertheless continued to have a strong influence on the progress of the movement.[3] In radically ascetic Christianity, conversion would continue to be the primary experience of entrance into the religion.

Some of these important questions are beyond the first-century purview. But criticism of Nock's work offers a clear path into the study of Paul. We must place Nock's perceptions about conversion in the special social contexts of the first century and investigate the effect of conversion on the life of a group in general, looking specifically at the effects of conversion on the special groups in first-century Judaism.

Recent studies have pointed out that the highest degree of commitment is apparent only when sudden conversions are followed by and supplemented with other members' thorough education to the values of the group. Since all communities establish what Peter Berger has called a "plausibility structure," a state in which beliefs seem self-evident and need no proof, an exact analysis of the relationship of commitment to conversion is necessary.[4]

Viewed from the perspective of social commitment, conversion resembles a new and conscious choice to socialize to a particular group—a resocialization.[5] The convert builds up a new structure of reality, corresponding to the structure of the group joined. The values of the new group forms the convert's new reality. The degree of resocialization depends on the distance the convert must travel between the old and new communities and the strength of the new commitment. Conversion can take place within a single religion, where less resocialization is needed. This is important for judging the differences between the kind of conversion that Paul underwent and that of his mostly gentile followers, who had a different experience when viewed from a social perspective. Paul began as a highly committed Pharisee and became a highly committed member of an apocalyptic form of Judaism, whereas his converts began as pagans and entered a new, ambiguous group whose relationship to Judaism shortly became a vexing issue.

Christianity was not yet defined as different than Judaism. Because of its newness, it is important to Jewish scholarship. Further, it is the only sect in first-century Judaism—including Sadduceeism, Pharisaism, and Essenism—whose origins are well known. Thus it gives Jewish historians data about the birth of first-century sects that are otherwise unavailable. Though Paul underwent a transformation, he did not lose his memory or his commitment to Judaism; he chose to express that commitment in an entirely novel way, by participating in a gentile community. No convert forgets everything previously known. Rather, the convert changes a few key concepts, revaluing everything else accordingly. Old doctrines often remain intact but are completely changed in significance through the imposition of a new structure.

These observations lead to several conclusions: (1) A convert is usually someone who identifies, at least retrospectively, a lack in the world, finding a remedy in the new reality promulgated by the new group. This is another aspect of the convert as a religious quester and biographical reevaluator. (2) The central aspect of the conversion is a decision to reconstruct reality so that (3) the new group the subject enters supports that reality by its self-evident assumptions. (4) Finally, the talents and attitudes that the convert brings into the movement are greatly affected by the previous socialization, no matter how strongly the subject affirms the conversion or denies the past. Though conversion is one of the sources of a particular person's commitment to a religious group, it is not the only one. Conversion necessarily involves strong emotional commitments, but conversion itself is not enough to preserve the commitment to the group after initial entrance to the group, unless the other social mechanisms of commitment act in concert with it. These other sources of commitment are noticeable even in groups where conversion itself is not a primary value, but they are linked to conversion within sectarian groups that depend on conversion. This is crucial for our understanding of Paul, since it both clarifies the strength of Paul's commitment to Christianity, which initially begins in his mystical, apocalyptic conversion experience, and the expression of it in consonance with a gentile Christian community.

CONVERSION AND THE STRENGTH OF RELIGIOUS COMMITMENT

In the religious life of most communities, the commitment of converts is legendary.[6] Scholars have also noted the relationship between strong religious commitment and conversion. In *Commitment and Community*, Rosabeth Kanter examines the psychology of commitment while investigating the factors influencing the survival of apocalyptic communities.[7] After studying nine successful communities and many unsuccessful ones, Kanter defines commitment not in individual terms but in terms that serve the community: Commitment consists of internal controls that support the group. Personal commitment and conversion become two aspects of the same dynamic of socialization in sects and apocalyptic or utopian communities. Whenever a group is made up almost entirely of converts, its cohesiveness tends to be much greater than a group whose membership is filled by casual affiliates or those not decisively rejecting other choices. Chronologically, however, conversion most often precedes commitment, so that the phenomenon of commitment includes more aspects than merely conversion. Conversion merely begins a process of commitment to the group, though it is often considered the culmination of it. Kanter observed that groups that present new moral communities, such as those where members share property and resources to form a single household, evince the highest degree of cohesiveness. This is a common feature of Jewish and Christian sectarianism, relevant to first-century Judaism and Christianity. One characteristic of sects that are highly dependent on conversion for membership is that they also tend to be highly cohesive, stressing the differences between themselves and the outside world.

In analyzing the history of these groups, Kanter observed three principal types of commitment and the processes by which the types are enhanced. Her three aspects of commitment are: affective commitment, instrumental commitment, and moral commitment.[8]

Kanter's theories allow us to distinguish between these differing definitions of conversion. Instrumental commitment is characterized as a commitment to the organization and its rules, affective commitment as commitment to its members, and moral commitment as commitment to the ideas of the group, as spelled out by its leaders. This results in three major characteristics of commitment in a particular group: retention of members, group cohesiveness, and social control. Since these are observations based on evaluations and interpretations of narrative data and not based on quantified data, they cannot be treated as strict definitions of every society's mechanism of commitment, but they are important descriptive tools in helping to analyze why conversion galvanizes community and ensures success.

Two mechanisms for each major aspects of commitment are described by Kanter. The first mechanism tends to separate the individual from other groups, and the second tends to attract the individual to the special group; for instance, in regard to affective commitment, Kanter discusses both renunciation of former ties and communion with the new group. Conversion is more likely to occur in people who have few affective commitments to other groups. For this reason, groups with active missions in the United States have become a commonplace at airports, where the proselytizers look for backpacks and other signs of transiency and rootlessness in the potential convert.[9] The new converts are then deliberately isolated from their other affective ties in an attempt to make them renounce them. This helps to account for the enormous number of converts to new religious movements among the children of nonobservant Jews and Christians. In place of the affective ties, ties of communion with the new group are developed. As one climbs up the ladder of the internal hierarchy from new convert to novice to member to leader, the individual makes an affective investment in the group and gains respect from other members.

Closely associated with this phenomenon is an instrumental level of commitment. The new member must be convinced that continued association with the group is worth the time and effort it demands. Hence dissonance (see appendix) operates at the cognitive level of commitment. On the negative side, the individual sacrifices various commonplaces of ordinary life in the larger society. Devotees may be forbidden alcohol, dancing, drugs, sex, or comforts in order to continue life with the group. The group may hold all property in common, requiring an enormous price from wealthier members, ensuring that these become the most committed members. On the positive side, these sacrifices are balanced by investments that yield a return of status or enjoyment through continued association with the group. Becoming a leader or making public announcements may have this desired affect.

The third level of commitment refers to obedience to the norms and values of the group. Kanter calls the negative mechanisms that separate the member from previous associations *mortification*, and she calls the positive force of attraction *transcendence*. Grouped under mortification are the disciplinary measures of the group, often a public confession of faults, which can in itself stimulate exhilaration because it indicates to the subject that the group cares about the person's behavior and thoughts. Difficult and painful psychological pressures such as these also serve to raise the cognitive dissonance, hence the commitment of the new member. On the positive side, the successful indoctrination and practice of the rituals, morals, and ethics of a group lead to a feeling of transcendence of one's individuality and a sense of ultimate meaning.

Although radical conversions relate to the affective side of group commitment, they may also have ramifications on the other two scales as well. Gradual conversions typically address all three aspects of group commitment as part of the training process. This explains why successful groups encourage gradual conversions. But some radical conversions are also important for the development of commitment, since emotions are typically important to religious groups. Radical conversions exemplify the ecstasy or bliss sought within the movement and give dramatic urgency to the claims of the group. For the stability of the membership, it is important to balance the emotional contribution of radical converts with the steady enthusiasm of gradual converts, who appropriate the rules and roles of the group more thoroughly and so add stability.

Even in conventional religious groups, affective commitment has a disproportionate effect in cohesion. Gerhard Lenski has noted that communal involvement and close affective interpersonal relationships with members is a crucial variable for the cohesion of a religious organization or institution.[10] This would also account for the high level of commitment among participants in a religious movement even when they do not seek or attain high office. Although the moral factors may be primary in terms of personal goals and meanings in a religion, the affective commitments chronologically come first in most believers' experience.

One result of such analyses in the modern world has been the observation that the most rapid church growth tends to be among the most conservative and demanding denominations. A liberalizing movement from sect to denomination is the general rule for most religious groups in American institutional religious life. Liberal churches and sects often do not attract members as quickly or retain them as surely as conservative churches, which rely on conversion, strict moral standards, and large investments of time and money to develop higher degrees of commitment. People join conservative churches, whereas others tend to disaffiliate from the liberal ones, ceasing to have affiliations with any church.[11]

Several psychologists have investigated the relationship between conversion and commitment by examining the language of converts. David Snow and Richard Machalek[12] proposed that the surest way to identify the phenomenon of conversion would be to look for changes in the subject's "universe of discourse."[13] Studying the Nichiren Shoshu Buddhist movement, they suggested that converts can be identified by four "rhetorical indicators": (1) adopting a master attribution scheme; (2) biographical reconstruction; (3) suspending analogical reason; and (4) embracing a master role. Subsequent research has shown that these four rhetorical indicators are important for locating religious commitment. Only one indicator—biographical reconstruction, where the subject actively reinterprets past experiences or self-conceptions from the vantage point of the present in such a way as to change the meaning of the past—is a clear indicator of religious conversion.[14]

Our literary analysis of Paul's writing has anticipated these conclusions about conversion in the modern period. The most obvious mark of Paul's conversion is his revaluation of his previous life on the basis of his experience of Christ. Besides the fact that biographical reconstruction is one of the most significant aspects of Paul's conversion, this recent finding points out the close relationship between religious conversion and commitment. Many of the indicators for conversion are also indicators of commitment. Only a few subtle factors can accurately separate the convert from the committed yet unconverted religionist. But high levels of personal commitment to a religious affiliation are clearly part of the individual's most significant attributions.

These analyses of commitment can be easily applied to Jewish society of the first century. There, they point out how Christianity among the Jewish sects tailored the conversion process in close consonance with its social goals and destined it for quick and effective proselytism. The conversion process among Jews and the sects of Judea exemplifies the remarkable success Christianity found in the wider society of the Roman Empire.

CONVERSION AND COMMUNITY IN HELLENISTIC JUDAISM

Before Paul's work in the gentile world can be understood, the various kinds of commitment that existed in the Jewish sects of the first century must be surveyed. There have been many studies of proselytism and conversion in Judaism. Rather than review all the evidence, I merely interpret it within the purview of Paul's conversion. A strong argument rages over whether or to what extent Jews proselytized. Few fully recognize or analyze the obvious fact that different Jews and different Jewish sects reached different opinions about proselytism and behaved accordingly. Attitudes ranges from a total denial of a mission to the gentiles to an extreme interest in one.[15] Not everyone realizes the background against which Jewish conversion should be evaluated: Conversion was a rare but not unprecedented experience in antiquity. And few scholars discuss the differences in perspective that would naturally occur among ancient authorities on the definition of conversion; for instance, a Roman government official would necessarily have different interests than a Jewish community leader in defining a conversion—after all, a conversion might affect not only a person's private status but also his or her tax bill.

Christianity was not the only proselytizing sect within Judaism. Its proselytizing style was rooted in Judaism, though Christianity and Paul in particular might have relied on missionizing more than other sects, transforming Jewish heritage by moving beyond the Jewish milieu into the wider world. Other Jewish sects, like the Essenes, the monastic group that left us the Dead Sea Scrolls, depended on converts regularly and operated successful propaganda programs for the purposes of educating the populace to the value of repentance. But they seem to have limited their mission to other Jews. This group, with its enormous interest in purity rules and the responsibilities of priesthood, qualifies as a highly cohesive, communitarian movement. Without doubt it was the most cohesive sectarian group in Graeco-Roman Judea, even when Christianity is included. But unlike Christianity it was totally uninterested in a gentile mission.

Since Hellenization also took place at different speeds among the various classes of Judea, several different and competing sects and denominations arose in the first century—among them the Pharisees, Sadducees, Essenes, and later the Christians, representing different ways in which Hellenistic religious values could be interpreted in Judean culture. This sectarian life was functional to the extent that it constructively channeled conflict between manifold expressions of Hellenistic Jewish life. But it also prepared the way for a new concept of religious change—conversion among the various sects of the day and into Judaism itself.[16] Although Christianity eventually surpassed the bounds of its sectarian status within Judaism, becoming an international Hellenistic movement, it began by disturbing greatly the equilibrium of sectarian life within Judea by virtue of its success in converting gentiles to something that resembled the other varieties of Judaism but also differed from them.

The perception that strong personal decisions lead to highly cohesive groups can be profitably applied to sectarian life in Judaism. One rule can be promulgated initially: gradual conversion was the typical and expected pattern for virtually every sectarian group in Judaism, although sudden and emotional conversion may have occurred occasionally. Admittedly little is known about the many messianic movements that left no documents, and even the community formed by John the Baptist cannot be defined. But Graeco-Roman Judea valued the learning of special meanings of difficult texts. In providing instruction in the truths of the sect, each of the sects set up the closest thing to an educational institution in Jewish society.

This phenomenon is best illustrated by Josephus's autobiographical statements. In his *Life* 7–12, Josephus reports, rather immodestly, that he was a wonder child. As the child of a priestly family, his fame quickly became known to the priests in Jerusalem, who would come to listen to his childhood lectures. He opted for a formal education (9–12)[17]:

> At about the age of sixteen, I determined to gain personal experience of the several sects into which our nation is divided. These, as I have frequently mentioned, are three in number—the first that of the Pharisees, the second that of the Sadducees, and the third that of the Essenes. I thought that, after a thorough investigation, I should be in a position to select the best. So I submitted myself to hard training and laborious exercises and passed through the three courses. Not content, however, with the experience thus gained, on hearing of one named Bannus, who dwelt in the wilderness, wearing only such clothing as trees provided, feeding on such things as grew of themselves, and using frequent ablutions of cold water, by day and night, for purity's sake, I became his devoted disciple. With him I lived for three years and, having accomplished my purpose, returned to the city. Being now in my nineteenth year I began to govern my life by the rules of the Pharisees, a sect having points of resemblance to that which the Greeks call the Stoic school.

Higher education of Josephus's day was by tutoring, or by learning in small groups, and in the hands of the various sects.[18] Josephus says that he tried all the sects, by which he means the three major ones. He also makes a point of stressing the hard training he underwent, illustrating the ancient world's distrust of quick conversions. His studies could hardly have been more than a quick sampling, because he entrusted most of his four years of higher education to a man called Bannus, with whom he lived for three years in the desert. Alternatively, Josephus's report indicates that he grew up as a Sadducee, spent three years with Bannus, and then pursued a public career, which meant submitting to the Pharisees. From Bannus, with whom he obviously did endure special hardships, Josephus learned to practice a regimen similar to that of the Essenes and John the Baptist. Of special interest is Josephus's report that Bannus practiced a simple life with frequent ritual immersions for purity's sake. If anything in Josephus's life could be considered a conversion experience, this is it, since he states that he became Bannus's devoted disciple (*zēlōtēs egenomēn autou*).

The systems of catechesis developed in each sect were obviously not publicly sponsored educational institutions but were systems devoted to the creation of disciples. Not everyone who attended the educational facility actually converted. Josephus's claim to be a *Wunderkind* and a religious quester is, however, a conceit, for it certainly is part of his attempt to recommend himself as a knowledgeable historian of the Jewish people. In fact, the motif of spiritual quest was itself a literary convention, functioning throughout the Roman world to establish an author's credentials as a religious commentator.[19] Josephus's religious sentiments were more impressed with Bannus, not with the other sects. He does not leave Bannus until his (religious) inclinations are satisfied (*epithumian teleōsas*).

His decision to join the Pharisees is hardly more than a matter of convenience. This interpretation is at odds with the majority of Josephus scholars, who see Josephus as a Pharisee. But they read too much into Josephus's description. Although many English translations have rendered *ērxamēn politeuesthai* as "I began to conduct myself," or some other phrase that reflects religious conversion, it is more likely that the accurate translation is something like: "I began to study civil law, for which purpose I entered the society of the Pharisees."[20] Josephus, then, never actually converted to the Pharisees; he only relied on them for his legal education since their popularity made his political career possible.

This clarifies Josephus's many pro-Sadducean statements and his continuing enmity with the Pharisaic leadership during the First Revolt against Rome in 68 C.E. When he states in *Antiquities* 18.15 that the Pharisees are extremely influential among the townfolk, and that all public rituals are carried out according to their precepts, we get an inkling of his motivation for seeking out their education. Since Josephus is most likely a Sadducee by birth, he must do as he himself says all Sadducees do: "For whenever they assume some office, though they submit unwillingly and perforce, yet submit they do to the formulas of the Pharisees, since otherwise the masses would not tolerate them" (*Antiquities* 18.17). When Josephus wrote, the Pharisees had become one of the most powerful groups in Judea and not just a sect. He was not a great sympathizer with their cause, but he was a practical man and understood the necessity of being guided by them. This also sheds light on his later defection to the Roman side during the war. Josephus was a pragmatic man throughout his life.

Pragmatic though he was, Josephus does illustrate the range of religious decisions possible for a Jew in the first century. Josephus can talk about his religious feelings, which he calls *epithumia*, as Paul does (Rom. 7), and he may be talking about a conversion experience when he became Bannus's disciple. He also evidences the converse phenomenon, what Nock called adherence and what many social psychologists call alternation, in his education by the Pharisees. We can see that a Jew's association with one of the Jewish sectarian positions—either Essenism or Pharisaism—might have involved a radical change of some aspects of existence. But at the same time, it might not be a radical change in every respect. Alternatively, one might go to some religious figures or communities for educational purposes, without anticipating a conversion experience.

Had Josephus actually joined the Essenes, as well as lauding them, he would have had to become a convert, although conversion to this group was normally envisioned as a gradual process of internalizing group norms. Essene membership came only by conversion. Even an orphan would have had to go through the same lengthy initiation as any other convert. Virtually no member of this group could be called merely an adherent because all members adopted a radically different life-style.[21]

The single most obvious characteristic of the Essenes or Dead Sea Scroll sectarians was their dualism. Strongly apocalyptic, the community divided the world into a battle between the children of darkness and the children of light. This should not be confused with a philosophical impetus toward dualism, for they believed in a single deity. The distinction, rather, has as much to do with sociology as theology. Their dualism was parallel to their division of the world, which served to separate members of the group from everyone else. From another perspective the dualism was parallel to the strong distinction between pre- and postdecision cognitive dissonance in their community. It functioned to keep the new member away from contradictory information. It is interesting how thoroughly this distinction affects their thinking, for they virtually identify themselves with the community of the saved at the end of time. There is thus a perfect symmetry between their personal decision-states in joining their community and their views of the ultimate purpose of history.

In this respect the Qumranites are quite close to the modern group expecting salvation from "flying saucers," which Festinger studied in the classic *When Prophecy Fails*,[22] or to many of the new religions today, which set up monastic, ascetic, or retreat communities based on the notion that they alone will survive. Although ecstasy appeared to be part of their rites, the Qumran group did not describe conversion in ecstatic or emotional terms, stressing the stages and rigors of the life of purity instead. They prescribed ritual immersion for purity, as did the Pharisees. But it had a mark that was unequivocally Essene. Ritual immersion made the Dead Sea Scroll community pure enough to fight with the angels at the end of time. Hence, the member could be saved at the final battle. The practice fills in the gaps between rabbinic views of community and Christian ones, as it adds the missing steps between Jewish ritual immersion and Christian baptism. Because of the Dead Sea Scrolls we can investigate the internal organization of the Essenes and see that they would score high on the scales of commitment developed by Kanter.

CONVERSION AMONG DIASPORA JEWISH GROUPS

Conversion among Jewish groups was a subspecies of the phenomenon of conversion known throughout the Hellenistic world. Philosophers in particular specialized in redeeming their contemporaries from human error; philosophical schools resembled religious associations as much as anything else.[23] Philosophers used the same term as did Hellenistic Judaism, *epistrephein* or *epistrophe,* to describe the turning or coming to oneself. The Septuagint's vocabulary came from this philosophical usage. Occasionally the philosophers even used the term *metamorphosis,* which Paul himself uses so significantly. The philosopher's audience was observed to experience a quickly changing palette of emotions, including repentance, joy, or wonder, "and even have varying facial expressions and changes of feeling as the philosopher's speech affects him and touches his recognition of that part of his soul which is sound and that which is sick."[24]

Normally, the conversion process was a gradual process of interest, followed by commitment. But it could also be miraculously fast, stimulated by some personal crisis like a shipwreck, financial or political ruin, or exile. The accounts of conversion in response to speeches tend to stress the spontaneity of the conversion as a way of underlining the power of philosophical speech and reason.[25] Christian stress on the speed and completeness of conversion seems equally to stress the power of the spirit. We can expect that Jewish proselytism relied on similar tactics to praise the power and rightness of its converts' choices.

Hellenistic Judaism, deeply influenced by classical thought, was the majority Jewish culture of the day. Even within the small area of Judea and the slightly larger area of the land of Israel, which included Samaria and the Galilee, we have evidence of a large number of Hellenized Jews. These Jews produced the majority of the material evidence that has come down to us from the first centuries. It is their culture whose ruins we find scattered over Israel and the Mediterranean landmasses. Josephus mentions the "representations of animals" that Herod Antipas put in houses in Tiberias (*Life* 65). Although the Galilean synagogues with their beautiful mosaics—containing zodiacs, the seasons, and depictions of Helios—date from the third century and later, they show the extent of Jewish acculturation to Hellenism, the willing interplay of Jewish and pagan beliefs—as long as some major tenet of Jewish belief was not flagrantly violated. In the Jewish Diaspora, acculturation can only have been all the more evident.[26] Philo, the spokesman for Hellenistic Judaism, evinces a large degree of universalism. He discusses the wisdom of the Greeks as one standard of truth in the world. He takes pains, of course, to show that everything good in Greek thought is paralleled by Jewish thought and that Judaism contains moral and philosophical truths only hinted at by the Greeks. He never explicitly mentions an active Jewish mission to convert gentiles.[27] He sometimes appears to believe, however, that gentiles can attain to salvation, as gentiles without conversion, just as Jews can attain to the philosophical mind. He does not actively promote a mission to gentiles, as he was a sensible Diaspora Jew and is sensitive to gentile fears. Though he mentions with pride that some gentiles have even sought fit to convert to Judaism and exhorts Jews to accept them, he seems to believe that there are some gentiles who have the advantages of a moral and philosophical life without conversion to Judaism (*Special Laws* 1.52; 1.308–9; *Virtues* 103–4).[28]

This is a minor topic, however, compared to the apologia that both Philo and Josephus mount for proving the truth of Judaism in *Against Flaccus* and *Against Apion* respectively. Indeed, scholarship has been needlessly detained trying to distinguish between the two different motives: missionary literature or apologetic. It seems best to assume as a general rule, as I try to demonstrate below, that apologetics were the primary motivation of Jews living within the Hellenistic cultural sphere, whereas missionary literature was characteristic of less acculturated Jews. It is, of course, possible that apologetic literature was used for missionary purposes, as well as for their more obvious use in gentile education. Even *Joseph and Aseneth* seems more suited for the education and training of previously identified proselytes than for the missionizing of gentiles.

Several arguments crop up repeatedly in the apologetic literature. Among the proofs of Judaism's truth are both its ancient history and its success in gaining converts, which was also noted by several prominent and hostile classical writers. Horace states that the Jews can compel a person to be one of the strong (*cogemus in hanc concedere turbam* [*Satires* 1.4.139–43]). Tacitus, the Roman historian, says of proselytes to Judaism: "The earliest lesson they receive is to despise the gods, to disown their country, and to regard their parents, children and brothers as of little account" (*Histories* 5.5).[29] Such statements testify to the success that Judaism had in proselytism. But they also show the social threat that Judaism and Christianity presented to Graeco-Roman society. Abraham Malherbe suggests that both Philo and Josephus's use of the so-called *Haustafel,* the idealized ethical portrait of a household common in pagan ethical treatises, was partly an attempt to counter polemics and fears that Judaism was antisocial or would undermine pagan society.[30] This is logical because Jewish rights in diaspora were dependent on the good will of the rulers. It was not wise to antagonize them. Roman historians record what happened when Romans felt threatened by the Jewish community.[31]

This perception is more important after the birth of Christianity, since both Jewish and pagan society shared exactly this distrust of Christianity. Jesus' message, according to the New Testament, did contain advice to leave parents and families. Later Christianity found the same and greater need to apologize for possible family disruption as did Judaism, as the *Haustafel* in 1 Peter testifies.

Before and after the rise of Christianity, Jews proselytized, and their proselytism gained them both friends and enemies. According to Valerius Maximus, the Jews were expelled from Rome in 139 B.C.E. because of their attempts to "transmit their holy rites to the Romans" (*qui Romanis tradere sacra sua conati erant*). Very likely this was the same reason for their expulsion under Tiberius in the first century, for according to Dio Cassius they were expelled because "they were converting many of the natives to their customs." One may question whether Jews actively sought out proselytes in an aggressive way or whether they just developed out of philosophical interest or the attractiveness of Jewish services and lifestyles. But the undeniable truth was that they did convert in sufficient numbers to cause anxiety in the pagan world. In the first century B.C.E., the Maccabees were also said to have conquered the Idumeans and to have forced circumcision on them. This can be considered conversion of a sort, but of an exceptional nature. The circumstances and the duress involved excludes this from consideration in our psychological and social portrait.

Jewish proselytism was both real and controversial. Jews gained proselytes but did not overwhelm the pagan world, because becoming a Jew was never merely a decision to join another religious club. Judaism was exclusive; it decried the other religious associations and therefore was sometimes seen as intolerant. Joining Judaism was primarily a decision to join another *ethnos*, which was a step not taken lightly and always accepted with some suspicion.[32]

We should not assume that there was a single definition of conversion within Judaism. That there were differing standards for the acceptance of converts to Judaism, attributable to the different orientations of the various sects, is evident not only from the rabbinic discussion but from a few precious reports from Josephus. Josephus claims that the Jews of Antioch "were constantly attracting to their religious ceremonies multitudes of Greeks, and these they had in some measure incorporated into themselves" (*Jewish War* 7.3.3 [45]). Some Jews preferred that potential converts remain semiproselytes because such in-between stages provoked fewer backlashes than did disrupting pagan families by converting wives, children, or husbands. Jews of the Diaspora, in the ancient world and today, equate visibility with vulnerability. Problems of family disruption only underline the fact that most conversions took place on a person-to-person level, spreading through organizations and families one member at a time. Such patterns, as in Mormon preaching, are well known today and are bound to be significant evidence for the process by which Christianity spread as well.

Just as they received converts from pagan society, many Jews, even those who wished to retain their Jewish identity, acculturated to pagan society. As in the modern period, the Jew's predicament as "marginal man" could be solved by leaving Judaism entirely, by downplaying the value of Judaism, or by reforming Judaism to make it more acceptable to gentiles.[33] Obviously, some assimilated completely, losing their Jewish identity and often gaining citizenship in the Greek polis.[34] There were many accommodations short of apostasy. Philo believed that the special laws of Judaism had to be practiced literally, but he also wrote that some intellectual Jews did not practice them. Although these intellectuals studied Torah, they understood the laws only as allegories and did not see fit to observe them. This implies that a Jewish education was received by most of the community, though different Jews may have stressed different values. Philo does not agree with these "extreme allegorizers," but his criticism stops short of hostility. He is satisfied with satirizing them as persons who try to "live as souls without bodies, as though they were living by themselves in a wilderness" (*On the Migration of Abraham* 89). Philo appears to mean that the customs of Judaism are designed to be practiced where they enforce moral standards within society. Philo describes the extreme allegorizers essentially as philosophers, misguided for having forgotten that universal values must be envisioned through particular material circumstances.[35]

The leniency of Philo's reproach of the extreme allegorizers can be seen in comparison with apostates, for whom he has less kind words: "being incontinent . . . [they] have sold their freedom for luxurious food . . . and beauty of body, thus ministering to the pleasures of the belly and the organs below it" (*Virtues* 34, 182). This discussion is reminiscent of 3 Maccabees where the apostates are called "those who for their belly's sake had transgressed the divine command" (7:11). The apostates are not virtuous but merely indulge themselves in degradation. Desiring complete assimilation, they make no attempt to live up to the virtues of Judaism. The extreme allegorizers continued to consider themselves Jews and maintain the moral laws of Judaism, though they neglected the special customs.

The ferocity of hatred directed against gentiles by some of the apocalyptic literature should be noted. Jubilees stresses the strict separation of Jews from the gentiles, who are their inferiors in morality (15.31). Jubilees considers the gentiles to be demonically related to the evil powers. The Qumran texts outlining the war of the children of light on the children of darkness depict the gentiles in similar villainy. Fourth Ezra too condemns the gentiles after the destruction of the Temple (6.55–57). These are hardly discussions of Jewish identity or conversion, but they show the range of choices available to Jews of the time and the range of opinions about the gentiles. Conclusions about such modern ideas as assimilation and conversion can be teased out of the context because some of the social conflicts are quite similar to those of the modern world.

Shaye Cohen (among others) has suggested that Jewish identity in this period resembles citizenship because it was usually determined by birth and was not easily obtained otherwise. The Greek *Ioudaios* and the Latin *Iudaeus,* like the Hebrew *Yehudi,* meant "Judean," describing more geographical and national connotations than the word *Jew* in modern languages. The analogy is not complete because a Jew could become a citizen of another place through naturalization without losing his Jewish identity. Citizenship in Greek cities was jealously guarded, but it was sometimes bestowed on foreigners on the basis of habitation, property ownership, religious rite, and, primarily, local benefactions.

The Jewish path to citizenship was still not an easy one. Jews in Alexandria aspired to and obtained citizenship on an individual basis, but because of civil conflict between the Jews and the Greeks, the best the Jews could receive was *isopoliteia,* separate-but-unequal rights to citizenship.[36] The legal issues surrounding Jewish rights were closely associated with their status as a *collegium licitum* or possibly a *religio licita*.[37] The situation in Alexandria was, of course, unique, but it is likely that fear of Jews multiplied anywhere in the empire where enough Jews settled to become politically, economically, and socially powerful. The history of each community differed, but some of the underlying forces were universal.

Some Jews were satisfied with such gains, content to develop independently; other Jews were not. Still other Jews, like Philo, probably came from families that had been part of the citizenry for generations. Paul was apparently a citizen of the empire. Citizenship was often bestowed on the basis of religious preference, rather than the other way around, which meant that it was never easy for Jews to become citizens of other areas. One way to become a citizen of Athens was to seek initiation into the Eleusinian mysteries.[38] This kind of religious devotion to a foreign cult was obviously more difficult for a Jew than other natives (one could own property in Athens without being a citizen) seeking citizenship. One should not expect to find many practicing Jews in civic office before the edict of the emperors Severus and Caracalla (between 198 and 210 C.E.) because of the special religious nature of jobs imposed on officeholders. Thereafter it was less rare, for Ulpian adds to his description of the ruling of Severus and Caracalla that the emperors did not infringe on the *superstitio* of Jewish officeholders.[39] Jewish identity in parts of the Diaspora was like foreign nationality, as it is today, though it is hardly identical with the ancient understanding of citizenship. Jewish identity in the ancient world could often be subject to the same stresses as it is even in the modern secular American Jewish community, which has its many examples of apostasies to both established religion and the new religious cults, based on psychological needs as well as perceived career necessities.

There is a Diaspora Jewish sensitivity to the whole issue of conversion. Unlike Paul, the Septuagint does not use terms associated with *metamorphosis* to any special advantage.[40] Philo uses *metamorphosis* three times, describing: (1) Emperor Gaius Caligula's insane attempt to become Apollo (*Gaium* 95); (2) Moses' transformation to a prophet by means of divine inspiration (*Mos.* 1.57); and (3) the virtue of piety, which is transformed by the slightest alteration (*Spec. leg.* 4.147). Speaking about Moses, Philo brings together the notions of prophecy and religious transformation, which we see in Luke's biography of Paul and to a lesser extent in Paul's writing itself. For the greatest religious leaders, Philo uses the language of transformation freely, without the satirical bite of his description of Caligula. Philo believes that Moses was a unique figure, a divine figure in many ways, and the perfection of earthly paradigms for prophet, priest, and king. In other writings, Philo avoids *metamorphosis,* stressing the patient progress (*prokoptein*) by which humanity is made perfect (*teleios*). This usage reflects the popular stoic conception of Philo's day.[41]

Philo believed that people do not see God directly but through a mirror (*On Flight* 213). The concept of perfection can refer to any philosophically minded human being, according to his or her abilities. Gentiles as well as Jews are capable of the journey, though Israel, whose name means *he who sees God,* is specially gifted in the search because of its possession of the biblical text and moral catechism. If conversion is a part of Philo's scheme, it is the kind of conversion characteristic of long training. Philo mentions converts to Judaism, but he never speaks of mission as a Jewish national purpose. He must have been sensitive to the issue of Jewish mission and tried to dispel pagan fears.

We have few explicit discussions of conversion in Hellenistic Jewish literature: Jewish adjustment to Hellenistic life often made proselytizing uncomfortable and dysfunctional. John J. Collins has shown, however, that among Hellenistic Jews there was a liberal attitude toward gentile interest in Judaism.[42] A body of apologetic or propaganda literature was designed to inform gentiles of the value of Jewish life. The Sibylline Oracles contain a public relations offensive. They praise the Jews as a most righteous race (3.219). Specific features proving Jewish moral superiority are enumerated: the practice of social justice (218–64) and the avoidance of idolatry and homosexuality (573–600). In a number of passages the sibyl speaks directly to the Greeks: "To what purpose do you give vain *gifts of the dead*[43] and sacrifice to idols? Who put error in your heart that you should abandon the fact of the great God and do these things?" (547–49). Within the Sibylline Oracles, salvation is sought in this world. Jews and Greeks alike can attain to a peaceful life, free from war and subjugation. Salvation can be attained by Greeks if they abandon idolatry and offer sacrifice at the temple of the great God in Jerusalem (624–34). In these cases it is extremely difficult to tell where apologia ends and mission begins.

The Letter of Aristeas makes no direct appeal for conversion, but there is certainly an apologetic or propagandistic attempt to portray the merits of Judaism. The letter purports to be written by one Greek and sent to another, but there is a Jewish hand behind it. The God of the Jews is described: "the overseer and creator of all things, whom they worship, is He whom all men worship, and we too your Majesty, though we address him differently, as Zeus and Dis; by these names men of old not unsuitably signified that He through whom all creatures receive life and come into being is the guide and lord of all" (16). Judaism is presented as a non-violent, nonaggressive philosophy and especially not as an exclusive or closed fraternity; rather, it is a gift to all humanity, since God's providence is universal. If this characterization evinces a sensitivity to pagan charges, there can be no doubt as to why proselytism is downplayed. It is not suggested that God will show special consideration for the Jews simply by virtue of their being Jews. The Jews follow their own rites, which attain a desirable religious end, but the same end can be attained by moral Greeks, though their rites are different.[44] Some of the most acculturated Jewish writers apparently soft-pedaled conversion when it was viewed as threatening by the gentile community, arguing that monotheism and virtue would be rewarded wherever it was found. These Jews asked gentiles to worship the one true God, which entailed a rejection of idolatry or, as it was often expressed, worship of the dead, and avoidance of sin, with emphasis on adultery and homosexuality as the two characteristic gentile sins. Both proselytism and the avoidance of it can thus be seen as characteristic of aspects of the Jewish community.

In spite of Jewish sensitivities to the charge of breaking up gentile families, some Jews welcomed converts. A brief mention of conversion occurs at the end of the book of Judith, which is probably from the Hellenistic period. After Judith has killed Holofernes, Achior the Ammonite general is so impressed with the saving acts of the Israelite God that he becomes a believer, even accepting circumcision. He is thus incorporated "in the house of Israel forever" (14.10). No doubt this is meant to illustrate the highest possible form of pagan admiration for Judaism.

The romance of *Joseph and Asenath* is an account of gentile conversion to Judaism set during Joseph's sojourn in Egypt, but it is meant to be the model of proselytism in the Hellenistic world. Since Asenath is a woman, the issue of circumcision does not arise. The ritual that is mentioned, however, is completely puzzling. Joseph is described as eating the blessed bread of life, drinking the cup of immortality, and anointing himself with the blessed oil of incorruption. When Asenath converts after throwing her idols away, she attains to these rites, which are apparently symbolic of Jewish life in general rather than representative of a specific conversion ritual.[45] The rabbinic document Shabbat 17b forbids gentile wine, bread, and oil: "the bread and oil of the heathen on account of their wine, and their wine on account of their daughters, and their daughters on account of idolatry." The symbols can be used conversely to illustrate Asenath's entrance into the community. The context of *Joseph and Asenath* is apposite to the rabbis' warning, implying that the rules of commensality were broadly understood in the Judaism of this period as safeguards against the idolatry of gentiles. We also learn that Joseph does not eat with the Egyptians, though he is ruler of all Egypt (7.1; 20.9). Asenath is described as "dead" before her conversion, which represents her journey into life. In this document, immortality is the benefit of conversion. She thus enters Judaism the way Paul suggested gentiles should enter Christianity.

The choices available to Hellenistic Jews were manifold, implying many different adaptations to the Jewish-Hellenistic cultural exchange, allowing for a variety of different opinions toward conversion in the Jewish community. Philo and the Hellenistic writers give evidence for the liberal end of the spectrum of commitment to Judaism: some self-identified Hellenistic Jews were still committed to Judaism, but the sources of their commitment must have been entirely different from the Essenes, who produced a sectarian, inward-looking, and highly cohesive society, separate even from the majority of Jews. The Hellenistic Jew could have been involved in many transactional relationships with the larger Hellenistic world while maintaining close ties with other Jews as well. Hellenistic Jews often needed both sets of relationships to pursue their livelihood. Though the upper levels of Hellenistic Jewish society may have felt deprived of the full rights of citizenship that many non-Greek or non-Roman gentile Hellenists had attained, most Jews felt at ease in Hellenistic society and trade, accepting the restrictions on their lives as given and seeking to remove as many nonessential boundaries as they could justify. They sometimes endeavored to remove a cause of suspicion between themselves and their gentile neighbors by saying that all moral people could enjoy God's blessing by righteousness. Few sought to convert their gentile neighbors, for this would have risked a gentile backlash. But some Jews did.

One cannot call Hellenistic Jews a unified group, much less a social grouping. Group commitment was built in quite different circumstances. Hellenistic Jews, with a variety of differing accommodations to Hellenism, were the majority of Jews of the time. Yet they could not have felt the social cohesion of the Essenes. Further, modern studies show that liberal positions do not grow as quickly as conservative ones. Some liberal members can be assumed to fall away from a group, giving up any religious identification, while more conservative groups are able, if they desire, to attract new highly committed members, even when there is a generalized, gradual movement toward more liberal positions. The conservative Essenes were a highly cohesive group, while the liberal Hellenistic Jews were hardly a unified group at all.

Unfortunately these meditations are of limited value for the study of Paul's past, because we know so little of his life. If Luke is correct about Paul's early life, he came from the acculturated Jewish community of Tarsus, but his family belonged to a group of Pharisees living there (Acts 22:3). Though Acts 21:40 and 22:2 mention that Paul spoke a Semitic language at home, there is no evidence that he wrote in any other language than Greek. Paul may have had experience with the part of the Jewish community most likely to be tempted to convert, but according to Acts he was not of that community. Rather, he was part of a more zealous minority in the Diaspora. Paul, however, did journey to Jerusalem for advanced religious education, already having had a taste of Hellenistic and Pharisaic Jewish life. Unlike Josephus, who was from a leading Jewish family in Judea but not a Pharisaic one, Paul was not a convert to Pharisaism, if we can believe Acts; rather, he was brought up as a Pharisee in an atmosphere that offered many other kinds of Judaism and religious life in general. But Acts is not automatically a reliable authority about Paul. We know too little about Paul's life before he became a Christian (and barely enough afterward) to make firm judgments about Paul's personal motivations. Further, Paul's conversion to Christianity may well have been through the dominant Jewish mode of patient education, even after his conversion experience. It is Luke who wishes to pattern the emotional nature of that experience for gentile conversions.

THE GOD-FEARERS OR SEMI-PROSELYTES TO JUDAISM

God-fearer is the term used to refer to those gentiles with varying degrees of commitment to Judaism, all of whom have been attracted to the synagogue but who are unwilling as yet to become full proselytes. Acts uses the terms *sebomenos,* literally a worshiper (sometimes *theosebes* and variants suggesting a worshiper of God most high), or *phoboumenos,* literally a fearer of God. Fearing God is merely the normal Hebrew idiom for describing worshiping Him. The term *God-fearer* is used directly in Acts 10, where Cornelius is described as one and also as a donor to the synagogue. But the term is not a Lukan invention, for Josephus uses it as well (to describe gentiles in *Antiquities* 14.110), as does Julia Severa, a cosponsor of the synagogue building in Acmonia.[46]

A. T. Kraabel has proposed that the presence of these people in the synagogues where Paul preaches is Luke's invention, introduced for the purpose of showing "how Christianity had become a gentile religion legitimately and without losing its Old Testament roots."[47] Kraabel's skepticism was based on his contention that we lack firm archaeological or inscriptional evidence for *God-fearers* in any synagogue site, though he himself describes the synagogue at Sardis as designed to be a showplace of Jewish ritual for the gentile passersby.[48] But the evidence is less one-sided than Kraabel suggests, since the term does exist in a few inscriptions, where its interpretation is moot, as it may refer to a Jew or a gentile.

The literary evidence contradicts Kraabel's methodological reserve. Many pagan writers attest to the attractiveness of Jewish ways of life, reporting that gentiles were interested in some Jewish ceremonies but did not convert. Plutarch speaks of the freedman Caecilius "who was accused of Jewish practices [*henochō tō 'ioudaizein*]" (*Life of Cicero* 7.6). Seneca may be referring to Judaism when he says that he became a vegetarian in his youth (*Letters* 108.22). Dio Cassius says that in 41 C.E. Claudius forbade the Jews in Rome from holding meetings because they had increased so greatly in numbers (*Historia* 60.6.6). He also says that many who were drifting into Jewish ways (*ta tōn 'Ioudaiōn ethē*) were condemned for atheism (67.14.1–3). Suetonius suggests that the persecution of Domitian was against "those who followed the Jewish way [*vitam*] of life without formally professing Judaism" (*Domitian* 12.2). The precise behavior among potential converts to Judaism occasioning these attacks is probably not consistent. But the fear and derision of the gentile observers is obvious enough.

Two recently published inscriptions from Aphrodisias in Caria seem to settle the question of the existence of God-fearers.[49] Besides identifying Jewish donors, with a mixture of Jewish, biblical, and Hellenistic names, the texts identify a whole group of people with exclusively Greek names as *theosebeis,* some with likely gentile occupations such as city councillors. Within the list there is a sprinkling of people with biblical names who are described as proselytes. God-fearer is a title with a special technical meaning, distinct from Jews and proselytes. The inscriptions indicate that some gentiles were fellow travelers with Judaism, supporting the synagogue but not converting outright. They can be thought of as similar to the well-attested, noninitiated, but interested throngs who visited the public ceremonies of a mystery cult; from this group came the more seriously interested fellow travelers with the cult, and eventually some declared their allegiance through conversion. In the case of the Aphrodisias synagogue, one can assume that the commitment of God-fearers varied from monetary support to participation in some of the synagogue's customs, including the establishment of a soup kitchen, if Reynolds and Tannenbaum's interpretation of *patella* is correct. God-fearers could be committed to some Jewish customs. After the destruction of the Temple, one custom was permitted for the highly committed God-fearers that was legally forbidden to Jews—sacrificing in Jerusalem, for Roman law forbade any Jew from entering the city. Luke might have construed the presence of God-fearers in the synagogues of the Hellenistic world as consonant with his own theology. God-fearers nonetheless existed, possibly in large numbers. These people formed a reservoir of gentiles with widely varying interests in Judaism for whom Christianity would have had a natural appeal.

God-fearers, as their name implies, were not an easily definable group; rather, many levels of commitment can be imagined. Their affiliation with Judaism ran all the way from casual interest to complete commitment. One can imagine a number of purely political reasons for a gentile to support a prominent local synagogue, yet among the God-fearers Philo would certainly have numbered some gentiles who could achieve the status and privileges God had promised to the Jews—after all, benefaction was one of the accepted routes leading to adhesion with the group. Possibly some God-fearers were content with adhesion because they were unable to consider conversion. These people were surely held in high respect by the community, since their gifts were accepted and recorded for posterity. The rabbis held similar but not identical concepts of righteous gentiles.

God-fearer might equally mean someone with high degrees of commitment to Judaism. The God-fearer could eventually become a full convert. This impressed Juvenal, who wrote a satire on the increasing Judaization of those who were first impressed by the rite of the Sabbath[50]: "Some who have had a father who reveres the Sabbath, worship nothing but the clouds, and the divinity of the heavens, and see no difference between eating swine's flesh, from which their father abstained, and that of man; and in time they take to circumcision. Having been wont to flout the laws of Rome, they learn and practice and revere the Jewish law, and all that Moses committed to his secret tome, forbidding to point out the way to any not worshipping the same rites, and conducting none but the circumcised to the desired fountain. For all which the father was to blame, who gave up every seventh day to idleness, keeping it apart from all the concerns of life" (14.96–106).

Juvenal's writing caricatures a gentile conversion to Judaism through progressive learning of God-fearers and culminating in the acceptance of Jewish ceremonial law. It also illustrates the dangers of gentile backlash inherent in Jewish proselytism, explaining the willingness of some Jews to consider God-fearers their equal in righteousness. God-fearers were probably asked to make their commitments slowly and with great care for fear of gentile backlash. Others in the Jewish community surely saw a providential progression in gentile interest in Judaism, just as the pagan community did, though they evaluated its divine sanction differently.

CONVERSION AMONG THE PHARISEES AND RABBIS

We cannot be sure that the rabbinic reports about conversion reflect Pharisaic practice of the first century. Rabbinic rules grew out of first-century practice, but without outside corroboration, we cannot be sure how or exactly when any particular custom developed. Some scholars have maintained that the Pharisees converted only Jews to their special sect and were unconcerned with gentiles. To claim this, they have ignored an enormous body of material about gentile conversions in later rabbinic writing, when conversion had grown yet more difficult. The rabbis clearly know of both kinds of converts. Although Akiba was a famous rabbi who came to Pharisaism only in his middle years, the rabbis also tell many stories of gentiles seeking admission to Judaism. They developed special vocabularies for both types of converts. So the hypothesis of a solely Jewish mission among the Pharisees seems wildly off the mark.

With regard to commitment, both Pharisaism and early Jewish Christianity would have fallen into intermediary positions between Hellenistic Judaism and Essenism, the two extremes of commitment, since both accepted converts, viewed themselves as a sect, but lived in the community rather than in monastic orders. It is probable from the description in the New Testament that Pharisees did not attain or need the same social cohesion that early Christianity evidenced. Pharisees did not live communally, for instance, though they surely lived close to each other. Conversion into the Pharisaic order of the first century meant accepting a new level of cohesion, although whether the community was limited by the rules of the *haburoth*—taking on the purity regulations at table, giving heave offerings, and being meticulous in observing the tithing regulations—is a moot point. The haburoth may have been special groups within the Pharisees. These regulations, as Jacob Neusner has pointed out, were used to create a self-contained community defined by its ability to marry within its ranks, eat in its own houses and touch only its own implements. At first, the Pharisaic order would have been sectarian in nature: most of those who entered the order would have been socialized to Judaism.[51] The later rabbis, reflecting on their traditions, idealized the legal situation in the first century and certainly held out high standards of entrance: "The rabbis say: 'If a proselyte takes it upon himself to obey all the words of the Torah except one single commandment, he is not to be received'" (Sifra, Kedoshim 8). This rule would apply to both gentile and Jewish converts to Pharisaism. The rabbis never imply here that proselytism was limited to Jews. Gentile conversion to Pharisaic Judaism certainly existed and would have required a more serious case of resocialization.

The study of gentile conversion to Judaism must confront the problem that most of the information available comes from rabbinic evidence whose date and disinterestedness is difficult to establish. The evidence of Christianity, if used effectively, can push back our knowledge to the first century. This would mean accepting Christian proselytism as evidence that some first-century Jews were interested in proselytizing gentiles. Such a conclusion has at least some limited validity. But that merely begs the question of the extent of the Jewish mission. The rabbinic evidence reproduces what we assume must have been the case in the first century. Later talmudic tradition presents an idealized range of opinion: "A foreigner came to Shammai, saying, 'Make a proselyte of me, on condition that you teach me the whole of the Torah while I stand on one foot.' Shammai drove him off with a measuring stick he had in his hand. Thereupon he repaired to Hillel with the same proposition. Hillel received him as a proselyte and taught him: 'What you do not like to have done to you, do not do to your fellow. This is the whole of the Torah; the rest is explanation of it. Go learn it'" (b. Shabbat 31a).

The convert (foreigner) is most likely a gentile. This story is one of three examples of the difference between Hillel and Shammai, two early rabbis who lived just prior to Jesus, on the issue of conversion. There is no way to be sure that the stories contain any historical value for the study of the first century. The gentiles in the three examples are meant primarily to point out a difference between the schools of Shammai and Hillel, which flourished later. They might also represent different positions in the group of potential proselytes. The three stories in the rabbinic anthology emphasize the more lenient approach to Hillel, the dominant rabbinic sage, on the issue of conversion over the strict position of Shammai, who does not appear to be interested in making converts. The three gentiles may even represent varieties of opinions among converts to Judaism: those who convert to non-Pharisaic Judaism (no oral law and only some of the laws of the Bible), those who convert out of ambition (to become the High Priest) and finally the one quoted above, who converts for moral principles and to whom is given the famous answer of Hillel: "What you do not like to have done to you, do not do to your fellow." The important part for the rabbis is the instruction to go out and study. If each of these groups represents an actual possibility, then some gentiles could be accepted into Judaism by non-Pharisaic Jews without having to accept the whole law, a category that Paul discusses as well.

The problem with the rabbinic evidence lies not only in what it means but also in the date in which it became the standard practice within Judaism.[52] Like the Essenes, the rabbis favored the slow conversion of a highly indoctrinated convert over the rapid conversion of an emotionally involved one. What became rabbinic doctrine may have only been a formalization of earlier general practice within the Jewish community or it may have been the explicit beliefs of the first-century Pharisees. One effect of Hillel's answer is to encourage the convert to enter the stages of training to become socialized as a Jew. This is why gradual conversions are emphasized: Gentile conversions to Judaism were decisions to leave one kind of cultural milieu and enter another, moving from one socialization to another. They therefore demanded long training. Whether or not an emotional crisis precipitated conversion, the rabbis emphasized the process of education. The rabbis here must mean study in whatever rabbinic schools of study then existed. The stories of Rabbi Akiba do not emphasize the suddenness of his decision so much as the stringent training he undertook so late in life. In later tradition, the cultic requirements of conversion were three, as the statement attributed to R. Judah the Prince (fl. 200 C.E.) makes clear: "Rabbi says: Just as Israel did not enter the covenant except through three things—through circumcision, through immersion, and through the acceptance of a sacrifice—so it is the same with proselytes" (Sifre Num. 108).

The story establishes the rabbinic model for the acceptance of proselytes: the Sinai theophany. To the three ritual obligations one must add the fourth obligation to know and practice the Torah of Israel, as interpreted and taught by the rabbis. When the rabbis said Torah, they meant the written and oral law, but other kinds of Jews practiced a less-exacting Judaism. For purposes of legal precedent, all Israel is assumed to have been circumcised, been baptized, and made sacrifices before Sinai. By the end of the second century, the ideal of the rabbis was to insure that proselytes kept every single aspect of Torah (e.g., t. Dem. 2.5), but there is no telling how close actual practice throughout Judaism, including non-Pharisaic Judaism, came to this ideal, nor when the rabbinic ruling became normative for the entire world community of Jews. Yet this statement does not contradict the practice of Hillel in first-century B.C.E. Judea.

There is evidence outside of rabbinic literature of Jews seeking converts. Matt. 23:15 reports that the Pharisees were zealous to make converts. The most famous of Josephus's accounts, the conversion of the royal house of Adiabene (*Antiquities* 20.2.3–4 [34–48]), illustrates the importance of the Pharisaic opinion in matters of conversion. It also gives us a sense of how the differing views of conversion worked in real cases. A Jewish merchant named Ananias visited the royal house of Adiabene and taught the king's wives to worship the Jewish God.[53] His efforts to convert began with the women and were continued on a person-to-person basis. Through the harem, he won over the crown prince, Izates, but his mother, Queen Helena, had already been won over by another Jew.

The issue of circumcision becomes problematic in this conversion account, since Izates is a male and needs circumcision to convert. In fact, he wishes to be circumcised. But his mother disagrees, thinking that his subjects would reject him as king if he practiced Judaism openly. Interestingly, Ananias takes the part of Queen Helena, not recommending circumcision under the circumstances. Josephus has Ananias recommend that Izates remain a God-fearer, since "he could worship the divine [*to theion sebein*] even without circumcision, if he had fully decided to be devoted to the ancestral customs of the Jews, for this was more important than circumcision." These words are Josephus's, not Ananias's, but they do articulate a rational and defensible position within Judaism, one which is compatible with the archaeological record about God-fearers. It shows us how the problem of conversion was actually handled, outside of the prescriptive, legal requirements discussed by the rabbis. Malherbe and other scholars' suspicion is confirmed: many Jews simply preferred that a God-fearer bypass formal conversion when a complex social situation was involved, relying on the universalism that God loves all moral people. In this case, Izates is ready to accept circumcision but his mother prevents him for reasons of state. Whether or not Josephus agreed with the practice, his narrative implies that becoming a God-fearer was the functional equivalent of becoming Jewish. More important, it saved the sensitive Hellenistic Jewish community from the ire of the convert's relatives or, in this case, the irate subjects of the convert. Such a tolerant position could hardly have arisen from one of the Jewish sects. It is another example of the acculturated, culturally plural universalism characteristic of the Diaspora. But this is not the end of Josephus's story—Eleazar, a pious Jew from Galilee, arrives and requires Izates to undergo circumcision, although the rite is performed by his physician, not by a *mohel,* the ritual circumciser (if the occupation then existed).

The story hints at Josephus's opinion: all things being equal, being Jewish is better than being God-fearing. The story ends happily: the populace accepts Izates as king, whereupon he and Helena become famous as benefactors of Jerusalem, donating generously toward the improvement of the city, and again showing the importance of benefaction in establishing a new identity. This incident suggests not only that there were differences in definition of conversion throughout the Jewish community, but that for acculturated Jews being a God-fearer was virtually the equivalent of being a Jew, especially since non-Jewish peoples could react hostilely to attempts at formal conversion. It also shows that while some Jews were content with making God-fearers sensitive to the hostility that was generated by attempts at formal conversion, others risked themselves and possibly the welfare of the Jewish community by promoting conversion.

Although Eleazar comes from Galilee, he has some characteristics of the Pharisees. Like them and the rabbis after them, he was characteristically strict in the performance of ritual. But the story does not reflect Josephus's own opinion of circumcision, which had grown more liberal in his stay with the imperial family. Josephus's personal opinion about circumcision has become much less strict:

> About this time, there came to me from the region of Trachonitis two nobles, subjects of the king, bringing their horses, arms and money which they had smuggled out of their country. The Jews would have compelled them to be circumcised as a condition of residence among them. I, however, would not allow any compulsion to be put upon them, declaring that everyone should worship God in accordance with the dictates of his own conscience [*kata tēn heauton proairesin ton theon eusebein*] and not under constraint, and that these men, having fled to us for refuge, ought not to be made to regret that they had done so. Having brought over the people to my way of thinking, I liberally supplied our guests with all things necessary to their customary manner of life (*Life* 113).

Forced conversions, which were an abuse of power under the Maccabean kings, appear to have survived into Roman times, especially during the revolt in which Jews were trying to assert their ancestral rights. The extent of the practice remains unclear. Forced conversions are a product of Jewish military domination, which is rare in this period. Were it not for the aberration of the revolt, Josephus would not mention it as an incident of such great import. Josephus is criticizing a forcible conversion, not trying to make a convert himself; he is trying to ingratiate himself with his new Roman overlords by articulating Roman opinions about circumcision; he might be claiming credit for an opinion that was widespread in Israel. He relies on the vocabulary of God-fearing to describe the religious practice of the refugees and justifies his claims by citing the universalism of God-fearing.

Eleazar might represent the Pharisaic position. Although nothing in the story establishes the historicity of first-century rabbinic practice, Josephus strongly hints that the rabbinic practice of allowing conversion only with the observance of all the law was known in the first century. Otherwise, the story would have ended with Izates' adoption of semiproselytism. The committed convert, Izates, wanted to express a stronger religious commitment, which was laudable given the happy outcome, even to those who did not feel conversion to be universally required. Though explicit rabbinic practice cannot be demonstrated from this report, we can assume something like it to make sense of Josephus's story.

Later rabbinic traditions illustrate how careful and sensitive the rabbis were to the issue of the intent and motivation of a convert. To illustrate the issue clarified in the story of Izates' conversion, later traditions can be drawn on. Strong conversion decisions, which include circumcision, help to make more committed converts:

> Our rabbis taught: A proselyte who comes to convert at this time, we say to him: Why did you decide to convert? Do you not know that Israel at this time is afflicted, oppressed, downtrodden, and rejected, and that tribulations are visited upon them? If he says, "I am aware, but I am unworthy," we accept him immediately, and we make known to him a few of the lighter commandments and a few of the weightier commandments, and we make known to him the penalty for transgression of gleaning the forgotten sheaves, the corner, and the poor man's tithe (i.e., rules of charity, protecting the poor). And we make known to him the punishment for violating the commandments . . . And just as we make known to him the punishment for violating the commandments, so we also make known to him their reward. . . . We are not too lengthy with him nor are we too detailed. If he accepts this, we circumcise him immediately. . . . Once he has recovered, we immerse him immediately. And two scholars stand over him and make known to him some of the lighter and some of the weightier commandments. If

he is immersed validly, he is like an Israelite in all matters. (In the case of a woman, position her in the water up to her neck, and two scholars stand outside and make known to her some of the lighter and some of the weightier commandments.) (b. Yeb. 47a–b)

This incident represents itself as the practice of the tannaitic rabbinic community before the third century, while the document and the reference to the fallen condition of Israel suggests a date later than the first war against Rome, which ended in the destruction of the Temple in 70 C.E. But it does underline the same motivations that seemed obvious in Josephus's story of Izates' conversion.

In setting high standards for conversion, the rabbis intended not to discourage conversions but to make committed converts. Yet, if one looks at conversion within the broad context of the whole Jewish community, which the convert entered when he or she finished training, is one justified in calling first- to fourth-century Judaism a high-conversion community? The answer is certainly less positive than in regard to the Qumran community, a sect within first-century Judaism that was heavily oriented toward conversion. Many Jews were simply born into Judaism without undergoing any conscious decision to join the religion. There were also some Hellenized Jews who could be called adherents in Nock's terms. Finally, there were a variety of different possibilities available for a loose and incompletely defined group called God-fearers, who might be fellow travelers, benefactors, or who, although attending synagogue, had not taken decisive steps to become Jews.

In measuring the frequency and effect of conversion in the Jewish community at large, if such measurements were possible, we would have to be satisfied with some expression of a mean or average, saying that pockets of conversion experiences were correlated with high group coherence in various Jewish subcommunities. But the special laws of Judaism functioned more strongly than conversion to develop group cohesion. Nock's generalization might still be maintained, but only in a carefully nuanced way. Within sectarian and apocalyptic Judaism, conversion was an important aspect of Jewish cohesion. In other parts of the community, the special laws functioned to keep community commitment high.

Many varieties of both Judaism and Christianity proselytized, each using a method that was uniquely suited to itself—ranging from monastic social organizations like the Dead Sea Scroll community to the Pharisees, including their stricter *haburoth* fellowship communities, to loose affiliations based on social class and sacral function in the wider Hellenistic world. Within Christianity as well, different varieties of community sprang up. The earliest Christian community apparently contained representatives of both the most exclusive and the most open attitudes of the Judaism of the day. The Christian record is evidence that these attitudes existed in Judaism and should not be treated as unique examples of a Christian revolution in Jewish sensibilities. The problem raised by Paul was not one of universalism so much as the recommendation that the ritual distinctions between Jews and gentiles be removed entirely, which shocked Paul's fellow Christians.

The ancient world of Judaism knew of both highly emotional conversion experiences, like the infusion of the spirit in the early Christian community, and the ritual catechism of the Qumran community. There were a variety of ways to approach the issue of inclusion, and the rabbinic solution was to enforce a standard definition. Although the rabbis try to make highly motivated and sincere converts, ecstatic experience is never discussed. Circumcision, however, is fully discussed and universally demanded. Paul's entrance into Christianity was accompanied by a vision. Luke makes the ecstasy itself important. Unlike Christianity, where, because of Luke and 1 Timothy, emotional content is conventionally expected in some contemporary evangelism, the rabbinic community was uninterested in ecstasy insofar as it had no legal ramifications for conversion. The frequently cited controversy between Rabbi Eliezer and Rabbi Joshua (j. Yeb. 16a) does not imply that some rabbis accepted converts without circumcision; rather, it underlines a legal question of some importance for the convert—namely, at what moment does a conversion actually take place and thus when does a convert take on all the responsibilities of a Jew?

Jewish literature describing conversion leads us to believe that ecstatic experience was not always absent in conversions to Judaism. Revelations and ecstasy had other uses in the community. In the story of Joseph and Asenath,[54] conversion is accompanied by ecstatic experience. Asenath is valorized as a sincere gentile convert to Judaism. Her conversion and marriage to Joseph is viewed as a movement toward new purity—even a holy marriage (*hieros gamos*). The structures of oppositions that frequently appeal to converts (because they eliminate cognitive dissonance) are strongly present. The bread of life, immortality, and incorruptibility adhere to the true convert, the opposite to her detractors. This dualism is enforced by the appearance of Michael, the chief captain of the Lord God and commander of all the host of the Most High (14.7). He is not only the morning star and a messenger of light but amazingly is the twin of Joseph, except that his features glow and sparkle, a conventional description of a heavenly being. He announces Asenath's glorification and underscores that she has, by virtue of entering the community, entered eternal life. He then returns to heaven in his fiery chariot. He is everything we normally expect from an angel, demonstrating that parts of the Jewish community believed in heavenly guardian angels, who were the twins of those on earth. Whether this is meant to take place in an altered or normal state of consciousness is unclear.

The visit from the heavenly being is meant to verify the reward of the true convert as Enoch's heavenly ascent justifies continued belief in reward and punishment. There is a clear relationship between stories of heavenly journeys and the granting of immortality in the ancient world. In many cultures of late antiquity the journey itself confers a guarantee of astral immortality. In *Joseph and Asenath*, the messenger from heaven merely confirms that the ethical and spiritual position of Asenath will be confirmed by astral immortality. Ecstasy, the motif of heavenly journey, the theme of conversion, and the resultant dualism are important categories in analyzing Paul's experience. In Christianity, the themes are united by the passion and resurrection traditions.

Commitment in the ancient world was formed in the same way it is formed in the modern world. There was an instrumental aspect, where a person develops a willingness to carry out requirements of the group. These instrumentalities can start out as symbolic or ritual actions in which commitment is cemented and developed, but end in moral or evaluative dimensions where a person continues to uphold the beliefs of the group outside of the ritual context. Behind this is, in Kanter's words, a cost-benefit ratio in which the individual invests his or her psychological energy into the group. This seems to be the strategy of rabbinic conversion where the ritual qualifications yield both a highly cohesive group and a strong commitment to continue acceptable moral behavior. The special laws and the other rituals, rather than many conversion experiences, would have been the basic tool for enforcing the commitment.

The standard practice of the rabbis in trying to dissuade proselytes once they had signaled their desires had nothing to do with being opposed to proselytes in general. Rabbinic dissuasion was for the purposes of selecting highly motivated converts, discouraging others who might become immoral or lax and hence give Judaism a bad name. Further, we know from the New Testament that the Pharisees were particularly zealous in trying to make converts, in spite of the danger of inadvertently admitting a Roman informer (Matt. 23:15). We may suspect that the

Palestinian rabbis did not normally face the same kinds of pressures and threats of reprisal that Hellenistic Jews did. Rabbinic discussion about policy was accompanied by the most rigid instruction, change of life-style, circumcision for men, immersion and sacrifice for all, followed by a strict and permanent regimen of purity and dietary prohibitions. The dangers of undergoing circumcision as an adult, given the state of medical knowledge, is reason enough to believe that conversion to Judaism was itself a high-dissonance-producing situation (j. Yeb. 16a). We also know that converts rejected their previous friends and relations, an attitude that was fostered by the decision for a new faith. Others were ostracized by their old friends.

PROSELYTISM AFTER THE WAR AGAINST ROME

After the war against Rome (68–70 C.E.), Jews and Judaism went through a period of disfavor. Henceforth, the tax owed to the Temple was extracted by Rome. The emperor Domitian instituted a system of informers to ferret out anyone who converted to Judaism.[55] His successor, Nerva, seems to have abolished the system of denunciation. Later, Hadrian outlawed circumcision, as a kind of castration, and possibly Jewish proselytism entirely. Whether he did so before or after the second Jewish revolt against Rome in 132 C.E. is of great significance in weighing the causes for that unfortunate conflict. But the date of the edict has less significance to the history of proselytism; its effect was uniformly to oppress the practice of Judaism, consequently stopping proselytism as well. Under Antoninus Pius and thereafter, the penalties for circumcision were rescinded for Jews and presumably for Jews alone. Jews could circumcise Jewish children again, but circumcising gentile proselytes still remained illegal and dangerous. It is not known whether these rules were Antoninus Pius's or if they were enforced after his reign. Becoming a God-fearer or a Christian rather than a convert to Judaism must have gained in attraction after the two revolts against Rome. We should not dismiss the effect of these second- and third-century facts on Christian missionary movements. Judaism might have been as attractive to a motivated gentile as Christianity, but the choices were narrower. God-fearing and Christianity were safer choices. Jewish proselytism and Jewish Christianity remained a force in the Roman world long after the canonization of the New Testament. It was from this group of semiproselytes that many of Christianity's converts came, for they were an anomalous group, alienated from their gentile past yet not fully Jews, or fully accepted as such by the rabbinic definition, and under some suspicion. To take the final step into Judaism was a dangerous operation surgically and often politically inexpedient. Such people were attracted to the message of Paul during the first century. They must have been yet more easily evangelized.

WHY DID JEWS, GREEKS, AND ROMANS CONVERT?

Most Hellenistic texts stress that the attractiveness of Jewish life was its moral superiority. But if there was no need to convert to Judaism explicitly because of the virtual equality of the God-fearers, why then did some gentiles seek conversion? There are no simple answers because of enormous variability in the phenomenon of conversion itself, as well as the different kinds of people who converted to Judaism or Christianity, or changed from one sect of Judaism to another. Judaism was clearly attractive to God-fearers, perhaps because it ended a kind of double marginality. Further, the paucity of historical sources and the constantly changing historical circumstances make attempts at generalization tentative. Assuming that people in the Graeco-Roman world had as complicated motivations as people do today, there can be no single reason. Because conversions have a number of common traits, some generalization is possible. The most obvious conclusion, however, is again a reversal of normal methodology in the study of the first century. The phenomenon of Christian conversions, about which we know something because of textual evidence, is better evidence for the conversion of gentiles to Judaism than is the rabbinic evidence. This is because the rabbinic evidence is later, having been edited authoritatively from the end of the second century to the beginning of the third. It is prescriptive rather than descriptive, and it is confined to the legal consequences of the conversion. Though the New Testament is certainly not free of prejudicial statements (what historical document is?), it is a discursive history and remains one of the best documents available for reconstructing Judaism of the first century. In outlining the reasons why gentiles converted to Christianity, we are also outlining the reasons they might give for converting to Judaism. After the similarities are displayed, the differences, as seen in Paul and Luke's writings, become evident.

Apocalypticism and Millenarianism in Judea

Judea was not only an occupied country, it had been severely repressed by its governors. The Maccabean revolt in 165 B.C.E. against the Syrian king Antiochus IV had been but the beginning of a number of revolts, either actively political or religious. The opposition was located in a number of differing sects whose membership was gained by conversion. The Roman occupation made the situation worse. The rule of the pro-curators, who tried to enrich themselves personally during their brief time in office, made the situation worse still. But under these political extremes, and in a country with a strong tradition of providing religious explana-tions for historical events, the stage was set for messianic and apocalyptic cults.

The evidence available about conversion in Judea is confined almost entirely to recountings of the conversion of Jews from ordinary Jewish practice to a specific cult. The motivation of people joining these move-ments was manifold but difficult to define. We must confine ourselves to motivations known to operate universally in movements of this type. Deprivation, either absolute or relative, should be considered a prominent one. Converts often feel deprived of something, either material or spir-itual, that seems present in the lives of others.[56] The deprivation can be material and is often due to colonization and exploitation, but it can also be deprivation from the sources of religious meaning in the society. The deprivation can be as subtle as the achievement of a certain status or prestige in life, which might not even be valued highly by the society as a whole. Or it can be as great as feeling unable to gain access to the rewards of religion.

Status ambiguity was another common problem in the Graeco-Roman world, where trade provided an avenue for economic advancement but status was strictly defined in legal terms. A range of people, from those who were newly (barely) self-reliant in economic terms to those who were affluent, found no legal avenue for advancement commensurate with their economic and personal achievements. Some were tempted to join cults, where their accomplishments were viewed with more respect. For these social concerns to galvanize into religious movements involving the classic phenomenon of conversion, rather than into purely political movements, there must be a predisposition in the society to explain events in religious ways. These factors came together in first-century Judea to produce differ-ent religious movements of which the Qumran Dead Sea Scrolls sectarians and the followers of John the Baptist and Jesus were prime examples. The groups differed widely in most areas, and prominently in their political positions. They also differed greatly in the ways they sought and gained converts; for instance, the Essenes appeared to have been attractive to young aristocrats, as both Philo and Josephus testify. They might have attracted others as well, but only aristocrats left us their memoirs. More generally, the underlying forces that stimulated the differing kinds of conversion in each group could have been similar. The forces that made one group more attractive than another to a specific religious quester are best outlined after the commonalities are described.

Conversions in Diaspora Judaism

Jews in Diaspora should have been more tempted to convert to other cults than those within sectarian Judea. The phenomenon of the God-fearers and Jewish involvement in trade make the Diaspora situation more complex and subtle. The evidence of Christianity as well as the meager Jewish sources show that a wider variety of gentiles were attracted to Judaism and Christianity than simply the materially disadvantaged.[57] The issues of millenarianism do not disappear. Christianity appears to be a major source of the spread of Jewish apocalypticism in the Roman world. No doubt this is one reason that it was viewed as dangerous by Jews and Romans alike. The high level of commitment in Judaism and Christianity is, as we have seen, one important reason for their success in conversion. According to reports in Paul, Acts, and Josephus, targets for conversion also included a number of well-placed, prominent women, whose positions were marginal, exemplifying status ambiguity.

In this situation, no one theory of conversion can explain the attractiveness of Judaism and Christianity. A number of anthropological studies of conversions in other cultures can be helpful in suggesting additional motivations for gentiles to convert. Robin Horton has outlined a relevant African cosmology of two tiers, in which events in the microcosm are handled by the lower, local spirits, whereas events in the wider world are handled by the high god.[58] Horton contends that Africans tend to convert to Islam or Christianity, if they enter the wider world of trade contacts with the West, for both Western religions have more sophisticated rites directed to the high god than traditional African religions. The mechanism and applicability of this observation has been challenged, and some antithetical phenomena, such as the function of keeping African rites alive in

England, have been noted. But the possible application of Horton's comments to Hellenistic Judaism cannot be dismissed. Other cults besides Judaism dealt with the wider issues of life, and some of the God-fearers must have been adherents to the synagogue in Nock's sense of limited commitment, perhaps because some public contribution was helpful to their office or career. But other God-fearers probably converted to the religion of the Jews (without taking up full Jewish nationality). They may have been attracted for any number of reasons, including a universal understanding of the purpose of history, not to mention international trade contacts with Jerusalem and other Jews. The attractions of international trade and the awareness of salvation were parallel in the sense that they both involved perceptions of human significance beyond the local level. Judaism was one religion to provide both.[59]

Another phenomenon leading to conversion was the continuing demonization of the religious world of the empire. Peter Brown and others[60] have noted that although Christians and Jews were often accused of magic, promise of protection against magic also played an important role in conversion to Judaism and Christianity. Since both Judaism and Christianity subordinated earthly powers to God they could function as anti-witchcraft cults do in African religion. They can free the convert from subjugation to these forces. The *Golden Ass* contains the most famous example of antiwitchcraft as a motivation in conversion. It is not strictly speaking historical data and does not involve either Judaism or Christianity, yet its point is more general than Lucius's attraction to the Isis mysteries. As the goddess Isis frees Lucius from his animal state, brought on by dissolute and carefree curiosity about magical powers, so the mystery cults free the convert from fate to a new destiny of salvation.[61]

Whether millenarianism, antiwitchcraft cultism, status ambiguity, or something else was the motivation for joining Judaism and Christianity would depend on individual case histories, which are few and far between in the extant historical record of the ancient world. One or another mechanism can be more applicable on average to a particular situation in the church, but they must all be mentioned as possibilities. None of these motivations are particularly relevant for understanding the conversion of Paul, though they are likely to be important to the converts that Paul made after his conversion. Paul's discussions about conversion, however, help explain the dynamics of Jewish acculturation in the Roman world. Paul's preaching had a particularly important role in the later distinction between Judaism and Christianity for a potential convert.

MESSIANISM AND CONVERSION

Messianism and Conversion in Apocalyptic Judaism

Not only is the language of transformation occasionally part of Jewish mystical speculation, it is also part of messianic longing.[62] This double location is significant for Christianity. In 1 Enoch 107.1, the transformation is implied but not stated in a vision where the children of men become righteous and worship God.[63] One also finds words indicating transformation in relation to the cosmic process of redemption. First Enoch 45.5 reports that God says that he will transform the earth to make it a blessing. God will transform the spirits who were born in darkness (1 Enoch 108.11–13), presumably another reference to the conversion of the gentiles. In 1 Enoch 90.37f, the saved become transformed into white bulls, which are symbols of the messiah.[64]

The Qumran community envisioned a cosmic battle at the end of time with a subsequent transformation of the world called a time of renewal (hadash). The vocabulary for the individual's behavior is closely related to Philo's vocabulary of perfection. The term tamim (perfect) occurs in many passages (1QS 2.2; 3.9; 8.10; 18, 21; 9.2, 5.9; CD 2.15, etc).[65] These transformations of the earthly environment parallel the personal transformation (see Chapter 1).

Messianism and Conversion in Christianity

The best evidence about the continuing relationship between conversion and messianism comes from Christianity. The Jesus movement in its Palestinian setting and the evidence of Paul in the Diaspora not only supplements what we know from our fragmentary reports in Jewish literature, but it helps considerably in filling in gaps in our knowledge of first-century Jewish life.

The Gospels present specific evidence about two different but related movements—the followers of John the Baptist and the followers of Jesus of Nazereth. Whether or not they were overtly political movements, the Romans interpreted them as a political threat, as is evidenced by the martyrdom of the leaders of each movement.[66] Both have been credibly described as apocalyptic, millenarian movements, though they contained other elements as well. Jesus was surely a wisdom teacher, even if few of his wisdom sayings can be indubitably ascribed to him. (We demand originality for a saying to be indubitably ascribable to Jesus. The ancient world demanded wisdom but not originality.)

Both John the Baptist and Jesus are pictured as teachers demanding *metanoia,* or repentance, which is the Hebrew condition for a gentile conversion or return to the Jewish fold. That John converted members by means of baptism is evident, but Jesus' common practice seems to be less formal. Although John baptized his followers for the forgiveness of sins, we do not know how commitment was maintained after baptism. The New Testament is an outside observer of John's movement, believing that John's mission was fulfilled in the teachings and resurrection of Jesus. Thus, we can learn little from the New Testament of the internal structure of the group that followed John closely.

In the case of Jesus' movement we learn a bit more. There is no question that the early church demanded an enormous commitment from the new member. Those who joined were warned that they may have to give up their obligations to parents or spouses (Mark 3:31–35; 10:28–31; Luke 9:54–60). The early followers of Jesus must be considered converts, if not into broader Judaism then at least into a new, dynamic revival movement within it. This counts as a conversion, according to the modern vocabulary. What the early conversion experience was like is unclear. We know that those closest to Jesus followed him, often after memorable conversion experiences, and learned from him after the conversion experience. The well-known New Testament theme of the stupidity of the disciples appears to underline the necessity for the further training of disciples after conversion, as well as illustrating the utter unexpectedness of Jesus' death and resurrection. It does not matter whether the process of conversion was viewed as short, as in the emotional conversion of Aseneth, or long, as in the period of initiation for Qumranites. The Jesus movement, by preaching conversion of Jews first, and then conversion of all peoples eventually, fits squarely into the Palestinian scene, where movements of a politicoreligious nature were common. Christianity's choice of a passive political role did not mean that it would not be viewed by the religious establishment of Romans and Jerusalemite priests as an active political threat.[67]

The language of transformation was evidently used by two evangelists to describe Jesus' transfiguration. It is quite possible that the transfiguration itself was supposed to be a model of transformation for the believers as well as a sign of Jesus' own identity as God's principal angelic manifestation. According to Mark and Matthew, what happened to Jesus at the transfiguration was a transformation (*kai metamorphōthe emprosthen auton* [Mark 9:2; Matt. 17:2]). Luke, who does not use this vocabulary, probably had sensibilities similar to Philo in not wanting to sully true spirituality with a pagan language of deification. The transformation is a common sign of divination in the Hellenistic world and may be what Mark has in mind. Instead Luke says simply that the appearance of Jesus' countenance was altered (Luke 9:29). The relationship of these terms to the heavenly journey motif in Jewish mystical apocalypticism is unmistakable. Further, in the hands of Paul they also reveal an explicit conversion setting. Evidently, the evangelists were trying to use the language of transformation to express an aspect of Jesus' divinity and its acceptance by his disciples. Paul can express the same sentiments, but he uses this vocabulary to discuss the conversion of believers and their occasional visions of the risen Jesus. So the traditional view that the transfiguration is a kind of misplaced resurrection appearance is correct in an ironic way. It is an anticipation of the way in which converts come to know Christ.

The Revelation of John, the last book of the New Testament, is a treasure trove of apocalyptic images of transformation. According to Rev. 1:18 the son of man, clearly identified with Christ in this place, affirms: "I died, and behold I am alive." At the end of his discourses to the seven churches he says: "He who conquers, I will grant him to sit with me on my throne, as I myself conquered and sat down with my Father on his throne" (Rev. 3:21). In Revelation, *to conquer* is virtually synonymous with undergoing martyrdom.[68]

In late antiquity then, there were at least two major ways to deal with gentile interest in Judaism: (1) some Jews favored conversion for the gentiles; (2) others recommended that gentiles give up their sinful ways and recognize the one God, but they need not convert—this appears roughly to correspond with what Luke and other sources call God-fearing and was favored by those Jews who feared a gentile backlash against Jewish proselytism of pagans. Some sectarian Jews, as represented by Jubilees, felt that only those circumcised on the eighth day could be part of God's plan for the future. Conversion became the dominant Christian solution to the issue of gentile interest, because Paul's definition of conversion was more popular with gentiles than the traditional Jewish definition of conversion. The Noahide commandments became the dominant Jewish solution because of the opposition to conversion from the Roman world.

It would be unfair to say that Judaism stopped proselytizing. The Romans often felt that persecuting Jews was not worth their while; perhaps the rule against proselytism was entirely rescinded for a time. As the Christian church gained in power, however, it had quite a different view of these laws and strengthened them. Jewish proselytism and Jewish Christianity, however, probably remained a force in the Roman world after the canonization of the New Testament.

This permanently alters an easy understanding of the sociology of Jewish life. First, Christianity must be placed within the realm of sectarian Judaism where conversion was the norm rather than the exception. Second, Paul takes that characteristic of conversion religion, an apocalyptic trait of the most sectarian aspects of Judaism, and successfully transfers it to the Diaspora where conversion was much less common, because God-fearing and ethnic pluralism were the rule. Paul is suggesting that Jews as well as gentiles need to undergo a significant transformation before they can enter the new community. This would contrast with the position attributed to James, who felt that the teaching of Jesus and his messianic mission can be accommodated within the sphere of traditional Judaism. It means for Paul, as it cannot for James, that to be a Jew who has accepted Christ is not enough. For Paul, the Jew as well as the gentile must be converted, and the new community that Jesus founded must be a community of converts.

Paul has retained the more sectarian and millenarian notion of conversion, though he has chosen to speak to the gentiles. Unlike Philo, who envisioned a slow degree of progress to perfection for every philosophically minded person with Jews having a divinely revealed advantage in the progress, Paul sees a stronger moment of decision, though he shares Philo's opinions partly by cautioning against the excesses of emotionalism. Further, after outlining the radical decision of conversion, presumably in baptism, Paul also talks about a period of training and growth. Paul discusses the metamorphosis of believers from one degree of glory to another through the action of the spirit (2 Cor. 3:18), suggesting that the transformation process is on-going in the life of the believer. Further, Paul never forgets that the new Christian must live in an unredeemed world (e.g., 1 Cor. 5:10). Thus, no simple contrast between quick conversion and long training separates Paul from Philo. Quick conversion is not mentioned often in Judaism, though visionary experience of recent converts are occasionally part of the tradition. Paul shares the first century Jewish suspicion of emotionalism. He is reticent in 2 Corinthians 11–12 to give emotionalism much credence. The same cannot be said of Luke, who uses Paul's experience to model Christian conversion.

In one respect the impetus toward quick conversion seems stronger in

Pauline Christianity than in other sectarian forms of Judaism. Paul effectively gives gentile and God-fearing pagans the ability to join Judaism without the drawn-out period of education in the special laws and without the necessity of circumcision. This is an effective promise, but it carries the danger of lower commitment. The concern about this danger is obvious in Paul's pastoral writings. Paul also shares some of the attitudes of Greek-speaking Jewish Hellenism in that he intends to view God-fearing gentiles as the complete equals of Jews.

Although Pauline Christianity theoretically lacks the degree of commitment that circumcised converts to Judaism and Jewish Christianity exhibit, the Pauline community presumably developed different mechanisms of commitment, based on the conversion experience itself, apocalyptic ideas of the quick return of the messiah, and the moral rules of community entailed by that coming. The cost of leaving Pharisaic Judaism was also not a small one. The special laws of Judaism were a source of solace and pride to all who observed them. The commitment that Paul made in giving them up should not be undervalued. As he himself says, he gave up everything of significance to follow the consequences of his vision. So would all those who followed him out of Torah-centered Judaism.

¶ PAUL THE CONVERT

CHAPTER FOUR

℘ THE CONSEQUENCES OF CONVERSION: PAUL'S EXEGESIS

Viewing Paul as a convert is a productive model. Taking Paul's conversion seriously shows the differences between Paul's letters and Acts and can explain Paul's own writings. Mystical experience started or aided Paul's conversion. Whether the conversion took place gradually or suddenly, the effect was an about-face. Whether or not Paul also tried to missionize Jews, the change is most easily described as a decision to change commitments from one religious community to another.[1] In Paul's case, the change was from Pharisaism, in which Paul received his education, to a particular kind of gentile community of God-fearers, living without the law, and the change was powered by Paul's absorption into the spirit. The influence of the gentile community on Paul's understanding of the content of his religious vision is crucial to explaining his religious vision. Paul did change religious communities. The effect of that change was volatile and unpredictable, apparently even to Paul, because it took him many years to understand what was demanded of him and his converts.

The structure of Paul's thought contains the same patterns of antinomies that characterize conversion to highly cohesive groups today. Paul does not forget his Jewish past, rather he bends his Pharisaic exegesis to new ends. Paul describes the differences between his previous life in Pharisaism and his present life in Christ in the strongest possible terms. George Lyons thus considers contrasts—and specifically the contrast between Paul's former life and his present situation—to be the most characteristic theme of the autobiographical sections of his letters.[2] The grammatical counterpoint between *formerly* and *now* (Phil. 3:6; 1 Cor. 15:9; Gal. 1:23) opposes Paul the persecutor to Paul the persecuted teacher. One thing is clear from this language: Paul is no longer a Pharisee.

In 1 Tim. 1:12–13, Ephesians, and Colossians Paul's conversion has become paradigmatic for the conversion of all Christians.[3] The predisposition to revalue one's past life on the basis of a transformation is the main characteristic of modern converts according to Snow and Machalik, Staples, and Mauss.[4] Paul's experience and work fall squarely within this rubric.

The effect of conversion can be seen in the way Paul argues his position and analyzes Scripture. The passage that most clearly illustrates Paul's Jewish past in creative tension with his Christian future is Gal. 3:6–14:

> Thus Abraham "believed God and it was reckoned to him as righteousness." So you see that it is men of faith who are the sons of Abraham. And the scripture, foreseeing that God would justify the gentiles by faith, preached the gospel beforehand to Abraham, saying, "In you shall all the nations be blessed." So then, those who are men of faith are blessed with Abraham who had faith. For all who rely on works of the law are under a curse: for it is written, "Cursed be every one who does not abide by all the things written in the book of the law, and do them." Now it is evident that no man is justified before God by the law; for "He who through faith is righteous shall live," but the law does not rest on faith, for "He who does them shall live by them." Christ redeemed us from the curse of the law, having become a curse for us—for it is written, "Cursed be every one who hangs on a tree"— that in Christ Jesus the blessing of Abraham might come upon the Gentiles, that we might receive the promise of the Spirit through faith.

This is ostensibly an exegesis of Genesis, not a description of conversion. Paul argues that Scripture shows the gentiles to be included in God's plan for salvation. He describes the relevant social groupings on the basis of Scripture, but his conclusion comes from his conversion experience, not from Scripture. As a Jew and a Pharisee, Paul learned to judge the meaning of his experience by reading the Scriptures. After becoming a Christian he does not abandon his previously learned methodology, even when his predominantly gentile audience would not understand his references. The uniqueness of his conversion experience causes unexpected turns in his argument.

In this passage, his ire is most obvious. He defends his mission to the gentiles against the idea that all new converts need to be circumcised. The procircumcision position of his Judaizing opponents is not a Jewish ploy; rather, it is the natural perspective of Jewish Christians and is completely at odds with Paul's own experience. So he begins with the strong statement of antagonism that not only is Torah irrelevant for community definition, but also that those who rely on the works of the law are under a curse. Not content with vituperation, Paul demonstrates his point exegetically with the deftness of one who trained as a Pharisee—a tour de force based on Deut. 27:26, which states that those who do not live by the law are under a curse. The puzzling part of this quotation from Deuteronomy for any Jew is that it also proves the converse of Paul's claims: those who live by Torah are blessed. The lack of exegesis of the full and plain meaning of the passage sounds like a non sequitur. We are likely missing something that Paul took for granted. Perhaps it is the accusation against Christianity that Christ's death was cursed, because he was hanged (crucified). Paul may have learned of it in his Pharisaic days or he may be responding to an opponent. There is no way to tell; it is clear that he has a new perspective on the passage that he wants to disclose. Paul might also be opposing a midrash that suggests that the Torah is a blessing to Jews and a curse to gentiles.[5] To defeat it, he does not cite the success of the gentile mission in making God-fearers. Instead, he brings in the specific transforming role of Christ that turns the curse into a blessing.

In Paul's context the passage from Deuteronomy functions as a proof that Christians do not need to keep Torah in a Pharisaic way. Paul appears to have foreshortened an argument that would warn his hearers that if they adopt Torah they must adopt the entire Torah, observing all the ordinances of Torah (including the Pharisaic oral Torah), or live with the curse of Torah.[6] It is possible to overinterpret this paradox. Paul does not imply that Torah is wrong, rather that the oral Torah, as understood by the Pharisees, is an all-or-nothing proposition, shaming his less-pious Jewish Christian opponents by comparing them to Pharisaic standards of morality. This is the special perspective of the Pharisees, and, as we have seen, not necessarily the view of other Jews of the time. Paul himself will advocate a social arrangement that looks more like a Diaspora Jewish accommodation rather than the strict Pharisaic view of Torah—based on faith, not on a watered-down version of Jewish observance or on a culturally plural idea of God-fearing.

Paul's wider audience is gentile Christians who are also potential converts to Judaism. He calls them "those who are under faith" (*hoi ek pisteōs*), a phrase defining his audience sociologically, describing how they entered Christian community. These are in turn contrasted with "those who are under the *works* of the law," defined as those who must do everything in Torah. By stating that one must observe the entire Torah, Paul reflects the Pharisaic view of conversion. If one desires to convert, according to the Pharisees and the rabbis after them, one must be willing to take on oneself all of Torah, ignoring not even one light ordinance.[7] This piece of rabbinic lore has entered Paul's argument (hence it can be dated from the first century), but it is transformed by him from a Pharisaic doctrine into a taunt against the Jewish Christians, less pious than the Pharisees, who yet oppose Paul's understanding of a faith conversion. It functions as a warning to his readers, enemies and friends alike, that if they desire to adopt Jewish law they must be prepared to do it all, as he had done before he became a Christian: "Cursed be he who does not confirm the words of this law by doing them" (Deut. 27:26).

Paul speaks rhetorically. He has already rejected the Pharisaic approach to conversion and surely did not want his hearers to adopt it. He counts on the impossibility of such a strict life for his gentile hearers, but his insistence on a firm decision for the new spiritual, unfleshly way of life is the core of his understanding of Christianity. The fact that, as an ex-Pharisee, he could claim more piety than any of his opponents makes his arguments stronger. His perspective on the meaning of Scripture has changed, reflecting the change from one community to another. This shows up in his entirely new assumptions about the meaning of Scripture, which he does not argue so much as present. His job is to reveal the implications of his revelation as he sees it. This is what makes him a convert.

His exegesis takes another unexpected turn, which argues for a new direction to the Christian mission. He shows that Deut. 27:26 conflicts with Hab. 2:4: "He who through faith is righteous shall live." There would be no contradiction between the two statements for a Pharisee; both faith and the commandments are integral and noncontradictory parts of the love, obedience to, and worship of God. For Paul, whose conversion turned him from being a righteous persecutor of the church to a persecuted believer, the two statements cannot both be true any longer. His new faith based on spiritual absorption into the risen Christ, not his observance of Torah, followed his conversion. He attempts to impress this on his gentile Christian audience. However much he may have attempted to preach to Jews in his early mission, by the time he wrote his letter to the Galatians he had lived in a gentile Christian community for a long time. He now represents their position and also sees the unexpectedly good result of his gentile mission. Searching for a precedent for gentiles who have strong faith yet did not perform the ceremonial observances of Torah, Paul finds Abraham, whose faith was great enough to leave his own home and to risk sacrificing his son without the ordinances of Torah to guide him. This is not merely an adventitious example, for it is quite likely that Abraham had been used by the Pharisees as a role model for potential converts, as he was thereafter by rabbinic Judaism. Because Abraham left his gentile home and made the great journey to the one God, rabbinic and Philonic Judaism, as well as Christianity, use him as an example of conversion.[8]

The truly extraordinary aspect of the passage is the new meaning that *faith*—faith in Christ—has for Paul. It goes beyond any doctrine of the inherent value of God-fearing in Jewish tradition. Abraham's faithfulness would not have been denied by any Jew. But faith means more to Paul than remaining faithful and steadfast to the covenant. It is not something that Judaism or Jewish Christianity exhibits, but it *is* inherent in gentile Christianity. The paradigm for this type of religion is Paul's own conversion from the surety of his Pharisaic observances to the freedom and uncertainties of his gentile Christianity. By faith, Paul essentially means a radical reorientation and commitment, as social science describes a radical new commitment in contemporary conversions. This also means a radical change in the community to which Paul gives allegiance. Those who are faithful are those who believe in Christ without the works of the law, the gentile Christian community.

Instead of trying to define Paul's new faith and the nature of his audience, most exegetes of Paul have pursued the implicit contrast between law and faith, supposing that since Paul believes that Jesus was the messiah, the law must be wrong.[9] Such a tack is mistaken in two respects: (1) Paul does not here say that Torah is wrong, rather he asserts that its meaning is different from what he thought at first and that properly performing Torah is an all or nothing proposition; (2) he is not pursuing an intellectual argument about the value of abstract concepts; rather, he is exegeting a passage from the perspective of his experience of conversion, hence his justification and anticipated salvation. He is trying to legitimate a new concept of gentile community. Further, he is trying to show that those who have faith can also count themselves as part of the covenant relationship with Abraham.

Judaism before Paul could conceive of gentiles as righteous without their following the explicit ordinances of Torah, believing that this righteousness is part of God's plan. But Paul must have known that the one thing that did not follow from these traditions is that the gentiles were part of the Mosaic covenant. So Paul trots out all his Pharisaic acumen to underline his new invention. His exegesis also depends on his conversion experience and his postconversion experience living with gentiles, though he addresses that experience through an analysis of biblical texts. Hab. 2:4

is clarified by means of Lev. 18:5: "You shall therefore keep my statutes and my ordinances, by doing which a man shall live: I am the Lord." Paul thus claims that the two concepts come into full contradiction: either the Torah brings life or faith brings life.

Such passages seem contradictory to Paul. For any Pharisaic Jew without Paul's experience of conversion they would have been corresponding aspects of the same idea. The text itself does not support Paul's distinction. He is approaching the text in an entirely new, unexpected way. It is not the biblical text itself that has made this seeming contradiction evident to him. Because of his conversion from Pharisaism to Christianity and his subsequent experience of dealing with gentile and Jewish Christians, he now sees faith and law as two different paths. Paul perceives the new distinction in a social as much as a theological manner. He distinguishes between Jewish Christian communities, which augmented their Judaism by Christian commitment, and the community in which he now lives, a community based on the experience of transformation into the spirit through faith, which lives without the obligations of Torah. Paul recommends for everyone conversion to a life of spiritual transformation, not a life defined by ceremonial obligations. In so doing he takes the part of the gentile Christian community in which he lives. Paul's constant theme of the opposition of faith and law is a social and political justification for a new variety of community. It matches the opposition between Jewish and gentile Christianity.

In a possibly deliberate irony, Paul's language for expressing this subtle problem comes out of his Pharisaic past. Resolving contradictions is one of the basic methods of rabbinic exegesis. It would be standardized as one of fourteen or thirty-one classic rules of rabbinic argumentation. Though Paul could not have learned the rule in the form in which it is preserved in rabbinic literature, the method of argumentation has come from Paul's Jewish past.[10] Hence, Paul gives evidence of the antiquity of the technique. Paul's solution to the problem, while reflecting his Pharisaic training, is unique to his Christian perspective. Rather than resolving the contradiction by siding with one or another of the positions,[11] Paul brings in a third passage which shows how the contradiction can be avoided: "Cursed be he who hangs on a tree" (Deut. 21:23). Paul interprets this passage, without so much as a word of explanation, as referring to Christ. By taking the taunt of the opposition, that Jesus had died under a curse, Paul has assumed that no one would deny the applicability of the Scripture to Christ. In his present argument, however, he finds a completely different meaning from that of his persecutors. He does not say that this is an impossible attribution for the crucified Christ. He turns the passage around in a surprising way to make it a prophecy showing that the crucified Christ had changed the curse so that the blessing of Abraham might come on the gentiles. Later Paul can say that the law itself is under a curse, but here he means only to transform the Deuteronomic curse against a person executed by hanging into the biblical proof of vicarious atonement for the gentiles. It is on account of Christ's salvific death that the gentiles can be adopted into Abrahamic faith by the process of conversion; yet they do not have to keep the ceremonial law, because no one needs to keep it to be part of the community of faith.

The solution to the problem is rabbinic in method, although no rabbis would have understood the exegetical problem to be a contradiction of Scriptures. Paul's experience of conversion has made that perspective necessary, but it has also shown him how to interpret this law for the first time: as a prophecy for the saving acts of the crucified Christ. So Paul's conversion experience turns scripture on its head and makes it come true in an ironic, unexpected way, which can be schematized as follows: If the law is a medium of salvation, as Paul had believed when he was a Pharisee, then there can be no crucified Christ. Since he knows from his mystical experience that there is a divine, crucified messiah, then Torah cannot be the medium of salvation in the way he originally thought (although it will continue to be a moral norm for community, in ways that he does not specify).

The logic of this argument depends on knowing that the Jews believed in a messiah who would defeat their national enemies and usher in a period of tranquility. Such a concept virtually eliminated the possibility of a crucified messiah for Paul when he was a Pharisee. Since Paul knows from his personal, visionary experience that Christ was crucified and rose, and that his earthly mission had not only failed but ended in a curse, he still understands the Jewish position, but he can no longer accept it at face value. Rather, he transforms it into a new understanding of messiahship. He says in 1 Cor. 1:23, "but we preach Christ crucified, a stumbling block to Jews and folly to gentiles." Paul knows in ways that the later church cannot appreciate how difficult it was for a Jew to accept a crucified messiah and how difficult it was for a gentile to accept a crucified god or hero. Paul maintains that the difficulty is overcome by a conversion experience of the risen Christ, which proves that Christ is still alive and therefore annuls the curse of Torah on the gentiles, who do not observe Torah.

Following Marcus Barth, John Gager notes that the phrase "works of the law" occurs in contexts where the question of the ritual practice of the

gentiles is concerned.[12] Although "works of the law" is a direct translation of the Hebrew *Ma'asei ha-torah,* Paul is not referring to Torah but to
the *observance* of Jewish ceremonial practices. James D. G. Dunn says, "In
my view, however, 'works of the law' is precisely the phrase chosen by
Paul (as either already familiar to his readers or self-evident to them in its
significance), by which Paul denotes those obligations prescribed by the
law which show the individual concerned to belong to the law, which
mark out the practitioner as a member of the people of the law, the
covenant people, the Jewish nation."[13] "Works of the law" means the
ceremonial Torah, those special ordinances that separate Jews from gentiles. Dunn shows that the term is reflected in Qumran writings where
ma'asei torah, "deeds of the law," is understood as the day-to-day responsibilities of remaining within the community. Paul uses the phrase to mean
the typical ways Jews assert their identity (Rom. 3:19–20). This approach
is associated with boasting (Rom. 3:27–8; 4:2), paralleling Paul's earlier
attack on the Jews as a people of the law (Rom. 2:17–20, 23), with
circumcision serving as the primary sign of this identity (Rom. 2:25–9).
Dunn also shows that Paul makes the same point with his contrast between "within the law" and "outside the law," "of the law" and "of
faith" (Rom. 2:12–14; 3:19–21; 4:14–16; 1 Cor. 9:20; Gal. 4:5). The
distinction is between two different communities—those who keep the
law as a mark of their identity and those who can be identified by faith.[14]

What is important here, and what few New Testament scholars seem
to see, is that Paul is not theologizing. He is talking about the proper role of
Jewish observances in the Christian community. Works of the law are the
material effects of the special laws of Judaism on the unity of Christian
community; they are almost synonymous with dietary laws, holiday observances, purity, and circumcision. Throughout Paul's career, he will
attempt to specify case by case in what ways the ceremonial law can be
avoided. Observance of the law fixes a particular social identity as Jewish,
apparently encouraging in Jewish Christians a sense of superiority to those
gentile Christians who rely on their conversion experience and their abstinence from idolatry, immorality, and blasphemy. The legitimate question
posed to the gentile Christian is, How much of the ceremonial law should I
perform? Now that they are halfway to Judaism by becoming God-fearers,
should they not go all the way? Paul answers: "No." Paul says nothing
about the value of law-abiding or moral behavior. If asked, he would
certainly be in favor of Torah as a standard for moral behavior. He is
advocating a new definition of community in which the performance of
the special laws of Judaism does not figure. This new definition is an

attempt to enfranchise the community in which he lives, the community in which he learned the value and meaning of his religious conversion.

Many scholars conveniently drop Paul's interest in Jewish ritual from their discussion because it is an inaccessible world, whereas philosophical generalities derivable from Paul's discussions are not. This omission causes much confusion in understanding Paul. For Paul and his generation, ritual was not an empty form. Even for Hellenistic Jews—living outside of Pharisaic authority and having to deal with the problems of acculturation and assimilation—ritual, like prayer and certainly more than philosophy, became symbolic of the deepest religious commitments because it was characteristically and unambiguously Jewish. They argued, in fact, that the philosophy and prayers of Judaism were part of the rational heritage of humanity. Only the ceremonial laws were exclusively Jewish. The vexing issue of the ritual status of the gentiles—and not their salvation or even philosophical issues of universalism or particularism or the value of works' righteousness—directly occasions Paul's meditations on law.

PAUL'S NEW VOCABULARY OF FAITH: NO RIGHTEOUSNESS BASED ON LAW

E. P. Sanders observes in *Paul and Palestinian Judaism* that in Paul's thought the solution preceded the problem, meaning that for Paul, Christianity does not remedy some failing in Judaism.[15] Paul's Christianity arrived first, and in retrospect Paul sees the way not taken, in this case Pharisaic Judaism, in new, less positive ways. A radical change in point of view necessarily means overturning previous beliefs and arguments. Paul does not forget his Jewish past; rather, he inverts the values of his past in a way that is consonant with his new commitments. What Paul finds fault with in his previous faith is that it is not faith in the crucified messiah, which is a new revelation about God's purposes for humanity vouchsafed to him personally. Paul suggests to the Galatians that the relationship between the two experiences is chronological. God intended Torah to have sole validity for a time as the Jewish-gentile dichotomy was valid for a time. He intended to replace it by the appearance of Christ. This doctrine would be enormously controversial to almost any Jew. Even acculturated Hellenistic Jews respected Torah in spite of interpreting it differently. Paul's peculiar combination of departure from Pharisaic Judaism and strenuous and public reliance on rabbinic method to demonstrate Christianity was a dangerous path to choose. It was bound to cause trouble in the Jewish community. It became even more dangerous because Paul insisted that he remained a Jew.

These anomalous traits, which ultimately put Paul in danger, are rooted in the nature of his conversion experience. Paul is a person who has revalued his life on the basis of his conversion. The traditional dichotomies in Paul's thought can be seen as originating in his conversion experience. The dualism—of flesh and spirit, life and death, darkness and light, life apart from the law and under it—derives from the perspective of a person who is trying to look at his previous values within Pharisaic Judaism after having adopted a new basis for salvation in gentile, God-fearing communities of faith. He is also using older, apocalyptic imagery to express something new.[16] John Gager writes:

> Just as it would be inaccurate now to say that Christianity had not entered Paul's emotional involvements *before* his conversion, so it would be wrong to claim that the law ceased to play a role in them *after* it. Thus my contention is that the fundamental system of values and commitments is preserved intact in this sort of conversion. But it is turned upside down, reversed and transvalued. The religious goal or target remains the same in the sense that righteousness or justification continues as the focus of Paul's religious concern both before and after the conversion. But whereas the law had been the chosen path to the goal, and the Christ the rejected one, beforehand, their order is reversed after the event. (700)

Gager summarizes the immediate effects succinctly:

> —[Paul's] repeated statements that salvation results in a new creation, a new definition of humanity, a transformation in which our lower physical nature is supplanted by a higher spiritual nature.
>
> —Because of this extraordinary movement from previous life to present one, the most fruitful way of looking at Paul's or any other conversion is to look at their future consequences, not their past causes.
>
> —His affirmation that the law, as manipulated by the power of sin, plays an essential, if preparatory role in the divine plan of salvation; and his undying memory that his own persecution of Christians had been based on a zealous loyalty to the law.
>
> —And finally, his tendency to divide history into two stages, and to

characterize these stages as opposites—body/spirit, law/grace, law/spirit, death/life, sin/love, loss/gain. (702)

Each of these Pauline themes corresponds closely with modern data about conversion experience.[17] Further, as Festinger, Riecken, and Schacter observed in *When Prophecy Fails*,[18] one result of postdecision dissonance is a strong desire to proselytize, as if increasing the acceptance of the idea and the size of the believing group would bring about a world in which the new conviction would be vindicated. Paul himself exemplifies this phenomenon.

Paul also illustrates the other major mechanism for dealing with cognitive dissonance—hermeneutics. *When Prophecy Fails* has the methodological fault of concentrating on disconfirmation and proselytism to the exclusion of other dissonance-reducing mechanisms, but it does describe the close relationship between proselytism and religious decisions. Though no one could responsibly say why Paul felt called to proselytize, Luke says that the impetus came directly from his conversion. Paul himself says that his mission started in the womb but leaves the chronology of his decision unspecified. Such an idea would be a natural expectation of anyone who had read the account of Jeremiah or Ezekiel's commission as prophet. It is even more logical in the case where the commission to prophesy entailed an enormous change in religious sensibility. Thus, modern social theory corroborates Paul's own account of his commission in which he asserts that the impetus to proselytize was a central and direct result of his conversion experience. But it advises suspicion in Paul's chronology and characterizations of sudden change. Paul still respects Torah but does not give it ultimate authority for forming a new community:

But now the righteousness of God has been manifested apart from law, although the law and the prophets bear witness to it, the righteousness of God through faith in Jesus Christ for all who believe. For there is no distinction; since all have sinned and fall short of the Glory of God, they are justified by his grace as a gift, through the redemption which is in Christ Jesus, whom God put forward as an expiation by his blood, to be received by faith. This was to show God's righteousness, because in his divine forbearance he had passed over former sins; it was to prove at the present time that he himself is righteous and that he justifies him who has faith in Jesus. Then what becomes of our boasting? It is excluded. On what principle? On the principle of works? No, but on the principle of faith. For we hold that a man is justified by faith apart from works of law. Or is God the God of Jews only? Is he not the God of Gentiles also? Yes, of Gentiles also, since God is one; and he will justify the circumcised on the ground of their faith and the uncircumcised through their faith. Do we then overthrow the law by this faith? By no means! On the contrary, we should uphold the law. (Rom. 3:21–31)

Although Paul says that the law should not be overthrown, he also says that faith rather than law manifests the righteousness of God. By this he means faith in spiritual transformation, which defines a new community of believers. This statement is so radical for Judaism that it would have been impossible for Paul to have guessed the consequences of his conversion before he had lived with them for years, both in the gentile community and in polemics with Jewish Christians. When he was a Pharisee, Paul would have been incapable of saying that faith rather than law manifests the righteousness of God in any meaningful way. No other Jews in the first century distinguish faith and law in the way Paul does. For a Jew, faith fundamentally precedes anything as well, but there is no need to distinguish between it and law. Jews perform the commandments because they are commanded by God, not because they guarantee justification. This arrangement assumes a prior faith commitment and a prior act on God's part in justifying that never needs to be discussed. Paul distinguishes between these several concepts because he has experienced and learned his Christian commitment, and he now represents a community of faith, the gentile Christian community, in which Jewish ceremonial law is not a significant issue. It is his experience as a Christian that encourages the reformulation of biblical promises. He is not talking about Torah in general in these places. He only talks about the use of Torah to define the basic community. He says, in effect, that faith, not Torah observance, defines the Christian community.

Paul reflected on his personal experience in such a way as to make it a new model, raising faith to the level of a basic stance in life, a synonym for conversion. In doing so, he developed a new vocabulary of salvation in Christianity, both for the Jews and for the gentiles. The first principle of salvation is the same as the impulse to form a community: conversion. This is not the whole story: In order to understand the different views of Torah that Paul promulgates in Romans, one has to trace the progress of his faith through what little of his personal history we can reconstruct— conversion, apostolic acceptance, and internal conflict—outlining both his thinking on a variety of important issues in the new faith and facing a variety of difficulties within Christianity for his opinions. This cannot be chronological because we have only the vaguest ideas of Paul's chronology. So we must return to the problem of the role of Torah in later chapters.

Paul understands that the Torah is divine, that it provides the prophecies for the coming of Christ and, more important, that it is still and always was in some ways a standard of righteousness for Jew and gentile alike. This is partly in keeping with the general Jewish understanding of the universal value of Torah. Torah is the blueprint by which the universe is patterned (Midrash Genesis Rabbah 1.1). It is not only the special possession of Israel; even the gentiles must understand and keep its general moral insights.[19] Some moral precepts of Torah, the so-called Noahide Commandments, are incumbent on gentiles as well as Jews, according to the later Jewish doctrine. Only the special laws are incumbent on Jews.

It is thus possible to assume that what changed is Paul's view of righteousness and the medium of salvation for the *gentiles*. As Gaston, Gager, and Stendahl have said, Paul might see that all rests on faith but would maintain that Jewish faith should still include Torah.[20] This was empirically true of the Christianity of Paul's day, for many Christians continued to observe Torah. Further, this concept would be in keeping with the mature rabbinic view of the second century that salvation for Jew and gentile alike is to be based on righteousness and repentance, with the rules of law for the gentiles to exclude the special laws that apply to the Jews alone. But the church has certainly not understood Paul in this way, and Paul does not allow that the gentiles can be righteous according to less-exacting regulations in Torah, a concept of universality that would evolve in Judaism[21] and Christianity.[22] The important questions of the value of Judaism and Torah after the Christ event are not answered by Paul directly or, more exactly, they are answered by Paul in several possibly contradictory ways, depending on the specific question he is addressing. Paul's personal experience after conversion is what most affected both his theoretical thinking about the new basis for Christian community and the value of Torah within it.

Paul meant *at least* that gentiles should enter the Christian community without having to perform the ceremonial law, as Jews did. This new choice offered to gentiles explains why Christianity became so attractive a possibility: it was now possible to enjoy the promises of the Hebrew Bible without having to risk the dangers or social inconveniences of adopting the special laws of Judaism. Stendahl, Gaston, and Gager assert that Paul meant only this. Torah remains in effect for Jews; a new path is opened for gentiles. As we have seen, the same sentiment is present in Judaism before Paul. But the idea of two separate paths—salvation for gentiles in Christianity and for Jews in Torah—does not gain much support from Paul's writings. Were it so, Paul could not describe himself as a suspected transgressor, as he does in Gal. 2:18. Paul says that without faith he has merely left the fold. Paul instead advocates the notion that Torah has a chronological limitation, being added for transgressions (Gal. 3:19) and later to be replaced by faith as maturity replaces tutelage (Gal. 3:23–24).

Galatians 2 is the key to deciding whether Paul means that faith should exclude Torah for all or only for gentiles. The affirmation in Gal. 2:15–16 appears to be that *all* will be justified by faith. Thus Torah cannot be important for justification in Christianity[23]: "We ourselves, who are Jews by birth and not gentile sinners, yet who know that a man is not justified by works of the law but through faith in Jesus Christ, even we have believed in Christ Jesus, in order to be justified by faith in Christ, and not by works of the law, because by the works of the law shall no one be justified." Paul is saying that not only he and his Jewish Christian compatriots know that salvation is by faith, but they all have, like him, given up the law as a means of salvation. His faith in Christ, based on his conversion experience, made him feel righteous and justified him. This conversion experience, radical or gradual, had nothing to do with "works of the law," the observances of Judaism. As a Pharisee interested in the moral life of God-fearers he might have said a similar thing, so Paul is not innovating. But Paul seems to have learned the meaning of his Christian life most fully from his experience with gentile congregations; he holds up his own experience and those of other Jewish Christians who have taken up residence in the gentile community and given up conscientious practice of ceremonial law. For Paul, something critical happened to Torah, based on Christ's saving death. Paul knows that Torah must still somehow be true, because it comes from God and is necessary for understanding the meaning of Christ's mission and victory. He posits the idea, however, that the *complete* Torah law need not be the standard of righteousness, at least for the gentiles. Because he is talking about himself and his Jewish colleagues, he appears to be saying more. The context itself implies more than Stendahl, Gaston, and Gager are willing to admit.

This is the ambiguity: when Paul talks about the works of the law, he is talking about the ceremonial laws of Judaism. When he says: "By the works of the law shall all [*pasa*] not be justified" (Gal. 2:16), he can mean either or both of two things. Although it has most often been taken to mean *no one* shall be justified by law, it literally says that not by works of law shall *all* men be justified.[24] So it is possible that Paul means to set up a second possibility for salvation, faith, without denying the validity of the first, Torah or law, for all. Or perhaps the two contradictory passages are resolved chronologically: though the Torah and faith are both part of God's plan, the Torah was only valid until faith replaced it, as had happened in Paul's own life. The problem is central to Paul's theology but may be insolvable, given his disposition for bold statements.[25]

Paul begins by speaking personally. He tells why he converted and ends with the general statement about the exclusive value of faith for justification. Most of Paul's important meditations on Torah likewise begin from his personal experience and end in a generalization about the value of law universally, based on that experience. In this case the answer is that the law can justify no one: "because by the works of the law [ceremonial rules of Torah] shall no one be justified" (2:16). The meaning of justification is underlined by Paul's statement in Gal. 3:21 that "if a law had been given which could make alive, then righteousness would indeed be by the Law." In this context, Paul's understanding of justification is influenced by the ultimate purpose of justification—salvation through resurrection.

Lloyd Gaston has pointed out that the phrase "works of the law" is an allusion to Ps. 143:2, which Paul quotes in good rabbinic fashion. For Gaston and Gager, the resulting translation becomes: "We too became believers in Christ Jesus, in order that we might be justified from the faithfulness of Christ and not from works of law, because [as it is written:] by works of law *all* flesh is not justified. (Ps. 143:2)."[26] Gager and Gaston are right in cautioning us against relying on received translations and in showing that Paul is using the verse in a rabbinic way. But, as a student of rabbinic literature would know, and as we have seen in regard to another of Paul's exegeses in Galatians, rabbinic method does not commit Paul to interpreting the verse as the Hebrew Bible would or even to the often differing interpretation of the Septuagint. It certainly does not commit Paul to a rabbinic conclusion. The meaning of the verse for exegetes of this period did not inhere in any historical arguments about what the verse must have meant to the writers long ago, for the entire work was held to be the medium of divine revelation. Any acceptable meaning derived from the text, no matter how ingenious, was valued as revelation. The rabbis delighted in finding as many (acceptable) meanings as possible. By comparison, Paul seems to have a one-track mind because he speaks to a complex social situation in light of an overwhelming spiritual experience.

Paul's intent to exclude everyone from salvation through the observance of Jewish law comes out in comparison with his other uses of the same phrases. Paul wants to include all humanity in the term *flesh,* as he does in so many other places; for instance, in Romans 2, where Paul is also speaking about law and where he addresses largely gentile as well as some Jewish Christians, Paul uses the word *anthrōpos,* meaning all of humanity. *Sarx* (flesh) and *anthrōpos* (humanity) are indeed synonyms in the Bible; like the Hebrew Bible, Paul characteristically uses *flesh* to refer to all humanity without faith. Those who are converted through *summorphosis* have a spiritual body and are in Christ, as Enoch is in the son of man. Again, we see that Paul has adopted a language of opposition to describe the distinction between the converted and the unconverted. This language states clearly that all people must be converted. In Romans, Paul means to condemn both gentiles and Jews equally. There is no reason to suppose that Paul exempts Jews at this moment. The same appears to be true in Galatians. He means to include both Jews and gentiles in those who are excused from observing Torah. In Gal. 2:16, Paul uses the words *ean oē,* "unless . . . [he is justified] through faith in Christ" to underline his meaning.[27]

Paul was trying to make a specific point about the generality of faith. He uses himself and other Jewish Christian missionizers as examples of people who have come to the right conclusion. Paul uses the words "*ou . . . pasa sarx,*" literally "not . . . all flesh," in its sense of no one, no *person* or *human being,* to characterize those who are saved by "works of law," ceremonial observance. One cannot make this term mean "not all . . . flesh," hence excluding gentiles from those who are made right-eous by law, as Gaston and Gager do. Paul means that ceremonial Torah is of no significance for salvation for *anyone.*

Stendahl, Gager, and Gaston are right in cautioning against an easy or confident theological interpretation of Paul that does not take into account his personal and historical situation. They are also right to stress the importance of Paul's gentile mission as the context out of which Paul writes. In Galatians, Paul is speaking principally to gentiles and from the perspective of the spokesperson for the gentile community. Stendahl, Gager, and Gaston are right as well to stress that Paul does not want to exclude Jews so much as to include gentiles in the promise. He was defend-ing a gentile minority against a majority opinion in Christianity that they all must become Jews before they could be accepted as Christians. The mature Paul takes certain actions to prevent Jewish alienation. But what Stendahl, Gager, and Gaston apparently miss is the crucial importance that transformation plays in Paul's understanding of Christianity. All

Christians must be part of an evolving, redeemed, transformed community formed by their faith.

Paul's use of flesh and spirit, too, has an insufficiently appreciated social connotation. In this context, the persons of the flesh are probably those who do not come to the spiritual awareness of Paul's gentile community. They are fleshly because they trust in the flesh and the works of the flesh. They observe the rites of Judaism either as Christians or as Jews. The spiritual people, however, are those who are transformed by baptism in Christ. One can suppose that not all Jewish Christians treated baptism in the way in which it was practiced in Paul's community, although some found in it an even greater pride, as Paul's opponents in 2 Corinthians make clear.[28] The vocabulary of flesh and spirit distinguishes those who have been transformed by their experience of baptism from those who have not, on the one hand, and those who are "superapostles" and "puff themselves up with knowledge," on the other. Either or both of these groups might be Christians who continue to observe the Jewish law.

While Paul seems to be demoting Torah, he is not denying that Torah is from God, which would automatically raise the issue of apostasy.[29] He is advocating a change in practice that certainly included the abolition of circumcision as the entrance into Christian community. Whatever else may have been necessary to enter the Christian community may not have been clear to him at this point. It is important to realize that the Jewish community and the Jewish Christian community would not judge him on the basis of his ruminations about God's plan alone or about some nicety of theology. They would probably judge him on his personal practice and on the basis of his recommendations for others. In this respect, he is courting danger.

CONVERSION AND BAPTISM

Paul's major emphasis was on the equality of believers within their community, on trying to express a new unifying factor apart from the traditional ritual of Pharisaism. The circumstances that brought about this search were historically novel. Paul used his own experience of conversion to express that vision. He did so in a number of interrelated ways. Paul could define the unity of his new community in terms of a transformation of believers or an apocalyptic opposition of the world. He could also define the unity in terms of a common ritual experience within community. This experience is mentioned by Paul in Galatians immediately after his statement that the old unity of Jewish ceremonial law is outmoded: "For I through the law died to the law, that I might live to God. I have been crucified with Christ; it is no longer I who live, but Christ who lives in me; and the life I now live in the flesh I live by faith in the Son of God, who loved me and gave himself for me. I do not nullify the grace of God; for if justification were through the law, then Christ died to no purpose" (Gal. 2:19–21).

This image is closely associated with baptism. The idea of defining the conversion experience in terms of a ritual requirement is commonplace in Judaism. When Paul speaks of his death and rebirth through Christ, he is also expressing the meaning of his conversion experience. He needs a new vocabulary to speak of conversion, because the vocabulary of repentance is inapplicable to his experience, though probably not to the experience of the gentile community. He expresses several themes that attack the issue. He uses *becoming just,* justification, in a unique way. By speaking of his past commitments as death and his present commitments as life, Paul uses the kind of language that modern research associates with conversion experiences. In Paul's case the language of death and rebirth comes explicitly from his experience of transformation, though Paul gives no detail. He says that because he practiced the law, he experienced death through the law and that he has been crucified with Christ so that Christ lives through him. He lives through Christ and this experience is his faith. The law, through which he discovered Christ, is now dead for him. It died with his old self. Were it not so, Christ would have died to no purpose. The converse language implies that his experience of transformation is also to be understood as a death and rebirth. Consequently, his new commitments are spiritual and eternal, and his old ones seem fleshly and ephemeral. The difficulty is to see exactly what Paul means by the death of the law. Does this mean that Torah is abrogated? Does it mean that its importance has changed? I think the latter, though it still remains to show in what ways its importance has changed. In this case Paul offers concrete examples rather than principles.

There is something deeply mysterious about Paul's conversion experience, something that will never be available to scientific analysis. Paul does give us other hints as to what this experience is. In Romans 6, Paul links the experience of death and rebirth to baptism:

> What shall we say then? Are we to continue in sin that grace may abound? By no means! How can we who died to sin still live in it? Do you not know that all of us who have been baptized in Christ Jesus

were baptized into his death? We were buried therefore with him by baptism into death, so that as Christ was raised from the dead by the glory of the Father, we too might walk in newness of life.

For if we have been united with him in a death like his, we shall certainly be united with him in a resurrection like his. We know that our old self was crucified with him so that the sinful body might be destroyed, and we might no longer be enslaved to sin. For he who has died is freed from sin. But if we have died with Christ, we believe that we shall also live with him. For we know that Christ being raised from the dead will never die again; death no longer has dominion over him. The death he died he died to sin, once for all, but the life he lives he lives to God. (Rom. 6:1–10)

Paul links the experience of death in Jesus with baptism. Through that rite, each person of faith experiences death, and with death comes freedom from sin. Since Christ was crucified and then resurrected, the person of faith can expect also to be resurrected.

Paul speaks in Galatians about his personal experience of death and rebirth. In the Romans passage above he speaks of the same experience as part of baptism. It is not possible to tell how the three events—transformation, resurrection, and baptism—interrelate from this passage, though they all appear to relate to the Christian community at large. The community that Paul joined saw the experience of baptism as enacting the drama of birth and rebirth and the cleansing from sin. Thus Paul makes his experience consonant with that of his community's. Ever after he virtually defines what that experience is.

Paul uses a personal language, but some of his language of death and rebirth comes from Judaism. There was a strong emphasis on baptism in the communities that sought direct experience of the divine. This is because many different varieties of Jews believed that God demanded ritual purity for those who entered his presence, as can be seen from the ablutions of the Qumran sectarians. It is also true that proselyte baptism in Pharisaic Judaism signified the end of the process of purification from the sinful gentile world and its impurities; thus it eventually became a definitive mark of entrance into the Jewish community. When baptism was used for proselyte conversion, it also signified the rebirth of the convert, commencing a new identity in Israel. We cannot be sure when this language evolved in Judaism. Such language might have been part of Paul's gentile community of converts, but it would not have been personally relevant to Paul, who was Jewish and continued to think of himself in that way. Baptism would have been for Paul more like that of the Qumran community, since it signified his change in purity and status but not his conversion to a new people. Paul sought an experience that would unify all Christians.[30]

Many scholars think that Paul relied on a mystery vocabulary that he learned in his Hellenistic journeys or, less likely, in his original home in Tarsus. But if so, Paul did not make nearly as much of the analogy as would later church fathers, who likened Christianity to a mystery cult. There is no need to posit any particular relationship between Paul and any known or unknown mystery cult. The vocabulary was probably generally available throughout the Hellenistic world to express mystic empathy with the divine. Further, and most important, the language probably already existed in the Hellenistic church that Paul joined and that would have baptized him. To say that the language comes from Hellenistic spirituality is not to say that it was not also part of Jewish tradition as well. The cultures had had broad contacts. Language of death and resurrection, for instance, had been absorbed into Jewish apocalypticism. We have seen that Paul's language also has obvious parallels in Ovid's *Metamorphoses,* in the second- and third-century Hermetic literature (which has obvious Jewish influences), the so-called Mithras Liturgy, and the later mystery cults, where the initiate goes through a symbolic death and rebirth. In the Mithras Liturgy and Hermetic literature the adept explicitly takes in a part of the divine presence or is regenerated for future immortality. The experience of theophany functioned as a guarantee of immortality (promised through good deeds) in Jewish mysticism as well.[31] Though the context is not wholly parallel, the death of the mystical adept in ecstatic trance is mentioned as one of the many dangers of the journey.[32]

Beverly Gaventa's discussion of conversion concentrates on the imagery of darkness and light that adheres to Paul's conversion accounts.[33] The same, I maintain, is true of Paul's language of death and rebirth and his language of flesh and spirit. Paul experienced, mediated or unmediated by the language of his community, his death and resurrection with a new understanding of the value of law. Paul's decision cannot be seen as an affiliation with some messianic form of Pharisaism. It is a complete personal transformation to a new, immortal, and angelic status anticipated by continuing early existence. Paul's description of his conversion is often framed in terms of his symbolic death and regeneration in Christ (Gal. 5:24; 6:14). On the basis of this experience, he hopes for resurrection after the death of his body. For Paul, the language of death and rebirth does not imply generalized Hellenistic mystic empathy. It is specific to his own experience. This language had developed into a specific technical vocabulary in the Hellenistic Christian community, the community in which Paul lives and to which he writes. Paul adds only the distinction between fleshly and spiritual bodies. In the Christian community, resurrection language occurs frequently in the descriptions and liturgy of baptism. Thus, Paul's discussion, as other converts' discussion does, reflects the teaching of the church he entered.

For Paul himself, however, baptism retained a strong sense of present ideal: it defined a new moral community. Being in Christ, there is "neither Jew nor gentile," "slave nor free," "male nor female" (Gal. 3:28; cf. 5:6 and 6:15; Rom. 3:29; 10:12–13). This is the central definition of the new Christian community, based on the Hebrew purity ritual of immersion, reinterpreted so that, once done, its purification powers last forever. It is probable that this formula is pre-Pauline, transmitted through the baptismal liturgy.[34] But its importance to Paul cannot be gainsaid. All are equal parts in a community of the last days, soon to arrive. Everyone who is baptized goes through a symbolic death with Christ and is resurrected with him on rising from the water. Descent into the water was construed as being "buried with Christ" (Rom. 6:4; Col. 2:12), and rising from the water might signify "being raised with Christ" (Col. 2:12; 3:1; Eph. 2:6). The death of Christ is signified in the unclothing and reclothing of the believer. All who underwent baptism experienced resurrection liturgically with Christ.[35] So to be *in Christ* is another way to describe the experience of being a believer or convert. Afterward, according to Paul, the spiritual body will demand a new praxis.

Paul certainly encountered ritual immersion in Pharisaism and probably in mystical preparations for entering angelic company, as Qumran and the Jewish mystical corpus state. Baptism is a characteristic rite of purity in most Jewish sects, but as a rite it is amenable to easy reinterpretation. Baptism thus takes over in Hellenistic Christianity the crucial role of initiation ritual that circumcision combined with baptism had been for men in Judaism and Jewish Christianity. In Judaism, male circumcision was accompanied by baptism, followed by an animal sacrifice when the Temple stood. In the Hellenistic Christian community, Paul allegorized sacrifice as rebirth in Christ and accelerated the revaluation of baptism. For the Jewish community circumcision and baptism were necessary for entering the community. Some Christians saw no reason to change the practice; but others in gentile communities saw no reason to perform circumcision. Circumcision entailed entrance to Judaism, and God-fearing did not demand it. For Paul, who represented the God-fearing, baptism also signifies conversion, but it is a spiritual ritual symbolizing spiritual rebirth and leaving no mark on the flesh. Paul argues in his letter to the Galatians for dropping circumcision because God-fearing is sufficient. This change in the value of the ritual that Paul found in Hellenistic Christianity would spark one of the most divisive controversies of the early church.

Wayne Meeks points out that the effect of this practice was to define a new social unity: all Christians, so long as they are in the group, are brothers and sisters.[36] For Paul, they then become intimate enough to marry each other and to eat in each other's company. For gentiles and Jews to be able to eat together freely and marry was hardly a commonplace in Judaism in that time. The two biological drives of hunger and sex are treated through parallel rules of social acceptability in Judaism.[37] For Jews and gentiles to attain the same level of ritual purity so as to engage freely in these intimate social activities, there must have been a radical cultic boundary-crossing ritual. For Paul that ritual was baptism. By means of baptism the believers take off their old physical body and invalidate old identities. On reclothing they put on Christ (see Col. 3:9–10).[38] The religious meaning of baptism, as expressed here, has a higher priority than Paul's occasional criticism of the baptismal beliefs and customs of others (1 Corinthians 1).

DEATH AND REBIRTH WITHOUT THE LAW

Paul's vision is not only of the risen Lord but also of the crucified messiah, as his exegesis in Galatians shows. Inherent in that vision is the implication that the special laws of Judaism need to be revalued. In Galatians, Paul says that he died to the law that he might live in Christ, the messiah. This sentiment is developed in several places in Paul's work, notably in Rom. 10:4, where Paul proclaims that "Christ is the end of the Law." In Rom. 7:1, Paul goes further, using an obscure aspect of rabbinic law in a completely new context: "the law is binding on a person only during his life." In several places in rabbinic literature the legal maxim occurs that a dead person is free from the duties of the law (e.g., b. Shabbat 30a, 151b; b. Niddah 61b; b. Pesahim 51b; j. Kilaim 9.3). Limitations on the legal responsibilities of the blind and otherwise disadvantaged people are likewise derived in rabbinic writings from the principle that the dead are free from the law. Freeing a wife from the covenant of marriage, for instance, must be defined by the legally acknowledged death of her husband. In a metaphorical way, Paul uses a doctrine that has significant consequences for Jewish marital law. Most of the duties from which the handicapped are free, however, turn out to be ritual and ceremonial laws. They are obviously not free from moral laws.

In Paul's eyes the limitations of death have more far-reaching conclusions. Paul uses that legal instrument to discuss the end of Torah as well (Romans 7). Paul is not primarily interested in the legal ramifications of the principle. He uses the legal principle as a metaphor for his conversion, carrying the message that the convert need not worry about the law: the person who has died in Christ is dead to this aeon and has become free from the law (Rom. 7:6), for the messianic future era of the world has already begun. Paul states only that Torah is no longer the medium of justification and salvation. By this Paul does not necessarily negate the importance of Torah. Paul still understands Torah as the sacred story of Israel's salvation. What he negates is the value of observing Torah for the purposes of defining who is part of the community of the saved. Spiritual people are part of a spiritual process and should not take pride in the flesh. God provides justification first and the person should respond with faith. That faith is synonymous with conversion for Paul. So Paul is again saying that righteousness comes not from the law directly, but from God, who has provided a way to become a spiritual person. Any other Jew might say that God's action of justification is first, though there would be no reason to analyze action so carefully. But Paul wants to change the community's basic ritual requirements, because he has lived in a gentile community in which legal requirements are not primary, though faith in God is.

In post-Pauline rabbinic terms, Paul reveres Torah as *aggadah*, story, and prophecy, but he ceases to practice it as *halakha*.[39] Functionally, this works as a description of Paul's legal opinion, but it does not reflect Paul's own vocabulary for dealing with the issue. Paul promotes the experience of conversion, out of which faith arises, as the most basic response making for community. Paul's own experience of death, followed by his experience of life in Christ while living in gentile communities, lies behind his pronouncements. He assumes that with the conversion the convert will continue moral behavior or learn new moral behavior.

Paul has adopted God-fearing as the model of righteous behavior.[40] The metaphor is significant because, if one ignores Paul's conversion, this is the effect of his legal position. Pointing out the similarity between Paul's view of gentiles and the Jewish concept of God-fearers does not tell us everything we want to know about the situation, since God-fearing could encompass anything from minimal financial support to proselyte status. Further, when Paul missionizes, he evinces no sensitivity to the problem of changing affiliations. He is adamant that everyone declare to be *in Christ*.

And Paul does not merely adopt the prevailing rabbinic view of the responsibilities of righteous gentiles. He works it out within the Christian community based on its own precedents. What Paul's complex notion of metamorphosis in Christ meant about the practice of ceremonial Judaism had to be worked out case by case over the course of his ministry.

PHILIPPIANS 3

Philippians 3 can be considered a summary of the entire process of spiritual incorporation in Christ. This can be seen by departing from the conventional discussion of Paul's theology and examining the social situation in which he is writing. Paul represents and defends those gentile Christians who do not observe Jewish laws. He strongly opposes the Jews and Jewish Christians, who are in the majority or have taken an initiative against him. Otherwise he would not use such polemical language.

He begins by warning his readers to beware of evil workers, whom he also calls dogs, who attempt to circumcise. Paul is punning in Greek, calling the circumcisers mutilated or cut off (*katatomēn* [3:2]), while calling his followers the spiritual circumision, literally "*cut-around* worshiping in the spirit" (*peritomē hoi pneumati theou latreuontes* [3:3]). Paul's opponents are again a party of those Jews or Christians who wish to perform circumcisions to signify that the new Christian convert has also entered Judaism. The rite would only be relevant to the gentile community, since Jews were already circumcised. This in itself violates his sense that all must be transformed. Thus, his opponents are similar to the group in Galatia and also to the group in 2 Corinthians.[41] All opponents boast of the flesh (Phil. 3:3; 2 Cor. 11:18), since they hold their fleshly lives, their superior ritual status in Judaism over the gentile converts. The language of flesh and spirit is not allegorical. It is a reference to the two kinds of Christian community—one priding itself in the flesh, circumcision; the other defining itself by means of spiritual transformation, baptism, those who are converted in faith. He is again talking about Jewish Christians and gentile Christians.

Paul's rhetoric is ferocious; he immediately begins his well-documented argument that he has more to boast about than they do. He tells us exactly how law observant he was—circumcised on the eighth day, a Benjaminite and a Pharisee. Then he tells us of his zeal, ending with his claim of having overturned everything of worth to him for the knowledge of Christ, concluding that righteousness comes from Christ and not from the works of law (3:9). This is one of his few explicitly biographical statements, and it concentrates on his conversion experience. It says that his conversion, hence spiritual transformation in general, had nothing to do with the special rituals of Judaism.

We often assume that arcane and punctilious Jewish ceremonial food laws and observances can scarcely have been attractive to anyone. But Paul's ferocity belies this error. The opposing position appears in the majority. Many Jewish Christians must have thought that faith in Christ begins the journey toward righteousness, again God-fearing, but reaches its goal in complete conversion to Judaism, with its special obligations. This would be the normal expectation of any Jew concerned with the gentile problem. Yet Paul strenuously objects because it represents a complete negation of his idea of a community transformed by faith, showing that he is not merely equating gentile behavior with God-fearing. He wants a single community in which all share in faith.

Paul counters his critics by telling of his transformation in death by means of fellowship with Christ's sufferings ("koinōnian pathēmatōn autou, symmorphizomenos tō thanatō autou" [3:10]). This is a functional equivalent to discussing the consequences of his conversion. Because of this experience he is confident that he will know him (*gnonai auton*) and the power of his resurrection (*tēn dynamin tēs anastaseōs* [3:10]). It is even possible that the opponents of Paul used the same expression, "knowledge of God," to express their piety. Of special interest to us is the parallel: Paul is using knowledge of God as an explanation of his transformation. The process of transformation produced the knowledge of Christ and the knowledge of his resurrection. Paul discusses the knowledge of God in such a way that it can only be something gained in conversion. This, in turn, is knowledge of Paul's own resurrection because of his being conformed to Christ. The contrast is also between his previous pride in law and his new, reborn, and transformed character. Thus Paul never leaves the purview of his own experience. He is contrasting his own experience of the Pharisaic mode of piety, which he characterizes as confidence in the flesh, with his own experience of spiritual regeneration, the new justification that comes from Christ's actions. Then he uses that experience to generalize about Christian community.

Although the conversion must have taken place in a certain moment, Paul's use of the present participle *symmorphizomenos* shows that the process is continuous, as John Koenig points out.[42] This implies that there is a continual and communal process in which final salvation is to be worked out, but it is not a communal process that has anything to do with practicing the law. We can conclude from this that Paul's group is rather estranged from Jews and Jewish Christians. Paul confesses that he is not yet perfected (3:12), seemingly contrasting the finished and unchanging piety of his opponents with his continuous growth in the faith. This perfection appears to be associated with the future resurrection because he says that when Christ returns from heaven, he will transform the lowly bodies of believers into glorious bodies ("metaschēmatisei . . . symmorphon" [3:21]).

Paul's appeal to the gentile church depends on his knowledge that he is not only a Jew, but that he was the most observant Jew imaginable, a Pharisee. The circumcisers are not as pious as he was. But Paul now sees circumcision as fleshly religion, recommending instead spiritual transformation. Ultimate transformation occurs in the apocalyptic future when the Christ returns. In 3:15, however, Paul implies that he has already achieved a certain high level of perfection, because he uses the past tense. He and some of his readers have already achieved a great deal of the goal of perfection (*teleioi*). In this context, perfection appears to be a result of his transformation, the realization that knowledge of God comes not from Jewish law, but from being conformed to Christ, which is apparently a progressive process.

Although his initial insight may have come at conversion, Paul implies that the legal consequences of his conversion were worked out over time, as he began to understand what being in Christ meant for gentiles. He might be admitting here that there was a time after his conversion in which he continued to practice Torah. He certainly says that many have not yet learned the lesson. Thus, Torah as practice must be left behind, but the process of education is continuous, and some have not yet learned the true knowledge. Others have been tempted to raise their level of ceremonial observance. Those who glory in Torah are glorying in the shame of their belly and members (3:19), while those maturing are being remade into an eternal body through this both punctual and durative process of transformation. This is not an allegory. It is a literal description of the two Christian communities in conflict, with Paul representing the gentile Christian one. The Jewish Christians do glory in their physical ceremonial status; the spiritual community reflects the Glory of God.

In Gal. 3:19 Paul is using the Jewish polemic against apostasy and gentile immorality, which we have seen illustrated by Philo and others, against the very people who could use it against him. Ironically, he says that it is the observers of such ceremonial laws as circumcision who are glorying in their flesh, not the pagans. This is Paul's clearest linking of his own conversion experience and transformation with the necessity of giving up confidence in Torah. The entire enterprise depends on his previous experience. It is not a theological insight into the value of law; rather, it is the result of a spiritual experience. The spiritual insight that Paul receives can equally be seen as a summary of his experience in gentile Christian society. The alternative to ceremonial Torah is not lack of Torah but a new apocalyptic form of it, which is unique because it has at its center the identification of Christ as the Glory of God and the consequent irrelevance of all special laws of Judaism. This apocalyptic form of religion is viewed by Paul as the most mature form of piety, but it is one that could only have evolved in gentile Christianity, which is God-fearing transformed by union with the divinity.

CONVERSION AND PAULINE COMMUNITY

Paul's variety of Judaism (Christianity) is attractive to the gentile world and threatening to the Jewish one. In attempting to unify the Christian world, he threatens to rupture the Jewish and Jewish Christian world. Paul himself says that he abandoned Torah because of the success of the lawless mission to the gentiles: "To those outside the Law I became as one outside the Law—not being without the Law toward God but under the Law of Christ—that I might win those outside the Law" (1 Cor. 9:21).

Paul distinguishes among the Jews, those under the law, those outside the law, and the weak. He offers the law of Christ as an alternative to the law. Presumably, this law of Christ approximates the moral law with the ceremonial laws of Judaism made optional. His stated reasons for abandoning the law are to win those outside of it or, as he also says, to "win the more" (1 Cor. 9:19). Anyone who had Paul's experience of living in the gentile Christian community, learning there the content of the Christian message and coloring the meaning of the vision through the issues relevant to it, might come to the conclusion that the success of Torahless gospel was proof of its being protected by the spirit. Besides reflecting on his own personal conversion experience, then, Paul is reflecting on his postconversion experience in the gentile community and his career in converting gentiles. These experiences form the basis of his theology.

Paul's experience in gentile Christian communities also explains where and how he defines his theological battlegrounds. They are, as often as not, personal and legal battles with Jewish Christians about how to observe the Jewish law. Paul's radical thinking about Torah would naturally have been suspicious to Jews and even to Jewish Christians. The most obvious charge is that Paul is making it too easy to become a Christian. Paul directly answers this charge in Gal. 1:10: "Am I now seeking the favor of men or of God? Or am I trying to please men?" He denies that his gospel is meant to water down the teaching of Judaism. He is correct from his viewpoint. His new vision is far greater than an accommodation in the laws for gentiles. "If I were still pleasing men I should not be a servant of Christ" says Paul. His conversion is the direct answer to the question in Gal. 1:10. If he desired to please men he would not now be a Christian. He would continue to be a Pharisee.

But there is the opponents' perspective to consider as well. True, his life has been made infinitely more complicated by his new position on the observance of law, but this is hardly a complete refutation of the charge that he has watered down the strict Jewish rules about conversion. He refrains from telling us that the gentile path to full status in the community is thereafter made much easier, because no ceremonial laws need separate Jew from gentile, which is the point of the charge against him. He could be charged with seeking the favor of men rather than God. As we can tell from his vituperation, and from his deflection of the question, that his opponents have hit a nerve. His thinking is greatly affected by his experience in gentile communities and his attempts to represent their position to his Jewish brothers in Christ. Although Paul left Pharisaism behind, he did not intend to deny his Judaism, since he was discussing a whole new community within Judaism. But the effect of his mission was seen as a kind of apostasy by his Jewish Christian brothers, as his denials in Galatians prove.

Paul's famous protestations in Rom. 6:1 and 15 are similar: "Are we to continue in sin that grace may abound? By no means!" or "What then? Are we to sin because we are not under law but under grace? By no means!" The rhetoric is powerful,[43] yet the questions do not appear to be merely rhetorical. Both passages imply that Jewish Christians are charging him with the converse—the doctrine that a faith commitment without Torah legislates sinning. From their perspective, Paul is antinomian. Paul's famous "by no means" (*mē genoito*) in Rom. 6:1 and 15 imply a directly voiced criticism that his gospel is immoral, not merely lacking ceremonial law. The charge must be not only that he himself is a transgressor but that he may be an apostate, or that he is perverting the traditions of Judaism or even leading people astray. In Rom. 3:8 he states that he was falsely accused of teaching evil that good may come of it: "And why not do evil that good may come?—as some people slanderously charge us with saying. Their condemnation is just." Paul shares the sentiment that those who teach doing evil for good purposes are subverters of Judaism. He does not agree that he is guilty of the charge. But this is the reaction of some Jewish Christians to his doctrine that Torah is no longer as valid as it was before Jesus' arrival.

The irony is, of course, that by continuing to preach his position, by justifying it in Galatians, he is in danger of a greater charge than transgression or apostasy, that of leading others astray. Paul's direct report is that without faith his behavior would merely be transgression. Yet, whether Paul's theology is apostasy because it replaces fleshly, ceremonial Torah by faith in spiritual transformation is a moot point. For the rabbis it was apostasy to maintain that Torah was not from heaven. Although Paul does not maintain this, his behavior was subject to scrutiny and many different interpretations. Fortunately for Paul, Judaism of the first century did not seem preoccupied with theological rectitude.[44] Such issues, should they arise, were more likely to have been solved by a local community's attention to the suspect's behavior, as Luke's recounting of Paul's troubles in Acts makes clear. Paul too describes the Jewish Christian and later the Jewish community's inquiry into his motives as if his actions and not his theology first caught hostile attention. Although Paul's theological or, as I prefer to call it, ideological position is clear from his conversion and never wavers, his behavior changes on several occasions.[45] These changes arise in the context of Paul's discussion of the ritual requirements of gentiles. Paul's discussions of Torah begin as explanations and exegeses of his conversion, and his understanding of how to carry on his mission emerged from that conversion and his subsequent experience within the church. But both emerge concurrently; Paul's explanations were born out of his mission. They are statements that define Paul's conversion within his community, not primarily theological meditations, though one can make theological sense of them once the social context is clear. Whether they are transgression, apostasy, or leading astray—three offenses of ascending severity in Jewish law—depend on the evaluation of Paul's observers. More than his theology, his critics will seek to judge his actions.

Paul's conversion entailed a single factor, faith, for the definition of a new community, not two different and equal factors, which risked creating different communities separating Jews and gentiles within Christianity. Paul's drive for uniformity is typical. Conversion within an apocalyptic or sectarian environment normally produces a highly cohesive community, both according to modern observation and inferences from first-century data. Although Paul recognizes that Jews continue to exist, and he is aware of Torah-abiding Jewish Christians, he advocates a new community where all internal and external divisions are secondary to faith. In Christ, there should be no distinction between slave and free, male and female, and especially between Jew and Greek (e.g., Gal. 3:28). He is trying to forge a new unity based on faith in the promises of God and not in the distinctions between Jew and gentile. He is promoting not an end to the Jewish law or the Jewish people but an end to differentiation between Jew and gentile as status groups *within* the Christian community, though he is speaking primarily to gentiles.

The Stendahl-Gaston-Gager position that Paul only means to negate Torah among the gentiles is ironically close to Luke's portrayal of Paul. Luke's Paul agrees with the authentic Pauline letters in saying that the law is good but does not offer a way to salvation (Acts 15:10; 13:39). Luke says that the gentiles should not be required to keep the *burdensome* parts of the Law (Acts 15:10, 28). Paul himself denies any motivation of ease. The only statements about the ease of Torah Paul makes are in the context of criticizing others for being less observant than he was. Possibly, Luke was writing to effect a compromise position in a church that still contained an active and vibrant Jewish Christian community. He therefore needed to talk about the gentile mission in that particular way.[46] Given the number of voices objecting to Paul's solution, Jewish Christians cannot have disappeared as quickly as most scholars assume. But Luke's Paul does not say that Jews have misunderstood the law since the arrival of Christ, and there is no criticism in Luke of the Jewish desire to be justified by the law. For Paul these are the most significant issues.

Paul, unlike Luke, is not looking for a middle ground in his ideological statements about the status of the law. As a convert, he radicalizes the decision, excluding the middle ground. He states that those who proclaim the specific responsibilities of the law, including circumcision, often do not themselves adequately keep the law (Gal. 6:13). This is the judgment of an ex-Pharisee, and it is rhetorically powerful. Paul, having been a Pharisee, has complete disdain for the intermediate position. If one is to practice Torah, one should do it thoroughly. One should convert to Judaism practicing the law according to the position of the Pharisees. But that will be of no use: "We ourselves who are Jews by birth and not gentile sinners, yet who know that a man is not justified by works of the law but through faith in Jesus Christ, even we have believed in Christ Jesus, in order to be justified by faith in Christ, and not by works of the law, because by works of the law shall no one be justified" (Gal. 2:15–16). These statements, the results of years of experience in gentile community, mark a converted man. Paul insists that both Jew and gentile convert to the faith in Christ:

"For neither circumcision counts for anything, nor uncircumcision, but a new creation" (Gal. 6:15). The new creation can only be the transformed spiritual human being who has stood before the divine throne and partaken of divinity. For Paul the experience of conversion to a new faith is the only entrance to Christianity. Spiritual people have no need for fleshly customs.

That Paul, a Jew, provided the basic model for conversion experience for both Jew and gentile in Christianity is extremely important. Paul was not the only or even the first convert to Christianity, nor was he the first to preach to the gentiles. Because he had been a Pharisee and because he converted to a new view of salvation, he was the most effective spokesperson for the new rather than the old concept of community. This new community was, in fact, already existent in gentile churches that Paul joined. Paul only argues for their acceptance and for Jewish Christians to join them on their own terms. He does this better than anyone else could have done, because he had been part of the movement in Judaism that most strongly emphasized ceremonial laws. The proof of belonging to the new community lies in the radical reorientation of everyone, not just gentiles, in their entrance to Christianity.

Those who stress that Paul was merely a Jew whose messiah has come have missed Paul's point. Paul was a Jew who did not have to convert to become a Christian. Theoretically, he could have just slid over as an adherent by claiming Judaism was fulfilled by the messiah's arrival. In that case, he would have insisted that the rules of Jewish life be imposed on all Christians, as did the Jewish Christians. Or he would have insisted that the gentiles remain God-fearers and not become part of the community. But Paul, though Jewish, and because he had been a believing Pharisee, had to go through a radical reorientation to enter Christianity. Paul then said that everyone needs radically to reorient his or her way of thinking in order to become a Christian.

Although the absolute equality of gentiles and Jews was hardly a popular belief in Christianity in his day, the result of the growing popularity of gentile Christianity over the first and second centuries was that Paul and the gentiles' understanding of Christianity became ever more popular. Eventually, conversion—by which we mean Paul's understanding of universal spiritual transformation—became the operant model for both Jews and gentiles in a new entity that was later called Christianity. But it happened decades, perhaps more than a century, after Paul.

For Paul, being a Jew socialized to the extreme value of ceremonial Torah, the hallmark of Pharisaism, the subservience of Torah to faith meant a demotion in rank of an important concept—ceremonial law. To a gentile who had not the slightest understanding or experience with Torah, Paul's discussions of the irrelevance of ceremonial Torah meant its complete irrelevance. For Paul, giving up special claims to the performance of ceremonial Torah was part of his dissonance over leaving Pharisaism and entering an apocalyptic community based on faith. For the gentile, Torah was itself of a sinful world to be left behind, virtually on a par with paganism. For Paul, part of the value of Torah was carried over from one secondary socialization to another. For the gentile convert to Christianity, the new primary socialization to Christianity seemed to ignore Torah, since it did away with the distinctive parts of ceremonial Torah. Paul's analysis of community was far more sweeping for the gentile Christian than it was in his own experience. This situation made the kind of unity Paul envisioned more difficult to achieve in fact than in the formula of a baptismal liturgy. In the end, Paul's victories in forging the unity were limited to his theory, for the actual attempt at implementing the plan caused too much conflict during his own life.

No one should think that Paul's writing is a dispassionate or impartial theology of Torah. Paul's description of Torah is a consequence of his conversion experience, not the other way around; for conversions do not follow the pattern of philosophical questioning. Neither are Paul's statements a phenomenological description of Torah; rather, they are the result of cognitive changes in a man who has experienced dissonance in a sharper way than many other Christians, especially other Jewish Christians. Paul's personal experience of conversion to Christianity after having succeeded as a Pharisee functioned as one strategy, and eventually the dominant one, for including gentile Christians within the original Jewish apocalyptic sect. Paul's analysis of law, of course, goes far beyond Paul's personal religious stance, helping Christianity to define its new role in world history. But one must be careful not to homogenize Paul's thought on law into a single statement, nor to forget that Paul is speaking personally. Paul advocated that his new gentile converts need not practice Jewish law, and he tried to minimize the kinds of Jewish rituals that the community practiced. Though some of the rites of passage of conversion, such as baptism, were kept, largely through the influence on Christianity of John the Baptist's movement, they were received by Paul with a considerable new exegesis from his gentile environment and further transformed by Paul's understanding into an entirely new ritual.

Paul, like most Christians in his day, was also profoundly apocalyptic in his thinking. But, as we know from the study of modern conversion communities, Paul's formula of conversion allowed Christianity to stimulate a high level of sectarian commitment even after the apocalyptic beginnings of Christianity were left behind. Paul and then Christianity's use of conversion—with its attendant characteristics of high faith commitment and low practice of Jewish ritual—as an effective role model for a convert's behavior was a significant reason for the success of Christianity in attracting gentile converts. Paul's experience, stressing conversion within the structure of the community itself, helped bridge the gap between the apocalyptic Jewish sect and the normative Hellenistic mystery religion of piety and morality that Christianity was eventually to become. The language Paul used prepared the church for that transference, though it took place long after Paul. Paul himself was more interested in the consequences of his perception that Torah was no longer valid in the way he had supposed. He tried to understand how moral behavior was to continue in the new community of faith.

CHAPTER FIVE

℘PAUL'S NEW CONVERSION COMMUNITY AMONG THE GENTILES

Conversion raises the commitment level of the new convert, but without other sources of commitment, the effects of conversion soon evaporate. Paul's career was devoted to the unification of a conversion community. The roots of the long process by which conversion was institutionalized in Christianity—how it resulted in a committed and unified community—are to be found in Paul's letters.[1] But it begins in Paul's ecstatic vision in Christ. Paul's search for community assumes a group of believers who share in the spirit.

Since Paul eschewed some Jewish practices that functioned to raise Jewish commitment, Pauline gentile communities had to develop new ideas of commitment. Paul's idea of community based on faith was not a novelty. Many non-Pharisaic Jews in the land of Israel and in the Diaspora lived with a lesser degree of ritual than the Pharisees, developing strong sources of commitment in communities structured around synagogues— retaining a few crucial ceremonies such as the Sabbath—combined with social and business relationships. Nevertheless, the Pauline gentile community was more difficult to maintain than either the Pharisaic one or the minimally Jewish one, because it did not have at its boundaries the same easily understandable markers. For this reason many Jews who accepted Jesus as the messiah were still skeptical of gentile Christianity. Paul's letters show that conflict in its clearest form; indeed, the conflict between those who practiced some form of Jewish custom and those who did not was the most significant issue within Christianity's first two generations.

The attractiveness of Jewish law is an issue that modern Christians find difficult to appreciate because it rings no chords of sympathy in their lives. This puzzling phenomenon is most clearly seen in Gal. 4:19: "My little children, with whom I am again in travail until Christ be formed [*morphōthē*] in you!" In this passage, Paul is upset with a group in Galatia. That there are factions is underlined by his addressing more than one church there: "tais ekklēsiais tēs Galatias" (Gal. 1:2). Some of the Galatians are deserting Paul's teaching (Gal. 1:6) for the relatively greater security of traditional Jewish practice. They are observing "days, and months, and seasons, and years," which is for Paul a lapse back into life under law (Gal. 5:4)—ceremonial Torah. For them, it is not a lapse at all, rather another step forward in the direction of full entry into the Jewish community by conversion. But Paul suggests that conversion in Christ ought to be a spiritual transformation, not the ritual of circumcision and sacrifice.

Jewish practice is the temptation against which Paul warns. It brings security in a way that living under faith alone did not, partly because it must have been the Christian majority's way of addressing the issue. At the time Paul wrote, the practicing Jews among the Christians must still have been a majority. Also at stake is the well-understood nature of becoming Jewish. It must be assumed that a fuller identity within the Jewish community brought with it a more easily understandable source of identity and reduction of cognitive dissonance.

Paul uses the term *morphosis* to express the true Christian life. The tenses indicate that the Galatian Christians were formed in Christ, probably by baptism as with Paul himself (Gal. 2:20; 6:14); now they are backsliding and that formation needs to be done anew. Paul also sees he is "again in travail" (*hous palin ōdinō* [4:19]), implying that the *morphosis* he discusses is explicitly a language of new birth and maturation. This suggests that the formation of the likeness of Christ is both a punctual event, which is marked by baptism, and a durative process, which will culminate in the second coming, the parousia.[2] The process of maturation is to be undertaken in the community, meaning that Christians should stay away from the temptation to express their religion through Jewish ceremonial law. The effect of this perception emphasized and aggravated the social distinctions between Jewish Christians and gentile Christians.

PAULINE TRANSFORMATION AS POLEMIC AGAINST LAW

In 2 Corinthians 3, Paul interprets the rekindled brilliance of the new dispensation that had been lost in the old, the same brilliance whose embarrassing fading splendor Moses had to hide under a veil. Paul's theme is that the law itself is part of the dispensation of death. He says: "the letter killeth, but the Spirit giveth life" (2 Cor. 3:6 AV). He does not mean that punctilious observance of law destroys, though God's intent for the law makes it live, for such thoughts were not new in Judaism. *Spirit* in 2 Corinthians 3 does not refer to the intention of the law. It refers to the presence of the resurrected Christ in opposition to the demonic forces of this world. The definition of his community as those who have faith and who feel the work of the Holy Spirit is a mark of an apocalyptic community, defining itself as in Qumran as the children of light and the followers of the angel of truth. In this passage particularly, Paul stresses that the action of salvation in the world is from Christ in whose being the saved can share.[3] Paul means that the ceremonial laws of Judaism, understood strictly rather than allegorically, cannot bring one to transformation, as does the Holy Spirit. Paul expresses the subject of correct faith in eschatological, future terms as the spiritual glow, radiance or splendor, the special resemblance of Adam to God before the fall, which is imparted only to those who, like Moses, have been called into the presence of God. Paul implies that converted Christians have also received this glow from the presence of God. Paul has been called into Christ's enthroned presence by his conversion, as are all in the Christian community of faith. Only Christian community can maintain the radiance undiminished: "Yes, to this day whenever Moses is read a veil lies over their [i.e., the Jews' or the Jewish Christians'] minds; but when a man turns to the Lord the veil is removed. Now the Lord is the Spirit and where the spirit of the Lord is, there is freedom. And we all, with unveiled face, beholding the glory of the Lord are being changed into His likeness from one degree of glory to another; for this comes from the Lord who is the Spirit" (2 Cor. 3:15–18). This passage, which reflects Paul's mysticism of the *Kavod,* has a polemical purpose as well. The context for these remarks can help to explain its importance. It is quite possible that Paul is making explicit use of his opponents' arguments—perhaps a midrash on Exodus that has been used by a Jewish Christian community. Indeed, an enormous and rather subtle scholarly enterprise has been directed at separating Pauline comments from the possible Jewish Christian opponents' argument underlying it.[4]

I should like to suggest a supplementary hypothesis: Paul's metaphor of veiling is not only metaphorical, he is also speaking of a communal practice. When Paul says that "whenever Moses is read, a veil lies over their minds, but when a man turns to the Lord the veil is removed," he is referring to the ritual of veiling one's head in Judaism. This custom is not the one most often identified with Jews in commentaries on 2 Corinthians 3. Today some Jewish men do wear head coverings for prayer. The custom's origin is unknown; the Bible does not explicitly command either men or women to cover their heads. By talmudic times it was considered an expression of awe before the divine presence to conceal the head and face, especially when praying or studying mysticism (Hag. 14b; RH 17b; Ta'an. 20a). The custom of head covering was, however, restricted to honored persons; for a bachelor to do so was considered presumptuous (Kid. 29b). The synagogue illustrations of Dura Europos generally depict Israelites without head coverings. So it seems unlikely that head covering could have been a first-century Pharisaic custom, and it was unknown among Hellenistic Jews. It is possible that the custom was beginning to evolve in a way that the New Testament helps to clarify.

Because the origin of headcovering is unknown and not attested to in the Hebrew Bible, Strack and Billerbeck assume that it had not yet arisen in Judaism.[5] First Cor. 11:4 virtually clinches the argument: "Every man praying or prophesying, having his head covered, dishonors his head." Although Paul is exaggerating, perhaps for polemic effect, as both the high priest and the ordinary priests wore special headgear (Exod. 28:4, 37, 40), he is explaining the dominant symbolism of head covering: covering the head could be interpreted as an expression of grief, modesty, or embarrassment in biblical times (2 Sam. 15:30; 19:5; Jer. 14:3–4). Bar Kappara covered his head after the death of R. Judah the Prince (Tj Kil. 9:4, 32b; Tj Ket. 12:3, 35a). Lepers and members of the community ostracized by a ban were obliged to cover their heads (b. MK 15a), as were those who were forced to fast in times of drought (b. Ta'an. 14b). So Paul is writing before the custom of reverent head covering for worship had evolved.

It is possible that Paul was referring to another well-attested, existent custom in the Jewish community that he did not advocate for his gentile congregations: veiling the head with a prayer shawl or *tallit*. Jewish men wore prayer shawls in Paul's time (Mark 12:38). The tallit is the ritual garb that grew out of the command of the third paragraph of the Shema, which demanded the wearing of fringed garments (Deut. 6; see also Num. 15:37–41). Although the ritual of wrapping oneself in the tallit for prayer is ancient, a specific ritual garment developed only later, because in this period many Jews ordinarily wore a tallit or fringed garment, which distinguished them from gentiles. The rabbis regarded this as proper ritual attire, a mark of reverence for the divine presence (b. Shab. 10a), showing both that it existed and that it was not universal, probably because the garment itself was not a universal Jewish fashion. Wrapping oneself in the prayer shawl is an aid to attaining the proper mood of reverence for God (M. Ps. 2.99). It is also characteristic of mystical praxis, where wrapping oneself in a tallit is necessary for being in the presence of the divine.[6] The custom of wrapping oneself in the tallit, including veiling one's head with it, could itself have been the forerunner of head coverings (*kippot*) (b. Menachot 39b; b. Baba Batra 98a; especially b. Rosh Hashanah 17b), as piety provided that a tallit could be used to wrap or veil the head.

Veiling the head with the prayer shawl is a sign of the holiness of Torah reading, and it is an impressive aspect of orthodox services even today. Some strictly observant Jews always put the prayer shawl over their heads. It might reflect the ritual preparation necessary for divine encounters among Jewish Christian mystics.[7] The context of Paul's polemic can imply that the leaders of the opponents veiled themselves or that the entire opponent community did. Paul's community worshiped and read Torah without putting on a tallit, going bareheaded, because they did not characteristically wear such garments. Although there may be a Jewish Christian polemic behind Paul's argument, his communal defense begins with an issue of custom, against the practice of veiling one's head while reading Torah, not against a presumed Jewish Gnosticism. Paul assumes that the practice is Mosaic, since the ritual is prooftexted in Deuteronomy 22:12. He directly contrasts the practice of Moses with a new practice of the Lord, Christ. But this is not merely a literary figure, it is a symbol of two different ways of approaching Christianity. Jewish Christians brought Jewish custom with them into Christianity; gentile Christians obviously did not, but many Jewish Christians probably insisted that they learn the proper Jewish procedures. The issue of correct behavior during worship divided the community. Paul believes that the Jewish custom is immaterial. His comments on ritual practice point out that Christianity is an all-or-nothing decision. Of course, he is also making a striking point about Christ's participation in divinity, using the metaphor of the divine *Kavod*. For Paul, the Jewish custom of veiling one's face with the tallit is a symbol of faded glory, a disgraceful and underhanded tampering with God's word (2 Cor. 4:2). This is possibly an aside to the practice of interpreting the oral law. Those Christians who have put aside the oral law are with unveiled face beholding the Lord, therefore they commend themselves to every conscience in the sight of God (4:2).

The importance of ritual actions and their unwritten messages cannot be easily denied. Innovations in ritual would have been especially provocative to traditional Jewish sensibilities, as they were when tried again by modern Reform Jewish congregations. Although no doctrinal statement inheres in Paul's change of practice, its symbolic message about the value of Torah was radical, causing both Jewish Christian distaste and gentile Christian inquiry as to the reason for the Jewish criticism. Paul defends his lack of respect for custom by saying that the new Christian experience of Christ as Lord, based on a new understanding of Scripture, does not need the obfuscation that Moses inserted into Jewish rites. Paul is making a wider claim about the relationship between Torah-true Christianity and his abridged variety, basing his comments on a concrete ritual. Interpreting 2 Corinthians 3 in this way emphasizes the separation of the gentile converts from the Jewish and Jewish Christian communities. Paul's strong language underscores the social friction; one might assume an equally strong criticism from Jews or Jewish Christians occasioning Paul's vituperation. The Corinthian correspondence also implies a partial isolation of Paul's new gentile Christian community from the Jewish and Jewish Christian synagogues and possibly some pressure from the other side to conform.

The opponents whom Paul criticizes might well be Jews, even Pharisees; and they might also be Christians of some sort. We cannot be sure of the identity of Paul's opponents because the break between Judaism and Christianity was incomplete. Paul is also more interested in the divisions between Jew and gentile. Paul's discussion thus illuminates a giant social fissure opening up in early Christianity. In the midst of the polemic we discover some of the most intimate aspects of Paul's religious experience. Paul is intent on discussing the participation of faithful Christians in the Glory of God; this is the mystical and apocalyptic core of Christianity. But Paul was speaking to a difficult argument between Christians evangelized from Judaism and those from the gentile community in which he lived. He has knowledge of, and some sympathies with, each community. His basic position, however, is that of the gentiles, as is clear from this polemic: "And even if our gospel is veiled, it is veiled only to those who are perishing. In their case the god of this world has blinded the minds of the unbelievers, to keep them from seeing the light of the gospel of the glory of Christ, who is the likeness of God" (2 Cor. 4:3). Paul is opposing ordinary Judaism and Jewish Christianity to gentile Christianity in this passage. Gager, Gaston, and Stendahl would thus find it hard to maintain that Paul automatically included Jews within the community of the saved. Rhetorically, Paul has no problem in saying that the gospel is veiled from those who have no faith, provided that one understand that the veiling is an appearance. Paul might allow some people to veil as a custom in his congregation, as long as no special privilege is claimed for it. Other Christian communities might *require* it; he does not. To require veiling is to be blind to faith. Paul's mature ritual strategy maintains that since ceremony neither helps nor hurts, it should never be an issue between Christians.

Those who make veiling a significant issue have been blinded by the god of this world. They cease to focus their eyes on heavenly matters. They may not see *Kavod,* Christ, who is the *likeness* of God.

Second Cor. 4:3 shows that Jewish Christians who visited or joined the community in Corinth had rejected some of Paul's teachings, probably using the passage in Exodus as a prooftext. Paul turns his image around by saying that he and his followers see Christ clearly, without a veil, and although the true gospel may in fact be veiled, it is veiled only to those who misunderstand it. Paul's language shows a man well-versed in Jewish Bible interpretation and also Hellenistic diatribe. His statements also help us understand the nature of the Pauline gentile Christian community and some of the ways Paul approached his mission.

Paul reacts to opposition with a typical apocalyptic intuition about the world, mainly derived from living a life of strong conviction that is strongly disputed by one's neighbors.[8] In accordance with apocalyptic dualism, the "god of this world" in 2 Corinthians is obviously Satan or one of his principal envoys. Those who do not see the truth are under the sway of Satan. The opposition can seem like angels of light but they are actually ambassadors of Satan (2 Cor. 11:13–15).[9]

Whatever underlies this passage, Paul adds his explicit understanding of Christ as the image of God, the *likeness* of God that Moses saw (2 Cor. 3:18). Scripture is no longer the bright looking-glass for the image of God, nor is it totally vacant; instead, it is, like Moses' glowing face, a fading reflection of the experience of Christ, who has taken on the role of the transmitter of divine light. Paul believes that the Glory of God is something that one actually sees: "seeing the Glory of Christ, who is the likeness of God" (2 Cor. 4:4). He himself had visions confirming the identification of Christ with the Glory of God. This illumination gives him sure knowledge of the "Glory of God in the face of Christ" (2 Cor. 4:6). The center of Paul's gospel is the identification of Christ as the Glory of God.

But can Paul be saying that all converts must have the same vision that he did? I think not, otherwise he could not claim any special authority for his own visions, as he does in 2 Corinthians 12. Paul expects the faithful to accept his identification as revelation, because in 1 Cor. 15:49 he states that Christians will not fully bear the image of the man from heaven until the resurrection.[10]

The possible contradiction between Paul's present and future languages of transformation has been tentatively resolved by John Koenig in references to 1 Corinthians 4 and 5.[11] Paul parallels the contrast between the believer's present and future transformation to the contrast between the earthly and heavenly tabernacle in 2 Cor. 5:1. Koenig brings in several features of Paul's language to establish this hypothesis. The eternal weight of Glory, for example, corresponds to the heavenly garments of Glory that play a role in Jewish apocalypticism. In 1 Enoch 108.11ff, God promises to effect a metamorphosis of the good: "So now I shall summon their spirits if they are born of light, and change those who are born in darkness—those whose bodies were not recompensed with light, those who have loved my holy name, and seat them each one by one upon the throne of his honor; and they shall be resplendent for ages that cannot be numbered; for the judgment of God is righteousness, because he will give faith—as well as paths of truth—to the faithful ones in the resting place."[12] First Enoch 62.15–16, of more uncertain date, speaks explicitly of the clothing donned by the righteous at the last judgment, thus becoming garments of life (see 2 Cor. 5:4).

Like the Glory of God in 2 Cor. 4:17, the building of God (5:4) is also conceived as a garment, a spiritual tallit of sorts. It is put on (*ependusasthai*) so that the mortal nature may be swallowed up. Paul also uses the same imagery in 1 Cor. 15:53–54. The picture in both 1 and 2 Corinthians is of a heavenly garment to be put on by believers at the resurrection, in contrast to the special garments that Jews wear in this life. This language allows Paul to talk of being in Christ, while spirit language allows him to speak of having Christ in him. The passage connects with the rite of baptism, in which dressing in a new garment was a significant part, a symbol of the transformation to eternal life that had taken place ritually. It is at baptism that the spirit descends on Jesus as well. In 2 Cor. 5:1, this resurrection is a future conditional event, what would happen should the temple be destroyed.

In 2 Cor. 4:17, this Glory is augmented by the suffering of believers. Paul makes a sharp distinction between present suffering and future glorification. A vision of heaven is vouchsafed to but a few, although by faith in the prophecies the content of the vision is made known to all believers. It will happen to all believers and only to believers. When Paul speaks of his mission as bringing light out of darkness, he means "to give the light of the knowledge of the Glory of God in the face of Jesus Christ" (4:6). Paul's vocation is to make known the identification of Jesus Christ as the Glory of God, because others have not been converted in quite so dramatic a fashion and have not seen it as directly as he.

John Koenig says that the "garment of glory remains invisible, intangible and essentially inaccessible to believers on earth until it is 'put on' at the parousia (5:4)" (155). The process, however, is continuing presently in the spiritual life of the faithful. The phrase "from one degree of glory to another" (3:18) means that each individual's resemblance to the Glory is somehow accumulating, presumably in heaven. At the imminent last judgment, the Glory prepared for the believers in heaven (4:13; 5:5) will finally be manifested. Thus, in 1 Corinthians 6, Paul can say that the believers will be appointed judges of the world (6:2) and even of angels (6:3). Becoming one with the Son, they will be higher than the angels. Given their future role, he despairs of their present moral naïveté. Paul sees Christians as a congregation united by their absorption into Christ, the angelic vice-regent of God.[13]

Paul's understanding of the issue is thus exclusively mystical and apocalyptical, with one further proviso. The activity of the end-time has already begun. The Holy Spirit, evident in the success of the mission, and present in baptism, is a pledge that the process has begun. The transformation is a continuous process leading to the final consummation. Although the suffering of believers is only thus far made manifest, it is a sign that the glorification has already begun. This conversion process subsumes and explains all future activity, tying moral and community life to it, and it promises that each faithful action is itself a step toward the approaching final consummation. It also shows that Paul has not completely discarded ritual activity. Baptism obviously retains an important ritual place in his view of Christianity. The ritual defines a highly visible and strictly defined community of those in the spirit.

Paul's mysticism is combined with an apocalyptic sectarianism. It is an ironic apocalyptic sectarianism, for the Pauline gentile community is distinguished from its Jewish and Jewish Christian neighbors mostly by its lack of traditional Jewish praxis, rather than its strict adherence to law and denial of Hellenistic life, as is typical of the other apocalyptic groups. Paul's church is a group apart from the rest of Judaism, distinguished by its lack of most Jewish ceremonies. The separation is enforced by high group definition, as in the extreme, Torah-true apocalyptic groups.

PAULINE APOCALYPTICISM

Apocalypticism and mysticism were inextricably bound in first-century Judaism. Paul is himself a prime example of the way in which apocalypticism and mysticism were united phenomenologically. His writings define and describe a special, new way of living for an apocalyptic, Christian gentile community. One of the most widespread findings of psychological, anthropological, and sociological studies of apocalypticism has been a rigorous distinction between the community and the outside world, which is always parallel to the distinction between the saved and the lost. Thus, expulsion from the apocalyptic group can be the most serious penalty of the community. In the Qumran community, ostracized members starved to death because they would not eat the polluted food of the outside world. For this reason, the group often rescinded its interdiction at the last moment and accepted the sinning member back into the group (Josephus, *Jewish War* 2.142–44). Such clear differentiation between earthly communities often entails strict dualism within the heavenly community. Qumranic dualism was not driven by a philosophical impetus; the cosmic battle between the forces for good and evil explained the heavy opposition that the group faced on earth. Demonization of all outside of the group also characterized Christianity on occasion.

Paul's apocalyptic view of community is unique in two ways: first, because he understood that the final days had begun, and second, because he abrogated the special laws of Judaism in the service of converting gentiles. Paul's attention to missionizing the gentiles is an extraordinary aspect of his thinking when compared to other apocalyptic sentiments. Denying the relevance of many of the ancient ceremonial boundaries between Judaism and the world, his definition of the church as the community of those who have been justified and saved by their faith is based on apocalyptic sentiment. All else falls under the sway of sin, as the Qumranites believed that there was no possibility of virtue outside their community. Whether they have the law or not, all those within the community are saved and all those without are damned.

Paul's word for the special knowledge that he has received in his conversion is *apokalypsis* or revelation (Gal. 1:2). Yet he also uses the term *apocalypse* for the final future event in 1 Cor. 1:7, and in Rom. 8:19 he speaks of the coming revelation of the sons of God, awaited by creation with eager longing. In both cases he views the appearance of Christ, both incarnationally and personally to him through the Holy Spirit, as a precursor to the final consummation. Paul's expectation of the end is a consequence of his having seen Christ revealed as the Glory of God in his conversion experience, as Paul clarifies in Gal. 1:12: "For I did not receive it from man, nor was I taught it, but it came through a revelation [*apokalypsis*] of Jesus Christ." As in Daniel 7:9–13 and the Enochian literature, the appearance of the human figure of God was part of a larger scene in which judgment and reward of the righteous was prominently featured. What made this a Christian conversion is that Paul identified the figure with the Christ, Jesus.

Paul was not the sole apocalypticist in early Christianity. Apocalyp-

ticism was one salient characteristic of early Christian communities and
no doubt reflects an aspect of Jesus' teaching. Paul does not write florid
apocalypses, possibly because he was trying to temper the wild apocalyptic fervor of some of his readers—for example, his Thessalonian congregation, who were in danger of becoming full-blown millenarians. Paul does
encourage apocalyptic thinking whenever he discusses resurrection, true
to his mystic conception of the rapidly dawning new age. Paul's most
characteristic topics are typical of apocalypticism. Paul's discussion of the
body, both natural and spiritual, reflects an apocalyptic view of the world.
Paul does not distinguish between flesh and spirit within a single body.
Rather he distinguishes between the flesh, those who have not heard or
spurned the gospel, and the spirit, those who have accepted it, thus dividing humanity neatly into two categories, those within Christianity who
have become one with Christ's resurrection through transformation and
those who remain without.[14] Although Paul polemicizes against his enemies, he does not exclude either Christians or Jews from the saved. All
Israel is saved, he says, in typical Pharisaic manner (*pas 'Israel sōthēsetai*
[Rom. 11:26]). It is clear, however, that they will not be saved until they
are transformed spiritually.

Paul's tendency to divide history into two stages and to characterize
these stages as opposites is another apocalyptic trait. His distinctions
between flesh and spirit, law and grace, law and spirit, death and life, sin
and love, loss and gain, all reflect an apocalyptic dualism, though they
function in other ways as well. Like flesh and spirit, they sociologically
define an in-group and an out-group. These traits are also characteristic of
the thinking of a convert and a sectarian. These opposing terms define two
different groups within Christianity. These apocalyptic motifs augment
the commitment of the community, and they protect the recent convert
from disconfirming outside evidence. Wayne Meeks suggested that these
antinomies are related to the independent social organization of the early
gentile Christian community, as well as to the originally Palestinian apocalyptic movement.[15]

Paul's conversion brings an apocalyptic warrant to a new community,
which is stated in Gal. 1:4: "our Lord Jesus Christ, who gave himself for
our sins, in order to deliver us from the present evil age." This apocalyptic
end, brought about by Christ and perceptible through faith in him, allows
Paul to outline a new community. He speaks of his opponents who
preached "another gospel." From the point of view of the other Christians, of course, Paul is the innovator. He has radically renovated the
standards of Judaism by preaching that the gentiles can enter community

without circumcision and without the requirement to keep the Sabbath and festivals of the Jews.

For Paul, the innovations come not from him but from God. Paul emphasizes that his innovations are not based on human activities, as we have seen. His gospel was received through a revelation (Gal. 1:12; 1:16; 2:2). It is not he who says that Torah cannot be true in the way it had been before; rather, it is God himself who says this through the person of Jesus. In Galatians 3 and 4 Paul tries to explain this, giving examples that illumine his Pharisaic training in its new apocalyptic framework. The term *seed* in 2 Sam. 7:12 and hence also in Gen. 17:7 is used to refer to the messiah and is combined with Gen. 49:10: "Until there shall come the one to whom it belongs." Qumran also used this passage to discuss the apocalyptic end: "Until there shall come the legitimate Anointed One, the Shoot of David, for to him and his seed has been given the covenant of kingship for eternal generations" (4QPB 3). Paul takes this, as the covenanters at Qumran did, to imply a limitation solved by the arrival of an agent. But Paul goes further. He not only insists that the messiah has come but deduces that some ordinances were valid only until the messiah came. This includes (possibly progressively in his ministry) the whole body of commandments that distinguish Jews from gentiles.[16]

APOCALYPTICISM AND MILLENARIANISM IN THESSALONICA

Like the Qumran sectarians, Paul was an apocalypticist, differing in that he recommended that the community live within the world. Paul's sense of his duty was, however, urgent because he expected Christ's parousia imminently. The movements of Jesus and John the Baptist closely follow the patterns of other apocalyptic movements, which have been more carefully observed by modern anthropologists and sociologists.[17] In his possibly earliest correspondence, to the church at Thessalonica, Paul discusses his apocalypticism and its limitations. He writes first of his great pleasure that the Thessalonians had turned from idols to God (1 Thess. 1:9).[18] This suggests that the congregation was largely gentile. Further, he exhorts them to treat their wives as befits a Christian and not in passion and lust, as the gentiles do (1 Thess. 4:3–8). This can be seen as an answer to a specific problem that arose in Thessalonica or, more likely, as a standard part of Jewish proselyte paraenesis. The most striking aspect of this letter, however, is his discussion of his apocalyptic hopes:

But we would not have you ignorant, brethren, concerning those who are asleep, that you may not grieve as others do who have no hope. For since we believe that Jesus died and rose again, even so, through Jesus, God will bring with him those who have fallen asleep. For this we declare to you by the word of the Lord, that we who are alive, who are left until the coming of the Lord, shall not precede those who have fallen asleep. For the Lord himself will descend from heaven with a cry of command, with the archangel's call, and with the sound of the trumpet of God. And the dead in Christ will rise first; then we who are alive, who are left, shall be caught up together with them in the clouds to meet the Lord in the air; and so we shall always be with the Lord. Therefore comfort one another with these words. (1 Thess. 4:13–18)

Some of the community have died, raising doubts about the anticipated consummation. Paul turns his attention from those who have died to those who have felt the loss, consoling them with his confidence that the parousia will not be long delayed. As a confirmed apocalypticist, he speaks as though he himself will see it. Though Paul does not elaborate a vision of the end of time, he does volunteer, probably in answer to a direct question, a brief description of the awaited consummation: "For you, brethren, became imitators of the churches of God in Christ Jesus which are in Judea; for you suffered the same things from your own countrymen as they did from the Jews, who killed both the Lord Jesus and the prophets, and drove us out, and displease God and oppose all men by hindering us from speaking to the gentiles that they may be saved—so as always to fill up the measure of their sins. But God's wrath has come upon them at last!" (1 Thess. 2:14–16).

The Thessalonian problem comes from hostile gentiles, but Paul takes the opportunity to build a typology, showing them that the behavior must be expected since the Jews, the relatives and friends of Jesus and the disciples, also persecuted them. This is based on the tradition that prophets were persecuted by their hearers. But it goes far beyond this, certifying that the church already knew of and perhaps exaggerated Jewish opposition to the church. From the strength of the vituperation we know that the Thessalonians are in grave danger from their gentile neighbors. The deaths in the community might have been caused by persecution. It is the crisis of the martyrdom of the saints, who keep God's law, that most often raises the issue of resurrection in Jewish tradition (see Dan. 12:2, 2 Maccabees 7). Paul relies on Jewish tradition, albeit in a hostile way, to answer their question, illustrating one ironic way in which Jewish apocalyptic traditions entered the wider gentile world.

Paul is concerned about the commitment of his community in the face of this crisis. The letter begins by reminding them of their conversion, a commitment that they have already made: "What a welcome we had among you, and how you turned [*epestrepsate*] to God from idols, to serve a living and true God, and to wait for his Son from heaven, whom he raised from the dead, Jesus who delivers us from the wrath to come" (1 Thess. 1:9, 10). The use of the term *epestrepsate* signifies that the conversion is from paganism to the living God. Any pagan conversion to Christianity would have been thus, but the added dimension is that the Thessalonians must expect the arrival from heaven of God's son, who will protect them in the coming wrath. Paul also describes a conversion that led to a separation between them and their relatives and neighbors; hostility came from those who were formerly their friends (1 Thess. 2:14), as the disciples experienced hostility.

Wayne Meeks suggests that Paul's words of consolation, which use language of kinship and friendship, are meant to emphasize to the Thessalonians how they have become a new community of relatives together: "He even reflects the typical convert's experience of being 'orphaned' in the word he chooses to speak of his pain at being separated from them. Thus the letter itself becomes part of a process of resocialization which undertakes to substitute a new identity, new social relations, and a new set of values for those which each person had absorbed in growing up."[19]

In his first letter to the Thessalonians, Paul exposes his apocalyptic scheme and uses apocalyptic language in the service of community definition. His opening thanksgiving leads to both a description of a theophany and a discussion of judgment (1:7–10). The theme is vindication of the oppressed Christians and the punishment of their oppressors. The converse is also discussed: "love of each one of all of you for one another" (1:3), as well as "patience and faith" under persecution (1:4). In 1 Thessalonians, the definition of community life is implicit in Paul's admonitions. It aims at a quietness of life (*hēsouchia*). The apocalyptic language is thus meant to instill community values, and it parallels the community's social situation. More often the intent of the apocalyptic language is consolation for persecution (*thlipsis*), the primary reason for Paul's letter to the Thessalonians: "For brothers, you have become imitators of the churches of God that are in Judea in Christ Jesus, because you have suffered the same things at the hands of your own people as they at the hands of the Judaeans" (2:14).

The isolation of the Pauline gentile community is evident in Paul's most apocalyptic statements.[20] Any groups with whom they formerly shared ties of kinship became their enemies. Like the Jews and unlike the many clubs and associations that were part of civic life of the Hellenistic world, the Christians were exclusive in the sense that no *truly committed* gentile Christian could maintan cult membership. Thus, Christianity was subversive to the basic religious institutions of gentile society. The Thessalonian correspondence exemplifies the social forces seen also in the modern period, where a small committed group of millenarians is found to be a civic threat because it separates children and spouses from their families. This is one of the major points of tension between the early church and its pagan neighbors.[21]

The picture of the community that arises from the Thessalonian correspondence is one of a radical, apocalyptic movement, expecting the end imminently and alienated by hostility from the wider world. The Thessalonians' separation is more obvious than in the Corinthian case, where the synagogue may have ostracized the Corinthians because the congregation was eating meat sacrificed to idols. This charge implies that the Corinthian community was at least partly integrated in pagan society.[22] Since Paul was one of the founders and leaders of the Thessalonian church, it is likely to have been Paul himself who communicated Jewish apocalypticism to his gentile churches, even mentioning his inability to visit as the hindrance of Satan (1 Thess. 2:18). Like the Qumran sectarians, Paul calls his coreligionists "the sons of light" and predicts that those "of darkness" or "of the night" will be destroyed as suddenly as a thief attacks in the night (1 Thess. 5:1–5).

Some Thessalonians took Paul's apocalypticism to an extreme.[23] In the second letter to the Thessalonians, attributed to Paul but probably not written by him, the persecutions have grown yet worse (2 Thess. 1:4). The suffering of the congregation is interpreted as the first sign that the wrath of God will fall on the persecutors. But, in an abrupt turnabout, Paul or some disciple writing in his name warns the Thessalonian congregation against any false letters or reports that claim that the day of the Lord has come. Some Christians, either in the community or elsewhere, must have been prophesying not just that the judgment approached but that it had actually started. Such an exaggerated claim, along with a stern warning against idleness ("If anyone will not work, let him not eat" [3:10]), might indicate that some early Christian communities actually became millenarian cults, stopping work entirely because they expected the effects of God's judgment day immediately. The author of 2 Thessalonians warns that this is too radical. The community should continue its ordinary social and economic life with the confidence that God will bring his judgment soon and at a moment known only to him.

The whole Thessalonian correspondence shows how originally Jewish apocalyptic ideas could be transmitted to a gentile Christian community. Apocalypticism, like the European millennialism it spawned, operates like social revolution, except that it concentrates on reforming the religious symbols of the society rather than the political order (insofar as they can be distinguished). The potential converts must first be disposed to interpret their lives in religious terms and then must feel that commitment to the new religious movement remedies some lack in their lives or gives them some benefit that they do not already have. Otherwise, they will simply foment political rebellion. Apocalypticism was endemic to Roman occupation, in Jewish as well as gentile lands. Jewish apocalypticism appealed to the disadvantaged members of gentile society, and, as Paul clarifies in Corinthians and Romans, taught them to despise the conventional civic rites of the establishment in their town as idolatry. Active rebellion did not break out, but even passive resistance became dangerous when the Roman emperors of the second and third centuries demanded for themselves public civic rites as immortal gods on earth. The emperors' claims were ironically similar to the immortal transformation the Christians had been preaching for a century or more. The persecutions that followed the failure of Christians and Jews to respect imperial wishes often evinced apocalyptic notions, pointing to an underlying broad dissatisfaction among the potential converts to Christianity and Judaism.

Many Pauline scholars admit that Paul lived in an active apocalyptic environment, sharing many of its assumptions.[24] Our understanding of apocalypticism has changed enormously over the past few years by the renewal of research in noncanonical Jewish literature, by the discovery of the Dead Sea Scrolls, and by the work of Gershom Scholem, who has shown that Jewish mysticism was a central part of apocalypticism. Apocalypticism continued in Judaism as a living tradition only in the texts of the merkabah mystics, which had hitherto been supposed to be medieval.[25] Scholars have recognized the ecstatic and mystical core of apocalypticism, revising their understanding of these ancient phenomena. Paul's writing fits especially well into the reinterpreted apocalypticism. The Thessalonian correspondence shows that Paul's conversion also gave him an apocalyptic sensibility, with many of the more traditional accoutrements of apocalypticism: an expectation of the imminent end of the world, an extremely cohesive community ideal, and a vivid distinction between the community of the saved and the damned—what we would also expect from a reading of the modern data on conversion. Paul's mystical-apocalyptic conversion experience evolved into an ideal pattern for gentile conversion to Christianity, though Paul himself brought it up to define his apostolate. He applied the pattern to Jews as well as gentiles, articulating his belief that all Jews must convert to become truly faithful Christians. But Luke and the pastoral Epistles revised the experience as repentance, fashioning Paul's apocalypticism and mysticism into a model of conversion for the God-fearers and gentiles.

Paul promulgates some surprising modifications in apocalypticism. After the Thessalonian correspondence he did not stress the traditional apocalyptic terminology of this age against the coming age or the terminology of the kingdom of God or the day of the Lord. Though striking, these adjustments can be understood as necessary, not only because of the possible overinterpretation of his words in Thessalonica, but because of his positive conviction that Christ's resurrection has stimulated the beginning of the new age. These facts might have led Paul to eschew long apocalyptic speculations about the coming eschaton or the structure of heaven. Nevertheless, there is evidence in Paul's writing of the traditional vocabulary, antinomies, and dualism that characterizes apocalypticism, as well as Paul's vision that the end is coming: "Through him we have obtained access to this grace in which we stand, and we rejoice in our hope of sharing the Glory of God" (Rom. 5:2). This apocalyptic hope, begun by conversion experience and confirmed by the special rites of Pauline gentile community—baptism and the Lord's supper—was substituted for the special laws of Judaism and made a continuing commitment possible.

PAULINE COMMUNITY

As an apocalyptic Jew and a radical convert, Paul naturally envisioned strong boundaries between outsiders and insiders (1 Cor. 5:12; 1 Thess. 4:12; 2 Cor. 6:14–7:1). Wayne Meeks has catalogued a remarkable, if not exhaustive list of the apocalyptic terms used in 1 Corinthians.[26] In 2 Corinthians, Paul distinguishes between insiders and outsiders and excoriates his churches not to allow themselves to be fooled by those seeming Christians who do not support Paul's apostolate. They are outsiders and anyone who associates with them becomes an outsider. In such a bitter internal dispute, Paul uses language that sounds most like the exclusivity of the Dead Sea Scrolls:

> Do not be mismated with unbelievers. For what partnership have righteousness and iniquity? Or what fellowship has light with darkness? What accord has Christ with Belial? Or what has a believer in common with an unbeliever: What agreement has the temple of God with idols? For we are the temple of the living God; as God said,
>
> > "I will live in them and move among them,
> > and I will be their God,
> > and they shall be my people.
> > Therefore come out from them,
> > and be separate from them, says the Lord,
> > and touch nothing unclean;
> > then I will welcome you,
> > and I will be a father to you,
> > and you shall be my sons and daughters,
> > says the Lord almighty."
>
> Since we have these promises, beloved, let us cleanse ourselves from every defilement of body and spirit, and make holiness perfect in the fear of God. (2 Cor. 6:14–7:1)

The phraseology is not typically Pauline. This fact along with the strength of the invective has led some commentators to think that this fragment is non-Pauline, although it has been ascribed to Paul and is enclosed in the anthology of writings known as 2 Corinthians. The passage contains two requirements necessary for a scholarly judgment of interpolation. The subject matter of the passage has no real connection with its present context and the passage reads more smoothly with the section removed. It is also possible that the fragment was originally part of another Pauline letter to the Corinthians and has been included there.[27] However, the theme of God's residence in the community is crucially Pauline.

The discovery of the Qumran writings has thrown new light on this passage.[28] Paul is either directly quoting or otherwise relying on material that comes out of an apocalyptic environment similar to Qumran. The role Christ plays in the fragment substitutes either for God directly or one of the principal angels of Jewish apocalypticism, such as Michael, Melchizedek, the Spirit or Angel of Truth, or the Angel of Light, as at Qumran. The demonic opponent to the community is called Belial, as at Qumran. The world is divided into believers and unbelievers. Many of the terms dividing the world into light and darkness, the saved and the damned, the notion of the community as the temple of God, the need for purification, are direct parallels to Jewish apocalyptic in general and Qumran in particular. In the Pauline context, the fragment furthers Paul's recommendation that the Corinthians welcome Paul and not support those who refuse to welcome him. Paul says that not to welcome him is to behave like an unbeliever, for whom he has nothing but apocalyptic scorn. Paul could be talking about Christian unbelievers (2 Cor. 4:4) rather than outsiders, but in apocalypticism, as elsewhere, unbelievers and outsiders are equally scorned.

The passage might have been inspired by or copied from some lost Essene writing, making it possible that Paul rather than an editor took it for himself because it fit his context perfectly. In any case, Paul is using a style of invective that early Christianity inherited from Jewish apocalypticism; the social context of early Christianity presupposes an equally committed, highly cohesive group, such as was also found at Qumran, though most Christians did not live separate from society, as many of the Dead Sea Scroll sectarians did. Given Christianity's birth as an apocalyptic community, it would be surprising if invective like this did not surface occasionally.

Paul expressly identifies the Christian community with the Temple of God (cf. 1 Cor. 3:16–17). This concept of community is prominent in Qumran. Paul links the community to the purity rules of Lev. 26:12 by means of a loose quotation from Ezek. 37:27 (LXX), which he interprets in an eschatological manner. As in Ezekiel, the pronouns from Leviticus are changed from the original second person to the third: "I will live in them and move among them, and I will be their God and they shall be my people" (2 Cor. 6:16). For Paul, as it might have been at Qumran, this prophecy has been fulfilled. In Qumran the angels could be found in the sectarian community, because the sectarians themselves scrupulously enforced the necessary purity rules, making possible the angels' presence. Unlike Qumran, Paul finds the fulfillment of the verse in the incarnation of Jesus that has ushered in the beginning of the messianic age. But the purity rules are themselves irrelevant. The church has thus become the people of God, and as God dwells among them, they are now as holy as God's temple. By saying that the body is a temple and that God's spirit dwells in it, Paul has transferred God's presence from the physical temple, the center of the purity rules, to the believers and the community to which they belong. This dualism is typical of Qumran sectarianism, though Paul develops the theme uniquely, dropping out the cultic requirements and using his vocabulary of spirit (see Rom. 8:9).[29]

COMMANDMENTS AND PURITY LAWS

E. P. Sanders has shown that Paul sometimes relies on the vocabulary of law, which he is so much against in his discussion of salvation, when he is discussing communal ethics.[30] Paul calls the behavior of Christians "keeping the commandments" (*entolai*) of God (1 Cor. 7:19). The phrase "every good work" in 2 Cor. 9:8 implies the same, as does "any other commandment" in Rom. 13:9, since he states that the one law of love includes many commandments. Paul thus appears occasionally to approve of the commandments of Judaism and to recommend them as ethical models for Christian behavior, if the issue is ethical behavior rather than the salvation process. Such an ambiguous use of vocabulary leads to a logical impasse whenever a modern exegete attempts to write a systematic account of Paul's theology. But systematic theology was not Paul's purpose. Paul was not trying to outlaw Torah so much as he was trying to express how his gentile Christian society could maintain its concept of community and its commitment without what we would call the ceremonial laws. His principle was not systematically to avoid Torah or deny it categorically but to eliminate the special laws of Judaism from his definition of conversion to Christianity, thus stressing Torah only where clarification was needed or where anyone might talk about law.

E. P. Sanders does not maintain my hypothesis explaining Paul's behavior, but he sums up the paradox of Paul's use of law admirably by asserting that the negative statements of law arise only in the context of membership requirements, where faith is to be the only criterion. The positive statements derive from questions of behavior within the Christian community. When discussing the value of law, Paul sought to answer practical questions, and there he could rely on the usual Jewish language for dealing with the problems. Paul's search for ways to express his new concept of community was obscured by terms taken from his Pharisaic past, obscured even from those who know rabbinic Judaism because he begins from assumptions that no rabbi would make. But, like the rabbis and Qumranites, he often used the language of purity to discuss ethics.

Having located his churches in the houses of prominent patrons, Paul's discussions of moral precepts within the community resemble the traditional Hellenistic tables of household ethics. Paul often uses the terms of cultic purity, so strong in Qumran and other parts of the Jewish community, for describing the ideal state of morality within the Christian community.[31] Paul warns: "If any one destroys God's temple, God will destroy him. For God's Temple is holy and, that temple you are" (1 Cor. 3:17), again depending on the identification of Christian community with the attendant purity of Temple itself. Immorality is thus a crime of desecration against God's new Temple. Though Paul's ethical system is designed for the interim until the final consummation, the Christian community must still enforce purity on itself, as the Qumran community enforced cultic purity for the expected *eschaton*. But the concept of purity is reinterpreted in strictly moral terms. In 1 Cor. 5:1 the man openly living with his father's wife must be expelled from the community lest he further contaminate the group, as a little yeast leavens the whole loaf (5:2, 13). The dominant metaphor is the special laws having to do with Passover, which Paul has allegorized to bring out the distinction between malice and evil, to be put away like the old leaven, and sincerity and truth, to be fostered as unleavened bread for the festival. Paul also uses the ordinary rituals of Judaism as a symbol for his new community. One may not eat with sinners (1 Cor. 5:11). They are to be driven out of the group. Elsewhere Paul uses uncleanness (*akatharsia*) to mean impurity of any kind, but he links it with the crime of sexual immorality (*porneia*) (2 Cor. 12:21; Gal. 5:19).[32] The documents from Qumran show us that this is typical of Jewish mystical and apocalyptic thinking; cultic purity is demanded wherever God is to be encountered.

The clearest example of Paul's use of the language of cultic holiness is the passage in 1 Cor. 6:12–20 where he discusses the purpose of the body in God's scheme and warns against the sins of sexual immorality. The theme of impurity and the argument against sexual misconduct is the same in Jewish mysticism and apocalypticism, where the body must be kept pure to commune with the holiest creatures of God in his heavenly temple: "Do you not know that your bodies are members of Christ? Shall I therefore take the members of Christ and make them members of a prostitute? Never! Do you not know that he who joins himself to a prostitute becomes one body with her? For, as it is written, 'The two shall become one flesh.' But he who is united to the Lord becomes one spirit with him. Shun immorality. Every other sin which a man commits is outside the body; but the immoral man sins against his own body. Do you not know that your body is a temple of the Holy Spirit within you, which you have from God? You are not your own; you were bought with a price. So glorify God in your body" (1 Cor. 6:15–20). The metaphor is still one of purity but it functions without explicit allegiance to the special laws of Judaism.

Paul sometimes compares his work of proclaiming the gospel to that of the priests who serve in the sanctuary (1 Cor. 9:13–14), claiming his personal vocation as a temple servant. Like the priests, he is entitled to a share in the sacrificial offerings. As such, Paul justifies earning his living from the gospel.[33] Paul speaks of Christ as a sacrificial offering. In Rom. 3:24–25 he states: "Christ Jesus, whom God put forward as an expiation [*hilastērion*] by his blood, to be received by faith." Paul also envisions Christians as both priests and living sacrifices offered to God within the temple: "I appeal to you therefore, brethren, by the mercies of God, to present your bodies as a living sacrifice, holy and acceptable to God, which is your spiritual worship. Do not be conformed to the world but be transformed by the renewal of your mind, that you may prove what is the will of God, what is good and acceptable and perfect" (Rom. 12:1–2).

Rom. 12:1–2 is another example of the transformation imagery in Paul. It is interesting that this language, which is central to Paul's own conversion, appears in the context of a spiritual approach to God for sacrifice. He constructs the passage with the technical vocabulary for making sacrifices, emphasizing his suggestion that the Romans make the sacrifice of their bodies as a holy service and describing a mystical identification with Christ through suffering.[34] This parallels the role that Paul has outlined for Christ as a sacrifice. The whole concept of purity is bound to his idea of mystical identification with Christ. Parallels between heavenly sacrifice and the earthly service of the congregation are common both in rabbinic Judaism and Qumran. Paul uses a new vocabulary for describing the inner unity of the Christian church, a vocabulary that will make sense of the world's opposition and encourage believers to persevere in trials. Though it is new, it is not wholly unprecedented in Judaism. The language appears in rabbinic literature afterward as well. But it is not the central aspect of Pharisaic views of Jewish commitment. Instead, Paul plays on the approach to God again as the proper place to talk of transformation to a new being.

THE HOUSE CHURCH

Acts relates that Paul's missionary efforts within the synagogue met with considerable opposition, as occasionally did his efforts with pagans. Thereafter, so Acts claims, Paul withdraws to a private house in which he founds the church under the patronage of some prominent person. Acts might be exaggerating, but it credibly describes the typical process by which many kinds of brotherhoods and civic associations, including synagogues, were founded. As the new movement continued to attract followers, it became a separate body from the synagogue. Paul's own writing also leads us to believe that his churches existed separately from those of his Jewish Christian brothers, and even more so from the synagogue. Though Paul may have meant to reconstitute the remnant of Israel, the effect of his preaching was to create a third group, neither gentile nor Jew, because of the lack of acceptance that these ideas found within the Jewish and Jewish Christian community.

For Paul the ideal of community is to be realized immediately. After arising from the baptismal waters, the members of the new community are free to eat and interact with each other as equals. All are one in the new community risen with the body of Christ, found in baptism, and remembered in the eucharistic blessing over wine and bread. Paul used this language, rather than the traditional language of repentance and return in Judaism, because he had undergone such a baptismal experience when he entered the Christian community. The effect of the use of baptism as the central rite made women full ritual partners with men in Christian communities. Though women might actually have retained an inferior place in society, and though slaves, out of necessity, must have been returned to their masters, Paul felt that the distinctions between Jew and gentile, which were based on ritual status, could be erased by new rituals of unity. Perhaps in this he overestimated the effect of his writing or simply did not see that others' experience of Christianity was so entirely different that it would take years to bridge the gap.[35]

According to Wayne Meeks, the Pauline language of separation and the ritual of initiation defined a totally new form of community, in effect a ritually defined ideal to which the Hellenistic house church aspired. The gentile Christian communities that Paul founded and encouraged had little contact with the synagogues of the Diaspora. The church (ekklesia), this new church meeting in houses, is supposed to be marked by sacredness, homogeneity, and unity—that is, communitas.[36] Thus, it marks off a new community.

This church entered by baptism in Christ became known as the body of Christ. The terminology is apocalyptic, paralleling developments in the Qumran community, but there is an underlying social strategy as well. In Natural Symbols, Mary Douglas has shown that the human body is used as a symbol for society when the unity of the various parts needs to be stressed.[37] Paul's use of the metaphor of the body of Christ defines the social group of the new believers and suggests a pattern for ethics: all those who perform rites derived from but not the same as Judaism can enter the new community and are to be resurrected. Ethics arise because nothing that Christians do, either Jews or gentiles, males or females, slaves or free, should separate the unity of the saved. Thus all should treat each other with love, equality, and humility.[38]

THE EUCHARIST

Paul's writings give us less information about the other major ritual of early Christianity, the Lord's Supper (*kyriakon deipnon* [1 Cor. 11:20]). Both Jews and gentiles possessed religious customs associated with home entertaining. Festive meals were characteristic of the voluntary associations of the Hellenistic world, from the Jewish Sabbath and feasts to the rites of the mystery religions and the *symposia* philosophical schools. The Passover seder of Judaism was and continues to be deeply influenced by the customs and etiquette of Hellenistic dinner parties, though it certainly did not contain the lasciviousness of some Hellenistic entertainments.[39] The earliest church set about to memorialize and commemorate Jesus in ritual and tradition, taking their cue from the meal rituals ascribed to Jesus.[40] It would have been natural for the Christian community to have instituted such meals in ritual remembrance of Jesus' last meal with his disciples. The Eucharist was already a major theme of the meal during Paul's time: "This cup is the new covenant in my blood. Do this, as often as you drink it, in rememberance of me" (1 Cor. 11:24). Memorial dinners were even a feature of family piety in the ancient world, where burial clubs hosted such ceremonies for the deceased. But commemoration would have included not just Jesus' memory but the partnership of the believer in his death and an eschatological element of the commemoration quickening the time of his return.[41] That memorial rituals were common in Hellenistic homes underscores the new location of Pauline gentile congregations; rabbinic rituals associated with Passover prevent us from thinking that such rituals can arise from the gentile Christians alone.

Paul discusses the community's meal of commemoration in several places. In Galatians, which is notoriously lacking in apocalyptic themes because it is concerned with the threatened unity of the congregation, the antinomies of Jew and gentile are discussed in the most detail. In 1 Corinthians and Romans, the issue of communal dining threatens disunity. Paul states, unequivocally, that the old ceremonies of Judaism, especially circumcision, are of absolutely no account in the new community of Christianity. Discord must be overcome in unity. Since Paul himself had overcome the distinction between Jew and gentile in his own life, he saw no reason why the unity of Christianity could not encompass both; and he did not misjudge the issue. The bonds separating Jew and gentile could be overcome more quickly than the institutions preventing women and slaves' equality, though the boundary between Jews and Christians itself was not overcome quickly. Paul's baptismal ideal of Christian unity was never policy until the Jewish Christians were so small a faction as to be incapable of withstanding the pressure from the majority. In the end, they were declared heretics and purged, which is hardly what Paul had in mind. The issue for Paul is the management of diversity, so that it does not become divisive. Unity is possible if the diversity that can lead to disunity in the community is overcome.

JUSTIFICATION BY FAITH

So much has been written about Paul's concept of justification that a systematic discussion is impractical.[42] Rather, there is an aspect of Paul's discussion of this important topic that is illuminated by his status as convert and by thinking carefully about the community to which he was writing. Although Paul may not have meant to define a new theology by using the language of justification, he was trying to define a new apocalyptic community.[43]

Although Paul's use of the terminology of justification by faith is original, it is not unprecedented in first-century Judaism or Christianity. The precedents were not particularly evident until the Dead Sea Scrolls, the writings of the Essene community at Qumran, were read closely. A similar vocabulary of justification was used by the Qumran community in describing God's justice for the believer and the coming apocalyptic end. Given the similarity, it is possible that Paul was intimately familiar with Essene theology. His invective starting in 2 Cor. 6:14 has close affinities with Qumranite polemic. It is possible that before his conversion to Christianity Paul had observed the Essenes in close detail. Though the Essenes kept their secrets to themselves, they were also visible to the Jewish community and to travelers. Since Paul might have been a religiously questing intellectual, like Philo before him and Josephus after him, he might have been attracted to an Essene community.[44] But there is not a line in Paul's letters that gives us a clue to the relationship.

It is safer to assume that the relationship between Paul and Qumran was analogical, deriving from similar social situations. The community at Qumran was comprised of converts and Paul was also a convert, albeit to a different Jewish sect. Having converted, he might have developed ideas about the importance of God's actions in a fashion similar to other converts in the Hellenistic Jewish world. Although the idea of justification is not unique to Qumran or Paul, Qumranite and Pauline writings are the two major locations of the idea in first-century Jewish documents. The similarities are striking.[45]

Though the concept of justification is present in first-century Judaism, it is crucial to Paul, who works out the problem thoroughly. But there is an important difference between Paul and his Jewish contemporaries in discussing justification. The rabbis, for instance, felt that individuals maintained righteousness through observing God's commandments, but they were not convinced that humanity was helpless against sin. Paul maintains that it is through faith, as opposed to observance of the commandments, that righteousness is attained. The rabbis maintained that the commandments themselves are an aspect of God's mercy. Paul emphasizes that justification is something that God grants in response to faith, and though the rabbis would not disagree, they did not see Torah and faith in opposition. Further, they see salvation both as deliverance from personal danger and as admission to the world to come, benefits that God gives to those who practiced his laws. But rabbinic literature did not characteristically use this language.

Paul's desire to discuss justification is more characteristic of sectarian groups like Qumran than the rabbis; a more striking parallel with Qumran is his assertion that without God's direct intervention for salvation an individual is irretrievably lost. The part of the Pauline doctrine that bears the closest resemblance to Qumranite thinking is Paul's conviction that all humans are sinners, requiring the intervention of God's grace to be justified. This is a thought found often in the Dead Sea Scrolls (IQS 11):

For to God belongs my justification [*mishpati*]
And the perfection [*tom*] of my way [*darki*] is in His Hand, with the
  uprightness [*yesod*] of my heart [*levavi*]. And by His righteousness
  [*sidkato*] is my sin [*pish'i*] blotted out. (v. 2)

And from the fount [*makor*] of His righteousness [*sidkato*] comes my
  justification [*mishpati*].
The light in my heart are from his wondrous mysteries. (v. 5)

I am of wicked humanity, of the assembly of perverse flesh.
  My transgressions, my sins, my wickedness are from the depravity
  of my heart. (v. 9)

For although humanity has its own way, it cannot establish its own
    steps.
For justice [hamishpat] belongs to God
And from His hand comes perfection of way.
All things are by His understanding
Every being is established by His thought
Without Him nothing is made.

As for me, if I stumble
God's loving kindness [hisde el] is my salvation. (v. 106–12)

Nils A. Dahl, who noted the relevance of these passages to Paul, points out the difficulties in finding exactly the right rendering of the words, not only given their Pauline association but also given the way in which Paul is interpreted among Protestant communities (98). It is difficult to deny that in this and many other Qumran passages, there is an uncanny correspondence with Paul's expressions of justification by faith. Righteousness comes only through God's saving grace, since man is by nature sinful. God's justice or righteousness saves. God's righteousness is not strict justice in the sense of revenge, for it includes his mercy, as it does throughout Judaism, especially rabbinic Judaism. Though this parallel might show that Paul was influenced by the community that left us the Dead Sea Scrolls, it also shows that Paul's doctrines are not to be understood merely as opposition to midrash or the Septuagint, as others have assumed. A more complicated and subtle dynamic is operating.

The psychology of conversion suggests some reasons for the similarity between Pauline and Qumranite discussions of sin.[46] While there is a great deal of controversy in psychological literature about the actual psychological state of a subject before conversion, there is little controversy about the retrospective reports of converts about their states of mind before conversion. After conversion, converts report that their lives before conversion were troubled, describing conversion as the experience of salvation from their past, a free gift operating from outside them. Pauline discussions and especially Lukan characterizations of Paul have actively shaped conversion behavior in the West and continue to do so. Feelings of guilt and the act of surrendering, however, are characteristic of the reports of persons who have undergone *sudden* conversions in our society.[47]

Concurrently, converts report heightened feelings of purpose after conversion.[48] The theory of cognitive dissonance predicates that a highly cohesive group would better confirm and preserve an individual decision of such magnitude by erecting high boundaries between themselves and the disbelieving world. Thus, conversion communities tend to be both more cohesive than and hostile to the outside world. These feelings help maintain commitment to the group after conversion.

What is automatically seen as Paul's great theological insight was a chracteristic perception of sectarian groups in the first century. What the first century termed faith, we might see closely associated with the commitment that comes from living in a small embattled minority community. Justification therefore is probably one of the basic vocabularies of first-century Jews for discussing conversion and its subsequent high levels of commitment to a sectarian group, with its attendant feelings of salvation and subsequent personal meaningfulness. The language of justification, far from being only Pauline, appears also in John, the letter to the Hebrews, and even in 1 Peter and the pastoral Epistles. It is not, of course, as common elsewhere as it is in Paul, for whom it was a major topic. Hence the language of justification appears to have a definite origin in early Christian tradition, as the response and product of converted minds, possibly as part of the *kerygma* of the early church.

One example of the use of the term for justification elsewhere in the New Testament appears in Luke: the tax collector goes "down to his house justified" (18:14). The language was present in early New Testament traditions, and it is preeminently developed by Paul, though it is not his invention.[49] Paul could have learned the language of justification from his Christian compatriots after he entered the Christian community. It is part of the usual language available to Jews to express their feelings after conversion to a particular sect.

There are some unique aspects to Paul's doctrine, which not only distinguish Christianity from Essenism, but also distinguish Paul from other Christian writers. In 1 Cor. 6:9–11, for example, Paul stresses a fact that he regards as well-known: "Do you not know that the unrighteous will not inherit the kingdom of God? Do not be deceived; neither the immoral, nor idolaters, nor adulterers, nor sexual perverts, nor thieves, nor the greedy, nor drunkards, nor revilers, nor robbers will inherit the kingdom of God. And such were some of you. But you were washed, you were sanctified, you were justified in the name of the Lord Jesus Christ and in the Spirit of our God." Paul's rhetoric reminds his readers of something he assumes they already know: some of those justified needed repentance, demonstrating that the concept of justification was general in early Christianity, as well as Qumran. The progression of washing, sanctification, and justification suggests that Paul is relying on their experience, possibly even a liturgical fragment, making reference to baptism and the process of crossing the border into the community. The order is washing, sanctification, then being judged righteous. Interestingly, justification is not linked to faith explicitly but to the agency of the name of Jesus, suggesting again a special tradition of Jesus as the divine name in baptism.

The similarities between the Qumranites and Christianity should again be noted. Both were conversion communities; both used baptism. In each case, the rite formalized the distinction between the convert's previous life of sin and the new life within the saved community. Spiritual cleansing explicitly allowed the convert to enter the adopted community. Yet the parallelism highlights the difference between the Dead Sea Scrolls and the New Testament. Only those already initiated were admitted to the rite at Qumran, and the rite was performed as a daily ablution. Their rite of baptism was not strictly a rite of admission, but a rite maintaining the purity that was acquired by the initiate on entering the community. In both cases, however, the rite was associated with the community's claim that it approached the divinity in visions and had first-person witnesses of the divine presence. Ritual purity in Judaism was designed to enable one to approach God in his temple with a sacrifice. For this reason ritual baths are closely associated with the ecstatic journey to God's throne in heaven in Jewish mysticism.

The sociological location of Essenes and Christians is in sharp contrast. The Qumran community was a priestly community whose headquarters were far from the centers of civilization. It was also radically literal in performing the biblical immersion rituals. Primitive Christianity was ambivalent and sometimes hostile to issues of ritual purity in Judaism. Paul's version of Christianity was suited to gentile Christians living in proximity to the Jewish Diaspora but not part of it. To Paul the special laws of Judaism were to become entirely irrelevant. His teachings eventually helped turn the tide against the most ritually conservative members of the church in favor of the burgeoning gentile Christian community. Thus the unique aspect of the Pauline teaching of justification by faith is not the concept of justification. Paul's contribution is the role that faith (as opposed to ritual law) plays in it:

> Now we know that whatever the law says it speaks to those who are under the law, so that every mouth may be stopped, and the whole

world may be held accountable to God. For no human being will be justified in his sight by works of the law, since through the law comes knowledge of sin. But now the righteousness of God has been manifested apart from law, although the law and the prophets bear witness to it, the righteousness of God through faith in Jesus Christ for all who believe. For there is no distinction; since all have sinned and fall short of the glory of God, they are justified by his grace as a gift, through the redemption which is in Christ Jesus, whom God put forward as an expiation by his blood, to be received by faith. This was to show God's righteousness, because in his divine forbearance he had passed over former sins; it was to prove at the present time that he himself is righteous and that he justifies him who has faith in Jesus. (Rom. 3:19–26)

Nils A. Dahl suggests that this passage contains a rough paraphrase of a confessional formulation to which Paul has brought his personal emphasis of faith; for instance, the "through faith" (*dia pisteōs*) in verse 25 is likely to be a Pauline comment. Evidently, the pre-Pauline text spoke of the righteousness of God, rather like Essene thought. Paul agrees with these formulations of confidence in God's grace, as well as the structure of sinfulness prior to conversion, righteousness, sanctification, and redemption—in this case by means of Christ, rather than by God directly as in Qumran. It is likely that the contrast between prior and current states is drawn more sharply in Christianity than in Essenism, because Christianity uniquely in Judaism stressed a single baptism. Essenism centered on gradual initiations into the cult's ecstatic mysteries. The gradual initiation and purification ceremonies at Qumran were not designed to elicit a single emotional response. Rather, they were designed to slowly increase the ritual purity of the initiate until a few could be called on to learn the angelic names that mediate the divine presence: "He [the proselyte] swears, moreover, to transmit the rules exactly as he himself received them; to abstain from robbery; and in like manner carefully to preserve the books of the sect and the names of the angels" (Josephus, *Jewish War* 2.142). Christian baptism is all the more important because of its nonrepeated, single action, making the believer participate in the saving event of Jesus' resurrection from the dead, which is nearly contemporaneous with the action of justification. Christian literature constantly shows that this single action could be accompanied by strong emotional experience. Josephus and Philo, both concerned with justifying Jewish culture to a Roman audience, take pains to show how sober and rational are the Essenes, an appreciation that would be lost to us if we were to view them only from the Dead Sea Scrolls.

The social implications of these similarities are striking. A direct link between early Christian circles and the Qumran sect remains a possibility, but the similar language can also be understood as typical first-century Jewish reactions to similar social situations. Both in Qumran and early Christianity the process of personal salvation was inaugurated by membership in a religious sect, which considered itself a new covenantal congregation. The language of sin and justification reflects the high social cohesion that existed both at Qumran and the early apocalyptic Jewish community, because it deflects the hostility of the majority of the Jewish community at the same time as it obviously also generates hostility. Another function of the language, however, is to seal off the group from contradictory and conflicting evidence about the nature of conversion experience, which is typical of sectarian groups everywhere. But the particular language of sin and redemption is part of the vocabulary of first-century conversion literature in Judaism, as the romance *Joseph and Asenath* has shown. In that book, there is an angelophany, confirming the importance of the conversion, although there is little apocalyptic language.

Paul's doctrine of justification by faith alone and not by law goes considerably beyond what was current in the language of sectarian experience in the first century. It must reflect his own experience and insight, as it was revealed to him both in his conversion and his subsequent personal history within the church. Again we find that he is not working out a systematic theology; rather, he uses scripture to understand his own experience, both in conversion and in the community he joined. His explanation becomes the basis of more general discussions within the Christian community. Paul's discussion of faith begins in personal experience and involves itself in the text of the Scripture, as for any Jew, before attempting to generalize about the meaning of the experience for his society.[50]

The doctrine of justification by faith is illuminated for Paul by Hab. 2:4, which states that the righteous shall live by faith. In Gal. 3:12, Paul reads Habbakuk as contradicting the notion that Torah justifies. In Qumran the same verse was used to prove that those who observe Torah in the house of Judah will be saved (1QpHab 7.17–8.2). Paul returns to the converse conclusion. In Rom. 10:5, he states: "Moses writes that the man who practices righteousness which is based on the law shall live by it." Paul's exegesis depends on the presupposition that faith and works contradict each other, that they exclude each other and cannot be rectified. This is not a perception that any other sect of Judaism would have promulgated and I doubt that it was a serious part of Christianity before Paul. It is a perception that Paul traces to his entrance into the Christian community, when his Pharisaic meaning system was overturned by his experience of the crucified and risen Christ. It articulates a new community with a new moral understanding of gentile-Jewish relationships.

In Romans, which is usually viewed as Paul's latest letter and most mature thought, Paul returns to the theme, began in Galatians, that faith and law appear to be contradictory. Torah is from God, it was good and holy: Paul asserts that God never intended the Torah to last forever; rather, it was a temporary measure, valid only until the coming of Christ. Paul's own life could easily serve as the example for this, since he himself had passed from Pharisaism to Christianity. Again, it is no accident that the story of Abraham is used as the figure illustrating the limitation of Torah, for Abraham is used traditionally in Judaism to model the faith of converts.[51] For Paul, Abraham becomes not only the model for the faith of the convert but the model of the sinner who receives justification by faith. God promised and Abraham believed, even before he was circumcised; therefore, circumcision cannot be a precondition for the fulfillment of the promise. In midrash, Abraham's circumcision as an adult provided a different kind of exemplar. Although Paul's logic here can hardly be called airtight, his point is plain enough: the fulfillment of God's promises cannot depend on adherence to Torah. Those who believe in Christ, and especially those to whom his rhetoric is most turned, the gentile Christians, are the true children of Abraham. Gentile Christians need not become Jews, not even in part, in order to become full members of the church. According to Acts, much of the church accepted that gentile Christians do not need circumcision. So Paul hardly invented or singlehandedly promulgated the idea. He is merely its most famous proponent.

It is not by accident that we find in this context of a discussion of the doctrine of justification the quotation, "There is neither Jew nor Greek, there is neither slave nor free, there is neither male nor female; for you are all one in Christ Jesus" (Gal. 3:28; cf. 5:6; 6:15; Rom. 3:29–31; 10:12–13). This statement is the baptismal formula that defines the new church in Paul's thinking. Paul stresses that justification occurs specifically through faith, which is described by means of the baptismal formula; as a result, he can only mean that justification is brought about by faith in Christ. Faith and baptism belong together, because baptism is the social ceremony marking faith as present, signifying that the believer has entered Christ; undergoing baptism evokes the experience of death and rebirth in Christ, a sharing in his resurrection. Baptism does not mark the beginning of a life of Torah observance, dependent on circumcision, as it would in an ordinary conversion to Judaism. It marks the beginning of a new life not based on fleshly observances. Paul is not making an abstract theological statement in his discussion of justification. He is reflecting on his own experience, having himself retreated to the moral and ceremonial life of a God-fearer after having been first a Pharisee. This parallels Paul's experience and participation in the gentile Christian mission. That Paul's arguments are fitted to missionary work has been noted often before.[52] How his theology actually reflects community norms has not been adequately emphasized; indeed, one wonders how much of Paul's reliance on the exegetical intricacies of Jewish Scriptures was lost on his gentile audience. Paul was probably arguing these things out for himself, and the gentile church, which was not as skilled as he in the Pharisaic science of exegesis, became the heirs to his personal ruminations. Paul's concept of the salvation of gentiles was not an innovation in Judaism, but his reflections on his own personal experience are a unique definition of community.

Paul's new community was itself a kind of Pharisaism transformed and made applicable to gentile converts. Instead of Pharisaic rules of community differentiation, Paul substitutes a faith commitment and a pledge to keep the purity rules in a spiritual, symbolic way. The apocalyptic fervor that Paul expresses helped to bind the community in the same ways that the special laws of Judaism did for Pharisaic Judaism. So Paul's emphasis on righteousness was not only meant to replace Pharisaic Judaism but also to parallel and reconstitute Jewish moral imperatives among gentile converts. In this sense Paul's Christianity is an alternative religion, analytically complete in its own terms, based on Paul's experience within Pharisaism but transformed by his faith in Christ. For Paul it was not so much a moral transformation as a social one. But for the gentile convert, it was as complete a moral transformation as were the new religions of the sixties and seventies in the United States for the so-called hippies who flocked to them. Steven Tipton's description of the moral community offered by the new American religions to the youth in the seventies could easily apply to Paul's community of gentiles and Jews combined: "They bind together heretofore disparate elements within a pluralistic culture, revitalizing tradition as they change it. They are engaged in a constructive process of mediating and recombining existing meanings . . . ."[53] So too Paul attempted to mediate the bewildering moral differences within the culturally plural world, binding together previously disparate aspects of gentile God-fearers and Jews into a single community of the faithful. He tried to create the same single, moral community envisioned by Pharisaism and Judaism at large. He attempted to do so out of elements that were far more disparate than the Jewish community comprised, including Jews and gentiles within the same social organization and maintaining that they both could share the same spiritual purity.

Having begun with his personal experience, Paul thereafter expands the theory not simply to involve his own salvation, and the salvation of the gentiles, but also the entire history of humanity, from Adam through the rapidly approaching eschaton. Justification becomes the merciful acquittal of all humanity, equally guilty at first, of which he is one example, though he himself claims to have done no sin according to Jewish law. The implication is that sin is inherent in every creature whether they practice Torah or not. In effect he removes the benefit to the convert of complete membership in the Jewish community. Those who have had Torah have the advantage of knowing what sin is, but they are all the more intransigent for having spurned the message that Jesus is Christ. Yet one purpose of Romans is to warn his gentile flock not to boast of their religious accomplishments, against Jews as well as the Jewish Christians, who required that gentiles observe Torah. When Paul addresses the issue of justification, he is also attempting to create a single community where all share a single moral standard. His life as an apostle is thereafter devoted to solving the practical problems of creating a single community, based on being in Christ, out of two diverging ones with competing ideas about what community entailed.

¶ PAUL THE APOSTLE

CHAPTER SIX

¶ CIRCUMCISION AND THE NOAHIDE LAWS

Living in the spirit, or being in Christ, is the central fact of Pauline community. If that central experience is maintained, however, Paul appears to take a moderate view about a number of critical issues that divided the early church.

PAUL'S PERSPECTIVE ON THE JERUSALEM CONFERENCE

The controversy at Antioch and the Jerusalem conference clarify Paul's statements on circumcision in Galatians. In Galatians 2:1, Paul states that he took Titus, an uncircumcised gentile, to Jerusalem fourteen years after his conversion, where the issues of circumcision and food laws were discussed and settled.

Then after fourteen years I went up again to Jerusalem with Barnabas, taking Titus along with me. I went up by revelation; and I laid before them (but privately before those who were of repute) the gospel which I preach among the gentiles, lest somehow I should be running or had run in vain. But even Titus, who was with me, was not compelled to be circumcised, though he was a Greek. But because of false brethren secretly brought in, who slipped in to spy out our freedom which we have in Christ Jesus, that they might bring us into bondage—to them we did not yield submission even for a moment, that the truth of the gospel might be preserved for you. And from those who were reputed to be something (what they were makes no difference to me; God shows no partiality)—those, I say, who were of repute added nothing to me; but on the contrary, when they saw that I had been entrusted with the gospel for the uncircumcised, just as Peter had been entrusted with the gospel to the circumcised (for he who worked through Peter for the mission to the circumcised worked through me also for the gentiles), and when they perceived the grace that was given to me, James and Cephas and John, who were reputed to be pillars, gave to me and Barnabas the right hand of fellowship, that we should go to the Gentiles and they to the circumcised; only they would have us remember the poor, which very thing I was eager to do. (Gal. 2:1–10)

Paul goes on to discuss the issue of dietary laws, which he sees as directly pertinent to this conference. Circumcision and dietary laws are both special laws incumbent on Jews, but they are different bodies of law with different implications for the new Christian community, warranting separate discussions (see chapter 7 for a discussion of dietary laws).

Acts 15:1–29 and Gal. 2:1–10 are apparently discussing the same incident, the so-called Jerusalem Conference. There are several important differences in the two accounts: (1) In Gal. 2:1, Paul says that he went to Jerusalem with Barnabas and Titus. Luke reports that the community in Antioch sent Paul and Barnabas, as well as others, to Jerusalem. (2) Paul says that he went "by revelation," while Luke says that the reason was a theological controversy in Antioch instigated by some Jerusalemite Christians. Paul describes some false brethren who sneaked in to spy out Antioch's freedom and bring them into bondage (Gal. 2:4). (3) The Jerusalem Conference, in both Galatians and Acts, is about gentile Christians' legal responsibilities and is focused on circumcision. Luke expresses this by relating that the visitors in Antioch and the Pharisaic party at the conference claimed that circumcision was necessary for salvation (Acts 15:1, 5). Paul says that he lay the gospel to the gentiles before them and that not even Titus, a gentile, was compelled to be circumcised (Gal. 2:2, 3). (4) Both Paul and Luke distinguish between the Jerusalem disciples and a more conservative faction (Gal. 2:4 and Acts 15:5). (5) Luke portrays the conference as involving the entire Jerusalem leadership (Acts 15:6). Paul says that he explained his preaching before a larger group and then privately to those of repute (Gal. 2:2). (6) Paul refers to his recognition by the pillars (Gal. 2:9). Luke says only that they related what God had done through them among the gentiles (Acts 15:12). (7) According to both, the conference ends in agreement. Paul speaks of the right hand of fellowship extended to him and Barnabas (Gal. 2:9). Acts portrays Peter and James as speaking in favor of the law-free gospel in Antioch, bringing a letter of consolation back to them (Acts 15:7b–29). (8) Paul agrees to remember the poor (Gal. 2:10) and speaks about the acceptance of his apostolate to the gentiles, but Luke makes no reference to either. (9) Luke narrates the imposition of a set of restrictions on gentile Christians, known as the Apostolic Decree (Acts 15:20, 29), whereas Paul claims that nothing was imposed on him (Gal. 2:6). (10) In Acts the decree is promulgated at the conclusion of the conference. In Gal. 2 the conference is followed by Paul's brief discussion of Peter's behavior in Antioch. Thus, it is not clear whether Paul's letter to the Galatians precedes or succeeds the conference.[1]

Paul's account must take precedence over Luke's because he was an eyewitness. Paul, however, did not write from an objective perspective, since his letter is strongly influenced by polemic. The many puzzling details of the Jerusalem Conference, the incident at Antioch, and its possible conciliation with Acts,[2] are not pertinent to this study, but certain details of Paul's account are worth careful examination. First, Paul says that he went to Jerusalem by revelation (*kata apokalypsin*), stressing at the least that the meeting was intended by providence. Second, Paul says that he met privately (*kat' idian*) with the other apostles, so that some of the results of the conference were not public events. He also implies that the silence of the conference on the matter of Titus means that the whole church leadership agreed that gentiles did not have to be circumcised, a rather exaggerated interpretation in view of what follows. He claims that his deportment with his colleagues was secretly monitored by false brothers (*pareisaktous pseudadelphous*) who spied (*kataskopēsai*) on him. He also says that his apostleship to the gentiles ("apostolēn . . . emoi eis ta ethnē") was acknowledged by them, as Peter was accepted as the apostle to the circumcised. Paul evidently takes this as his own acceptance as an *apostle,* but he is careful to say only that they saw that he was entrusted with the gospel to the uncircumcised ("idontes hoti pepioteumai to evaggelion tēs akrobustias"). Finally, he says that they agreed, by the right hand of fellowship—that is, by formal, legal fashion—that "we should go to the gentiles and they to the circumcised" (Gal. 2:9).[3] This action is legally binding in Roman law and signifies for Paul that they recognized the validity of Paul's mission to the gentiles and probably Paul's apostolic authority, at least in regard to the gentiles. Again, Paul appears to take from this agreement the conclusion that his role as apostle was completely recognized and that the conference accepted the validity of a gospel to the gentiles without circumcision. The exact words that he uses, however, allow for the suspicion that less was agreed on than Paul claims.

Paul's language raises the issue of the extent of the agreement. The silence of the council on the issue of Titus's lack of circumcision cannot be considered an agreement with Paul's position on circumcision. Even the conference's agreement could not ensure or guarantee the agreement of all Jewish Christians on the issue of circumcision. Jewish law had an authority independent of the Christian community. These factors make for some possible differences between the events and phrases that Paul quotes from the conference and the way in which he reports them.[4] Even Paul's position as apostle is not acknowledged in so many words, though that is the conclusion that Paul tries to make of it. Paul seems to be maximizing the conclusions of the council, while being careful not to misrepresent the opposition's actual words. Though they might have acknowledged the existence and possibly the rightness of his uncircumcised mission to the gentiles, the issue of Jewish law was more complicated than Paul would have us believe here. Otherwise the Antioch incident could not have happened.

My approach to the problem is the following: Paul agrees to a position in Jerusalem that is not fully consonant with his private opinion because he feels that the Jerusalem conference does not explicitly contradict his opinion. Paul's private opinions are expressed in Galatians, where he says that the experience of faith overrides the ceremonial Torah by making circumcision unnecessary for anyone. As opposed to the extremist Judaizers, whose position is known by their proselytes in Galatia, Paul finds the unity of the church to be most important, so he can compromise with the opposition, though he disagrees with them. Some of the most important issues must have been left out, both in Paul's brief narration and likely in the conference itself, because the conflict flares up again whenever gentile and zealous Jewish Christians encounter each other. Possibly the validity of the gentile mission was all that could be agreed on at the conference, which means that the all-important question of the gentiles' status and ability to be a single community with Jewish Christians was not resolved. But the most important thing about this account is that it is only a brief theoretical statement. Even if the council agreed with Paul in principle, the formula would still remain to be worked out in actual cases. Paul counsels the Corinthian church not to exercise all the freedom it wants to arrogate to itself. But it is also possible that Paul accepted some limitation on his principle of freedom from ceremonial obligations in order to gain acceptance as an apostle.[5] He may then have been seen by others to have changed his mind on crucial matters, though he could maintain that he made no essential changes in his position.

Paul left with the impression that his apostolate had been validated. It would be unwise to overstate the level of cooperation between Paul and the other apostles. Paul's letters are full of the conflict that separated him from Peter and James. Further, almost no Pauline letter forgets to mention Paul's status as an apostle through God, underlining his constant need to establish his credentials in the face of Jesus' personal wishes in appointing only his immediate disciples as apostles. Acts does mention, however, that the conference endorsed Paul's stand on circumcision for the gentiles.[6]

LUKE'S PERSPECTIVE ON
THE JERUSALEM CONFERENCE

Luke has a different view of the Jerusalem Conference. According to Acts 15 the issue of circumcision arises at Antioch before the Jerusalem council, because emissaries from Jerusalem maintain that one cannot be saved unless one is circumcised into the people of Moses ("ean mē peritemēthēte tō ethnei tō Mōuseōs, ou dynasthe sōthēnai" [Acts 15:1]). Luke's chronology can be questioned because he is writing after the fact. It is possible that the conservative members of the church do not go along with the Jerusalem church's decision. The restrictive understanding of salvation is characteristic of some kinds of apocalyptic Judaism, but it is certainly not a universal doctrine within the Jewish community. Paul's opinion that gentiles do not need to be circumcised to be saved is, in turn, characteristic of Pharisaic and later rabbinic Judaism but emphatically not true of apocalypticism. In this case, the church issue reflects the spectrum of Jewish as well as Christian opinions.

It is not clear that Luke understands fully or reflects clearly these distinctions, since he equates the idea that there is no *salvation* without circumcision with the party of the Pharisees who say, "It is necessary to circumcise them, and to charge them to keep the law of Moses" (15:5). The two positions that Luke mentions in this passage are not identical. In the first instance, salvation is discussed; in the second, only proper conversion is being considered. Rabbinic Judaism allows that some gentiles can be saved qua gentiles, but it requires that all converts to Judaism be strictly charged to keep the law of Moses.

The rabbinic doctrine that the righteous of all nations have a place in the world to come is not evidenced by Luke. Whether this is a simple inaccuracy, a mistaken conclusion by Luke about what was being debated, or a completely accurate view of the debate can never be resolved. But we cannot understand the full consequences of the debate unless we look at the wider context. Rabbinic writings debate the issue of the salvation of the gentiles, as they debate most every issue.[7] It is possible that the Christian Pharisees were of the most conservative persuasion, although this seems unlikely. This issue is crucial for understanding Paul's program for Christianity.

Luke also maintains that, though some Christians spied on Paul, they were acting on their own initiative (Acts 15:24). According to Luke, the Jerusalem church agreed that circumcision was not necessary for the salvation of the gentiles and outlined a series of more lenient food laws for gentiles. Then Paul returned as one of the emissaries of the agreement. Although the principle that circumcision *of gentiles* is unnecessary for salvation is accepted in Luke's account, whether it is necessary for Jewish Christians and gentile Christians is ambiguous. Further, no one says that Gentiles cannot be circumcised if they want to be. Only Paul himself has said that he does not advise it, because it tends toward a confidence in the flesh instead of spirit. No one says that Jews should not be circumcised.

SYNTHESIS

The ambiguity about the actual apostolic agreement colors every assessment of Paul's intention in Galatians. Since Galatians may have preceded the conference, it may represent an earlier stage of Paul's thinking. Paul himself sees his position on law as vindicated and feels that his apostolate, though untimely born, has been accepted. Yet nothing in either story explicitly states that all the opposition agreed to accept Paul's position. At best we have an agreement from the centrist forces, represented by Peter, concerning some of Paul's program. Further, the legal implications of the agreement were untried and untested. The Acts version also presents more conservative positions than those of Peter; whether they agreed with anything that Paul represented is doubtful.[8]

The legal questions of circumcision and dietary laws can be understood by putting aside the accepted doctrine that Paul was committed to the theological principle that no human actions can produce righteousness. Instead, let us look at the question from the perspective of a man who was a Pharisee, who converted into a new community of gentiles with faith in God, and who strove to make a single community out of a chaotic group of Jews and gentiles united very loosely by their reliance on Jesus' teachings. If one takes a Jewish, legal perspective rather than a theological perspective about Paul's message, Paul's suggestions seem more flexible. If Paul were writing a systematic theology, there would be no reason to expect compromise. If the issue is legal, then a variety of different theologies can be accommodated by the same ritual actions. Paul is searching for a procedural solution to a ritual problem that we now know to be the symptom of a larger social problem. I maintain that Paul's approach is halakhic, even if the problem he addresses is one that cannot arise within Pharisaic Judaism.

Paul's polemics are part of a social strategy to maintain unity between Jewish and gentile Christians. This makes several of the stories that Acts attributes to Paul become more plausible. I do not maintain that both Acts and Paul's letters can be right all the time; rather, I suggest that when one takes into account the principles and precedents of Jewish legal reasoning, both describe the same phenomenon. In some places Paul argues the force of his own perceptions; in others he counsels reconciliation with people whose opinions differ. I try to show that although Paul accommodates his opponents, he does not do so on issues of ethical principle. His compromises follow the logic of the situation in the manner of Jewish law, and they are only accommodations based on magnanimity, for the purpose of maintaining church unity. Paul's discussions of circumcision and food laws demonstrate that he is familiar with Jewish customs and elucidates several first-century Pharisaic positions.

As Paul's apostolate was accepted, even provisionally and possibly in his own mind more than in those of his colleagues, before or after the conference, he had to balance two occasionally opposing goals: (1) to gain acceptance for gentile communities that did not observe ceremonial law and (2) to work for accommodation and reconciliation between the two opposing factions within the church. His first job was to try to describe the new unity that he envisioned inside the Christian community. Pious Jews insisted on circumcision for all Jewish males, most on the eighth day, as well as circumcision for all male converts to the religion. Jews also stood out from their neighbors because of their special rules of resting on the Sabbath. Further, they followed special dietary laws that affected the food they ate and the way it was prepared. These facts were noticed by others, but the motivation to observe Torah was not social aloofness or misanthropy, as they were charged; rather, it was the central duty incumbent on Jews to warrant their Torah-revealed priestly status, for God demanded these sacred duties as a mark of the Jews' service as priesthood. The laws functioned socially to mark Jewish identity for those both inside and outside the community.

For the Jewish community as a whole, the special laws, not conversion experiences, functioned to raise Jewish commitment and ensure Jewish survival as a nationality and religious group in the Diaspora. By seeming to recommend an end to the primacy of the special Jewish laws within Christianity, Paul was taking a radical position. Taking into account Paul's position as stated in Galatians, I maintain that Jewish law occasionally allows Paul to compromise in order to avoid open hostility, to avoid antagonizing Jews and Jewish Christians. His strategy failed, and the reasons are both specific to Paul's own life and crucial for understanding the split between the two religions. In order to understand what Paul's diplomacy was and how it failed, one must understand what he said and how his opinions were understood by his contemporaries. Consequently, it is difficult to grasp Paul's position. I think that understanding Paul's social position, his identity as a convert from Pharisaism and as a member of a gentile community of faith, will help clarify these complicated issues.

GENTILE CIRCUMCISION AND THE NOAHIDE COMMANDMENTS

After Paul converted and preached the crucified Christ to the gentiles, he concluded in Galatians that circumcision was not important to salvation, for the (special) acts of Torah were no longer essential for salvation. Waiving circumcision for gentile salvation was not in itself a startling conclusion, for not all Jews insisted that conversion was necessary for gentile salvation. There were a variety of opinions within the Jewish community concerning ritual observances and gentile salvation. Jewish Christians, because they were primarily Jews, must have had a similar spectrum of opinion.

From a legal perspective Paul did not startle the Jewish Christian community by saying that circumcision was unnecessary for gentile salvation per se. His claim that the saved Jews and gentiles could form a single new community and freely interact was more innovative. The issue was not how the gentiles could be saved but how to eat with them and marry them. For Paul, Pharisaism had set down the rules: Birth inside the people of Israel was a special honor, like priesthood. Unlike the priesthood, membership in the people of Israel was available through conversion to any who desired it. It was not necessary for a person to become Jewish to be righteous and thus have a place in the world to come, as it was not necessary to be a priest to be righteous. Instead, special laws were a special responsibility attendant on any Jew for the privilege of being part of Israel. But purity rules prevented the observant Jews from intimate contact with the impure. Several Christians, reacting from their previous understandings of purity in Judaism, were afraid to allow Jews and gentiles to form a single community, even in Christianity, because such actions would violate the purity laws. They were right: Pharisaism inhibited such interaction.

The fate of the gentiles is discussed in rabbinic Judaism through the doctrine of the Noahide Commandments. This rabbinic doctrine is derived from a midrash on the flood narrative in which God makes a covenant with *all humanity,* not just Jews, never again to destroy the world. God seals the covenant with the sign of the rainbow, as he thereafter seals the special Abrahamic and Mosaic covenants with circumcision, indicating membership in Israel. Conversely, the sign of the Noahide covenant, the rainbow, is available to all humanity to symbolize God's promise of safety. The rabbis assumed that the covenant with Noah also contained several revealed commandments defining just and humane behavior. Their exegesis of the flood narrative extends the benefits and some of the responsibilities of Torah to all the peoples of the world. The Noahide Commandments (e.g., b. Sanhedrin 56b) function like a concept of natural law, which any just person can be expected to follow by observation and reason. In Christian theological language, it is available by God's grace to all humanity.

In rabbinic midrash, the Noahide Commandments include monotheism, avoidance of murder, organizing courts and promulgating justice, avoiding incest, theft, blasphemy, as well as avoiding eating the flesh of living creatures and, sometimes, recognition that the Lord, the God of Israel, is the one true God. All of these ideas can be derived from the Noah story in Genesis, if they are read together with the rules for sojourners, principally in Leviticus 17–26. These two passages are associated because they point to the origin of the laws for the legal treatment of resident aliens.

Mentioning rabbinic doctrine in the first century raises the issue of anachronism. To find out what was practiced in first-century Judaism we have to consult other varieties of Judaism. Although rabbinic doctrine, enumerating from six to ten Noahide Commandments depending on the version, cannot be traced to earlier than the third century, other versions of the Noahide Commandments can be found in Jubilees 7:20–21, which is pre-Christian[9]: "And in the twenty-eighth jubilee Noah began to command his grandsons with ordinances and commandments and all of the judgments which he knew. And he bore witness to his sons so that they might do justice and cover the shame of their flesh and bless the one who created them and honor father and mother, and each one love his neighbor and preserve themselves from fornication and pollution and from all injustice."

The ordinances thought to be universally humane by Jubilees call for establishing justice, eschewing incest, honoring parents, loving neighbors, and prohibiting adultery, promiscuity, and pollution.[10] In Jubilees, this short law code forms the basis of the judgment against the giants, which brings on the flood and sets the scene for the myths contained in Enoch.

It would be unwise, however, to assume that Jubilees is promulgating such ideas in order to find a basis for humane universalism. On the contrary, Jubilees has a strictly dualistic view of the world, both on the divine and human level, in consonance with the ideas of Qumran sectarians, in whose library it figured prominently. Israel is identified as a good kingdom. God selected them as special and above all other peoples (2:21) to be marked by circumcision (15:11). They alone can participate in the Sabbath and the other festivals ordained by God. The other nations are condemned, and God has placed spirits in authority over them to lead them astray. Jubilees 22:16 warns Jews not to eat with gentiles. Jubilees forcefully says that there is no salvation without circumcision on the eighth day (15:26–27). This means that conversion of the gentiles is virtually impossible. Even a charitable reading supposes that only the children of converts can enter the community: "And anyone who is born whose own flesh is not circumcised on the eighth day is not from the sons of the covenant which the Lord made for Abraham, since (he is) from the children of destruction. And there is therefore no sign upon him so that he might belong to the Lord because (he is destined) to be destroyed and annihilated from the earth and to be uprooted from the earth because he has broken the covenant of the Lord our God. Because of the nature of all of the angels of the presence and all of the angels of sanctification he sanctified Israel so that they might be with him and with his holy angels."[11]

The obvious reason for the inclusion of the Noahide Commandments in this place is to provide Jubilees with a legal warrant for condemning the gentiles. This is appropriate to a sectarian position, where the gentiles and all but a saving remnant of Israel are scheduled for divine destruction. We know from this evidence that there were sects within Judaism that did not subscribe to liberal ideas about the capabilities of gentiles; the relatively liberal rabbis in later times added only a few more commandments than we find in Jubilees and deleted the explicit pollution requirement (whose essence is subsumed under incest). The rabbis also clarified that when a child is not circumcised, his future reward is not automatically imperiled.

Such a lack is, in the opinion of the later rabbis, a sin of his father (*Shulḥan Arukh,* "Yoreh Dea" 260.1). Sabbath laws took precedence over circumcision laws for children born by cesarean section. In rabbinic tradition, it was thus not necessary to be circumcised on the eighth day to be Jewish, part of Israel, or deserving of the world to come.

The early date and apocalyptic setting of the Noahide Commandments is clear from the Jubilees reference. But law, like reason, is a two-edged sword. It condemns the guilty and also upholds the innocent. A legal structure amounting to the Noahide Commandments is found elsewhere in Jewish tradition, though its formulation differs depending on the exact purpose of the law. The converse to the Jubilees vision, that some gentiles are capable of righteousness, can also be found in Judaism in communities that were not sectarian or apocalyptic. It is found in rabbinic Judaism, although the estimate of the number of righteous gentiles was usually fairly low. Early rabbinic opinions about gentiles were at least partly formed by the experience of two disastrous wars against Rome and by observations of the level of gentile morality. We have seen the same issues surface in Hellenistic Jewish apologetic literature, which might have been used to missionize gentiles. It follows then that some Pharisees, as well as other Jews, would have considered God-fearers to be righteous gentiles.

Strangely enough, Luke again helps demonstrate that a positive use for the Noahide Commandments was known in first-century Judaism. Acts 15:20, 15:29, and 21:25 describe an Apostolic Decree defining a minimum of practice for the new gentile Christians. The specific decrees are derived from an exegesis of Leviticus 17–18,[12] probably under some influence from the Noah story. In the Christian version, the new Christian God-fearers had to abstain from meat sacrificed to idols (*eidōlothutōn*), from bloodshed (*haimatos*), or alternatively, from the flesh of animals not ritually slaughtered, from animals that had been ensnared and killed (*pnikton*), and from forbidden marriages, incest, and unchastity (*porneias*). Whether *haimatos* refers to a moral action or a ritual one is not entirely clear in church tradition, which has taken it in both ways.[13] The early Christians more closely approximate the ordinances of Jubilees than did the third-century rabbis.[14] It is possible that the reason the Christian version of the rules is stricter than the other Jewish versions is that a large section of the church was allowed to remain uncircumcised and impure from a ritual standpoint. Each version of these minimum moral laws not only articulates the responsibilities of the gentiles in God's plan but also reflects the historical situation and values of the particular Jewish sect promulgating it. The Christian Apostolic Decree is more positive than the rabbinic one. This is a necessity, as the Christian group had a larger percentage of gentile converts than other Jewish groups. The rabbinic version is from a time when the righteousness of gentiles, even in nonsectarian circles, was more controversial and proselytization could be considered a capital offense in Roman law. The rabbis mention several times that bad proselytes informed against the Jews. One can imagine a backsliding convert informing the authorities that he had been proselytized against his will and against Roman law, as today's deprogrammed counterconverts turn against their former communities. So it was wise to be careful.

The rabbis, like the Christians and unlike the apocalypticists, used the Noahide Commandments for a positive purpose—namely, to include righteous gentiles in the world to come.[15] Paul desired not only that the gentiles be among the community of those saved but that both Jews and gentiles form one community on earth. This was a step that many Jewish Christians could not accept. The concept of the Noahide Commandments is more antique and more widespread in Judaism than can be proved from the midrash, as the New Testament once again shows us.

The reports in Acts give a clear exegetical sense of how these rules were derived. Pinned to the Noahide covenant, so that they could apply to all humanity, they were more directly derived from the biblical rules encumbent on "the stranger in your gates."[16] Resident aliens were obliged to abstain from offering sacrifices to strange gods (Lev. 17:7–9), from eating blood in any form (Lev. 17:10ff), from incest (Lev. 18:6–26), from work on the Sabbath (Exod. 20:10f), and from eating leavened bread during the Passover (Exod. 12:18f).[17] The Christian version deliberately parallels both the order of laws for resident aliens in the Bible and the formulations of the Noahide Commandments: it does not merely leave out the special Jewish laws, otherwise it would not have specified that unkosher slaughter could not be eaten. The Christian form of the rules is based, like the Jewish ones, on the actual experience of accommodation between Jews and gentiles living together, within a Jewish state or a Diaspora community. Thus, the Christian form of the rules mentions only those issues that are likely to be a source of controversy between the Jewish and gentile Christians living together. The formulation of the Noahide Commandments in the rabbinic literature arises in the same way but reflects a later time, when the problem for Jews was how to live in gentile communities, not the other way around.

The issue of righteous gentiles had surfaced in the lives of sectarian Jews, as Jubilees makes clear. In the first century, the Jewish Sibylline Oracles specified those rules incumbent on righteous gentiles:

Happy will be those of mankind of earth
who will love the great God, blessing him
before drinking and eating, putting their trust in piety.
They will reject all temples when they see them,
altars too, useless foundations of dumb stones
(and stone statues and handmade images)
defiled with blood of animate creatures, and sacrifices
of four-footed animals. They will look to the great glory of the
one God and commit no wicked murder, nor deal in
dishonest gain, which are most horrible things.
Neither have they disgraceful desire for another's spouse
or for hateful and repulsive abuse of a male.
Other men will never imitate their way
or piety or customs, because they desire shamelessness.
On the contrary, they deride them with mockery and laughter.

(Sybilline Oracles 4:24–39)

Murder, theft, and other specifics are again mentioned as primary prohibitions for all humanity to observe. Sacrifice is forbidden. In the Apostolic Decree some issues were taken for granted because they were obviously eschewed by all Christians, leaving the ceremonial laws of Judaism as the most significant questions.[18] The appearance of idolatry was also important, so Acts 15:20 mentions it, as does Paul in 1 Corinthians 8, 10, and again in Romans.

The poetic fragments of Pseudo-Phocylides also mention the general principles of Jewish ethics without mentioning the ceremonial Torah. One of the witnesses of this poem reports that it ended with the exhortation that "purifications are for the purity of the soul, not of the body" (*Charlesworth* 2, 582, 11. 228–30). Aristeas likewise says: "Honoring God is done not with gifts or sacrifices but with purity of soul."[19] These sentiments come from the prophets, who rebuked the misuse of the sacrificial cult. They are used in Hellenistic Judaism to argue against the necessity of temple worship, both for Jews in Diaspora and gentiles. It is also part of a proselyte literature designed to convince pagans of the inherent morality of Judaism and to persuade them to become God-fearers or converts. Slow progress convinced the community of the convert's sincerity and also defused the perceived threat from the gentile family left behind.

The rabbinic version of the Noahide rules does not contain any of the positive special laws of Judaism, such as *Kashrut* or circumcision. The Apostolic Decree does contain special laws of Judaism, demonstrating that within the Christian community Jews and gentiles were expected to eat together regularly. Paul, however, did not insist on any Jewish customs in his gentile mission. He says that he himself adopted the rules of gentile God-fearers in his mission to them (Gal. 4:12; 1 Cor. 9:21).

As the Sibylline Oracles and other Hellenistic literature show us, the social location for the promotion of God-fearing and conversion is Diaspora Judaism, where prospective threats from gentile neighbors mitigated Jewish enthusiasm for gentile conversion (see chapter 3), encouraging a preference for God-fearing over conversion. The Pharisees, largely a Palestinian phenomenon, had no such scruples. They desired committed converts. But the rabbis also promulgated Noahide Commandments, perhaps with the same social strategy as Jewish missionary and apologetic literature. Many rabbis simply assumed that becoming Jewish was not the only way to gain God's love. For the believing Jew, cultic and ceremonial laws reflected moral principles. Hellenistic Jewish writers chose to emphasize the moral principles, not the ceremonial laws, in discussions with gentiles. For many varieties of Judaism, a gentile was not excluded from the rewards of the righteous because of the accident of birth.

Likewise, Paul does not say that all law is worthless, only that its meaning has changed. Paul's missionary writings occasionally assume that gentiles are under the law. The Noahide laws help us understand what he means. As Raeissaenen has shown, Paul's use of the first-person plural in Gal. 3:23–29 implies that the gentile hearers are equally with the Jews under the sway of the law.[20] The law is a custodian or prison guard and a tutor both to him and the Galatians, who are addressed directly in the second person: "for in Christ Jesus are all sons of God, through faith" (Gal. 3:26). In this respect he includes himself as well, since he has undergone a radical conversion: "that *we* might be justified by faith" (Gal. 3:24). He has retreated halakhically from Pharisaic observance to that level demanded of God-fearers, though he still considers himself to be Jewish.

In Gal. 4:5–6 Paul repeats the pattern of preaching: God sent his son to redeem those under the law, who receive the status of children. Because *you* are children, *we* have received the Holy Spirit. This is not a double concept of law, sometimes referring to Torah, at other times to a more general, moral law. For every Jew, moral law and Torah were coterminous, and Torah was conceived as a transcendent natural law, as well as a set of ordinances. Paul knows that because of the Noahide Commandments (an anachronistic term in the first century) Torah is the moral guide for gentiles as well as Jews.[21]

In Romans, Paul again seems to assume that gentiles, as well as Jews, can get the rewards of Torah, though they do not observe the ceremonial laws: "All who have sinned without the law will also perish without the law, and all who have sinned under the law will be judged by the law. For it is not the hearers of the law who are righteous before God, but the doers of the law who will be justified. When gentiles who have not the law do by nature [*physei*] what the law requires, they are a law to themselves, even though they do not have the law. They show that what the law requires is written on their hearts, while their conscience also bears witness and their conflicting thoughts accuse or perhaps excuse them on that day when, according to my gospel, God judges the secrets of men by Christ Jesus" (2:12–16).

Paul does condemn what he considers to be Jewish misapplication of law. He appropriates an argument from Judaism to condemn Jews by their own standards. Paul states that all sinners are judged by the law and the righteous are upheld by it. This judgment is equivalent to natural law (*physei*), since Paul says that humans know this law by nature. He also says that this doctrine is what Jews teach (2:21).[22] In characterizing a Jewish position in order to defeat it, Paul ironically gives us evidence for the importance of the Noahide Commandments in Judaism. This is another example of how reading Paul's letters helps us date and understand the evolution of rabbinic thought. In the first century, Pharisaic thought could both debate and admit that righteousness among gentiles was equivalent to righteousness among Jews, which would become normative among the rabbis. It is possible that Paul did not like this idea during his most zealous Pharisee stage, but it seems likely that it was already part, if a debated part, of Pharisaic teaching in the first century.

ONE COMMUNITY OF CIRCUMCISED AND UNCIRCUMCISED

The lack of specifically Jewish customs was appropriate for a group of gentile Christians living alone, but it became a problem for the unified group of faith, made up of both Jews and gentiles, as Paul envisioned. Such a group existed at Antioch where Paul and Barnabas eventually assumed church leadership. Paul's understanding of the status of gentiles proved to be controversial when discovered by the flourishing Jewish Christian community, which assumed that all new converts to Christianity would become Jews as well, since that was the only way for Jewish Christians to eat with them, to celebrate the Eucharist, or to intermarry with them. Thus, the stage was set for an unprecedented fight in the Christian variety of sectarian Judaism, precipitated by the new forces unleashed in Christianity.

For various sects of Jews, the gentiles could either be damned entirely, saved by conversion, or saved as gentiles as part of their own communities. But if they were saved as gentiles, Pharisaic Jews would not seek to compromise Jewish ritual purity by intimate contact with them. Although ordinary Jewish practice was more lax than Pharisaism, especially in the Diaspora and in the Greek cities of Judea, purity laws theoretically held throughout Judaism. One can allow a fairly high amount of laxness without assuming that the lax Jews were automatically apostates. It depended on the perspective of the actors in the first century.

The effect of Paul's preaching and his vision of a new, unified Christian community was the destruction of the *ritual* distinction between Jew and gentile within the Christian sect. Paul was breaking down a ritual boundary in Christianity, not a boundary between saved and unsaved. The same ritual boundary existed in all Judaism. Many Jews admitted that righteous gentiles were saved, but they differed wildly in estimating the number of saved gentiles. Many Jews insisted on ritual distinctions between Jewish and gentile communities.

Paul's action was an extremely provocative if not unprecedented development within Judaism. The unique aspect of Paul's mission was that he recommended that gentile converts ignore the ritual law to become one community with the Jewish Christians, something that could easily appear as sinning to a Jew, although it fulfilled the purpose of Torah. Paul risked the charge of apostasy for these ideas, as he ironically characterized himself with the epithet transgressor (Gal. 2:18) from the perspective of a faithless Christian. Paul, of course, denies that he is a transgressor, since the application of Torah has been overturned by the crucifixion and resurrection of Christ: "But if, in our endeavor to be justified in Christ, we ourselves were found to be sinners, is Christ then an agent of sin? Certainly not! But if I build up again those things which I tore down, then I prove myself a transgressor" (Gal. 2:17, 18).[23]

Paul's rhetorical point is that if he should return to the law, he would be admitting that he was a transgressor of it. Paul does not call himself an apostate; yet in admitting that, without understanding the primacy of his new faith in the crucified messiah, he can be called a transgressor from the opposing position. He testifies that others see him as an apostate. The definition of apostasy is a matter of perspective. On the basis of his experience of the risen Lord, he can abandon circumcision for the gentiles. If he were to abandon his faith and return to the position that gentiles needed circumcision, he would become a Jewish sinner in retrospect, not a faithful Christian. This is what his opponents think of him. This is also what he thinks of his Jewish Christian opponents who do not stress the primacy of faith.

There is precedent for Jews contemporary with Paul who abandon Torah but do not consider themselves apostates. Philo mentions not only apostates who gave up Judaism, but also some who remained within the community and allegorized the law instead of practicing it:

> There are some who, regarding laws in their literal sense in the light of symbols of matters belonging to the intellect, are overpunctilious about the latter, while treating the former with easy-going neglect. Such men I for my part should blame for handling the matter in too easy and off-hand a manner: they ought to have given careful attention to both aims, to a more full and exact investigation of what is not seen and in what is seen to be stewards without reproach. As it is, as though they were living alone by themselves in a wilderness, or as though they had become disembodied souls, and knew neither city nor village nor household nor any company of human beings at all, overlooking all that the mass of men regard, they explore reality in its naked absoluteness. These men are taught by the sacred word to have thoughts for good repute, and to let go nothing that is part of the customs fixed by divinely empowered men greater than those of our time. (*On The Migration of Abraham* 89–93)

Paul's policy resembles Philo's description of the extreme allegorizers, except that Paul was advising potential gentile proselytes and Jews alike to ignore the special laws, if they could. The reaction to Paul's teachings in Jewish Christianity and Judaism was more severe than the reaction to Philo's ambivalent rebuke of the extreme allegorizers because Paul was more public in his polemical criticism of the law than the extreme allegorizers and he took this criticism to Jerusalem, where the most conservative members of the Jewish community had enough power to enforce their jurisdiction over him. Paul's experience ought to be linked to Philo's report of antinomianism in Judaism as part of a larger question of the observance of ceremonial laws in an acculturated, first-century Judaism.

The problem of Jewish-gentile separation was greater than the specially Christian communal issues, but the problem became acute in Christianity only because of its successful gentile mission. Some Hellenistic Jews might wink at the improprieties of the committed but insufficiently observant radical allegorizers mentioned by Philo, but they could be seen as apostates by less charitable Jews. Probably few wanted to go out of their way to indict Paul or his sympathizers. But Paul traveled from city to city disseminating his ideas. He confronted the Jewish Christians, hence also the Jewish authorities, with his idea of a single community where ritual was not important. Apparently, he traveled widely enough and his thinking was radical enough within Christianity itself to attract the attention of the zealous factions of Judaism.

Paul recommends an allegorization of Jewish practice, as Philo's extreme allegorizers did. But there is no evidence that the extreme allegorizers insisted on transformation or conversion. Philo does not report that they proselytized or insisted that gentiles be a single community with them. We lack the most elementary information about their lives, but it seems out of character for an extremely acculturated group to insist on gentile conversion, whereas Paul made gentile conversion his life's mission. Paul also says, as a moral principle, that ceremonial Torah is an all-or-nothing proposition. Either one should perform it flawlessly as a Pharisee would or one should not do it at all. The extreme allegorizers, I assume, would never see the necessity of the choice. They might allegorize some customs and even continue to practice a few others ("treating the latter with easy-going neglect"). There is no evidence that they accepted any Pharisaic opinions of how to practice Judaism. After his conversion, Paul came to reject the Pharisaic notion totally. Moreover, Paul insists that all convert, according to his definition of conversion. He insists on the faith that makes transformation possible. This makes Paul a convert, whereas the radical allegorizers are apologists for acculturation.

Paul has adopted God-fearing as the model of righteous behavior. This description of the change in Paul's view has merits over previous explanations.[24] Unfortunately, it does not tell us enough about the situation. When Paul missionizes, he evinces no sensitivity to the problem of changing affiliations. He is adamant that everyone declare to be *in Christ*. The meaning of this complex notion had to be worked out case by case over his ministry, for Paul does not adopt the mature rabbinic view of the responsibilities of righteous gentiles. Paul has partly retreated to the position that gentiles can be judged as God-fearers, but the analogy is incomplete because God-fearing could encompass anything from minimal financial support to preproselyte status and behind it often lay a strategy of gentile appeasement.

How the special laws, ceremonies, and Sabbath observances must have appealed to God-fearers in Paul's day remains unappreciated. Paul's vituperation against those who preach circumcision is evidence for its attractiveness, but pagan writers are equally short-tempered with potential converts to Judaism. Once a God-fearer had become attracted to Judaism, there must have been benefits to ending marginal status. Many God-fearers must have been willing to convert, as Josephus's story of Izates shows us. Conversion of God-fearers was an explosive issue both for Christianity and for the entire Jewish community. Paul's solution to the inner Christian fight, that Jewish rules—ceremonial Torah—would not be significant for any Christian's justification, inevitably and logically meant Christianity's exclusion from Judaism. It confirmed Christianity's status as a Jewish heresy. This new idea was a historical progression, not a logical one, dependent on the interaction of a variety of Jewish and Christian communities. Several generations were to pass before new borders could be clarified. These new borders, representing new definitions of the terms Christians and Jew, were not apparent until after the death of Paul.

In going from a Pharisaic community to a gentile one, Paul made an enormous move. His actions about the law came as a consequence of a conversion. He had to work out for himself what the conversion meant for his understanding of Torah. Perhaps something important in the law had to be transmuted, as Paul himself had been transformed by his conversion and call to missionize the Gentiles. For Paul this meant that Torah's primary function became propaedeutic and prophetic. It could no longer be the symbolic mark of the community's border. But by proclaiming his new idea of community, he alerted the Jewish community to what they could see as a potential new apostasy.

For Pharisaic Jews, circumcision was the sine qua non for conversion of a male gentile. Paul could not ignore this issue, though he wanted acceptance of his God-fearers within the single community of Israel. The critical difficulty lay within the Christian community, not the Jewish community at all, as Paul must have seen. Many Jewish Christians, who were also Jews of the more conservative variety, felt that gentiles ought to become Jews too before they entered the community. This would remove any bar to full social intercourse with them. Paul believed that Jews and Christians must be one community based on the same experience and equality within. The unifying factor was the experience of Christ; both had received baptism in the crucified messiah. Both had the same faith; thus, both must recognize that they have the same faith. As he had learned in his fourteen-year sojourn among gentile Christians, this transforming mystical identification with Christ had nothing to do with circumcision. The Jewish community was also alerted to the problem by Christian preaching in synagogues, but the critical issue was an intramural Christian one. Circumcision was necessary for the gentiles to be allowed to eat, join the community, or marry with Jewish Christians.

Traditional Jewish ceremonial definitions of status explain the opposition to Paul. Paul's conversion to gentile Christianity explains his position. Cognitive dissonance explains the ferocity of the battle between the two Christian groups. Those gentiles who became Christians by undergoing the difficult operation of circumcision, in effect becoming Jews, necessarily had strong feelings about their new identity. We know that adult circumcision was a difficult and painful operation in that day, to say nothing of the anxiety that naturally attends this kind of operation for an adult male. And we know that it was undertaken both by converts to Judaism and some converts to Christianity. To make matters worse, the Roman world often confused Jewish and Egyptian circumcision with the Syrian practice of initiation into the priesthood of Kubele (Cybele) by castration. Hence circumcision and the anxiety associated with it seriously complicated gentile entrance into the Christian community, as it complicated entrance into the Jewish community. Those gentiles who embraced Christianity through circumcision are likely to have had extremely high levels of cognitive dissonance, meaning that they would have had strong opinions about the value of the path they had taken and stronger opinions about those who did not undergo the same entrance requirement. Festinger's theory of cognitive dissonance allows us to elaborate the sociological dimension of the ferocious fight between Paul and the Judaized Christians.

Paul's preachings would have offended the circumcised, ex-gentile Christian. Paul took the role of representative of gentile Christianity seriously. Thus we have a double irony. Circumcision was defended by gentiles who had undergone circumcision to become Jews, and the gospel of the uncircumcised was defended by a former Pharisee. Paul became a uniquely valuable spokesperson for the liberal sentiment in gentile Christianity because he opposed circumcision and he could express his objections in a Pharisaic Jewish way. Given the vituperation in his own letters, it is hard to believe that he faced an easy time recommending his position, in spite of Luke's report of the conference. It was the eventual success of the gentile mission over a long period of time, not Paul's arguments, that allowed his position to prevail. After the Bar Kochba war against Rome, performing a circumcision became a crime. When order was restored, Jews regained the right to circumcise their children, but the right to proselytize and circumcise gentile converts was never officially regained.[25] The

Jewish community did not want a large number of new converts around, especially when their presence might indict them of a crime. Whenever gentiles defended their family members from the influence of Judaism or Christianity by invoking the laws of the principate, the Pauline position became a more attractive way to enter the covenant. In a Christian empire, the Pauline Christian position was the only practical way to make converts to Christianity, just as God-fearing was the only practical way to associate with Judaism. These developments took place centuries after Paul's life and were never evident to him, but they ensured the success of his position. Paul's position made the success of the Christian community possible, though in ways Paul never anticipated.

The considerable reports about both Noahide laws and God-fearing say that circumcision was unnecessary for gentiles to partake in the benefits of the life to come. Paul thus had precedent for saying that gentiles need not be circumcised to become true worshipers of the one God; otherwise, this position would not have been accepted by James and Peter. If these thoughts had appeared only in Paul, one could say that he was the innovator. But Josephus echoed Paul's sentiments in his writings. Whereas Paul may have been a religious genius, Josephus, writing shortly after Paul, must be close to being Paul's polar opposite—a complete opportunist. Josephus could not have been directly influenced by Paul; nor could he have come independently to such a position, were it an intellectual breakthrough. So Paul's position about the righteousness of gentiles was not an innovation. What was innovative was Paul's insistence that all should become one community in Christ, by virtue of the transformation that all believers were experiencing and that he himself experienced in his conversion.

Paul's conversion formed the basis for his opinions. But without circumcision Paul's male gentile converts to Christianity could not be considered Jewish by either Jewish Christians or Jews. As a result Pauline converts were different from both their Jewish and their pagan forebears. They existed by themselves, in some tension with both the Jewish Christian church and the Jewish community. They could not have been actively involved in Jewish life without stirring up trouble.

CIRCUMCISION IN PAUL'S LETTER TO THE GALATIANS

Evidence for this fight over circumcision in Christianity is Paul's letter to the Galatians, beginning in chapter 5 and immediately following the passage explaining why Christ has changed the curse of the law into a blessing for the gentiles. This exegesis is crucial to the case because it reflects Paul's own experience of conversion, which in turn is a summary of more than a decade and a half of Christians trying to mediate between the two communities. Paul writes to clarify his position to the Galatian community, a place where he had been active as an apostle to the gentiles.

His opponents in Galatia are a circumcising party (*peritemnomenoi*), Christians who accepted circumcision when they converted to Christianity and proselytes of a conservative Christianity in which conversion to Judaism was a necessary prerequisite. During his absence, the circumcising party recommended that Paul's converts also undergo the operation, suggesting that Paul himself circumcised others (see the circumcision of Timothy below).

Paul does not treat his opposition charitably. He minces no words with the circumcisers, at one point suggesting that they should mutilate themselves (5:12). He rhetorically plays on the Hellenistic confusion between circumcision and castration. The bitterness of the controversy can be attributed to the emotions of cognitive dissonance aroused by these two opposing varieties of conversion within Christianity. On one side is Paul, whose conversion brought with it a new commitment to gentile missionizing. On the other side is that part of the gentile church converted to Judaism, whose decision for circumcision brought with it an equal and opposing conviction of the value of Jewish ceremonial law in opening the Jewish community to Christians. Those gentiles left their families and found a whole new life in the Jewish Christian community, separate from their old gentile life. The cognitive dissonance on both sides—a Jew who decided it was appropriate to live as a gentile as against gentiles who decided that it was necessary to become Jews—virtually eliminated the possibility of compromise. The conflict did not merely concern circumcision. At stake was the source of commitment to the new social group and the uniqueness of its self-definition. For the Jewish community, special laws provided the sources of commitment and identity. For Paul, who experienced the opposition of other Jews and the acceptance of a gospel without purity rules, special laws could be replaced by conversion. In opposing circumcision Paul was opposing the traditional view of Jewish identity. Insofar as it impinged on Christianity, he was claiming that the presence of Christ created a new community that superseded the old one. The source of this opposition to circumcision can only be his own experience of conversion. He insists that kerygma, the central proclamation of Christianity, which he received by revelation, releases gentile proselytes from ceremonial Torah.

Paul does not miss the chance to castigate the circumcisers for ritual practice less exacting than his own when he was a Pharisee. The circumcisers, for all their zeal to perform this commandment, ironically are less observant than was Paul the Pharisee. Additionally they lack faith and hence are not true Christians: "For freedom Christ has set us free; stand fast therefore, and do not submit again to a yoke of slavery. Now I, Paul, say to you that if you receive circumcision, Christ will be of no advantage to you. I testify again to every man who receives circumcision that he is bound to keep the whole law. You are severed from Christ, you who would be justified by the law; you have fallen away from grace. For through the Spirit, by faith, we wait for the hope of righteousness. For in Christ Jesus neither circumcision nor uncircumcision is of any avail, but faith working through love" (Gal. 5:1–6). Paul says that Christianity is a radical new community where faith justifies and saves. Pharisaism, too, is an all-or-nothing proposition. The absolutes oppose each other unalterably. Paul radicalizes the issue, eliminating the position of easygoing neglect of law. His opponents felt that some law was important, but they are evidently not as stringent in applying cultic rules as Paul had been when he was a Pharisee: "For even those who receive circumcision do not themselves keep the law, but they desire to have you circumcised that they may glory in your flesh" (6:13). Paul believes that there is no need to compromise the protorabbinic position. It is simply irrelevant in Christianity. Paul underscores the irony by saying that circumcision severs from Christ. Indeed, it simply makes the convert Jewish by watered-down standards. Paul does not mean that a convert *cannot* be a Christian if circumcised as an entrance into the Christian community. His legal position is: "For in Christ Jesus neither circumcision nor uncircumcision is of any avail, but faith working through love" (Gal. 5:6). His point is that circumcision without transformation is contradictory to Christian faith, not that circumcision alone is contradictory to it. Romans 2:25 makes the same point, stating, "Circumcision indeed is of value if you obey the law; but if you break the law, your circumcision becomes uncircumcision." Those who wish to be circumcised should become completely observant, as pious as he once was. Otherwise, circumcision is just another pagan ceremony, as it is when performed by the Egyptians. Ironically, Paul retains his Pharisaic opinions. Anyone who becomes a Jew should become as pious as the

Pharisees; but those who convert to (Pharisaic) Judaism lose the specific value of their faith. Paul polarizes the positions in order to stimulate a radical choice.

Paul has no intention of recommending that his community adopt Pharisaism. That appears to be a choice only for a few Christians, a kind of reduction to absurdity in the community. The benefits of the spirit without law are all that Christians need, since they bring miracles (Gal. 3:1–5) and freedom from the demonic powers that inhabit paganism (4:8). He appeals to the gentiles from his personal experience: "Brethren, I beseech you, become as I am, for I also have become as you are" (4:12). There can be no doubt that Paul himself has not only preached the end of ceremonial laws, he has given up his adherence to them, though obviously not to their ethical impulse and statutes.[26] He is saying that the power of Christ's sacrifice has made the route of conversion to Judaism unnecessary and absolutely outmoded. Paul has decided to live as a righteous gentile or God-fearer.

CIRCUMCISION AND THE MEANING OF TORAH

In order to answer his Galatian critics, Paul states that uncircumcision is not a special dispensation to make gentile Christianity easier than Jewish Christianity. It is a result of revelation from God, not his private decision. His apostolate and his opinions emerge directly from his conversion and subsequent revelation, though we know that the meaning of these ecstatic experiences is normally mediated by socialization within the believing community. But what Paul says about his own conversion differs from the effect of his words on a largely gentile audience intent on conversion and puzzled by the proper way to effect it. As different as Judaism and Christianity might appear to us today, they appeared similar to first-century gentiles; indeed, they were often indistinguishable. Gentile motivations for converting to either Judaism or Christianity would also have been similar. The same people tempted to convert to Judaism would have been tempted to convert to Christianity as well. The converse is also true: potential converts to Christianity might decide that if Christianity is good, Judaism is better. We know from Paul's argument that at this point the people who were interested in Christianity were also tempted by Judaism. Paul's argument was that Christianity had the same benefits as ordinary Judaism. Paul's success is based on this fact: entering the community of the saved without Jewish law was easier for the gentile convert than entering the same community with the law. He fights against other apostles who want to impose the requirement of Torah after the fact. Paul is not in favor of lower moral standards, but he is in favor of changing and, in fact, dispensing with many ceremonial rules.

Paul is talking to the gentiles in Galatia about their faith, not giving a phenomenological analysis of the continued existence of Judaism after the Christ event. The issue for Paul is the basis of salvation for the Christian. One cannot become the equal of a Christian by becoming Jewish. It is unnecessary and insufficient to become a Jew because Judaism does not include the faith in Christ (Gal. 2:16). Thus, in Gal. 3:2–5, Paul is opposed to the works of the law and to any attempt to follow the special laws of Judaism, presenting in its place the preaching of faith (*akoēs pisteōs*).

There are three important reasons for Paul's anger in Galatians. First, the way in which he expresses himself on the issue of law depends on the context in which he writes and the question asked of him. Second, the decision to give up the specific laws of Judaism was an enormous step for Paul. Third, and more important, publicly to advocate overthrowing the law of Judaism would have been seen not only as transgression, which Paul admitted was a possible interpretation of his behavior, but as true apostasy. Paul, because of his rhetoric, could be accused of subverting Torah or leading others astray, a crime that could theoretically be punished by death, though the Jewish community's ability to carry out any capital sentence, either in the Diaspora or in Jerusalem, would be strictly circumscribed.

At the end of his letter to the Galatians Paul reveals some otherwise undocumented evidence about the range of feelings of the Jewish community about circumcision: "It is those who want to make a good showing in the flesh that would compel you to be circumcised, and only in order that they may not be persecuted for the cross of Christ. For even those who receive circumcision do not themselves keep the law, but they desire to have you circumcised that they may glory in your flesh. But far be it from me to glory except in the cross of our Lord Jesus Christ, by which the world has been crucified to me, and I to the world. For neither circumcision counts for anything, nor uncircumcision, but a new creation" (Gal. 6:12–15). Paul questions the motivations of those who recommend circumcision as much as those who accept it. Many do so only because they are afraid of being persecuted by the Jewish community, but ironically they themselves do not keep Torah sufficiently. Here again Paul gives us interesting information about actual Jewish behavior in the first century. We reach the same conclusion whether Paul is discussing gentile converts to Jewish Christianity or ordinary Jews. Some Jews performed a minimum of Jewish practice, less than a Pharisee would have done. They were considered Jews by their colleagues, though they may have been disparaged by Pharisees (and others) for impiety. This evidence suggests that on several issues the record of the Christian community is useful for understanding the feelings of the Jewish community. Paul's Pharisaic training affects his judgment about the piety of these less observant Jews. He states that those who boast of their entry into Judaism are simply not up to his standards of piety, so their boasts are empty. Some Christians may have even accepted circumcision as a mere formality, with no intention of any further Jewish practice, to avoid any problems from the Jewish community. Paul testifies that the ritual standards of ordinary Jews overlapped considerably with those of God-fearers.

Paul's discussion of Torah in Galatians is heavily affected by this concrete situation. But in Gal. 3:21, immediately after his chiastic interpretation of the curse of hanging on a tree, Paul attempts to formulate the meaning of law:

> Is the law then against the promises of God? Certainly not; for if a law had been given which could make alive, then righteousness would indeed be by the law. But the scripture consigned all things to sin, that what was promised to faith in Jesus Christ might be given to those who believe. Now before faith came, we were confined under the law, kept under restraint until faith should be revealed. So that the law was our custodian until Christ came, that we might be justified by faith. But now that faith has come, we are no longer under a custodian: for in Christ Jesus you are all sons of God, through faith. For as many of you as were baptized into Christ have put on Christ. There is neither Jew nor Greek, there is neither slave nor free, there is neither male nor female; for you are all one in Christ Jesus. And if you are Christ's, then you are Abraham's offspring, heirs according to the promise. (Gal. 3:21–29)

Paul is discussing the value of Jewish ceremonial law. Since a principal issue in Galatians is gentile circumcision, Paul begins to tackle the larger issue of the meaning of Jewish (ceremonial) law in general for gentiles, a discussion that also makes sense only in terms of his own conversion. Paul's initial purpose is to chastise his opponents and to explain his position on circumcision, which is the more important issue to the first-century Jew on account of this action's symbolic value. Paul begins by denying that Torah is against the promises of God, because God ordained it. It is a complete and full system of salvation. Yet its period of instruction is over, because law simply cannot raise the dead. But raising the dead is precisely what transformation will do.

Jewish law provided for a death penalty, so Paul can describe it as a law that kills. But for him, faith in Christ achieves resurrection. As a Pharisee, Paul already accepted the doctrine of resurrection. Now he has experienced it. This polemic derives from his conversion, where his life/death imagery emanates, because it comes from the mystical experience of angelic transformation for the coming eschaton. Christ has not only been raised from the dead; faith in Christ will raise Paul from the dead. Paul says that faith is what "makes alive." It replaces law and forms a new community where being Jewish or Greek, being circumcised or uncircumcised, has no more ultimate value than being male or female, slave or free. With its explicit metaphors of death and life, dressing and undressing, Gal. 3:21–29 relies heavily on the liturgical language of baptism, probably indicating the gentile church's substitution of baptism for circumcision. Paul uses the imagery to discuss a whole new community based on faith, which has replaced the tutorship of the law. It also reproduces the chronology of Paul's biography. Now all have been adopted as sons of Abraham through faith. This mission is to create a single family or community of believers in Christ, who can eat together and marry.

Paul is ready to oppose anyone who dissents from his vision of unity. Even the pillars (*styloi*) of the church in Jerusalem cannot legitimately challenge his authority on this issue. He was ready to stand alone, if necessary, against those who follow James or Peter at Antioch or Jerusalem. The Galatians should not believe the rumors that Paul preached uncircumcision to them to please human beings (Gal. 1:10) or that he teaches circumcision elsewhere, as if others are more worthy of Jewish responsibilities. Paul has aligned himself against the continued practice of circumcision in his gentile ministry.

A fuller historical context for these strangely pointed comments is suggested by Luke. He talks about the conservative party of Pharisees in Jerusalem (Acts 15:5), who naturally regarded circumcision as the sine qua non for conversion and defended the complete validity of the Mosaic law for all Christians. This would be the expected reaction of any Pharisee—Jew or Christian—when asked about the rules for entering the Jewish community. Acts is not automatically trustworthy on these issues, yet it is interesting to entertain the possibility that it presents a view from a slightly different perspective of the same Paul that we have been studying. Acts does not endorse Paul's apostleship to the extent that Paul claims for his side, so its portrayal probably reflects a more circumspect view of the outcome. Peter and James could not have belonged to the most conservative group, at least as they are portrayed by Luke, since they eventually accommodate the gentiles wholly in regard to circumcision and partly in regard to dietary laws. Therefore, a wide spectrum of opinion existed among Christian communities in regard to the continued validity of the Jewish law.[27]

One need only compare Paul's position with the party that Acts 15:5 calls "the believers who belonged to the party of the Pharisees," to see how important was Paul's conversion to his religious convictions. Not every Pharisaic Christian was *converted* from Pharisaic Judaism to Christianity. Many Jews, including some Pharisees, saw faith in Jesus as the continuation and completion of their system of religious practice. Paul is unique in that he was not only Jewish but *a convert* to Christianity. His radical shift in religious sensibility comes out of that tension. The first and longest conflict was over circumcision. Other conflicts broke out as well. These conflicts brought Paul into court and ultimately to martyrdom, if church tradition is correct. But before the conflict was full-blown, Paul outlined his mature plan for the gentile Christian church.

In Galatians Paul is addressing his gentile converts to Christianity. He states his position that circumcision (hence ceremonial Torah) is irrelevant for justification. In the context of circumcision, the issue is theoretical, since only gentile Christians entering the community need to make a choice about circumcision. The Jewish Christians were already circumcised. In this respect the conference was a compromise. Paul's position is not accepted, but the conference did accept Paul as an apostle of an uncircumcised gentile church. Moreover, they did not necessarily accept Paul's idea of a single, united Christian community. In return, Paul might have left vague the implications for Torah of his position on circumcision. Paul appears to have won some support for his contention that circumcision is not necessary for gentiles, even if he made no progress on the more radical position that it had no significance for Jewish Christians either.[28]

Paul did not thereby give up his principle of freedom from the ceremonial laws. He chose not to emphasize the consequences of it. This is a generous or diplomatic accommodation to the feelings of the circumcised gentiles and Jews within Christianity, but it is not a compromise in principle. Church unity, to say nothing of Paul's continued acceptance as an apostle, must have been the overriding consideration.[29] Paul states this diplomatic accommodation in his first letter to the Corinthians: "Only, let every one lead the life which the Lord has assigned to him, and in which

God has called him. This is my rule in all the churches. Was any one at the time of his call already circumcised? Let him not seek to remove the marks of circumcision. Was any one at the time of his call uncircumcised? Let him not seek circumcision. For neither circumcision counts for anything nor uncircumcision, but keeping the commandments of God. Every one should remain in the state in which he was called" (1 Cor. 7:17–20). Paul does not shrink from using the language of commandments to discuss Christian responsibilities. If Paul were maintaining an uncompromising theological position about the value of Torah, he could not say this. Paul does not give up his principle of personal transformation through faith; he advocates an accommodation to the feelings of the circumcised. This is not a compromise of his ideological position, as he is not recommending that gentiles be circumcised. Instead, it is a commentary on Gal. 3:28, his baptismal formula of equality.[30]

Stendahl, Gager, and Gaston, in emphasizing the gentile audience of Paul's letter to the Galatians, have tried to prove that all of Paul's discussions about the law make reference only to gentiles, assuming that Paul thought Torah was appropriate for Jews but not for gentiles. They describe, however, the effect of Paul's accommodation or diplomatic position after the Jerusalem Conference. Paul's communal ruling in 1 Corinthians admits to this standard, but it is a record of his willingness to compromise for the sake of church unity. In fact, if Acts is correct, he goes beyond his accommodation in 1 Corinthians: he even circumcises Timothy, a Jew who was uncircumcised from birth. This is credible because the point of Paul's accommodation is that gentiles need not be circumcised and circumcision is of no benefit to the Jew either, but it may do no harm if the person already has faith. So Paul could easily have gone slightly further to accommodate the Jewish Christians. He says that the commandments of God are important, which would stymie any theologian assuming that Paul is opposed in principle to all works of righteousness. He is opposed to circumcision for gentiles, but he is in favor of church unity. He is able to accommodate other positions, provided that they do not insist on gentile circumcision and take out the entire force of his point about the centrality of faith.

It is misleading to hold Paul to a strictly ideological position about circumcision, for in the name of church unity he may make an accommodation to his opponents' position, whenever he can do so without compromising his ideological position (1 Cor. 7:17–20). Thus we have an interesting anomaly. He insists on the primacy of faith and the entrance of gentiles into the community, but he is willing to accommodate his opposition, as long as his principles are not directly violated by the action. He simply chooses not to exercise the freedom which he has defined for himself.

Paul appears to be thinking as a rabbinic Jew, not a theologian—a frustrating suggestion for subsequent Christian theology. Whenever there is a problem in rabbinic practice, the more lenient opinion naturally accommodates the less lenient, if the principle can be preserved, for the necessity of one overrides the predisposition of another. In modern life, many nonorthodox Jews wed and divorce according to orthodox law to avoid any chance of impropriety. Thus, Judaism can accommodate relatively large divergences in theological opinion by expressing symbolic unity in a conservative ritual.[31] No compromise of the magnitude that Paul suggested has actually been needed in Judaism. But Judaism has never been forced to face the basic issue of the Christian community—uniting gentiles and Jews into a single church. Rabbinic Judaism begins from the opposite premise: gentiles can be righteous but they are not the same community as Jews. Paul's method of thinking, rather than the solution itself, is a characteristic Jewish response. Alternatively, Paul's position itself represents an attempt to weld a single community of Jews and gentiles in Judaism, since the Christian and Jewish communities were not clearly separate then, although the vituperation shows that tension was growing fast. Jewish Christians rejected Paul's answer, which foreshadowed the later, more final break of Jewish rejection of Christians. The ritual actions of the community are important expressions of its unity. Further, Paul gained acceptance for his ministry with the other apostles with this accommodation, something he was unlikely to achieve on any other terms.

If Paul's letter to the Galatians were written before the church conference, there would be no real problem in understanding Paul's action, for it would represent his own opinion. Assuming that his opinions in Galatians are after the conference, which seems more likely, the situation in Galatians is different from Paul's charitable accommodations, for it is a flagrant violation of the church agreement by the opposing side. Some from the circumcising party have attempted to circumcise gentiles, which reneges on the agreement Paul thought he had achieved. This probably means only that the agreement that Paul thought he had achieved in Jerusalem was not automatically shared by all Jewish Christians. Paul might have overinterpreted the agreement, or some Jewish Christians may not have known about the agreement; others may not have assented to what was agreed in Jerusalem. Christianity was as disunified at its beginning as was the Jewish community itself at the time. It began as a group of interpretations of Jesus' message, not a single orthodox one.

Paul's statements in Galatians show us his ideological position and his sense of righteous indignation that Jewish Christians have not all accepted his mission as outlined by the Jerusalem council. Paul does not advocate twin paths to salvation. He argues that circumcision is of no real account for *anyone*. In his ire at the lack of respect for his authority and the doubt it puts on his position (Gal. 1:6–10), he states that the ceremonial Torah of these Jewish Christians is ancillary to God's purpose, having been added because of Jewish transgressions and having been given by angels or a mediator instead of God (Gal. 3:19–21).[32] Violations of the council's actions bring out strong language in return; but such strong statements would have confirmed Paul's apostasy to Pharisaism. Again, postdecision dissonance explains the strongly held opinions on both sides.

It is possible to accept Acts' reconstruction of the events without giving up Paul's essential legal position, if one realizes that the Jewish community dealt with this issue as it dealt with most others: practice had decisive import, not theology. This means only that Acts *might* be right about Paul's strategy for accommodation. As long as both parties stuck to the agreement outlined in Acts, there might have been little difficulty between Paul and his opponents, assuming that they lived in different communities. If some conservative members of the community did not accept the agreement, if others went back on it, or if there was a battle for dominance within a community, as at Antioch, a breech could not be avoided. Paul's ire is the natural result.

The most conservative members of the church advocate gentile circumcision, hence conversion to Judaism. Paul represents those who feel circumcision to be irrelevant, but the compromise allows gentile entrance into Christianity as God-fearers. This difference of opinion in the Christian community is an extension of the spectrum of Jewish positions about the salvation of gentiles. Some Jews thought that all had to be converted to be saved; others thought that gentiles could be righteous according to the Noahide Commandments. The Christians inherited the conflict in a particularly pointed way because such apostles as Paul desired to make one community of all believers in Christ.

Scholars have speculated about the outcome of Paul's conflict in Galatia. Wilckens, for instance, is quite pessimistic about Paul's ability to establish his side of the controversy, seeing in it the seeds of Paul's later unsuccessful fight with Jerusalem.[33] Whatever the outcome among the congregations of Galatia, the accommodation could continue only as long as there were no mixed congregations with Pharisaic influence, since those Jewish Christians could not eat together or intermarry with the gentiles. In a mixed congregation like Antioch, Jerusalem, or Rome, the separation was disturbed because Paul's own preaching could be judged apostasy.

THE CIRCUMCISION OF TIMOTHY: AN EXERCISE OF IMAGINATION

Although Acts may not be an accurate historical source, Paul could have held the opinions expressed in his letters and acted in the way described by Acts. If Paul's only motivation were the theological purity of his discussions of works of the law, no compromise would be possible. But if, as I suppose, Paul were asking himself how far he could accommodate his practice for the purposes of church unity, many accommodations would be possible. The freedom that Christ imposed on him offered the opportunity for magnanimity.

We can investigate the portrayal in Acts of Paul's actions in regard to the circumcision of Timothy. The purpose of the Acts story of the circumcision of Timothy is to illustrate how accommodation between Jewish Christianity and gentile Christianity is possible. Acts 16:1–5 contains this puzzling report: "And he [Paul] came also to Derbe and to Lystra. A disciple was there, named Timothy, the son of a Jewish woman who was a believer; but his father was a Greek. He was well spoken of by the brethren at Lystra and Iconium. Paul wanted Timothy to accompany him; and he took him and circumcised him because of the Jews that were in those places, for they all knew that his father was a Greek. As they went on their way through the cities, they delivered to them for observance the decisions which had been reached by the apostles and elders who were at Jerusalem. So the churches were strengthened in the faith, and they increased in numbers daily."

This story is puzzling because it appears to contradict Paul's strong opinion in Galatians. Many scholars assume that Acts has gotten the issue wrong, perhaps because of misinformation. Perhaps Acts deliberately invented a story in order to illustrate its concept of church unity.[34] This short incident plays a role in two extremely important motifs in Acts. The first is the general theme of Jewish opposition to Paul's message and Paul's great care to avoid conflict with the Jewish community. Second and more important, the story comes immediately after the Jerusalem conference in which the circumcision of the gentiles was deemed unnecessary by the centrist church forces. The Pharisaic party of Christians presents its position: "Unless you are circumcised according to the custom of Moses, you cannot be saved" (Acts 15:1). Paul, Barnabas, and some of the others present their side of the issue. The council decides with Paul: "For it has seemed good to the Holy Spirit and to us to lay upon you no greater burden than these necessary things: that you abstain from what has been sacrificed to idols and from blood and from what is strangled and from unchastity" (Acts 15:28, 29). The position of the council is supportive of the theory that the mature rabbinic doctrine of the Noahide Commandments was being discussed in first-century Judaism, although the rabbis may have framed the problem differently in their exegesis.

The story of Timothy follows, demonstrating the effect of the council. After the messengers of the council came, testifying to the agreement about ritual status in Judaism, the faith of the church was strengthened. It was Paul's behavior, at first in doubt, later confirmed by the Jerusalem messengers, that helps the success of the church. The issue is made even sharper by the portrayal in Acts of Paul's later troubles in Jerusalem. There, the Jewish Christians fear the condemnation of the Jews who will say that "you teach all the Jews who are among the gentiles to forsake Moses, telling them not to circumcise their children or observe the customs" (Acts 21:21). In Acts 21:28, the Jews of Asia do cry out that Paul is the man "who is teaching men everywhere against the people and the law and this place." The point of Timothy's circumcision from the point of view in Acts is that, although he has a gentile father and is regarded as a gentile, he is in fact Jewish. Paul abides scrupulously by the compromise of the Jerusalem conference, going so far as circumcising a Jew, because Jewish law requires that Jews be circumcised. The criticism of the Jewish Christians is therefore unjust.

Whether Acts reflects what actually happened is irrelevant for the moment. Timothy's mother and father are Jewish and gentile respectively, although the rabbinic rule about personal status following the mother is not explicitly stated. It does not need to be; otherwise, the entire incident is pointless. But the moral of the story is that Timothy is legally Jewish, though he appears Greek, so Paul obeys the Jerusalem council. The only thing standing in the way of such an interpretation is the twentieth-century notion that Paul could not have done so and still logically kept to his theological principles. But Paul does not violate his principle by circumcising Timothy, if Timothy were an uncircumcised Jew. He was merely forbearing from the freedom that he has attained. In so doing, Paul was solving the problem from a halakhic point of view, not a theological one. Further, Timothy's status follows the usual practice in Judaism, that a child of a Jewish mother is Jewish, so there is some support for the idea that the matrilineal principle existed in first-century Judaism.

If the moral issue is situational rather than a test case for a theology of works, Paul has more latitude than is normally ascribed to him. It is certainly possible to imagine a situation in which Paul could have acceded to Timothy's request, if one assumes that his method of adjudication was based on Pharisaic analyses of the individual nature of each event. Let us assume, for instance, that besides being Jewish Timothy himself *wanted* to be circumcised to return to the Jewish people in his acceptance of Christ. Not having been circumcised cannot itself make Timothy a sinner accord-ing to the Pharisees, if he corrected the error of his father by undergoing the rite himself. The commandment of circumcision in rabbinic tradition is encumbent on the father, but it does not affect Timothy's status as a Jew. If the father will not perform the rite, rabbinic authorities are to do so. Timothy's identity as a Jew would be uncontested even in rabbinic halakha though his circumcision may be lacking. But if Timothy under-stands the value of faith, feels a complete part of the community without it, and regularly takes part in Paul's community, would Paul have under-stood an ethnic or nonreligious reason for desiring to be circumcised?

If Paul's point had been that circumcision is not to be done under any circumstances because it represents an attempt at self-salvation, he could never have done so, as many scholars have pointed out. But we know that Paul may have agreed that circumcision is possible for Jewish Christians, if the Acts account has any validity. It is irrelevant that he might prefer a stronger position. He says only that circumcision is not to be effaced, nor is it necessary for someone who is not already circumcised, for it is of no relevance to salvation at all. If Paul's motivation were to gain acceptance for his gentile mission and insure unity in the community, then he would have performed it for Timothy, especially if that is what Timothy wanted. Would Paul have forbidden a Jew to be circumcised who wanted to be circumcised? That would have been a legal folly in Paul's day, when the Jewish community understood the penalty for such an action to be death! Thus, if Acts is correct, Paul's letter to the Galatians can be understood as an answer to his gentile converts, who see in this an inconsistency with his previous preaching. For gentiles to go on to circumcision proves the weak-ness of their faith. For a Jew to do so, in spite of the fact that it is unneces-sary, is only his legal right. But it all depends on the conclusion that Timothy is Jewish; otherwise, Paul is inconsistent.

Luke portrays Paul as true to his principles. Luke makes Paul's act of circumcising Timothy an extreme generosity, since he accommodates more than he recommends as necessary in 1 Corinthians. Paul would not have compromised his principles, if his principles were that circumcision is of no hindrance or help to salvation. Paul's action would have been ritually appropriate to a Jew regardless of his position on the issue of salvation and especially if Timothy understood exactly what Paul's position was and accepted it.

Whether this story shows that the matrilineal definition of a Jew existed in the first century is moot, because Luke is not necessarily a credible narrator on points of Jewish law, especially when the narrative has such a clear agenda. It appears that the usual procedure in Jewish laws of personal status is in effect. Further, considering the diversity of first-century Judaism, it would be a mistake to consider the Pharisaic practice normative, even if it later became the basis of the rabbinic one. To interpret the story as Paul's circumcision of a gentile convert to Christianity, and as evidence that the contemporary Jewish definition of a Jew did not exist, is simply unconvincing. The only thing that is clear from the story is that early Christianity attracted certain persons who were anomalous to Judaism, as Timothy's identity certainly was. Therefore, Acts is not relating a historical incident but it *might* be historical without affecting Paul's stated position that circumcision is unnecessary for the new Christian community. Such behavior on Paul's part would have generated the question, Was Paul now recommending circumcision for gentile converts? To have given his right hand to Peter and the other apostles would have raised the same issue. Thus, Acts may have more validity viewed from the perspective of legal precedent than from the perspective of Reformation theology.

THE PROBLEM OF PAUL'S SON: ANOTHER EXERCISE OF IMAGINATION

To investigate what Paul's opinions meant in practice, we can ask an interesting theoretical question. Raymond E. Brown asks what he calls a facetious question: "Would Paul have circumcised his son?"[35] The question is facetious because Paul never had a son. As it is easy to imagine a situation in which Paul would have agreed to circumcise Timothy, so it is possible, though less easy, to imagine a circumstance in which Paul would have circumcised his own son. Raymond Brown's question underlines the delicacy and subtlety of Paul's position against circumcising gentile converts, if Acts is correct. According to his ideological position, Paul would have found a circumcision unnecessary for salvation. But, if he were following the compromise of the church, he might have circumcised his son anyway, merely to have claimed for him his rightful place in the ethnic community of Jews, though maintaining that it was unnecessary for Christian faith or salvation. The question of the circumcision of Paul's son would have been crucial for establishing the truth of the allegation that the Jewish Christians leveled against Paul: that he was teaching Jews to forsake their Torah and give up circumcision. If Paul had a son and failed to circumcise him, he would certainly have been called a transgressor. If he had made a public display of his teaching, he might have been accused of apostasy and been prosecuted wherever possible.

Paul was not a typical case of a Jew quietly leaving Judaism through assimilation. He made a public display of his christological interpretation of Judaism and his interpretation of Torah in the synagogues before he was forced to withdraw to his own communities, as Acts makes clear. He also openly challenges rabbinic law by consorting with gentiles and disseminating his theories of the limitation to Torah. Further, Paul constantly makes reference to his conversion as a proof of the power of the Spirit, using his own history and experience as a paradigm for believers. This tactic, as I maintained, had certain and unavoidable consequences within his missionary enterprise.

In Acts, Paul and his compatriots almost unfailingly go first to the synagogues, finding opportunities to speak and debate at the regular services. When they meet resistance there, they withdraw to the households of sympathetic individuals, where they continue their preaching (16:13–15; 18:2). In Philippi, Lydia helps (16:15), in Thessalonica it is Jason (17:5–9), in Corinth Priscilla, Aquila, and Titius Justus (18:2–4, 7). Lydia is a gentile worshiper of Judaism, a God-fearer, showing one example of how Christianity spread and to whom it most appealed. Such stories confirm the uniquely isolated position of Paul's congregations. They also show that Paul's presence could not have been unnoticed among those Jews and Jewish Christians who disagreed with him.

Fortunately for Paul, there was no certain evidence to convict him on the question of circumcision. Though Acts takes great pains to disprove the allegation, Timothy's circumcision can be viewed either way: as a strong denial of the allegation or as a sensitivity to the truth of the allegation that Acts wants to cover up. Paul himself was an apocalypticist, believing in the imminence of Christ's kingdom. He clearly felt that his position was an interim one and that the problem would shortly be solved by the parousia. Though he never married, he avers that others might do so (1 Cor. 7:25–40). He was celibate, the state he recommended for everyone, citing as a reason the shortness of time until the parousia. A fortunate corollary of Paul's beliefs about sexuality is the prevention of any critical evidence about the rite of circumcision for Jewish children. If Acts is correct about Paul's circumcision of Timothy, however, he allowed that Jewish Christians could continue to circumcise their children, even if he recommended not doing so. Paul's position on marriage may, however, be parallel to his position on circumcision. Ideologically he sees no reason to continue either custom, but he may allow both marriage and circumcision in order to prevent unnecessary social dislocation.

Paul has not violated his ideological principle in regard to circumcision, for he feels his policy is entirely consistent: "But if I, brethren, still preach circumcision, why am I still persecuted[?]" (Gal. 5:11). His letter, written to the Galatian gentile congregation, clarifies the issue. If his position on circumcision is consistent with his position on marriage, he advocated neither but would accept either as an interim ethic. His formula of equality therefore brought not the end of distinction, but the end of the importance of the distinction (1 Cor. 7:17–27).

Most important, circumcision was not a trivial issue of style, custom, or hygiene. It had overriding symbolic importance for the Jewish community of the first century. For Jews, circumcision had become the first and most obvious sign of the covenant of Judaism, the mark of belonging to the Jewish people. Further, the first-century Jewish community remembered that scarcely two hundred years previously the Maccabees fought and had been martyred to free the Jewish people in Judea from the tyrant Antiochus IV, who had forbidden circumcision. According to the famous story in 1 Maccabees, which was in wide circulation in Paul's day, Antiochus was helped by some renegade Jews who felt that circumcision was no longer necessary (1 Maccabees 1). Thus, the dangers of apostasy were already emphasized by the narration of the Maccabean revolt. The result of the war was the independence of the Judean state until the arrival of the Romans, so circumcision became linked to both religious and national aspects of Jewish identity. To ignore it, neglect to do it, or deface it was apostasy and treason. With good reason Paul and the church after him was careful not to lay itself open to the charge of opposing circumcision for Jewish Christians. Nevertheless, in this most important area, Paul's preaching constantly risked just that dangerous charge, which Paul himself realized when he admitted that without the fortification of his revelation to abandon Torah and proselytize the gentiles by faith he was merely a transgressor. To the Jewish community, and to the Jewish Christian community, who gave no credence to Paul's special commissioning or to his conversion, Paul was an apostate.

CHAPTER SEVEN

¶ROMANS 7 AND JEWISH DIETARY LAWS

For Paul, the critical issue for faith was to be in Christ. For people of the spirit, the flesh was secondary. Nevertheless, Paul's community needed advice on fleshly matters. The issue of dietary laws appears to have given Paul as much or more difficulty as the issue of circumcision. Although circumcision is a physically difficult and painful operation for adult men, psychologically raising cognitive dissonance, it is a rite that need only be performed once, cannot be easily undone, and is not normally available to public scrutiny. In Paul's growing discussion of Jewish law, dietary laws prove to be the more difficult case; as public rites easily open to view, they are constantly an issue. It is also possible to vacillate between customs. Thus dietary laws become central to Paul's discussion of Jewish ceremonial law in a way that circumcision had not. This irony, that the less severe laws are the most troublesome ones, has been insufficiently appreciated.

By analyzing the symbolic issues inherent in the performance of dietary laws, the difficult and much debated passage in Romans 7, in which Paul makes some personal remarks about Torah, can be clarified. In the thicket of Pauline scholarship, Romans 7 is no doubt the center of the darkest, thorniest, and most disputed territory. In this passage Paul speaks in the first person about his inability to do the good that he desired while he was keeping Torah. Readers of the New Testament from the second century onward have argued about Paul's meaning. He appears to be meditating on the problem of volition and self-salvation. Is Paul speaking about his personal experience? Does he have a guilty conscience? Does he refer to experience before or after being a Christian? All the logical possibilities have been investigated, though none seems to satisfy all the data. If Paul is

speaking about his Christian experience, why is he making uncharac-
teristically critical statements about the Christian life? If he is only speaking universally, with no reference specifically to himself, why does he
adopt the first person so straightforwardly? Any argument about the
meaning of these passages must begin with a new exegesis that appears to
fit Paul's words.[1]

Some scholars have suggested that Paul's first person is an impersonal
figure of speech signifying all Israel, citing the Psalms and especially the
Hodayoth of the Dead Sea Scrolls as example of an impersonal "I."[2] But
the most convincing analogies produced in biblical and later Qumranic
Psalms come from confessional poetry appropriated into liturgy, which is
quite a different *Sitz im Leben* from Paul's letters. Throughout his letters
Paul uses the first person in the ordinary way. In Romans he addresses
himself to his readers both in the first person singular and plural in order to
generalize from their mutual experience to conclusions about the life of
faith.[3] But Paul cannot here be using liturgy.[4] Rom. 7:22–24 makes an
impersonal reading of Romans 7 virtually impossible: "For I delight in the
law of God, in my inmost self, but I see in my members another law at war
with the law of my mind and making me captive to the law of sin which
dwells in my members. Wretched man that I am! Who will deliver me from
this body of death?" This is not liturgical language but is a purely private
observation. The most obvious interpretation of Romans 7 begins with the
idea that Paul is speaking personally.[5] This does not mean that Paul feels
his experience to be eccentric; rather, he mentions his own experience
because, he believes, it illustrates a general religious truth with which he
hopes his audience will come to agree.

PAUL'S JEWISH AUDIENCE

The letter to the Romans is addressed to the church (or church-
es) in Rome, which evidently included both Jews and gentiles. The mixed
population makes it one of the crucial tests of the Christian community.
Much of the letter cautions the gentiles not to act superior to the Jews and
Jewish Christians because of their understanding of the obsolescence of
Jewish ceremonial laws. Chapter 7, however, defines a special audience
for the letter. Paul speaks to his brothers (*adelphoi*), "those who know the
Law" (Rom. 7:1). The context clarifies the identity of his brothers as
primarily the Jewish Christians and their followers in the community at
Rome, as Paul immediately mentions Jewish marriage and divorce law.
Whether or not he implicitly speaks to the audience he expects in Jerusa-

lem or has a specific problem of the Roman community in mind, he deliberately assumes a shared experience with the Jewish Christians in Rome. By first examining this experience and then raising the issues cf doctrine that depend on these experiences, Paul hopes to convince his compatriots of his position.

Paul's basic point appears in Rom. 7:4–7, in which he says that the Jewish Christians, having entered the Christian community, are discharged from ceremonial Torah, are dead to what held them captive, giving them a new freedom. He made a similar point to the gentile Christians in the Roman community with regard to sin. With the Jewish Christian community he finds it necessary to add a few personal notes; like him, they had come to Christianity from a Jewish past where Torah is paramount. Romans 7 makes good sense when read as a personal statement.

Yet Rom. 7:9–12 is troublesome: "I was once alive apart from the Law, but when the commandment came, sin revived and I died; the very commandment which promised life proved to be death to me. For sin, finding opportunity in the commandment, deceived me and by it killed me. So the law is holy, and the commandment is holy and just and good." These verses appear to state that he gave up Torah at a particular point and then returned to it. Paul nowhere explicitly states that he stopped observing Torah, and many New Testament scholars justifiably maintain that Paul continued to be an observant Jew throughout his life.[6] If this report is to be taken as personal, Paul is saying that there was a period of time when he did not observe Torah. For some reason he returned to it, and when he did, sin revived in him. This passage seems to contradict Paul's statements in Galatians and Corinthians where he says he gave up the law!

There are five logical possibilities for making sense of this statement:

1. Paul might be speaking generally rather than about himself, but we have seen this to be unlikely. Many scholars suggest that he is referring to the prelapsarian period. A personal reading of Romans 7 would logically rule out this meaning. Moreover, Paul's language is clearly inappropriate for a description of Paradise.[7]

2. "Apart from the Law" could refer to the time before Paul reached thirteen, the age of legal majority (i.e., what would later be called *bar mitzvah* [see *Avot* 5.21]), but this seems artificial: Paul's minority in Torah learning, like every other child's, would have made him subject to Torah before he became responsible for keeping Torah.[8]

3. There could have been a time before Paul became a Pharisee when he did not keep the law. Acts records that Paul came from a Pharisaic family

in Tarsus (Acts 23:6), but several scholars have questioned the meaning of being a Pharisee in the Diaspora.[9] Paul might then have been following a pattern of religious questing when he became a Pharisee, before he entered Christianity. Though this theory has much to recommend it, I find no evidence supporting it in Paul's writing.

4. Paul could be describing his life as a Pharisee when he talks about his inability to do the good that he wants: though Torah is good and holy, it led him to some wrong conclusions and, therefore, needs to be revalued. Paul's statements in Galatians 1 and Philippians 3 of the blamelessness of his behavior as a Pharisee argue against understanding Romans 7 as a reference to his Pharisaism. This is not conclusive since Paul may have been guilty of no infraction against Torah yet had a guilty conscience as a Pharisee. Some modern converts report a great dissatisfaction with their previous life so the interpretation is plausible, but in this case his statement of being outside Torah is too obscure to unravel. The most cogent argument against this position is that Paul had a "robust conscience."[10] Paul's discussion of these issues proves to be less ethereal and more practical.

5. Paul could be describing his experience with Torah *after* his conversion. This is not a new interpretation: Augustine and various other Latin fathers, as well as Luther, Calvin, Barth, Nygren, and Cranfield (among others), have read Paul in this way.[11] I think that this is the most profitable possibility. We have raised the possibility that Paul continued to keep Torah for a while after his conversion, and his fourteen years in gentile community slowly convinced him of the irrelevance of Torah. The testimony of Acts that Paul circumcised Timothy is not impossible either. In neither of these cases, however, do we have direct testimony from Paul to corroborate the change. In the case of the dietary laws, we have evidence that Paul did practice them on occasion, when he was present in Jewish communities (1 Cor. 9:20–22).

The strongest and most often raised objection to interpreting Romans 7 as Paul's experience after conversion can be found in Romans 8. Many scholars have noted that the two sections naturally set off each other, so that chapter 7 describes a person under Torah, and chapter 8 describes a person redeemed by grace. This makes simple theological sense, but it may not be the kind of sense that Paul wanted to make. It does not necessarily follow that Paul is distinguishing between Judaism and Christianity. He could as easily be talking about the distinction between two types of Christianity—being under Torah as a Christian and being saved by faith as a Christian, for the distinction between the two religions was not clear in Paul's day. The sense is apposite because he is trying to convince Jewish Christians of his personal view of salvation by faith. Since Paul is a kind of Jewish Christian, and since it has become clear that he is speaking personally, Paul must be speaking as a kind of Jewish Christian to other Jewish Christians about the value of Torah to Jewish Christians. In Rom. 8:3, he can be describing both pre-Christian and Christian observance of Torah from the point of view of a Christian. He would then be saying that Torah has no positive value for salvation even for the Christian redeemed, though it might continue to be meaningful as prophecy and divinely directed history. This is what he has said many times before. But to understand what he means by saying that he returned to the law, we must return to Paul's discussions of Jewish ceremonies.

THE WEAK AND THE STRONG IN CORINTH

Paul's circumcision strategy could allow a variety of accommodations, as long as the principle was not compromised. In regard to Jewish dietary practice, Paul used the same strategy, except that the consequences are more obvious because dietary laws relate to ongoing rituals, as opposed to circumcision, which is performed but once. There is considerable evidence in Paul's letters that he did change his practice whenever he could compromise in the name of unity while avoiding a violation of his principles.

Evidence that Paul did change his opinions about observing the ceremonial laws of Torah begins with his statement about his devotion to his mission: "To the Jews I became as a Jew, in order to win Jews; to those under the law I became as one under the law—though not being myself under the law—that I might win those under the law. To those outside the law I became as one outside the law—not being without law toward God but under the law of Christ—that I might win those outside the law. To the weak I became weak, that I might win the weak. I have become all things to all men, that I might by all means save some" (1 Cor. 9:20–22). Paul claims participation in a Jewish mission as well as a gentile one. Possibly his participation in the Jewish mission ended with the Jerusalem council. The context of Paul's statements is crucial for understanding his referents. Paul is not just discussing Torah in general or how to honor local customs while missionizing. He is discussing the issue of the *weak* and the *strong*, his terms for parties in the controversy about things sacrificed to idols (*eidolothuta*), an issue that deeply concerns dietary habits. Paul takes up the issue of dietary laws again in Romans, though in a different context.

He admits to abridging Torah when he mentions his own behavior, for only someone who thought Torah to have a limited role would be able to say that he or she merely followed the conventions of the community he or she was visiting. A Jew fully following Torah does not have this choice: "Food will not commend us to God. We are no worse off if we do not eat, and no better off if we do. Only take care lest this liberty of yours somehow become a stumbling block to the weak" (1 Cor. 8:8–9).

In 1 Corinthians Paul is definitely speaking to gentiles. Much as the Pharisees may have shared in feelings for the universal salvation of humanity, they could never have said that food will not commend us to God. Gentiles, of course, do not have to keep the same laws as Jews, and it is strictly true for Pharisees as well that observing the dietary laws is of no possible benefit to the non-Jew. But what of possible converts and God-fearers? The situation is moot. Paul is risking the charge of becoming a violator of Torah and leading the innocent astray. His congregations, committed to this liberty, would themselves antagonize the more conservative members of the Christian community. Thus, Paul counsels moderation. It is clear that he feels that the dietary laws are not of primary concern for anyone, even for Jews. But theological interpretations of Paul must be suspect: A person committed entirely to the destruction of a works-centered righteousness that commits the sin of self-justification could not in principle exercise the freedom to return to it. Many scholars have pointed to the idealism of Paul's ethical principles in these passages. But few have pointed out that the passage appears as well to be an apologia of Paul's own behavior: "This is my defense [*apologia*] to those who would examine me" (1 Cor. 9:3). It is interesting to speculate as to how formal an examination Paul is anticipating. If it is a legal process, we see a hint of a more serious problem behind these details of Jewish observance. Paul's defense must be against those who saw this behavior as apostasy or subverting Torah.[12]

The opponents of Paul in this instance are likely to be Jewish Christians who pride themselves on their legal practice.[13] A likely possibility, then, has been insufficiently investigated in New Testament literature: In Rom. 7:9 Paul could be reflecting on his personal experience after giving up serious allegiance to the ceremonial Torah. He still sees reason to return to various customs afterward as a courtesy to those whose sensibilities might be offended by his private beliefs. But the moment he *returns* to Torah is a crucial one in which sin, especially the sin of pride, can affect his actions, making him think that the ceremonial laws are important. It is a significant factor in his troubles within the Jewish and Jewish Christian communities.

Paul's position about observing food laws is spelled out in terms of ritual requirements as often as it is in terms of principles, in keeping with the Pharisaic approach to the problem of law. Moral principles are adduced through legal principles or cases, which become boundary-marking precedents for the community. He uses the same method for discussing the overriding principles. He warns the Corinthians not to eat meat sacrificed to idols. He approves of eating meat at another's house (even if the ritual circumstances of its slaughter are not known), yet he disapproves of sharing in the sacrifical meal at a public temple service of a pagan cult. Christians must not be seen at idolatrous sacrifices because this gives the impression that Christians believe in the idols. Though pagan *gods* have no real existence, behind them are *demons* tempting the righteous to destruction, because those who eat the pagan sacrifices become communal partners (*koinonoi*) with the demons (1 Cor. 10:18–22), as Christians become communal partners with Christ. Many New Testament scholars skip over the precise way in which Paul defines each ritual occasion, assuming that all rituals of this sort are exploded by Christian theology. Paul is, however, attacking the problem situationally.

In Gal. 2:11–12, Paul says that he opposed Cephas and James. Cephas ate with gentiles but then drew back and separated himself, fearing the circumcision party. Paul criticizes Cephas for changing his stance and jeopardizing the unity of the Christian community. There is a crucial difference between Paul and Cephas. For Cephas the change in practice was motivated by indecision about the value of Torah; for Paul, who had clarified his opinion about the limitations of Torah, the issue was not the distinction in purity between Jews and gentiles but church unity. Paul would not tolerate any distinctions among the saved within the Christian community and, one assumes, he would not have altered his practice for the purpose of making distinctions between Christians, only for removing them. This has obvious repercussions in how Peter and Paul would have analyzed the question of food laws. For Peter (Cephas) in the Pauline letter as well as for the Peter described by Luke, the issue might have been the continuance of the kosher laws per se, as Acts maintains. But for Paul, writing decades earlier, the basic issue might have been narrower: the correct procedure for eating with gentiles. This is discussed as a separate question from food laws in general in the Mishnah, and it appears to be directly apposite to Paul's circumstances, since he lived in a gentile community.

Many New Testament scholars miss subtleties in this argument by assuming with Luke (Acts 10:27–48) that Jews could have no intercourse with gentiles at all and especially could not sit at table with gentiles. To the contrary, there is no law in rabbinic literature that prevents a Jew from eating with a gentile. Although eating only with one's coreligionists is not a law explicitly enjoined on Jews, Paul, when he was a Pharisee, could not easily have eaten either with gentiles or impure Jews, because they carried ritual impurities to the table and were ignorant about how to prevent impurities from being transferred to the faithful. He might not trust a gentile host to know which foods Jews cannot eat.[14] If rabbinic rules were in effect, the Pharisaic Paul also would have been careful to avoid eating certain foods with gentiles on account of idolatry.

The Pharisaic position represents a very conservative approach to Jewish dietary law, because the Pharisees were noted for their punctilious observance of food laws. We do not know exactly how other Jews may have behaved in these circumstances. It is quite likely that Jewish practice of the time encompassed every strategy from total abstinence to virtual commensality. We can perceive some of the possibilities from tracing Paul's behavior. From his Pharisaic past Paul learned how important table fellowship is for unifying a community. Paul carried the oral, unwritten law and his legal acumen into his new community, but he left the specific rabbinic solutions behind.

Although Jewish commensality was frequently noted by Roman and Greek writers, we do not know how ordinary Jews, as opposed to strict Pharisees, observed the dietary laws in the first century. Since there was no explicit law forbidding Jews and gentile from eating together, we must assume that some, possibly many, ate with gentiles, despite qualms. There was obviously a range of practice that we cannot precisely reconstruct, since we have to rely on the mishnaic laws, codified a century and a half after Paul, which represent a prescriptive idealization by the successors to the Pharisees. We can find some hints in rabbinic literature. It is too inexact to consider that the issue separating Peter and Paul is *kashrut*, the special food laws for Jews, as many scholars have done.[15] The issue in the Corinthian community is how gentiles are to eat with Jews. They are trying to come to terms with the fact that some Jews say that they may only eat with them if the Corinthians abstain from certain foods thought to be dedicated to idols. So the issue has more to do with *idolatry* than food laws. Rabbinic law actually discusses similar problems to Paul's in mentioning the kind of foodstuffs produced by gentiles that can be eaten. Mishnah *Avodah Zarah* 2.3 specifically mentions that gentile wine and meat offered to idols should not be eaten: "These things that belong to gentiles are forbidden, and it is forbidden to have any benefit at all from them: wine, or the vinegar of gentiles that at first was wine. . . . Flesh that is entering in unto an idol is permitted, but what comes forth is forbidden, for it as *the sacrifices of the dead* [Ps. 106:29]—the words of Rabbi Akiba."

These rules could not overrule the other laws of kashrut: a Jew who eats foodstuffs produced or marketed by gentiles is assumed to be following the rules of kashrut. Eating meat that has been dedicated at a temple is thus forbidden, though eating meat obtained from gentiles itself is not. This leniency—that is, in allowing some meat obtained from gentiles to be eaten—in regard to idolatry only is usually attributed to its great expense. Since meat was too great a luxury to be wasted, close definition of avoiding the stigma of idolatry was deemed appropriate. Such leniency is characteristic of rabbinic writings; in fact, they are in some ways more accommodating than Paul, suggesting that Paul was a very conservative Pharisee.

Buying and using gentile wine is also forbidden because it is assumed to have been used for a libation. The "sacrifices of the dead" are probably discussed in relation to all gentile foodstuffs and are elsewhere mentioned both by rabbis Akiba (d. 135 C.E.) and Simeon (Aboth 3.3. See also Ps. 106:28, Prov. 15:8; 21:27). By the mid- and late second century, these reviled gentile customs probably referred to the commemorative libations for heroes and ancestors, which were frequent at Graeco-Roman dinners and which evidently displeased the rabbis. Analogously, the central rite of Christianity, the Lord's Supper, may have attracted rabbinic suspicion, since it commemorates a person who died and is worshiped as a god. (In regard to idolatry, other differences in moral sensibility between Christian and pagan dinner customs could be overlooked.)[16]

Much can be learned of the rites of first-century Judaism by comparing the differing solutions to the problem in the various Jewish and Christian communities. The rabbis may well be codifying in the second century what was common practice in the first. A Pharisee who observed the purity rules and tithes would have difficulty eating with any Jew who did not observe these rules. We can speculate about other possible areas of conflict between Paul's congregations and a variety of Jewish Christians; for example, if a Jewish Christian were observing rules about wine, he or she might have insisted that the Eucharist be dispensed by a Jew to avoid the problems associated with a gentile serving wine. Whatever else may have been at issue, Paul certainly has to deal with the questions of serving meat and wine.

Implied in the mishnaic laws is that whenever there is a question, many Jews would entirely avoid eating with gentiles—as Cephas himself does—or, as a lesser safeguard, limit the food consumed to vegetables, bread, and fish (assuming that the other laws could be observed). Since ritual vegetarianism avoids issues of slaughter and possibly some of the issues of tithing, which had specific implications for produce of Israel's land, it continues to be the natural choice for some Jews in a similar situation today. Paul seems to bear out that this ritual strategy was in use in the Christian community, in discussing the difficulties between the strong and the weak.

We have other evidence besides the New Testament that vegetarianism was an ancient as well as a modern alternative to total abstinence in the company of gentiles. In the court tales of Daniel, a similar issue is broached. Daniel resolves not to eat at the king's table or drink his wine, no matter how rich the fare, because the food defiles his ritual status (Dan. 1:8). Confident of God's favor, he proposes a test: "Test your servants for ten days; let us be given vegetables to eat and water to drink. Then let our appearance and the appearance of the youths who eat the king's rich food be observed by you" (Dan. 1:12–13). The vegetables can be procured from the same gentiles at whose table they will not eat. Daniel and his companions, of course, were in better health than the courtiers at the end of the period, demonstrating the correctness of Daniel's behavior. The steward thereafter gives the whole court vegetables. Thus, Daniel does not object to eating at the king's table, he merely objects to eating meat and wine there.

This story is fable, but it is an ancient one, earlier than Paul. It also illustrates one ritual strategy for eating with gentiles. Gentile meats and wine are considered impure. Proper Jewish behavior demands not the total avoidance of gentile tables, but the avoidance of wines and meats, even those as tempting as the king's. The fable's reward for this piety is God's favor. The same position is hinted at in Jth. 12:1–4, when Judith refuses to eat and drink the wine provided by Holofernes. Esther too tells how she has not eaten at Haman's or the king's table (Esther 14:17 LXX). And Josephus commends the priests taken captive to Rome who supported themselves solely on nuts and figs (*Life* 14). These cases are evidence for the opposing position to Paul, which he evaluates as weak because it does not allow gentile pollution to affect pious Jews' dietary habits. But it is the opinion recommended for proper Jewish piety. Paul is opposing ordinary Jewish practice in regard to gentile food.

THE WEAK AND THE STRONG IN ROMANS AND ELSEWHERE

In Romans, Paul discusses his gentile converts with a partly Jewish audience, stating his own private opinions about the irrelevance of food laws. He may, in fact, be talking about all the dietary laws of Judaism, since he does not mention food offered to idols in particular. He is not dealing with a different issue in Romans so much as the converse side of the issue in Corinth. In Corinth, Paul specifically addressed gentiles, answering their query by explaining Jewish sensibilities about idolatry and its relevance to the gentile church. He tells them why Jews will not eat with them and cautions them against any behavior that would raise Jewish suspicions about idolatry, such as eating in a pagan shrine. Thus, the problem in Corinth might be that gentile Christians are actually attending pagan shrines. This is the reason why Jews refuse to eat foods that are normally kosher when offered by gentiles. But this is not the whole story. Whatever they are doing, they are being chastised for their behavior by some Jewish Christians who refuse to eat with them, endangering the unity that Paul envisions.

Though Paul does not personally see the necessity of continued dietary prohibitions in Christianity, he cautions the gentiles against falling back into idol worship (1 Corinthians 8 and 10:25–30). According to the Mishnah, idolatry is the issue that necessitated the prohibition against eating gentile meat and wine, so Paul is probably expressing a Pharisaic sentiment. He has brought his Pharisaic sensibility into an entirely new environment, where the issue has become acute as a communal problem, rather than a problem for an individual Jew as he or she pursues his or her livelihood.

In Romans, Paul explains to Jewish Christians why his radical opinion of food laws is correct.[17] Speaking about food prohibitions generally in Rom. 14:1–6, 15–20, Paul argues that all Christians should eat together without fear. He addresses two different groups—the weak, who eat only vegetables with their comrades, and the strong, who eat together with their fellow Christians with no qualms or reservations. The strong position represents mostly gentile Christians, and the weak position in Romans and Corinthians reflects Jewish sensibilities. This does not mean that they are strict ethnic denominations, for Paul himself is an exception to the rule. Any person, Jew or gentile, who embraced the strong position would naturally point out that the rule applies to all food prohibitions and all religious holidays, hence it must apply to all parties within the church. No matter which audience he addresses, Paul cautions against scorning the other position, which is consonant with his general theme in Romans of the danger of pride, as well as his constant interest in the unity of the church. It also implies, although it does not prove, that the strong position is the dominant position in the Roman church at that moment.

In harkening to the criticism that gentile Christians might be idolators, Peter (Cephas) is probably urging another position from ordinary Jewish practice found in the early Christian community. The New Testament again might be inadvertently recording some of the ritual strategies available to ordinary Jews in the first century for dealing with commensality with gentiles, the kind of evidence that we cannot get from the Mishnah because it is a prescriptive legal theory and is redacted a century and a half after Paul. The weak and strong positions could even have originated before Christianity—among more acculturated Jews, for instance, who were forced by commerce into closer association with gentiles. But the Jewish legal issue is evidenced by Christianity alone in the first century because of two facts: (1) the Mishnah did not approve of the strong position, which violated ritual status, so it would not discuss such open accommodations, and (2) avoiding meals with gentiles was not an appropriate communal strategy for Christians, according to Paul and his supporters.[18] Partial commensality, then, appears to be one practical solution among the Diaspora Jews who encountered difficulties of dietary laws before the rise of Christianity.

So far as Paul is concerned, even partial commensality is an inadequate ethical solution to the problem. His personal opinion, that the rules are totally irrelevant now, is unique and radical, similar to the most acculturated position one can imagine in pre-Christian Judaism. The ethical function of Paul's position is the same as the function of food laws among Jews: to preserve the unity of the community. Though Paul's opinion of ritual observance opposes his Pharisaic past as well as much of ordinary Judaism, Paul also represents a Jewish perspective in warning the Corinthians not to fall back into idol worship.

Paul considers himself among the strong (cf. "we who are the strong" in Rom. 15:1). He can confidently say that no food is unclean of itself, only to him who thinks it so (Rom. 14:14). His personal opinion, perhaps a result of his vision of the crucified Christ, could be argued as communal rule according to his interpretation of Deut. 21:23. But in his capacity as apostle he is prepared to make an accommodation. It is possible to call this strategy a compromise, though Paul does not have to compromise his position to carry it out; rather, he again simply refrains from the freedom that he has prescribed for his churches. From Paul's perspective the accommodation is a kind of magnanimity. He outlines two axioms, an ideological position of strength and a diplomatic principle of conciliation. All Christians should eat with each other, even if doing so means that the strong diplomatically avoid foods that the weak despise, a position that he argues to each side of the controversy (Rom. 14:15; 1 Cor. 8:12).

Paul feels that the church's unity is more important than any food prohibitions or even the principle that all foods are clean: "Do not, for the sake of food, destroy the work of God" (Rom. 14:20). The ritual laws of Judaism are supposed to unite the community. So the dietary laws of the new community should unify it, not separate it. In 1 Corinthians Paul cautions against giving offense to either Jews or Greeks. Neither should offend the other in the interest of Christian unity. His personal behavior is the pattern for all to follow: "So, whether you eat or drink, or whatever you do, do all to the glory of God. Give no offense to Jews or to Greeks or to the church of God, just as I try to please all men in everything I do, not seeking my own advantage, but that of many, that they may be saved. Be imitators of me, as I am of Christ" (1 Cor. 10:31–11:1).

Paul's ideological position, as commonplace as it might seem to Christianity today, was an extreme position in his own time; his diplomatic principle of reconciliation would have been controversial in the church, to say nothing about the Jewish community. The Apostolic Decree sets aside the radical ideological position of Paul, regardless of Acts' contention that Paul was a participant in the decree (Acts 15:20, 29; 21:25).[19] Revelations predicts damnation for any who put a stumbling block in front of Israel by leading them to eat food sacrificed to idols (2:14, 20). For the *Didache*, proper behavior includes keeping away from all food offered to idols. It uses language that is more reminiscent of the Mishnah than Paul's letters: "Now about food: *undertake what you can. But keep strictly away from what is offered to idols, for that implies worship of dead gods*" (*Didache* 6.3). The *Didache* exhorts Christians to observe as many of the dietary laws as possible. It even mirrors the mishnaic warning against worshiping the dead, interpreting the phrase as pagan gods now known to be dead. Throughout early church history, the dominant position is more like the *Didache* or the Apostolic Decree than Paul's ideological position.[20]

PAUL'S ACCOMMODATIONS

With his opinions, Paul could no longer have been a practicing Pharisee, though he considered himself a Jew and honored Torah in other ways. Paul's ideological position could only be seen as yet more extreme by the Jewish community than by the Christian community. To the Pharisees it could only be seen as a radical antinomian revolution. Paul had no qualms about maintaining that the value of Torah had changed. As C. K. Barrett points out, Paul is nowhere less Pharisaic than when he states that food laws are of no consequence. This position can be seen as transgression of the dietary laws, or it can be seen as leading other Jews astray, a more serious crime. It is no wonder that Paul counsels a diplomatic principle of conciliation, rather than insisting on his position.

Having come to a radical analysis of the situation, Paul's principle of reconciliation takes him in the opposite direction of the weak position. If Acts is correct in regard to circumcision as well, Paul was willing to accommodate in order to preserve the unity of the church. In the case of circumcision, we have Paul's statement that all should remain as they are, but we do not have complete evidence about the extent of his attempt at reconciliation. We must judge the account in Acts to be questionable (see chapter 6 above).

In 1 Corinthians Paul does not merely recommend that the strong be respectful of the misguided weak sensibilities; he himself swears not to eat any flesh, if eating flesh offends his fellow Christians. This oath is in the first person singular: "If meat offends my brother, *I will not eat meat forever, lest I offend my brother*" (1 Cor. 8:13). There is no reason to believe that this oath was rhetorical. It is an honest obligation taken in writing. Since it is a written and unambiguous pledge, it would even be valid in a rabbinic court (see Mishnah Nedarim 1).[21] Using oaths in this way is a sensible ritual strategy in later Judaism, pledging to avoid a material of suspicious purity. Thus, Paul again evidences Jewish practice otherwise unmentioned in the earliest rabbinic writings but known from later ones. The legal situation raised by communal meals in Christian communities is unusual for first-century Judaism. Paul personally might have thought that food laws were entirely irrelevant. His accommodationist position may have been only to avoid meat when the idolatrous connection might tempt others to sin. He also takes the principle of reconciliation to its extreme, volunteering to abide by a more conservative position, stricter than either the Corinthians' weak position or the Jewish practice outlined in the Mishnah. He goes further than Pharisaism to make his point. By seeking the most stringent answers in matters of ritual, Paul adopts the traditional Pharisaic means of avoiding situations in which doubt could be thrown on his ritual status.

There must have been a serious reason for such an accommodation.

Since Paul says specifically that he would swear to avoid offending his fellow Christian, he wants at the least to avoid an open breach with some of the more conservative Christians. He might have his fellow Jews in mind as well, for it is likely that first-century Jewish opinion encompassed legal positions far more conservative than the rabbinic one of the second century. It is possible that the Apostolic council intervened, and the church took a more conservative line than Paul was preaching. In this case, Paul himself might easily have taken a more conservative tack in order to maintain his recognition as an apostle and to preserve church unity.[22]

It is important to see the gravity of Paul's behavior and the possible reasons for his accommodations. Not only is Paul recommending ideologically that gentiles not eat kosher food, he is also saying that Jews need not do so, as he believes that he himself need not do so. This endangers not only himself but every Jewish Christian, who would thereafter come under suspicion for apostasy. What Paul might consider to be a behavior justifiable by his faith might be seen as transgression or apostasy to Judaism by others and as leading astray by yet others. To counter the charge that he is unclean or untrustworthy for having eaten meat sacrificed to idols, he swears that he is willing to become a vegetarian. For the most stringent Pharisee, this would eliminate the issues of acceptable slaughter of meat, idolatry, and possibly even tithes on fruit, leaving only the relatively minor problem of tithing vegetables, which was irrelevant outside the land of Israel. But, in approaching Jerusalem, it would have removed the major issue preventing Paul's full acceptance by observant Jews, whether or not they be Christians.

Acts maintains that Paul also took a Nazirite vow (Acts 18:18) in Cenchrea on his way to Jerusalem. Although Acts does not specify what the oath was, and the ambiguous syntax allows for the alternative interpretation that Aquila performed the rite, Acts appears to describe the unique conditions under which (temporary) Nazirite vows can be terminated, if a minimum of a month had passed after the vow.[23] After cutting his hair, Paul needed to bring a temple offering, which would mark the completion of the vow. Acts implies that this is what happened. It records that Paul was indicted in Jerusalem in spite of his attempt to prove his loyalty to Judaism by paying for the guilt and thanksgiving sacrifices of four other Nazirites who underwent purification with him (Acts 21:17–26). We do not know if Acts is historically accurate, but paying for the sacrifices of others completing Nazirite vows was another act of contemporary Jewish ritual piety and would have been understood as a desire for communal respect.[24] From the perspective of Paul's detractors, his behavior could be seen as dissembling or hypocrisy.

For Paul to have taken on a Nazirite vow would, of course, have had serious implications beyond the immediate context of table fellowship with gentiles. But taking on any obligation would have meant subjecting himself to Jewish ritual law again. When salvation itself is not the issue, and especially when church unity *is* the issue, Paul, however, seems ready to accommodate. The compromise might even have been that if the Jewish Christians abide by the Apostolic Decree, so will Paul, though his own personal position is far more radical. Although this is a compromise ritual position, Paul is not compromising his ideological position. Since Paul believes that this ritual is of no importance for salvation, whether he observes it or not is irrelevant. He chooses not to exercise his freedom to ignore them.

In Acts this conflict is expressly linked to Paul's last visit to Jerusalem and his pilgrimage to the temple. Even his most conservative behavior does not assuage the ire of some Jews, who accuse him of teaching others to overthrow Torah. Acts, of course, implies that the charge is false. Although Acts is not above reproach as a historical source, it could be correct in portraying Paul's decision at this juncture, for Paul himself tries to avoid open conflict (e.g., 2 Cor. 1:23). Jerusalem is a logical place for these issues to come to a head. The charge against Paul is also logical, because Paul comes close to advocating overthrowing Torah in his opinion of its inapplicability to food laws or circumcision. From his own letters we know that Paul's conservative Christian brethren are angry (and Paul himself is angry as well). Other parties in the Jewish community could only have reflected still more conservative sentiments.

If we consider the nature of the charge, there is a sense in which it is true from some Jewish points of view. Paul could have lived as a Jew "in order to win Jews" in Jewish communities, and he could also have lived "lawlessly" around gentiles in order to win them (1 Cor. 9:20). But he could not have done both at once, which was exactly the problem when Jewish and gentile Christians ate together. In Jerusalem, with both communities present, Paul could not have practiced both. Nor would the strategy have worked as well where the Pharisaic issues of tithing fruits and vegetables were relevant. Paul's compromise fails when members of the two communities eat together or directly confront each other. Thus, as soon as Paul leaves the gentile Christian environment, he is judged according to Jewish law; his strategy of conciliation is a tightrope walk between transgression and apostasy or subversion. The issue is not merely what Paul himself did; it is that his practice reflected the gentile community's definition of piety, which he then advocated for Jewish Christians, and Jewish Christians were Jews as well. The result, according to Acts, is that Paul's life is put in danger by the allegations of Jewish Christians who denounce him to the Jewish authorities. This begins the process that brings him to Rome and, as legend has it, to his martyrdom.

Even without Acts' contention, the one place where Paul could not have avoided open conflict is Jerusalem. Paul's insistence on the presence of his gentile brother, Titus, as well as other unnamed members of his party, is likely to have been a provocation (2 Cor. 8:20–23). Paul not only left open the option for compromise with his colleagues, he also made sure that his ideological position was properly represented. He offered both the compromise and the confrontation. But to see the full issue one must realize that Paul offered a clear compromise (which was rejected by the most conservative members of the church in Jerusalem).

PAUL'S CLARIFICATION TO THE GENTILE COMMUNITY

Paul's actions in swearing not to eat meat and possibly in taking a Nazirite vow would have been troublesome to almost anyone in the church, including his gentile followers, the strong. By promising not to eat flesh, Paul appears to reverse his opinion and observe Jewish law. If Paul were abiding by the compromise of the Jerusalem council, the issue would only be sharper. Paul's response to the Galatians made it appear to some converts that Paul was preaching circumcision (Gal. 1:10). Finally, if Acts' account of Timothy's circumcision is to be believed, the question is acute, because Paul might have circumcised the Jew Timothy, who looked like a gentile. Neither Jews nor gentiles, hearing the reports at a distance, could be expected automatically to thread the legal argument that makes these stances consistent. Thus, there is no reason to reject Acts ipso facto. Paul's conciliatory actions cast doubts on his own position, as outlined in Corinthians, that the ritual laws are no longer relevant in Christianity.[25]

If Acts is correct the whole picture is consistent. Parallel issues, however, can be adduced from Paul's own writing itself. With the conservative methodology of accepting only Paul's own testimony, more must remain in doubt, but the importance of the symbolic messages that Paul sent throughout the Jewish world can still be noted. Paul's vow in 1 Cor. 8:32 had halakhic consequences and would itself have led to ambiguities in his position on his Christian freedom. As Paul himself says in Galatians, where the primary issue is circumcision but where issues of food laws surface immediately: "But if, in our endeavor to be justified in Christ, we ourselves were found to be sinners, is Christ then an agent of sin? Certainly not! But if I build up again those things which I tore down, then I prove myself a transgressor" (Gal. 2:17–18). It is an excruciating dilemma, brought about by the two opposing notions of community among Jewish Christians and gentile Christians. In Romans Paul was rebutting the charge that he had again subjected himself to the law, accepting the designation *transgressor,* or even *apostate.* Paul also entered the one jurisdiction, Jerusalem, that could easily try him for these crimes. Since Paul was arguing that other Jews do the same, the issue was not academic, since those who led others astray were subject to the death penalty according to biblical law.

In his role as apostle, Paul was not being inconsistent in retreating to a diplomatic compromise with the conservative position in the church. He was not removing his freedom, only refraining from exercising it. But this consistency would not necessarily have been evident to anyone else, especially in light of the Jewish Christian opposition to Paul's view of community. The fact that we do not know exactly what happened probably differs little from the perspective of most of Paul's contemporaries. Since few Christians were eyewitnesses to any of Paul's confrontations, most would wait for clarification in his statements and letters. Paul would need to resolve the seeming contradiction between his conciliatory actions and his ideological position, especially since these are complex legal issues that might be argued and construed in a number of ways.

Paul uses his letter to the Romans to clarify and justify his behavior and, in so doing, to meditate on the value of law. Thus, Romans 7 describes neither a psychoanalytic nor an existential predicament. It is the apologia of a pragmatic man who formulated a radical solution to the problem of food laws in Christianity, but who, as an apostle, was willing to compromise when his solution was not accepted by the more conservative members of the Christian community. His job is to explain his position in Romans and to show that it is consistent.

ROMANS 7

With the historical context in mind, the puzzling soliloquy in Romans 7, which comes just before Paul's discussion of the weak and strong, makes more plausible sense:

> I was once alive apart from the law, but when the commandment came, sin revived and I died; the very commandment which promised life proved to be death for me. For sin, finding opportunity in the commandment, deceived me and by it killed me. So the law is holy, and the commandment is holy and just and good. Did that which is good, then, bring death to me? By no means! It was sin working death in me through what is good, in order that sin might be shown to be sin, and through the commandment might become sinful beyond measure. . . . I do not understand my own actions. For I do not do what I want, but I do the very thing I hate. Now if I do what I do not want, I agree that the law is good. . . . (Rom. 7:9–15)

The death that Paul mentions might be linked to baptism, as many scholars have noted, but this explanation does not correspond to the chronology of Rom. 7:9–12. Paul mentions rebirth when describing his baptism, but chronologically the death he mentions here must come after his conversion. He may be speaking elliptically of the risk of losing the salvation he has gained or even anticipating capital punishment if charges against him are sustained.

Paul seems to be talking about his experience as a Christian after rejecting Jewish observance. He begins in medias res as a convert without the law: "I was once alive apart from the law." Sin is thereafter pictured as "deceiving," bringing death, "finding opportunity in the commandment" (7:11).[26] Paul's opinion in Romans 7 is that the law is good, though flesh is under the sway of sin, and the law is concerned with flesh, thus bringing one to death. Paul may be suggesting here that going back to the law imperils his future life because it risks his salvation. Reading this passage along with his description of transformation makes such an interpretation the most likely alternative. Having achieved a state of transformation, in which the laws that govern the body become pleonastic, he states that his return to ceremonial Torah makes him a transgressor.

Paul's observation could be based on legal difficulties in Paul's life: he is aware that he can be condemned by means of the law. It is misleading to theologically analyze the human situation when Paul emphasizes his personal experience by use of the personal pronoun. His deception by sin by means of the law began not when he was a Pharisee and not when he lived without the law as a gentile Christian, but afterward. Possibly it began before he completely understood his role as apostle to the gentiles or, more likely, when as a Christian he accommodated to it out of concern for Christian unity. By journeying to Jerusalem, he would have been subjecting himself to scrutiny by Torah-true Christians and Jews alike. Thus, to journey to Jerusalem was to put himself in real danger and to realize that he was caught in a situation that might prove his downfall.

In spite of the dire straits Paul has encountered or may be anticipating, this meditation is a softening of Paul's other positions on law. Paul virtually equated law with both sin and the flesh (see Gal. 3:19; Rom. 3:20; 4:15; 5:20; 6), in keeping with a strictly apocalyptic view of the fallen world and its depraved inhabitants and in keeping with his contention that concern with the rules of the flesh was unspiritual behavior. This crucial passage, based on Paul's personal postconversion experience with the law, seems to many scholars a less radical intuition about the place of law. The law is just, but the flesh brings about law's failure to give life.[27] He is, however, simply reiterating his position that the ceremonial laws are irrelevant to the fleshly lives of Christians. Does Paul say this out of a human desire to persuade his readers, since the Roman church might contain more Jewish Christians than do the other churches to which he has sent letters? He could anticipate an equally mixed audience in Jerusalem, where his writing would have preceded him. It is likely that the mixed audience, consisting of Jewish and gentile Christians, also presents Paul with an opportunity to try to unite the entire Christian community with a thorough treatment of the issue of law and Israel's place in God's plan.

When Paul quotes the tenth commandment, "Thou shalt not covet" (*ouk epithumeseis*), many scholars have assumed that he is speaking specifically about lust, following an exegesis of Eve in the Garden of Eden. But the term *epithumia* is a general term, more like desire than lust in Greek, thus covering all kinds of desires including religious ones. Josephus uses the same term to discuss the satisfaction of his religious desires during his stay with Bannus. And Paul uses *epithumia* in a positive sense in 1 Thess. 2:17.

Paul could be thinking of Israel's rebellion in Num. 11:4–34, where the people crave the meat of Egypt, as he does in 1 Cor. 10:6–10. Paul is speaking about desire in general (*pasan epithumian* [Rom. 7:8]), including the covetousness of depending on fleshly marks for religious justification—desiring the benefits of Torah—while ignoring the spiritual value of being made over in the image of Christ. The desire to be justified by keeping the law is one that he understands. It is a desire that he still has and that he now sees as a misguided emotion. Paul is talking about the joy and security of doing Torah, a feeling with which most New Testament scholars cannot empathize and therefore miss. Paul is saying that he enjoys doing the ceremonial Torah, but it is a trap for him. Though many Christian exegetes present this passage as a discussion of sexuality under the old covenant, I think that a critique of sexual license would be out of context here. He turns to such issues in the Corinthian correspondence, but sexuality is not the primary referent of his desires in Romans. He speaks of covetousness, envy of the position of religious surety presented by a life under the commandments, because he wishes to contrast the life of ceremonial Torah, a life of the body, with the life of transformation in Christ, a life of the spirit. The ethical aspects of Torah, however, are still important. In Rom. 13:9–10 he lists four specific prohibitions—adultery, murder, theft, and covetousness—showing that he considers each to be different. He uses them as examples, not as an exhaustive list of unacceptable behaviors. Among the objects of covetousness is a life depending on the fleshly ordinances of law but without faith.[28]

The basic issue is a political one caused by the social breach in the community. Paul's attempt to mediate between the different customs in the early church created misunderstandings in his own community and alienated his opponents so completely as to put him in danger. Placed in this position, his conclusion is breathtaking. He shows that his personal difficulty is neither accidental nor abstractly existential. It is the same material predicament of all Christians under Torah. He discusses the good that he wishes to do and suggests that attempting to follow the ceremonial Torah *as a Christian* inevitably leads to sin, whether intentional or not: "For I do not do what I want, it is no longer I that do it, but sin which dwells in me" (Rom. 7:16, 17). This could be another statement to his listeners on not recanting his position on law. He might not have foreseen at first that the effects of his compromise put him in real danger (7:15). Paul reiterates, as he always believed, both that Torah is good and that he enjoyed fulfilling it when he was a Pharisee, but Christ has saved him from observing those laws because he was converted, died, and was reborn in Christ and was transformed to a spiritual being who needs to put fleshly desires and covetousness behind him.

This is not a theoretical or theological discussion of why humanity is unable to keep the law. It is the self-description of a man relating his personal experience: his attempt to find a compromise between the two sociological groupings in Christianity and discovery that he could not. It is the confession of a man who could and did live as a Pharisee but finds ceremonial Torah a backsliding temptation after his transformation to a new spiritual body. He still has desires to live as a Pharisee; indeed, it is a simpler position because it is easier to observe the laws than to try to walk the fine line between the two communities of Christians. But he overcomes his desires and continues to live a life of faith.

Paul is not a man who was constitutionally unable to practice the law. In this passage he appears to be a man who still feels the desire to observe the law. Paul is tempted to return to the law, since he enjoyed it and since it might prevent some internal dissension within Christianity. He represents the struggle in this way: "For I delight in the law of God, in my inmost self, but I see in my members another law at war with the law of my mind and making me captive to the law of sin which dwells in my members" (7:22, 23). This is analogous to the desire to perform ceremonial law. Though the law is holy and good, the ceremonial laws, in dealing with circumcision and proper food are literally and metaphorically the laws of his members, bring him under the sway of sin again, possibly because they tempt him to pride and actually misrepresent his position on law to his congregations. Keeping the law, for whatever reasons of conciliation, is not a means for his salvation, though Torah is good and holy and points out what sin is.

His perception that the law of sin dwells in his members arises from his diplomatic struggle to find an accommodation to ceremonial laws in the new Christian community. It is a struggle that Paul cannot win, because he cannot both observe the laws and ignore them at once, and both communities appear to be watching him for guidance or criticism. It is a struggle that no Christian can win as long as Torah observance is a serious option within the Christian community. But Christianity can win the battle by ignoring observance of the special laws of Torah entirely. A lawless gospel is the only Christian solution that will yield a single community. Stendahl described the problem in Romans as salvation history, but he is right only when one realizes that the crisis that precipitated the discussion is a personal and legal crisis in Paul's life. Thus, Paul uses his own experience as an apostle in trying to mediate the dispute, to show that the only solution is faith and faith alone. Paul is not discussing sexual desire in this passage. He is talking about the temptation to covet the religiously easier life of the Jewish Christians, with their emphasis on law. Those who live according to the spirit are those Christians who have participated in the spiritual baptism, which unites them with Christ. Those who live in the flesh are the Jewish Christians, who still have confidence in their special laws. Those who live in the spirit are transformed by Christ and look forward to a complete spiritual transformation with him, though now they are only united with him in being reviled and in suffering.

A NEW VOCABULARY FOR DISCUSSING TORAH

Throughout Judaism, among both the Sadducees in the land of Israel and other sociological groupings in Diaspora, there was room for various degrees of piety with regard to Torah. But no Jew or gentile observer of Torah before Paul made a systematic distinction between ceremonial and ethical laws. Neither does Paul in so many words. Many Jews lived as Jews and justified a good deal of laxity with regard to the ceremonial laws, but for Paul and other religiously committed Jews, Torah was a body of divine wisdom that had to be adopted in its entirety, however that entirety was defined. The only question was how Torah was to be interpreted; by means of allegory, *pesher,* or midrash first-century Jews found grounds for latitude in practice. Though Paul had given up Pharisaism, he did not simply recommend that his community observe the ethical requirements of Torah and ignore the ceremonial parts. There was little precedent or vocabulary for such a policy. Yet Paul's argument has that force. Paul begins with his own situation in the law and in Romans 8 discusses a relationship between sin and the law, based on his own post-conversion experience. There is no ready-made vocabulary on which Paul can depend. Paul takes an unprecedented position when he says: "With the mind, I serve the law of God, but with the flesh, the law of sin" (7:25b). He thus invents a new, personal vocabulary for dealing with the ceremonial laws. His vocabulary partakes of Hellenistic philosophy and apocalypticism simultaneously. Though Paul's mature position about the special laws is unique, it does have certain affinities with the extreme allegorizers to whom Philo gives credit for having found philosophical wisdom. Philo criticizes the extreme allegorizers for trying to be souls without bodies; such a criticism would make sense against Paul as well, although Paul uses a concept of spiritual body instead of a soul in the philosophical sense. Further, Paul's conflict is the result of a conversion defined by his movement from a Torah-true Pharisaic environment to a gentile community of God-fearers in which Torah had a smaller part.

Although Philo criticizes the extreme allegorizers for their attempt to ignore daily life, imagining themselves to be disembodied souls without bodies, he tempers his criticism by recognizing their higher purpose. Philo does not believe them to be merely apostates; rather, they make the mistake of thinking that they live in the wilderness and "overlook all that the mass of men regard" (*Migration* 90). This would suggest that Philo, had he known Paul, would have considered him one of the radical allegorizers.

Though Paul certainly did not ignore the body, he preached its transformation through death and rebirth in baptism and through a mystical identification with Christ, which opened him to a criticism similar to Philo's when he claimed to have left behind the body of flesh and entered the one spiritual body of the Lord (1 Cor. 6:17). Further, Philo's observation that extreme allegorizers "overlook what the mass of men regard" would be an understandable criticism of Paul from a Jewish perspective, and it probably represents the closest we will get to a contemporary, moderate, philosophical (perhaps Hellenistic Diaspora) Jewish reaction to Pauline Christianity. If Acts is right, both Jewish Christians and some pious Jews were far more critical of Paul's view of the ritual aspects of Torah than Philo would have been. Philo would not necessarily have seen any apostasy in Paul's actions, but the Jerusalem community and the more conservative members of Judaism elsewhere saw a greater danger—that of leading the faithful astray.

Paul would have been well advised to have remained figuratively "in the wilderness" and literally to have stayed away from Jerusalem, where the conservative members of Christianity had more strength and where the pious parties of Judea had significant political clout. But this is exactly what Paul could not do, because he hoped to bring an acceptable charity collection and, in gaining acceptance for his gentile brethren, produce a single church community. He must have seen his visit to Jerusalem as an attempt to heal the incipient fissure in the church, though ironically it was just this desire to make sure that Jewish and gentile Christians could eat and pray together that put him in greater danger than any radical allegorizer. The irony is that Paul's desire for Christian unity, not specifically his thoughts about Torah, brought him into danger, since he apparently could have sidestepped the issue of unity by not going to Jerusalem.

Romans 8 deals with the contrast between being under law and being under faith. It is a personal distinction in Paul's life as a Christian. There was a period in Paul's Christian life during which he struggled with Torah "in the flesh," as he says, before he understood that its true value was "in the spirit," as prophecies of the coming of the Christ: "in order that the just requirement of the law might be fulfilled in us, who walk not according to the flesh but according to the Spirit" (8:4). During this period he may have observed Torah in Jewish Christian contexts, ignoring it in his gentile mission. That is indeed what Paul advocated to his communities whenever the issue of food laws was raised by the so-called weak. But this was an unacceptable compromise to those who still valued Torah because episodic observance was inconsistent.

Ironically, the so-called weak were vastly more powerful around Jerusalem because they could rely on the feelings of their Jewish brothers. Paul's final ideological point is always that, although the law is spiritual, it is played out in the flesh, which is unredeemable. Faith is spiritual and conquers fleshly attempts at salvation. The law has been replaced by faith (8:2), though the Torah-true converts might seem more vociferous. All of this is an understandable intellectual position, but it is not possible to make a single acceptable ritual practice out of it. Therefore, whenever Paul encountered a group of Christians composed of Jews and gentiles, as when he entered Jerusalem and deliberately created a mixed group, he was doomed to be misunderstood by one side or the other, if judged on the basis of his ritual actions: "For the law of the Spirit of life in Christ Jesus has set me free from the law of sin and death. For God has done what the law, weakened by the flesh, could not do: sending his own Son in the likeness of sinful flesh and for sin, he condemned sin in the flesh" (8:2).

It is also ironic that Paul should make his strongest statements about the relationship between Torah and grace in Romans, in the context of having to justify a retreat. But he conquers the bitterness of his misfortune, turning it into an occasion for meditation. By means of his personal predicament, he illustrates that it is the flesh and not the law itself that causes the law to bring men to death rather than to life. His rhetoric has the added advantage of addressing his Christian listeners in the same position, those who were wondering whether and how to keep the law of the flesh after they had become persons of the spirit. Paul does not begin with an evaluation of Torah in general so much as describe his experience. He feels he can generalize in warning people that their new Christian commitment has implications in regard to all Jewish Christians' previously learned attitude toward Torah. One can avoid the foods that offend the sensibilities of the weak and one can even swear to avoid all flesh in order to satisfy those who demand it, but it is faith and not fleshly observance that brings about salvation. He could be warning his readers that his attempt to compromise is unwise, but the letter appears to address gentile Christians who are not affected by the compromise in the same way. To them he preaches forbearance, tolerance, and understanding of the opposing opinion.

There are limits to Paul's toleration. For him, the life of faith is life immortal, life under the law ends in death. In Romans 8 Paul talks about the social manifestations of the distinction between law and faith. There are two communities, one defined by law and the other defined by faith. Those who are defined by law are a fleshly community:

But you are not in the flesh, you are in the Spirit, if in fact the Spirit of God dwells in you. Any one who does not have the Spirit of Christ does not belong to him. But if Christ is in you, although your bodies are dead because of sin, your spirits are alive because of righteousness. If the Spirit of him who raised Jesus from the dead dwells in you, he who raised Christ Jesus from the dead will give life to your mortal bodies also through his Spirit which dwells in you. So then, brethren, we are debtors, not to flesh, to live according to the flesh—for if you live according to the flesh you will die, but if by the Spirit you put to death the deeds of the body you will live. For all who are led by the Spirit of God are sons of God. For you did not receive the spirit of slavery to fall back into fear, but you have received the spirit of sonship. When we cry, "Abba! Father!" it is the Spirit himself bearing witness with our spirit that we are children of God, and if children, then heirs, heirs of God and fellow heirs with Christ, provided we suffer with him in order that we may also be glorified with him. (8:9–17)

Paul is again speaking of the transformation of believers, which he links to baptism and faith. Paul strongly contrasts the life in the spirit to that under the flesh. Life in the flesh corresponds to life dedicated to the special laws of Judaism, whether as Jew or gentile convert to Christianity ("for if you live according to the flesh you will die, but if by the Spirit you put to death *the deeds of the body* you will live"). Paul contrasts this with the spiritual life of his community, in accordance with his apocalyptic vision. Those who put confidence in the works of the law are condemning themselves to death, as the body itself dies. But those who put their confidence in the spirit of God, which has entered their lives through baptism, will become sons of God. Paul is relying on a metaphor of adoption. Roman law provided that even slaves could be adopted as the master's children and heirs.[29] Paul relies on this exceptional change in status to express the value of the speaker. The adoption metaphor must have seemed especially apt for a gentile, who in entering Christianity could be adopted into Israel's destiny.

The adoption image develops in multiple ways in Paul's mind. His argument moves forward by association; he states that this spiritual process culminates in being glorified with Christ, although all that is evident to earthly eyes so far is a likeness in suffering. In this context Paul plays on another implication of sonship:

I consider that the sufferings of this present time are not worth comparing with the glory that is to be revealed to us. For the creation waits with eager longing for the revealing of the sons of God; for the creation was subjected to futility, not of its own will but by the will of him who subjected it in hope; because the creation itself will be set free from its bondage to decay and obtain the glorious liberty of the children of God. We know that the whole creation has been groaning in travail together until now; and not only the creation, but we ourselves, who have the first fruits of the Spirit, groan inwardly as we wait for adoption as sons, the redemption of our bodies. For in this hope we were saved. Now hope that is seen is not hope. For who hopes for what he sees? But if we hope for what we do not see, we wait for it with patience. (Rom. 8:18–25)

In the context of the travail of creation, adoption and sonship become synonymous with redemption. Paul mentions the liberty of the children of God that will be evident when the sons of God are revealed. Since sonship in this case appears related to the apocalyptic end and since sons of God in 8:19 appears to refer to angels, it is possible that Paul is again referring to the apocalyptic transformation that is central to his spiritual experience. The spiritual Christians will live eternally by virtue of their sonship, their angelic status. But even in describing the apocalyptic hope, Paul is discussing his sense of how God's plan differs for the two different Christian communities. Observing law in these end-times is of no concern. What is important is spiritual transformation, which will soon be made evident to everyone at the last judgment. Paul's language of social distinctions is sectarian, resembling the Qumran community in some respects. But his vision goes beyond anything that has so far been discovered at Qumran. One can expect opposition to Paul's vision. For this reason, he councils patience in the face of opposition and persecution. Paul takes his own sufferings over his legal perspective as exemplary of unification with Christ's sufferings and counsels his churches to take the same patient attitude. Soon the glorious aspect of identification with Christ will also be evident.

ROMANS 12

Paul discusses several interesting aspects of Torah with his Jewish Christian brethren. He also speaks to the gentiles, showing that the Roman church was a mixed group, containing both Jews and gentiles. In fact, Paul speaks far more often to the gentile Christians than to the Jews.[30] It is possible that the tensions in the Roman community were a result of the Edict of Claudius, expelling the Jews in 49 or 50 C.E., followed by their gradual return to a predominantly gentile community.[31] Romans 12 should thus be seen as an appeal to the gentiles for tolerance and understanding, first for the sudden departure of their Jewish brethren and then for their slow return. They are not to pride themselves on the defeat of their opponents but to recognize that despite their differences they form one body in Christ (12:4–6); indeed, they must compete with one another in showing honor (12:10). The chapter seems to be an enumeration of what toleration is: "contribute to the needs of the saints, practice hospitality" (12:13), "live in harmony with one another, do not be haughty, but associate with the lowly," "never be conceited" (12:16); "take thought for what is noble in the sight of all. If possible, so far as it depends upon you, live peaceably with all" (12:17–18).

The strong are adjured not to be tempted to return to Jewish Christian practice either, but only to tolerate it where necessary. Their sacrifice is to be spiritual. As John Koenig has pointed out, it is quite striking in this context that Paul should appeal to his readers to present themselves as "living men" (*zōntas* [6:13]) and as "a living sacrifice" (*thusian zōsan* [12:1]). This must mean that the living sacrifice he demands in 12:1 is related closely to the baptismal speech in Romans 6, where believers are not to yield their members into sin but to "yield yourselves to God as men who have been brought from death to life, and your members [*ta melē humōn*] to God as instruments of righteousness" (6:13). They are not to submit to circumcision or to be tempted by such desires, but their whole bodies are to be sacrificed through the immersion in baptism to the new spiritual understanding of law. Since they ritually die as they are sacrificed, the special ordinances of Judaism no longer apply to them. These phrases refer to and contrast with a Pharisaic understanding of the requirements of ceremonial law. He warns the Roman community not to yield to ceremonial law as he appeared to do; moreover, he explains what his position actually is.

The commands not to be conformed (*mē syschēmatizesthe*), rather to be transformed (*metamorphousthe*), are in the present tense, showing that the action is continuous. The temptation to rely on a fleshly Christianity is continuous. The pressure to conform is constant. It is clear, then, that Paul has continually felt the pressure to return to the observance of Jewish law; thus, he assumes that others in his congregation also feel it. He wants to combat this desire, which is foreign to modern Christians, who have largely missed the significance of these statements.

Returning to Torah, according to Paul, shows lack of faith. The true sacrifice is to avoid these practices, even though observing Torah might forestall criticism. Those who are already in the spirit (7:6, 8:4, 9) must be called on to resist evil by submitting to the workings of the spirit (8:9–13; Gal. 5:25). If they do not follow Paul's advice, they themselves will be caught up in his previous agonizing conflicts, an inner war between the mind, which delights in the law of God, and sin, which continues to dwell in the body. They could even be caught in the same web of legal complications in which Paul finds himself.

Living in the spirit, however, brings its own variety of suffering, since it is distinguished from the future glorification of believers, when each shall be fully Christ's image. Thus Rom. 13:14 says: "Put on the Lord Jesus Christ and make no provision for the flesh," which means that they are not to allow themselves to be part of Jewish practice. The battle, as the parenesis that follows in Romans 12 and 13 shows, is not only ethical and ritual but also social. Living in faith apparently causes suffering for the believers, perhaps directly from Jewish persecutors or indirectly by the Romans for not observing Judaism, thus not deserving the protection of Judaism's legitimacy. But the believers are to hold firm, to be transformed in mind and not conformed in body. Paul calls this whole process transformation. We know this to be another term for the conversion process. Conversion is always understood by Paul as a personal transformation, either from a life of ceremonial law or a life or gentile impurity, to a new life of faith.

In Romans, Paul is talking about his own experience. Like many Jews of his time, he argues about the intentions and symbolic meanings of the rites of Jewish practice. His later readers, for whom the context of the symbolic value of ritual in Jewish life is lost, jump immediately to the theological implications. Paul's reflections are an obvious aspect of the highly debated issue of Jewish law in Christianity. Paul feels that his experience was relevant to the legal point because he was counseling tolerance of antinomian Christians to the Jewish Christians of Rome and vice versa. He is pointedly asking Jewish Christians to understand his behavior on the basis of a presumed shared experience—a move that has rhetorical motivations as well as personal and doctrinal implications. In doing so he illustrates an entirely new understanding of the value of Torah. He is also exhorting his gentile Christian brothers in Rome not to be tempted to follow Jewish practice, an exhortation that seems unnecessary now but countered a great though sporadic temptation throughout the first several centuries of Christian life.

Therefore, any doctrinal conclusions from Paul's discussion must begin with an appreciation of Paul's personal voice and the reasons for his apologia. Paul's intention was to meld two communities together; the result was that he himself was brought into danger. Paul's own commitment to Christian unity and to bringing the Jewish and gentile wings of the church into fellowship spelled disaster for him. Though neither Jewish nor Christian tradition has sufficiently appreciated it, Paul's soliloquy in Romans 7 is his own reflection on his attempt to make a single community by accommodation in ritual but not in principle—the issue that brought him into trouble at Jerusalem. Romans 7 is the stuff of tragedy.

CHAPTER EIGHT

♌ THE SALVATION OF ISRAEL

PAUL'S CHOICE AND CONFRONTATION

Paul not only accommodated his practice in going to Jerusalem, he also confronted the Jerusalem church with an entirely different and apparently offensive way of understanding the new Christian community. Though Paul was willing to retreat on all issues for the sake of one community, he was unwilling that there be two, separate communities. He insisted that Titus and at least one other uncircumcised Christian accompany the offering to Jerusalem (2 Cor. 8:20–23). Acts 20:4 names several other gentiles, thus calling into question the nature of Christian community. Would the Jerusalem church be one community with Sopater of Beroea, Aristarchus, Titus, and the others? Paul is adamant in his desire for a single Christian community; but Acts portrays Paul's attempt as a failure. There is no reason to disbelieve Acts on this subject, since we have seen the evidence for the failure within Paul's writing itself. There is, however, no reason to believe that the specific events transpired as Acts maintains.

Neither the Jewish community nor the Jewish Christian community shared Paul's conception of a single community of Jews and gentiles. The gentiles appeared to have been as happy as the Jewish Christians to remain separate. Jewish ritual, either present or absent, was bound to symbolize a communal conflict. First the Jerusalem church and then, with its instigation, the Jewish community itself raised strong voices against Paul. From their perspective, he had encouraged the people to give up their ancestral customs. If he had preached that a gospel without Jewish ceremonial laws was appropriate for gentiles, then the hostility of the Jewish Christian community would have been less vehement. Many Jews would have sym-

254

pathized with Paul's mission to enjoin morality on the gentiles and would have agreed that they need not keep the special laws of Judaism. The problem was that he wanted to create a single community with unconverted gentiles, which offended a sizable section of the Jewish church. Paul's life was apparently endangered by his preaching that Jews give up special laws. The audience Paul met first in Jerusalem and then possibly at Rome was hostile, for in Rome, as in Jerusalem, there was a significant Jewish community before the Christian community was formed, and the Christianity that first took root was one that accepted significant parts of the Jewish law.

We cannot assume that the Jewish-gentile argument was past history by the time of Acts. The continued importance of eating rules in Christianity in the second century, witnessed by such documents as the *Didache,* suggests that the Jewish mission was partly successful and that Jewish practices continued to be a question. Robert Wilken has shown that as late as Chrysostom (350–407 C.E.) there was a tendency in the Christian community to want to visit synagogues.[1] Gentiles were attracted by the special laws of Judaism because they were mandated by the Bible and performed with seriousness and dignity by the Jewish community. The influence on Christians of Jewish law observance, promoted by a Jewish contingent in the church, must have continued for centuries, though it became less critical. It certainly cannot be dismissed in a generation.

ROMANS 1 AND 2

It is generally acknowledged that Romans represents the latest extant statement of Paul and that it is, therefore, a summary of Paul's mature thinking. But the importance of Romans can be misleading, for nothing in the letter suggests that Paul means it to resolve or replace his earlier thought. It was also written at the verge of Paul's greatest disappointment, his (partly anticipated) rejection by the Jerusalem leadership of Judaism and the Jewish Christians. Though Romans may reflect his latest apostolic thinking, the situation to which it was written is also most pressing, so it is as occasional as the other letters, not a systematic theology. Paul's formula for Christian unity did eventually work, once the Jewish component of Christianity was attenuated enough to be powerless to oppose it. But it could not be practiced while the performative utterances of Jewish law were clearly understood by many Christians, since those messages envisioned an entirely different kind of unity and universalism.

According to Romans 15, Paul writes to Rome before he leaves for Jerusalem. He has left Ephesus, having completed his missionary work in the eastern Mediterranean (Rom. 15:19). He is probably writing from the vicinity of Corinth (see Acts 20:2–3), since he recommends to the Romans Phoebe, the deaconess at Cenchreae (Rom. 16:1), which was Corinth's eastern port. The Christian congregation's presence at the port city suggests a sociology similar to the synagogues of the Diaspora, invariably found at nodal points of trade and transportation where they served as safe hostels for traveling Jews. His stated purpose in going to Jerusalem is to bring a collection for the saints (Rom. 15:25. See also 1 Cor. 16:1–4; 2 Corinthians 8–9; Gal. 2:10). Paul probably had his Jerusalem trip in mind when he wrote the conciliatory words of his letter to the Romans.[2] Paul's impatient opinions about circumcisers in Galatians could not fail to be a divisive influence on community. It is likely that in Romans Paul, in turn, seeks to soften his anger, perhaps to restore a balance, partly by bringing a collection from the gentiles for the Jerusalem church. He fears that the collection will be rejected in Jerusalem (Rom. 15:31) but hopes that if it is accepted, it will cement the peace that he claims has been established by the previous agreements.

At the beginning of Romans Paul says that he wanted to come to Rome for a long time but had been prevented. Now, however, he is "hoping to reap some harvest among you as well as among the rest of the gentiles" (1:13). Paul's difficulties in coming to Rome may have been due to a previous agreement with the other apostles to work only among gentiles. Since the original Christian community at Rome was substantially Jewish Christian, it may have been off-limits to Paul's mission. The community to which Paul now writes has a strong gentile component. But these theories are speculative. What is clear is that Paul feels some anxiety about the hostility that he will incur in Jerusalem before starting for Rome, anxiety that turns out to be justified, according to Acts.

Jerusalem is not the source of his problems, only its focus, for Paul's theology of faith can be seen by Jews of Christian or non-Christian varieties as anything from transgression to apostasy to leading other Jews astray. Though Paul wrote Romans before his trip to Jerusalem (Rom. 15:25), he had experienced several scrapes with Jewish and gentile courts because of his missionizing activity (Gallio in Achaia: Acts 18:12–17; Aretas in Damascus: 2 Cor. 11:32–33. See also 1 Thess. 2:2; Acts 16:25–40; 2 Cor. 11:22–24; Acts 19:8–10; 1 Cor. 15:32). According to Acts, there was a plot against Paul's life in Damascus and later in Jerusalem. In Lystra, Paul was stoned and left for dead (Acts 14:19). He was imprisoned in Philippi (Acts 16:19–24). He was forced to flee Thessalonica (Acts 17:5–10). According to Acts, he was persecuted by the Hellenists in Jerusalem (Acts 9:29). He was constantly harassed by Jews (Acts 13:50; 14:2, 5, 19; 16:19–24; 17:5–9). He was even assaulted by the worshipers of Artemis (Acts 19:21–41). Paul's journey to Rome was ironically undertaken not to begin a mission in Spain (Rom. 15:24, 28) but to pursue the appeal against the charge of leading Jews astray—that is, inciting Jews to give up their ancestral customs. The charge is appropriate to the message that Paul delivered.

Even if one does not trust Acts entirely, it is hard to imagine that Paul's missionary life was not beset with constant danger and legal difficulties. He himself complains of the beatings and vilifications that he has withstood (2 Cor. 11:22–29; 1 Cor. 4:9; as well as several other times between 2 Cor. 4:7 and 7:4). The depictions seem to be real, though the *peristasis*, the catalogue of woes, is certainly part of any self-respecting Stoic's self-description. As a Hellenistic wise man, Paul uses the description of his sufferings to recommend his endurance and confidence in his task.[3] Nevertheless, the hardships seem real enough, providing a good description of the consequences of his chosen life—not merely trying to live as a Jew without the outward appearances of being Jewish but preaching antinomianism as virtue for Jew and God-fearer alike. Living as a Jew without the rituals of Judaism would have been difficult enough in those days. But when one tried to defend Paul's position, potential transgression could be seen as apostasy and, what is worse, as inciting others to abandon Judaism. The charge has some validity from the Jewish perspective, though what a Jewish court would have decided is a matter of speculation. Paul would have been well advised to appeal his case to Rome, had he been a Roman citizen and entitled to this consideration. There is no telling how much independence Jerusalem had in administering the death penalty. But the accusations against Paul carried a potential death sentence, whereas the Romans might overlook such charges as trivial or irrelevant.

We can be certain that wherever Paul's mission took him, trouble and persecution followed; this is an essential part of the background of his letter to the Romans. He uses the opportunity of his letter to the Romans first to write of his frustrations and then to address a larger issue, the fate of the people Israel, now that Christ has come—and not just the issue of the place of Jewish Christians in the Christian church, which he had addressed several times. Romans thus represents his most interesting and in some ways his most challenging writing. Though Romans states Paul's position clearly, it is also written in anxiety and in the hope of conciliation.

Paul's sense of foreboding is best expressed in Rom. 15:30–33: "I appeal to you, brethren, by our Lord Jesus Christ and by the love of the Spirit, to strive together with me in your prayers to God on my behalf, that I may be delivered from the unbelievers in Judea, and that my service for Jerusalem may be acceptable to the saints, so that by God's will I may come to you with joy and be refreshed in your company. The God of peace be with you all. Amen." The unbelievers in Judea might be Jews but they must also include some of the most conservative Jewish Christians who are unfaithful in the sense that they continue to insist on the Jewish ceremonial law for gentile Christians. The saints in Jerusalem are, presumably, the more moderate Jewish Christians living there, perhaps the family and immediate successors of Jesus. But Paul does not feel confident of their approval or acceptance, to say nothing of his acceptance by the unbelieving Jews.

Romans 2 should be seen in the context of Paul's scrapes with the law and his anxiety about coming to Jerusalem and Rome. It is also one of the most puzzling pieces of Pauline writing, because Paul appears to contradict his earlier discussions of the value of faith. Paul begins by quoting his favorite passage in the Hebrew Bible, Hab. 2:4, "He who through faith is righteous shall live," declaring that salvation shall come to all who have faith, "to the Jew first and also to the Greek" (Rom. 1:16). He still gives priority of position to the Jews because God called them first. By the end of the letter Paul will sadly admit that the order of the call to faith has been reversed. But immediately thereafter Paul depicts both Jew and gentile as condemned on the same basis, since God shows no partiality (2:11). The gentiles are condemned universally in Rom. 1:18–32. In chapter 2, he begins with a meditation on the limitations of law, addressing himself to "man"—that is, *humanity* in general.[4] He says ironically that God will "render to all persons according to their works" (2:6). And again: "For it is not the hearers of the law who are righteous before God, but the doers of the law who will be justified" (2:13). This starts a diatribe against the Jews who, though they have the law, are as sinful as the gentiles who do not have it. Circumcision is of benefit for those who possess the law, but it becomes uncircumcision to Jewish sinners, whereas a righteous gentile is to be regarded as truly circumcised. The true Jew is one inwardly and the truly circumcised man is one whose heart is purified.[5]

The difficulties with this passage are manifold. Although Paul states that redemption is through faith, he goes on to say that people are judged by the law (*nomos*). Instead of stating that justification is by faith, he assumes the Jewish position that justification is by doing the law. This is almost the exact opposite of what he maintained in his entire career as an apostle. If Paul's primary focus were to end a theology of self-justification by works, he would not say such things. But the audience and social context of these statements have been consistently undervalued by scholars. Paul is defending himself and gentile Christianity.

One way to understand this seeming turnabout is to emphasize the social context of his remarks: Paul has already suffered for his beliefs. He is now about to subject himself to the most conservative part of the Jewish community in Jerusalem. He takes the perspective of his opponents to show that it is inconsistent. In doing so, he states the Jewish idea that the righteous gentiles are as deserving of salvation as righteous Jews. In true apocalyptic fashion, however, Paul concentrates on the opposite: how few members of the saved remnant exist at all.

Paul states that, traditionally, justification for the Jew should come through *doing* the law, not *hearing* the law. He excoriates the gentiles, which might be a conventional piece of Hellenistic Jewish polemic,[6] but the importance of the diatribe is rhetorically to condemn the Jews yet more. The whole passage has an angry tone, which is puzzling unless it is seen as deriving from Paul's foreboding about his difficulties to come.

Paul says explicitly that those who condemn him and others for specific sins are themselves guilty of them.[7] The subject therefore is self-righteousness and hypocrisy. It sounds as if Paul had in mind someone who actually does some of the things in question. But Paul does not mean his remarks in quite the way that is usually understood. As usual, he begins his discussion of law with a personal statement about his unhappy experiences with it. He usually speaks of the limitations on the ceremonial aspects of Torah. Here he begins with personal observation not so much about Torah, or its Greek equivalent nomos, as about the courts that administer it. He is interested in the imperfect execution of the law.

Since the apostrophized audience in Rom. 2:1 is "humanity," the issue is Paul's difficulties with *human* law in both gentile and Jewish courts: "Therefore you have no excuse, O man, whoever you are, when you judge another; for in passing judgment upon him you condemn yourself, because you, the judge, are doing the very same things." This is a classic *tu quoque* argument. He is accusing past and prospective judges, either Jewish or gentile, of the same crimes for which he could be indicted, transgressing the law. He himself was once a Pharisee and guilty of no possible infractions of law. He feels he would be judged unfairly by (non-Pharisaic)

Jews or by Jewish courts using Torah, by judges who are likely to be as lax about practice as he is now and more lax than he was when he was a Pharisee, because ordinary Diaspora Jewish Torah practice was often no more pious or consistent than Christian God-fearing practice of Torah. As a lapsed Pharisee he would see all other Jewish practice as insufficiently pious. He is therefore questioning the assumptions by which he has been and could be judged. One difference between Paul's behavior and other nonpious Jewish behavior was that he recommended his practice to gentiles as an alternative to practicing the law, rather than simply practicing Judaism according to the dictates of his conscience. But from Paul's ex-Pharisaic perspective, any judgment against him by ordinary Jews was bound to seem hypocritical. This meaning emerges if Paul's use of nomos is completely understood. Paul normally uses nomos to mean Torah, for Torah had been translated into Greek as custom or law by all major Hellenistic Jewish writers. Many scholars have wrongly pointed out that nomos is a bad translation for Torah, since nomos can mean ordinary custom and Torah. Although Torah is partly legal enactment, it is essentially the story of the covenant, hence transcendent and revelatory.[8]

But nomos itself does not exactly mean law in our sense of statute or court decision. It is rather a procedure or practice. Greek papyri refer to marriage as a *nomos keimenos,* enduring practice, implying a mutual agreement, which is close to what the Hebrews called a covenant and has, in fact, been translated as covenant.[9] Further, nomos did have many transcendent connotations, especially in stoicism. When the Septuagint translated Torah as nomos it was not mistaken. Nor does Paul misunderstand torah as ordinance because of his use of nomos. Of course, no two words in different languages ever precisely translate each other. Paul, however, always understands Torah to be divinely given law. But because nomos means gentile law and practice as well as the Jewish Torah, he can use the same word to refer both to Jewish justice and gentile justice.

In Romans, Paul uses the ordinary Greek understanding of nomos as coterminous with the ordinary Jewish understanding of it. He is merely taking up felt injustices of Jewish and pagan law in turn. He is thus playing on the similarity in Greek terminology between ordinary civil, Roman law and divine Torah. Scholars have misunderstood the latitude of nomos, describing everything from divine law to human judgment. Hence they have misunderstood Paul's ability to depend on that latitude when necessary.

Paul is discussing the value of ordinary, civil legal procedure or custom, which can include Jewish law as well. He begins with the human value of law, commenting on the hypocritical way in which he has been indicted and the injustice of the proceedings against him, in both the Jewish courts and the gentile courts. Jewish courts were still considered to be the courts of the land in some limited spheres, for Judaism had achieved the status of a legitimate religion (*religio licitas*) in the Roman Empire. This is why he can speak of the purpose of all the ordinances as repentance (*metanoia* 2:4]). His terms for justification essentially express God's actions of forgiveness to those who do not observe the special laws of Judaism.

Paul is, as usual, talking about religious justification and salvation through the events and perceptions of his life, in this case through the naturally related issue of ordinary courtroom justice. He promises retribution for the injustices done to him and all other Christians: "But by your hard and impenitent heart you are storing up wrath for yourself on the day of wrath when God's righteous judgment will be revealed" (2:5). He continues, "All who have sinned without the law will also perish without the law and all who have sinned under the law will be judged by the law" (2:12), a conventional apocalyptic sentiment. Thus, his statement that those who do the law will be justified (2:13) does not directly refer to the process of salvation that he has discussed many times. He is adopting the argument of the Jewish Christians for the purpose of condemning them. It is an irony meant to underline the perversion of human justice. As a Pharisee he was far more observant than those Hellenized and non-Pharisaic Jews and Jewish Christians who attempt to judge him wherever he goes. Essentially he is saying that they are hypocrites, since they could not themselves stand up to scrutiny. The meaning is clear: those who do the law (not the hypocrites who know it but pervert it) will in turn receive justice. The rhetoric still leads to the conclusion that Jewish courts are the most corrupt, because they should know better than the gentiles. Paul is saying that he is being judged by lawless men, both Jewish and gentile. Of the two, the gentiles prove the less hypocritical because less is to be expected of them. This is hardly a compliment to anyone; but Paul is obviously angry and expresses his anger in apocalyptic language. It is not a violation of Paul's principles, provided one understands that he is more interested in describing entrance into the community without special law, not salvation by faith.

Paul uses the situation as an occasion for his further comments about Judaism, as he uses his personal experience of anguish in Romans 7 as the occasion for discussing Torah as a vehicle for salvation. In fact, both passages are part of the same discussion. The question he asks in Romans 3 is what one would expect after a discussion of the injustices done to him, in which Jewish disobedience is so clearly outlined: "Then what advantage has the Jew? Or what is the value of circumcision? Much in every way" (Rom. 3:1–2). When Paul speaks of the role of Torah in salvation, he points out that its purpose is to foretell the coming of Christ (Rom. 3:2), his least controversial understanding of its value to Christianity. Then, with the rhetorical change of direction typical of his writing, he begins a discourse that defends the value of God's law, maintaining that law's value is relative to the greater value of faith. In the midst of this discussion Paul meditates on the ultimate value of belonging to Israel (Rom. 9–11).

Paul uses the term *Israel* consistently to refer to the Jewish people, as opposed to the church fathers who formalized a doctrine of the church as a "New Israel."[10] He likewise does not use the word *Christian* to refer to the new religion, for either Paul did not know it (possibly it had not even been coined) or he objected to it. Had he used it, the term *Christian*, like the Pauline phrase *in Christ*, would not have necessarily designated a completely new phenomenon.

Paul's phrase *in Christ* represents his closest approximation of a definition of community; but he never allows that term to serve as a proper noun. Paul's lack of a specific term to refer to Christianity is puzzling, but it is understandable both in terms of Paul's polemical object, as well as his other goals of reconciliation between Jews, Jewish Christians, and gentile Christians. Paul did not desire to describe Christianity as a completely different phenomenon from Judaism, for, as he clarifies in Romans, he saw it as the fulfillment of Judaism and as part of it. *In Christ* is also consonant with the general use of language in the first century. Paul's imprecision of language is paralleled by other sectarian groups; for instance, at Qumran the term *Israel* is used for the whole people, though the community thought of itself as the only righteous remnant destined for salvation. Although one might ordinarily expect a strong and well-developed term of self-reference, Qumran had a variety of designations for itself, including *sons of light*. They apparently only refer to themselves as Israel when speaking of the apocalyptic future, when the unbelieving sons of Israel have been destroyed.

E. P. Sanders says, following N. A. Dahl, that a similar situation obtained in Paul's thinking. Paul normally uses such terms as *new creation* or *body of Christ*, to describe the church. Sanders maintains that he uses the term *Israel of God* (Gal. 6:16) to refer to the church. Sanders thinks that Paul might have intended this term to cover the future period when sinning Israel had been destroyed.[11] But this is controversial. Paul is as likely to have meant the historical Israel—that is, Judaism—in that place.[12]

Paul regularly uses a language derived from his conversion—being "in Christ" to describe the "new creation" (Gal. 6:15; 2 Cor. 5:17). He says in 2 Cor. 3:16 that those who "turned to the Lord" have the veil removed and become the sole inheritors of the promises of Abraham. He is referring to everyone, not merely himself, implying repentance, which he rarely mentions elsewhere. This makes sense in the context of his previous discussion of the depravity of all human legal proceedings, including both Jewish and gentile. Paul's spiritual experience, an experience closely paralleled by Jewish mysticism forms the basis for his thinking.

Some Jews who entered the Christian movement did not convert because their socialization in Judaism, their interest in Jewish law, would have continued to be relevant to their Christian identity. They would have been wary of meeting gentiles in community. But, Paul maintained, all had to convert. All had to undergo a metamorphosis. The process of completely revaluing one's life was essentially the same for both Jews and Christians. When Jews converted, they had to be willing to give up the factors that had traditionally separated Jews from gentiles, as the gentiles had to give up the factors (their idolatry and impurity) that separated them from Jews. Only in this way could a single community be formed. The result is that he uses the word *transformation,* not the traditional words for conversion in Judaism. The Hebrew word *gayyar* refers to gentile conversion only and *teshuva* refers to repentance from sinning. Neither was appropriate to the experience that Paul underwent or to the experience of the Jewish Christians.

What Paul did not wish and what he fought against is what eventually happened: The church became a new, third entity. Paul must have foreseen this as a possibility, since he lived a good part of his life among gentiles alone, who were separated from their Jewish brothers in Christ, but he did not desire it. Nevertheless, in the social atmosphere in which he lived, the construction of a new entity was the necessary effect of his teaching, both sociologically and theologically: The most conservative Jewish Christians would not eat with ritually impure gentiles, and some gentiles appeared to flaunt their new status before Jews. From the perspective of Jewish Christianity, Paul was indeed recommending that Jews give up Torah. It was of no account that Paul's accommodating legal procedure did not always require it.[13] E. P. Sanders writes:

Paul, then, we cannot doubt, thought of the church as the fulfillment of the promises of Abraham. In that sense it was not at all a new religion. Jews who entered the Christian movement did not have to convert in the way Gentiles did: they did not have to renounce their God, nor, at least in theory, observance of the law. Nevertheless in very important ways the church was, in Paul's view and even more in his practice, a third entity. It was not established by admitting gentiles to Israel according to the flesh (as standard Jewish eschatological expectation would have it), but by admitting all, whether Jew or Greek, into the body of Christ by faith in him. Admission was sealed by baptism, most emphatically not by circumcision and acceptance of the law. The worship of the church was not worship in the synagogue (though quite conceivably some members could have done both.) The rules governing behavior were partly Jewish, but not entirely, and thus in this too Paul's gentile churches were a third entity. Gentile converts definitely had to separate themselves from important aspects of Greco-Roman life, but they were not Jewish enough to make them socially acceptable to observant Jews, whether Christians or non-Christians. Jewish Christians would have to give up aspects of the law if they were to associate with Gentile Christians. Paul's view of the church, supported by his practice, against his own conscious intention, was substantially that it was a third entity, not just because it was composed of both Jew and Greek, but also because it was in important ways neither Jewish nor Greek. (178–79)

I agree with Sanders, but from a different perspective. I should also emphasize that it is foreign to Paul's thinking to say that many Jews did not have to convert in order to become Christian. Paul certainly desired them to convert, not just to enter Christianity, though the fact that many Jews could and did join Christianity without a prescribed conversion is an important reason why Paul's system failed to gain much Jewish support in areas where Pharisaism was strong. Paul's experience was quite unusual in this respect. As an ex-Pharisee who had himself given up substantial amounts of Jewish practice, Paul had hoped that other Jews entering Christianity would do likewise. But he in effect moderated his view for the purposes of church unity. Paul's preaching is, as he constantly reports with chagrin, better designed for gentiles than for Jews.

The first-century Jew's commitment to Judaism was increasingly influenced in the land of Israel by Pharisaism and hence more concerned with the ritual observances that Paul decries, for these rites functioned to construct Jewish identity by setting off Jews from their neighbors. Paul looked on non-Pharisaic Jews with the judgmental eyes of an ex-Pharisee. If they value the law, they should do it all—in effect become Pharisees. No compromise was possible. But for Paul there was a completely new way. The best approach to interest a Jew in Christ would have been to build on those rites, which is what Paul's opponents did. When Paul left Pharisaism, he took many aspects of his training with him, notably his desire to build a single community for all Israel. But the model of community that he formulated and the sources of commitment that he outlined were not those of Pharisaic Judaism; rather, they were those of mystical and apocalyptic Judaism, where the strict distinction between insider and outsider defined sectarian Jewish movements. Paul used that idea in a new way by abrogating the most difficult ritual requirements of Judaism and transforming the rest into a liturgical form comprehensible to gentiles. In so doing, he planted the seeds and indeed saw the first fruits (as he himself called them) of a new and overwhelmingly successful gentile mission.

If Paul's call for unity is taken seriously, he did not merely want to be the apostle to the gentiles. He wanted to be an apostle of all the church, for his vision was for a new community formed of all gentiles and Jews (1 Cor. 9:20–22). Paul's attempt to organize that community, parallel to his attempt to gain acceptance as an apostle, also ironically publicized his ritual position as apostasy and worse. A gentile apostle, had he preached the same, would not have run into the same problems. But the great power of Paul's vision and the great ferment that he caused came from the fact that he had been a Pharisee and then converted to gentile Christianity. This is an enormous leap and it was understood by those faithful to Christ to be a mark of the power of the spirit.

Forces of dissonance are always unleashed in a conversion, because the convert sees a great distinction between a previous life and a present one. But the Jewish Christians were not converted; they saw no necessary distinction between Judaism and Christianity. Paul's desire to find a formula for church unity also ensured his message's failure among Jewish Christians. It did ensure his message's success among gentiles, especially among those God-fearing gentiles who had been interested in Judaism before they met Paul. A God-fearer would have welcomed Paul's message with excitement, because it removed the status-ambiguity, the double alienation of being no longer gentile but not yet Jewish. Instead of being neither pagans nor Jews, God-fearers entered gentile Christian community as true equals, without having to undergo the seemingly irrelevant ritual conversion to Judaism.

Though the differences between Jew and gentile were not solved during Paul's life, whenever the social cohesion he desired was achieved within Christian churches it was by the means he suggested: transformation or conversion. In spite of the ferocious battles between Jewish and gentile Christians, no other Jewish sect developed the same kind of cohesion with gentiles that Christianity did—with both Jew and gentile wedded to one single concept of community, which is precisely what Paul wanted. Further, no other Jewish sect succeeded in producing a community so thoroughly adept at successful proselytism.

Paul was not the first convert to Christianity, but his life became a model for gentile Christians and Jews to follow. His work fueled the Christian community even after its apocalyptic vision of the world dimmed. All the variables that modern scholars see as important to the creation of social cohesion were addressed by Paul's concept of metamorphosis. Further, it was a spiritual or psychic phenomenon whose effects in the world could be transmitted to the next generation of believers by means of education and training. This balanced and emotionally predictable kind of metamorphosis, a continuously developing process of salvation, was more valuable to the growth of the community than a concept of a sudden, soon-to-arrive eschaton. All aspects of Paul's theory did not, however, find ready acceptance even in a largely gentile church; for instance, wherever charismatic leadership threatened to destroy church polity, Paul's theory still needed to be controlled by apostolic authority. Paul's idea of conversion into the community of repentant sinners was a potent factor in the success of Christianity, no matter how it might have offended the dominant Jewish Christian sector of the church in Paul's own day.

Paul's thinking was radical for the later church as well. He left open the possibility of Gnostic interpretation.[14] In fact, his letters became the principal New Testament texts of a large section of gnostic Christianity. In Gnosticism, the necessary control was also correlated with apostolic authority, which mounted an apologetic for the importance of Old Testament prophecy. Paul can no more be blamed for the free interpretations of his Gnostic readers than he can for those of twentieth-century scholars. Yet on the issue of Jewish-gentile relations, the basic issue of the earliest church, Paul was invaluable despite his failure to achieve his vision in his own day.

Once the gentile church came to predominate, the failure of Paul's attempt to effect a reconciliation in his own day was forgotten. The social ramifications of using Paul's experience as normative for all Christianity are clear. The conversion experience became more important because it helped Christianity to define its own unity. The dissonance that a gentile would feel on entering this new religion could be expected to be as great as Paul's if not greater, since it would probably entail a change of primary socialization. Yet on the issue of Torah, the ordinary convert would feel little of the anguish and ambivalence that Paul evinces in Romans. The gentile convert probably ignored much of Paul's meditations on Torah since it was foreign to him. Eventually, under the influence of theological reflection, Paul's personal statements could be turned into theological meditations on the insufficiency of law, which is almost the opposite of what they actually are. Instead, many statements reflect Paul's attempt to accommodate his beliefs diplomatically to the practice of Jewish Christians after he had retreated from the Pharisaic interpretation of law as a result of his conversion.

THE DIASPORA AND THE SPREAD OF GENTILE CHRISTIANITY

Although it is possible to overemphasize the role of gentile Christianity in the early church, in Paul's writings we can see some of the reasons for its eventual success. Though Luke's description of Paul's conversion is the definition of a "flash out of the blue," Paul did not live in a social vacuum. He was not the first convert either in the history of Christianity or Judaism, though he was certainly the most important one. Further, to say that Paul was the second founder of Christianity, as many Jewish and Christian scholars have, is not only to exaggerate but to obscure the communal mechanisms by which Christianity spread; Paul converted into a vibrant and dynamic albeit small gentile church, which provided him with a social context in which to continue his Christian education.[15] In the process he defined Christianity's gentile future by radically revaluing its Jewish past. Consequently, the importance of Paul's work was not fully realized until the church became largely gentile. But before Paul joined the church, it encompassed a significant Jewish and gentile population spread among the major cities of Asia Minor, Greece, and Rome.

Luke, who wrote in a world where the gentile mission had overtaken but not overwhelmed the Jewish one, used Paul as the model of gentile conversions. Paul would have disputed Luke's portrayal. Paul understood his own visionary experiences as crucial moments, putting him in the same category as the original apostles. But he was suspicious of other kinds of emotional experience, such as gifts of the spirit. Nor did he feel he had sinned in any way in his previous life. Luke and the pastoral Epistles saw Paul as a convenient model to pattern future gentile conversions. Paul the sinner and the emotional convert was a more relevant portrait for a burgeoning gentile church than Paul the metamorphosized Pharisee.

By contrast, Paul's letters represent the novelty and isolation of a number of gentile Christian communities seeking self-definition as a growing minority within the church. Paul records their first defense against some of the Jewish-Christian communities' criticism of gentiles. As Paul's letters outline a new idea for a unified community, so too they suggest the dynamics separating the two communities. The width of the chasm between them is suggested by Paul's vituperation. But the nature of the cohesion that internally bound each of the two communities and separated them from each other differed radically, preventing the kind of unification that Paul desired. The gentile Christians, like the rabbis, saw the distinction between Jew and gentile to be one of purity and impurity but no bar to gentile salvation, provided they remained in their own communities. They advised gentiles wishing to join with Jews in a single community to be circumcised and to practice ritual purity. Gentiles converted to Judaism would have found Paul's gentile Christianity without circumcision to be specious. Jewish Christians who found Christianity to complete their Judaism were in a peculiar bind, especially if their Judaism was heavily tinged with traditional Jewish apocalypticism, because Paul, speaking for the new gentile Christian communities, insisted on the total unification of the movement. In the gentile churches, surrounded by the larger gentile community, the wall separating unconverted and converted gentiles may on occasion have been higher than the one separating the ordinary Jew from a gentile, due to apocalyptic sentiments and cognitive dissonance. This wall was held up by the apocalyptic notion that outside the group all were damned and reinforced by the internal cohesion of a community based on conversion. The high number of conversion experiences in gentile Christianity would have reinforced group cohesion among the more gradual converts as well. The greater number of radical conversions, the higher the morale of the group. In the area of religion, as in other human endeavors, success breeds success. If Paul's letter are, however, representative of a split, the Jewish Christians could not trust gentiles to keep away from their former coreligionists. Jewish Christians probably were still part of the Jewish communities in several important ways, as the issue of meat sacrificed to idols suggests. The widespread success of gentile Christianity, with its differing possibilities of interaction with ordinary gentiles, made its incorporation into a single church an even greater desideratum, as Paul constantly reminds us.

There is nothing in Judaism to correspond to the determination and effectiveness with which Christianity missionized, though the dynamic that produced Christianity as a missionizing religion came partly from its Jewish roots. Paul himself shows us the importance of ecstatic conversion experiences and apocalypticism for building communal unity and breaking down traditional barriers within society. Abraham Malherbe, Gerd Theissen, and Wayne Meeks point out that by the time of Paul's letters, a scarce decade or two after Jesus, the church had begun to attract a larger cross section of the Roman world than one would expect from a Jewish apocalyptic movement solely of the disadvantaged.[16] In the purely Palestinian context of the Jesus movement, as in the case of Christianity in its Hellenistic setting, it is necessary to move to a much broader understanding of disadvantage, so that religious questing, the search for new answers, can also be included. The higher morality, with its communally sanctioned rules, would have appealed to some. No one knows for sure how the originally Jewish apocalyptic sect was able to cross into the gentile environment, but we can see hints in the ways that Paul speaks to his gentile parishioners. He tells them to avoid idolatry, the normal religious life of the civic-minded gentile; this gave an objective expression to the disaffection of the newly converted gentile Christian. Although many Jewish purity rules did not translate into the new Christian setting, apocalyptic dissatisfaction with the world found a ready audience among the disaffected gentiles, women, some Hellenistic Jews, and some half-proselytized God-fearers of the Roman Empire. The difference between Paul's apocalypticism and the traditional Jewish variety is that Paul brought with him the Pharisaic hopes for a gentile world won over to worship of the one God. He completely ignored the usual apocalyptic notion of condemning the gentiles for their sinning and mistreatment of Israel.

The Diaspora synagogue provided an initial setting for Christian missionizing activities, as well as some competition for the Christian cause, as Luke himself portrays. First, the synagogues of the Diaspora were public places where crowds assembled to hear messages tailored directly to their unique social position, the position to which Christianity most appealed. Jews were adapted successfully to Hellenistic life but were not accepted as full citizens in the Roman world. In addition to the Diaspora Jews, the gentile God-fearers, who were unable or unwilling to take all the conversion steps necessary to become Jews, also attended the synagogue. The most salient characteristic of this group was their double sense of ambiguity: having opted to change their ways, they could not be accepted fully into Jewish life until they were circumcised and began the practice of Jewish law. The attachment of this group of God-fearers to the synagogue varied from a neighborly financial support to potential conversion. Although women did not have to undergo circumcision in order to convert to Judaism and women in rabbinic Judaism also attained to an equality of status that was not guaranteed elsewhere in the Hellenistic world, the promise of higher status for women in early Christianity might have attracted some gentile and Jewish women alike.

As biased and ahistorical as Luke's reporting of Paul might have been, there was no reason for him deliberately to fabricate the details of the mission when they were known to him. If the social situation that Luke describes does not apply fully to Paul's time, it certainly describes the time of Luke, which is as important from this viewpoint. Luke reports that when Paul arrived in a new town, he often turned to the synagogue for lodging and support, as would any Jewish traveler, but also sought out the synagogue as a pulpit from which to advance his mission. Luke clearly has actual experience of this kind of proselytism, whether or not it corresponds to Paul's experience.

This mission would not have been turned exclusively to Jews, for there were always gentile listeners in synagogues. Many religions attracted gentile attention by virtue of their exotic beliefs and ceremonies or because of the ethics and morality with which they governed their lives, and Jews were no exception. We have evidence of the continuing attraction of gentiles to the synagogue. The Christian mission would have been most effective where Jews gathered and where there was a population of transients away from their closest family ties. Though Jews welcomed proselytes, it is unlikely that the synagogue itself indulged in the kind of missionizing that characterized early Christianity.

According to Luke, the results of Paul's synagogue missionizing were mixed. Gentiles were often intrigued but Jews were scandalized. Diaspora synagogues could have had understandings of Torah different from the early rabbinic movement, but they did not welcome the rancor and competition instigated by Paul and the Christian missionaries. Nor did they appreciate any interruptions of their services to discuss an apocalyptic end. The most obvious charge against Christian proselytism in synagogues, given the Lukan description, was disturbing the peace. This was not a misdemeanor, as it is in our society, but a crime that in theory risked capital punishment. A second charge, given the content of Paul's mission, might have been advocating that Jews give up their ancestral ways, subverting and perverting Torah, a far more serious charge in Jewish law that probably concerned the Romans but little. Either charge might have left Paul with the lashes he reports having received, since there is no guarantee that the later rabbinic rules of punishment were in force throughout the Jewish world of the first century. But the Jewish Christian missionaries would have been as sensitive to the charge of subverting Torah as the Jews. Why should Paul's outrageous remarks risk the safety of the Jewish Christians within the Jewish community? We can see from this that the opposition of the Jewish Christians might even have been stronger than that of the Jews!

After these events Luke reports that Paul retreated to his own community, separate from Jews. Luke's theology, rather than accurate knowledge of the events of Paul's life, controls this pattern. We cannot assume that every town reacted in the same way; at most we can assume that some Jewish communities in Luke's day reacted in this way. We know from Paul's own writings that his congregations were largely separate from the Jews and Jewish Christians. Thus, if Jewish Christianity were not already a distinct sect in itself, Paul made gentile Christianity into one. In doing so, he also planted the seeds for Jewish Christianity to become a sect. There were social reasons for the distinction, within both the Jewish community and the Christian one.

The social organization of the early Christian sect, with its apocalyptic expectation of a quick end of time, explains the enthusiasm with which earliest Christianity spread. Fervently expecting the end, living communally, and doing only what was necessary to support one's family in the interim, the cells of early Christian apocalypticists, of both the traditional Jewish type and the new gentile type, formed a highly motivated group of proselytizers, in terms of Kanter's scales of commitment, although they may have lacked the continuous level of commitment generated by practicing the special laws of Judaism.

Not all Hellenistic Christians, of course, were apocalypticists, as were the earliest Palestinian Christians. Nor need they have been, for conversion and other kinds of affective commitment, as well as instrumental and moral commitments, would have been high in such a cellular group without millenarianism. But without these social instruments, commitment is difficult to maintain. From the Pauline correspondence, there is evidence in Corinth, a gentile church evangelized by Paul and other apostles, that neither Jewish food laws nor the apocalyptic end were well understood. On the opposite extreme of gentile interpretation of apocalypticism was Thessalonica, where apocalypticism appears to have crossed the border into millenarianism. From the evidence of Paul's letters, apocalypticism and Jewish ritual law, with the attendant commitment to group maintenance, were still dominant in the majority of the early churches.

In spite of the occasional pulpit that Christianity found in the marketplaces and synagogues, it also spread by one-to-one evangelizing. The spread would not have appeared fast to the casual observer. Yet, over a generation or two, the results must have been clear enough to anyone concerned. Paul's record supports the idea that some Jews must have been proselytizing pagans; the Hellenistic literary remains leave no doubt that some Jews were interested in clarifying the status of God-fearing pagans. But Paul offered something that no other Jewish proselytizer had been able to offer—the promises of Judaism but with the peculiar responsibilities of the special laws entirely optional (Rom. 14:5–9). This was to be an explosive new formula that changed the spiritual picture of the late Roman Empire. It attracted Hellenistic Jews, like Timothy, as well as gentiles, like Titus. The stories in Acts underline the truth of the statements for his time more than for the time of Paul himself. It was Paul's clearly articulated transformation, his experience of conversion, that made this new insight possible. In the first generations, Paul's promise fell short because both the Jewish Christian community and the Jewish community viewed the inclusion of antinomian gentiles and observant Jews in one community with alarm.

Time was on the side of the gentile community. Christian communities formulated on Pauline conversion experiences might have had a higher degree of commitment than the Jewish Diaspora communities, for instance, which continued to observe Jewish law in an attenuated way. If the gentiles were an embattled group within Christianity, their commitment would have been far higher because of cognitive dissonance.

The gentile community eventually surpassed the Jewish Christian one. But even when the trend was overwhelmingly in favor of gentile Christianity, the balance would have depended on local populations for generations. As an embattled minority, ostracized by Judaism and Christianity, the Jewish Christian group could then have attained more commitment than the growing gentile one. There is evidence of their continued existence, but their political and economic situation seems to have deteriorated as the gentile Christian community increased and flourished. It is likely that Christianity continued to gain converts from the Diaspora synagogues, as well as from the God-fearers, but demography favored the increase of the gentile community.

Gentile Christian communities based on the Pauline model would have valued conversion experiences as a proof of faith. Jewish Christians, by contrast, lost touch with their Jewish past and were judged heretical by Jews. They were opposed by gentile Christians as well, as both Luke and Paul show us. Christians, even those socialized from birth, became imbued with the value of being in Christ through baptism and communion and tended to look at all ecstatic experiences as proof of the faith. Paul himself warned against abuses of ecstatic experience, when rational thought was the necessary remedy, but he still endorsed ecstasy, which was a popular religious form among later generations of pagans. Further, gifts of the spirit continued to be regarded as a sign of the imminent approach of God's kingdom; hence, they kept alive some of the springs of apocalypticism and the concept of conversion, though no actual decision was passed and so no dissonance would have been experienced. Occasionally, ecstasy and millenarianism broke out again, as in the Montanist movement. Such outbreaks may have been partly related to historical events and calendrical speculations, linking the prophecies in Daniel to the Jubilee years of the Jewish calendar. Further, Christianity's emphasis on rebirth and resurrection, promising life after death to its converts, was, if not unique, certainly one of the most cogent attractions of the new movement. This was gained through a radical conversion, or transformation, as it was known in pagan life, not through education and prayer, which came afterward.

Luke and such subsequent Christian writers as the unknown author of the pastoral Epistles transform Paul's special prophetic, apocalyptic, and mystical ecstasies, in which he learned the true meaning of his conversion, into a model for gentile Christian conversion. The significance of the ecstasy is that it signifies that a moral crisis, involving the recognition by the sinner of sinfulness and then forgiveness by God, is past. Paul never would have accepted such a characterization, though he used the same language to describe pagan and Jewish repentance. Paul becomes the model for gentile conversion in ways that are quite foreign to his own experience.

In the third and fourth centuries commitment seems to have waned. Although large numbers of people converted to Christianity, their conversions resembled the forced conversions of the Maccabean time. A new adherence was forced on an acquiescent population.[17] No religious decision need be assumed.

THE JEWISH REACTION

As Christianity spread, the rabbinic movement also spread. Both entered the cities of Judah and Galilee. Rabbinism, however, became most powerful in the smaller cities of the Galilee where Jesus preached, and Christianity spread most quickly in the large Hellenistic cities, where more anomolous and uprooted people were to be found. The social structure of the small cities and towns favored rabbinism. Within the Jewish community Christianity proved just as fractious. But the issue of law was not the only issue dividing Christianity from Judaism. The rabbis mention a heresy called "two powers in heaven," which must certainly refer to Christian beliefs, among others.[18] Rabbinism shows that the divinity of the risen Lord was a primary theological offense in the eyes of the Jews. There were, however, other Hellenistic and apocalyptic Jews of the first century who valorized one particular biblical hero or angel to the point of divinity. In those cases we cannot be sure whether the rabbis, or any other group in the Jewish community, would have called the sectarians heretics or done anything about it.

In the case of Christians there could be no doubt. Christianity firmly proclaimed the divinity of the second Lord and offered prayers to him as a god.[19] Breaking down the distinction between God and man directly paralleled their breaking down the distinction between Jew and gentile.[20] Thus, the rabbinic community evolved specific theological reasons for objecting to Christianity. The Christians against whom the rabbis railed were probably Jewish Christians. Most of the rest of Judaism was officially opposed to Christianity as well, though one can imagine that some less-committed members of the Jewish Diaspora community were attracted to Christianity. We do not know how often interested Christians listened to synagogue sermons or how much Jews cared about what was happening in the churches. But certainly some knowledge was transmitted through polemic. We find that the same terms used by Jews against Christians find their way into internal orthodox Christian polemics against Gnostics.[21] So as the rabbinic community gained strength, it fought the Christian community as a heresy; but if rabbinic records are accurate, the active confrontations were infrequent and involved vituperation or ostracism rather than punishment.

ACTS OF THE APOSTLES ON
THE PEOPLE OF GOD

This is a rough picture of the growing religious sect, no longer just of Jews, with which Paul came into creative contact. Although Paul described a single unity of all Christians in his letters, the social effect of his teachings was ironically divisive in the beginning. His letters, however, provide unique means for solving theological disputes and addressing legal rulings that might otherwise have hindered Christianity's acceptance. The social forces that were unleashed by the gentile mission in Christianity were not due to Paul. Paul attempted to solve an existent problem. The example he set in his conversion and career, his letters, and perhaps in his death changed the church forever.

The greatest significance of Paul's writings was to be felt after his death. At a decisive moment, Paul's experience and his writings allowed the church to analyze and solve the problem of its Jewish past by coming to terms with its gentile future. Because Paul's life as much as his writings embodied the solution to these issues, Christianity received the influence of his personality, giving the religion a characteristic Pauline cast. This Pauline cast can be seen in the image of Christianity as a missionary community of converts, the picture of community that would eventually dominate Christianity. But the immediate effect of the conflict on Paul's career might have been tragic.

Jewish Christianity probably continued to be the dominant form of Christianity for at least two generations and maybe for several generations after Paul. Even Acts, written in an environment of a more confident gentile mission, claims to be written from within Judaism. There is no theology of replacement whereby the church supersedes Israel in God's plan of salvation. Luke more than Paul believes that Torah is still relevant for Christians, though he reduces the number of ordinances to make the mixing of gentiles and Jews easier. Luke often stresses the Jewishness of Jesus where the other evangelists omit it. Jesus, for instance, has virtually no dealings with gentiles in the Gospel of Luke. Luke knows that Jewish practice forbids certain kinds of contact between Jews and gentiles (Acts 10:28).[22] For Luke, as for Paul, the struggle between Jews and Christians is a division in Israel. Jewish Christianity is a real force to be reckoned with. Rather than freeing gentile Christianity from Judaism, Luke attempts a conciliation with Jewish observance beyond anything Paul wanted. Luke appeals to the church to appease the feelings of the Jewish Christians, taking on the rules of the Jerusalem Conference. But Luke knows, with more historical distance than Paul, that the gentile mission is a crucial factor in the church's history. At the end of Acts, unbelieving Jews have simply given up their place within the saved remnant. Paul might suspect as much but he cannot be sure.

ROMANS 9–11

The emerging failure of the Christian message to the Jewish and Jewish Christian community informs Paul's discussion of the purpose of Israel. The end of Romans is Paul's mature thinking about the future of Israel. Though Romans 9–11 has often been read dogmatically as a meditation on free will and predestination, the conclusions for theology arise only secondarily, as a result of Paul's personal ruminations about the traditional role of Israel after Christ.[23] In Galatians, Paul had been concerned with clarifying that new converts did not have to observe Torah. In Romans, by contrast, Paul turns to the issues of the election of Israel and the ultimate fate of the Jews. These issues are not internal ones between gentile Christians and Judaizers siding with the Jewish Christians. Paul addresses the rejection of the Christian mission in toto by the majority of the Jewish community. Paul's argument divides neatly into three parts. First, he propounds that the failure of Israel to convert is not incompatible with God's promises to Israel (Romans 9). Second, he maintains that the hardening of Jewish hearts is due to their own lack of faith and is a response to their own guilt (9:30–10:21). Third, Paul maintains that the Jewish rejection of Christ will not last forever, for God will eventually show mercy and save all Israel (Romans 11).[24]

These statements are offered independently, and it is not clear that they can all be held simultaneously. But philosophical consistency was not the purpose of Paul's remarks; rather, they express Paul's sorrow that the rest of Israel has not followed him in seeing the truth of the Christian message, combined with his desire to protect the promises of the Hebrew Bible from the allegation of inconsistency, based on his novel interpretation of them. These are not likely to be theoretical issues, for they are criticisms that could have been plausibly leveled at him in discussions with Jewish Christians. His basic answer is that God has not changed his mind about the promises offered to Israel; they are still valid. But the way in which they are valid must be seen in a different light after Christ.

Paul states that not all who are descended from Israel belong to it. This is a natural sectarian understanding of the promises of the Hebrew Bible and illustrates how conflict enforces the pariah mentality of the sectarian. The prophets and the apocalyptic movements for which we have any literary evidence, from the book of Daniel through the Qumran community, held that only a righteous remnant of Israel would survive the coming judgment of God. There is nothing unusual in this thinking. But Paul's exegesis is quite different from those of the prophets and the apocalypticists, in the sense that he often adopts a rabbinic, midrashic approach to the Bible, which is consonant with his Pharisaic background, rather than an apocalyptic approach, which calls for the unraveling of the divine plan through *pesher* or special revelation.

Paul also distinguishes between God's promise and election in a way that would be impossible for a Pharisaic or rabbinic Jew. For the Pharisees and for the rabbis after them, there is no contradiction between election (God's promise in choosing Israel) and the ancestry of the people. But Paul sees that gentiles have been included in the new Christian community in a way that could not have been predicted from pre-Christian readings of the Hebrew Bible. He therefore cites the stories of God's pleasure with Isaac and Jacob and his displeasure with Ishmael and Esau as evidence that election and promise matter, but ancestry does not. Paul's usage is chiastic, opposite to the interpretation that a rabbinic Jew would have made: for the Jew, the positive fact that God chose Isaac and Jacob is important; for Paul the converse fact is equally important: God disinherited Esau and Ishmael in spite of their ancestry. God's differing plan for Jacob and Esau was not based on anything they had done. God chose one and rejected the other for his own purposes.

Paul also mentions the famous ethical problem of God's hardening of Pharaoh's heart: "For this purpose have I raised you up, for the very purpose of showing my power in you, so that my name may be proclaimed through all the earth" (Exod. 9:16). This is a particularly apt quotation for Paul's argument, since it implies that the hardening of Jewish hearts is for the purpose of showing God's power to the gentiles, that his name can be proclaimed in all the earth (Rom. 9:17). Paul puts the non-Christian Jews of his time on the same level as Ishmael and Esau and also with Pharaoh. This is a nonrabbinic conclusion, but the process of exegesis is strictly rabbinic, combining Paul's special religious perspective with the education he had received in Judaism. This method is emphasized in Rom. 9:25–26 where the appended text from Hos. 2:23 is used to prove that God has called his people from the gentiles: "Those who were not My people, I will call 'My people,' and she who was not beloved I will call 'My beloved.'" In place of saying, "You are not My people," they will be called "sons of the living God." Hence the gentiles have embraced the faith whereas the majority of Israel has not. The effect is that Paul's discourse in Romans comes painfully close to apostasy and would certainly have angered any Jew who was not already angered by his antinomianism. Paul risks these dangers for his new vision of community.

Paul makes a crucial statement in Rom. 10:4: "For Christ is the end [*telos*] of the Law, that everyone who has faith may be justified." Paul uses biblical exegesis to support this strong statement. He cites two pieces of Scripture that apply to the righteousness under the law and under faith. He contrasts Lev. 18:5, "The person who does them will live by them," with a whole section of Deut. 30:12–14 (amplified by such passages as Deut. 9:4, Ps. 106 [107]: 26 LXX), which begins: "Say not in your heart, who shall ascend to heaven?" Paul then adds his commentary: "that is to bring Christ down from above."

Anyone who has read the Midrash will recognize Paul's midrashic method. This passage is crucial for the understanding of religious choice in Israelite culture, for it is an exegesis of the passage in Deuteronomy where Moses exhorts the people to opt for the religion of God, providing the basic warrant for religious conversion in Judea (see introduction above). Paul, like Moses in Deuteronomy, is attempting to make his hearers understand the importance of their choice.

Like Moses, he exhorts them to choose life. He comments on "who shall descend into the deep" with the words "to bring Christ again up from the dead." Although this may seem like an unjustified reinterpretation, its form is not unlike many other rabbinic remarks in which the relevance of a biblical passage is asserted. The point of the passage, however, appears in Rom. 10:8 where Paul emphasizes that the word of faith that Christ teaches is near.

Paul has again set up a contradiction that would not have occurred to a believing Jew, for whom both passages would have applied to Torah as revealed on Mount Sinai. For Paul, after his conversion, the two passages conflict. On the one hand, he describes the righteousness of Torah, including all the ordinances and prohibitions, that promises life; on the other hand, he describes the righteousness of faith as close and easy to accomplish, because it is based on accepting Christ and not on performing all the details of Jewish ceremonial law. Paul does not deny either one, but tries to show that the Deuteronomy passage contains the universal statement about God's plan for humanity, whereas the Leviticus passage refers only to ceremonial Torah in the most narrow sense. His point here is to make the two paths equivalent because faith is the underlying point of similarity.[25]

The purpose of Paul's argument is not to eliminate Israel; rather, the problem continues to be what it always was during his life—the inclusion of the gentiles into the community. Further, as has become clear in his conflicts with Jewish Christians, all, not only gentiles, need to be evangelized. From Paul's perspective, most of the Jewish Christians have missed the point of Christ's presence. There has never been more than a remnant saved from Israel and now they who will be saved from Israel are those who have accepted Christ. His text at this point (Rom. 10:19) is Isa. 65:1-2 which concerns God's self-revelation to a nation that has not sough God, amplified by Deut 32:21: "I will make you jealous of those who are not a nation; with a foolish nation, I will make you angry."

In Rom. 11:1 Paul returns to his main point. Some Israelites are to be saved, as he has been, since he too is an Israelite, of the seed of Abraham, of the tribe of Benjamin. The hardening of heart of most of the Jews is not incompatible with God's promises in the Bible, because the number of faithful is always small, according to Scripture. Though Israel has not retained the prize, they are not disqualified forever. Through their intransigence, the Jews will forfeit their reserved first place and gentiles will be saved before them. As opposed to his statement in Romans 1 and Galatians that salvation comes to the Jew first and then to the gentile, he now sees that salvation will come to the gentile first and then to the Jews.

Paul begins his last argument in this section by emphasizing that he is speaking to gentiles, because he is the apostle of the gentiles. But he is speaking to the Christian community, not to the Jews or the unconverted gentiles. Paul says that God's promise is not removed from the Israelites; rather, the order in which salvation is brought has been reversed. It is possible to interpret this passage as a statement of double salvation, Jews by Torah, gentiles by faith. Since the passage is meant for gentile ears, it emphasizes faith as the path of salvation for gentiles by saying that it is the equivalent of Torah, hence Torah does continue to save.[26]

A double plan for salvation, however, does not seem to be the point here, as Paul's lament for the stubbornness of the Jews shows. The figure of the wild olive illustrates his hope that some Jews will be saved by the provocation of the inclusion of the gentiles and follow the gentiles into the church. Some of the olive branches are broken off, and a wild olive is grafted on. The broken branches represent the unconverted part of Israel, whereas the root must be the converted Israelites. One wonders whether Paul might not have excluded many Jewish Christians, who upheld the cultic differences between gentiles and Jews, for they demonstrated lack of faith as well. Only the faithful will inherit the promises. The faithful acknowledge the special process of transformation beginning in the world. It is to them that the gentiles will be grafted and they should not boast of their understanding of faith. Faith in Mosaic legislation is not the equal of faith in Christ, as Stendahl, Gager, and Gaston think. Paul only equates the faithful in Christ who observe Torah with the faithful in Christ who do not observe Torah. Paul argues that Jewish Christians (with faith) and gentile Christians (with faith) are equal, not that Jews and Christians are equal. This is the meaning of his statement in Rom. 10:12–13, "For there is no distinction between Jew and Greek; the same Lord is Lord of all and bestows His riches upon all who call upon Him. For 'Every one who calls upon the name of the Lord shall be saved.'" It would be better to take this statement literally, as the rabbis did, that all who fear the Lord (and therefore act justly) are assured a place in the world to come. In this passage, however, Paul is implying that the name of God is Jesus the Christ, as he himself had discovered in his ecstatic metamorphosis. Apocalypticism and Jewish mysticism consider that YHWH, the Lord, the proper name of God, could signify God's principal angelic manifestation, his Glory. Paul had seen the Glory of God in a vision, as Ezekiel had seen the human figure of God on his throne approach from his temple in Jerusalem and join the exiles on the banks of the Chebar River. The difference is that Paul had identified the Glory of God as Christ. Relying on Jewish mystical tradition and his private revelation that Christ is the principal mediator of God, Paul is interpreting the name of the Lord to be Christ and faith to be faith in Christ exclusively. Paul, however, does not draw a detailed picture of what he envisions at the end of time, when some of Israel will embrace Christianity.

Paul implies that only those who accept Christ will be saved, a momentous statement about the future of Israel; but, strangely, he does not actually state it. Paul's refusal to spell out the implications of his reasoning is extremely important. Having virtually committed himself to the proposition that only a remnant of Israel will be retained, the standard apocalyptic notion, he then surprisingly asserts the rabbinic notion that all Israel will be saved (11:26). That doctrine, which appears in rabbinic literature in Mishnah Sanhedrin 10:1, is thus proven to be first-century Jewish thought as well. It also demonstrates Paul's continuing allegiance to major aspects of the rabbinic understanding of Torah, in spite of his conversion. But, at this point, it adds mystery (11:25) not logical clarity to Paul's discussion. Rather than merely abandon the unbelieving members of the Jewish community, Paul asserts that God's promises to them are still intact: "For the gifts and the call of God are irrevocable" (11:29). Of course, he hopes that the remaining Jews will come to Christ as he did, freely and without coercion. Though the mission to the Jews has been a failure, God will eventually reveal the reason. Therefore, there need not be a continuing Christian mission to the Jews.

Paul does not state exactly how the process of redemption for Jews will come about. The ambiguity appears to be deliberate, as it is in line with

Paul's theme of the sovereignty of God. Probably Paul had not received a direct revelation specifying the future; thus he does not indulge in apocalyptic forecasting. Instead, Paul tries to answer the question, as the rabbis would, by pondering the meaning of scripture. But if Paul were interpreting scripture like a rabbi, he would have to admit that other, even opposing interpretations could be just as valid midrashically. Individual rabbis interpreting scripture knew that they were but one voice in a chorus of exegesis.

Paul's silence, his deliberate ambiguity, is as important as his exegesis, because Paul obviously does not want to impinge on the sovereignty of God in spelling out how God intends to fulfill biblical promises, when he himself has not been informed of a surety. Furthermore, Paul warns his gentile converts not to boast about their status, for God's judgment is unsearchable and God's ways are inscrutable (11:33). Though Paul anticipates the conclusion and is convinced of its speedy arrival, he does not state it explicitly, because to do so would presume to influence God's actions, which is a mistake of pride. To demonstrate his point he quotes Isaiah and Job (11:34–35) to the effect that no one can know God's plan or influence God's actions: "For who has known the mind of the Lord or who has been God's counselor?" (Isa. 40:13); "Or who has given a gift to God that he might be repaid?" (Job 35:7). Without explicit revelatory knowledge, Paul saw that it was pride to suggest how God intended to fulfill the promises to Israel.

As a believing Jew and a twentieth-century humanist, I could have hoped for a different outcome of Paul's interpretation of these passages. The theology outlined by Stendahl, Gaston, and Gager makes more sense for today than does Paul's actual conclusion. It would have been easier for today's Christianity had Paul embraced cultural pluralism more fully. But I do not believe that Paul meant his remarks to be prophecy for the necessary future of Israel so much as a description of the historical situation that he saw. He was a product of his past in the Pharisaic Jewish community and his present in the gentile Christian community. It is easy to see how a person with Paul's experience of metamorphosis and career of trying to represent the rights of gentile Christianity—risking all to bring the communities together and failing—would have ended his meditation in this way.

It would not be wise to overinterpret what Paul meant in this passage. Paul was not writing an eternal, systematic theology. He was trying to understand the meaning of events in the way that any pious Jew of his day would have done: by consulting scripture and comparing it with his experience. He was advocating a view of social reality. He had personally experienced a vision of Christ, followed by a successful career evangelizing the gentiles, and at the same time witnessing the largely unsuccessful attempt to evangelize the Jews. To his disappointment and horror he experienced the Jewish Christian and Jewish opposition to his view of life. Paul's interpretations of biblical passages are meant to be meditations on the events that he had experienced, not explicit prophecies of the ultimate fate and destiny of history.

What Paul expected did not actually happen. His journey to Jerusalem and Rome did not change the minds of Jews or Jewish Christians. It did not prompt their conversion to his vision of community. On the contrary, if Acts is correct, he spent two years imprisoned in Caesarea; his appeal to Rome evidently did not end in his exoneration or the unification of that prosperous Jewish community into a single Jewish and gentile Christian community. Suetonius's peculiar and ambiguous reference to the uproar among the Jews at the instigation of a man mistakenly called Chrestus rather than Christus (*impulsore Chresto*) shows that at Rome the conflict between Christians and Jews had deteriorated to the point of becoming evident to the authorities. Paul's resolution would have incited rather than quieted the conflict.

Israel as a whole has not shown any interest in accepting as God's principal angel the Christ whom Paul saw in his conversion experience. Nor has Judaism at large seen itself to be part of a gigantic transformation process mystically identified with that angel. Nor has the parousia happened. Nils A. Dahl has pointed out that the only thing that has surely happened is the thing that Paul warned against: gentile Christianity has boasted of its special knowledge at the expense of Israel. Paul's major warning in Romans against boasting has gone unheeded. Such an outcome would have saddened Paul. But, in Dahl's opinion, it probably would not have surprised him, for underlying this section of Romans is the point that God's grace is mysterious. The Lord is the one God, God of Jews and gentiles. Though God is faithful and just, no human being knows how God will perform God's promises. God's ways are not our ways.

Paul's discussions of Judaism change radically when read by a church with a comfortable majority of gentiles, a church not tempted to return to the law. Paul's angry rhetoric, trying to gain a hearing for his opinion, begins to sound like a radical condemnation of Torah and Judaism, which it never was. But over time, the historical context of Paul's writing was lost. Without the historical context many readers lose track of Paul the person, Paul the Jew, and Paul the convert. As a consequence, they com-

pletely misunderstand the program of Paul the Apostle, wrongly concluding that Paul's difficulty with Judaism was intellectual and theological—
for instance, interpreting Paul as opposing Judaism because it practiced
self-salvation and volition. They see Paul's discussion of justification as a
philosophical analysis, instead of a new way of talking about a conversion
experience to which both the repentant and the virtuous must submit.
They see election as a concept of supersession instead of a way to discuss
God's grace to Jew and gentile alike. But Paul had been a Pharisee and he
knew that Judaism was not mere boasting of human accomplishments.
Judaism was a response to God's prior action of justification, as was his
new faith. Both Paul and the rabbis cautioned against pride. Like any Jew
of his day, Paul was interested in conforming his actions to God's desires.
His experience gave him a unique (and from the viewpoint of Judaism
apostate) perspective on God's desires, but his purpose was the same as a
rabbi's: to understand what rites and actions God demanded of those
living in his community.

This book began by citing Deuteronomy to show that the possibility
for religious decision existed within Israelite society from first-temple
times. Paul's letter to the Romans is a meditation on Deuteronomy 30 in
which Moses offers Israel the choice between life and death. The rabbis
too found that Deuteronomy 30 was a major statement of their beliefs.
They used it in liturgy and Midrash, as Paul did, to call their people to a
moment of decision and commitment. Their view of Israel's purpose was
that it continue to be a people apart in a world that gradually learns
morality from them. The object of faith for Paul was salvation, eternal life
in Christ. As a Jew, Paul knew that it was easier to define what was moral
for humanity than to presume to understand what God would do in the
future. Both the rabbis and Paul, in spite of the depths of their disagree-
ments, saw that a decision to choose life meant to choose life in
community.

Paul's Christian career began with his ecstatic experience of the Lord.
It was this vision that convinced him of the need for the transformation of
all believers. He sought to realize that vision in his career as an apostle,
understanding the meaning of being *in Christ* as his life unfolded. Though
he used his intellectual gifts and his education both as an orator and a
Pharisee, he did not have the confidence in reason that systematic
theologians have attributed to him. He began his career because of an
experience, a conversion. His mystical vision of metamorphosis left much
unexplained. He began as a Pharisee and became a convert *from* Pharisaism. He spent the rest of life trying to express what he converted *to*. He

never gave it a single name. Whatever it was, he never felt that he had left Judaism. Like the early rabbis, Paul understood that God's ways are mysterious, hence human understandings must always leave room for ambiguities. Paul and the rabbis understood as well as anyone before or after that the truths inherent in the biblical text are manifold, complex, and sometimes opposing. Scripture is a gem that gives off a different glint each time it is turned in the light of analysis. It is time for us to realize this. Perhaps no single point of view can do scripture justice.

APPENDIX

¶ PAUL'S CONVERSION; PSYCHOLOGICAL STUDY

THE MODERN STUDY OF CONVERSION

Paul's experience can be described as a conversion, though he himself used the vocabulary of transformation and prophetic calling to describe it. But is the term *conversion* analytically helpful for understanding Paul? Conversion must be considered an *etic* term in regard to Paul. Nevertheless, the analogies between Paul's experience and modern day conversion are striking. For the term to be useful, it must conform to social-scientific usage. By tracing its history within the social sciences, trying to distill its most value-neutral definition, we can apply insights gained in the modern period to the ancient data. This task can never be completely successful, but it allows us to transport some successfully tested empirical distinctions back to the time of Paul.

William James brought the study of conversion to the public in 1902 in *Varieties of Religious Experience*.[1] James distinguished between the *once born* and the *twice born* who are compelled by their emotional and religious sentiments to realize a new faith. He defined conversion as "the process, gradual or sudden, by which a self hitherto divided or consciously wrong, inferior and unhappy becomes unified and consciously right, superior and happy, by consequence of its firmer hold on religious realities" (160). Though James allowed for gradual conversion, his most-sustained interest was in the sudden dramatic changes in religious sensibilities.

Like James, early scholars including G. S. Hall,[2] J. H. Leuba,[3] and E. D. Starbuck[4] concentrated on the psychological aspects of conversion and noted that conversions fall into one of two major groupings: (1) the sudden and emotional conversion in which the subject adopts a new and previously foreign religion; or (2) the markedly contrasting slow journey from one faith to another, in which training and the learning of new values

285

are the primary characteristics. Many writers mention Paul as an example of sudden conversion and thereafter concentrate on the sudden conversion experience as the most interesting psychological process. Almost all early researchers noted that age is a significant factor in conversions. Rapid conversions take place more frequently among the adolescent and young adult population. For instance, P. E. Johnson surveyed the major studies on conversion, which included more than fifteen thousand persons in total, and calculated the average age of conversion to be 15.2 years.[5]

A CRITICAL VOCABULARY

In an attempt to create a standardized vocabulary, psychological researchers call the religious change a conversion, even when the subjects themselves would call it a rebirth or a calling. Almost all researchers used the term *conversion* to describe a dramatic religious change, even if the change was between different denominations of the same religion. This is important to the study of Paul because he was aware of no change in religion when he entered Christianity. If the psychological vocabulary could be maintained systematically, consistency alone would justify the use of conversion to describe Paul. Yet, psychologists' definitions of conversion have also differed widely. Although many native vocabularies for conversion have been rejected by modern research, no standard definition has replaced it. Since empirical findings of early scholars have also not proven stable, the lack of a uniform definition might have affected the results of their research. Coe found that 31 percent of a group of seventy-seven converts had experienced a sudden or striking transformation.[6] E. T. Clark found radical conversion in only 6.7 percent of his 2,174 cases.[7] Among students entering theological schools the incidence of sudden conversions has ranged from zero in an Anglo-Catholic seminary[8] to 56 percent in an evangelical seminary.[9] In a 1978 survey of over a thousand American teenagers, 33 percent reported having had a conversion experience, of which 18 percent had sudden experiences. This included 20 percent of Protestant youth, 20 percent of the Southerners, and 14 percent of young Catholics.[10] Coe found 202 experiences among ninety-nine men, suggesting that multiple conversions are not uncommon.[11] Neither the figures nor the definitions can be directly compared because of enormous differences in the way conversions were defined and described by the researchers and the way in which the data was obtained.

In one attempt to clarify terms, Starbuck called the two types of conversion *self-surrendering* and *volitional* or *voluntary*. Others distinguished between active and passive conversions.[12] Ames, and others, wanted to restrict the word conversion to sudden religious changes and emotional experiences only.[13] Similarly, Coe carefully noted at least six senses of the term conversion but sought to restrict its use scientifically to those that are both intense and sudden.[14] The sudden, crisis-oriented conversion was the central object of early studies, following the attention given to Paul, Augustine, and other famous Christian conversions. The studies proved that conversion, if understood as a dramatic psychological event, is a significant feature in the history of Christianity and is still common in many Christian denominations, though more common in evangelical Protestant communities, where they are taken as a proof of faith, than in Catholicism and the established Protestant denominations.

CONVERSION AND GUILT

According to Starbuck and James, the convert's preconversion feelings of unworthiness, self-doubt, and self-deprecation are released or overcome by the conversion process. Psychologically, conversion becomes the solution to unbearable guilt and sin, which is in keeping with the traditional Lutheran view of Paul's conversion. In fact, many writers mention Paul as the prime example of sudden conversion. Starbuck distinguished between conversions that take place in early adolescence and those that take place thereafter. He found that feelings of sin and guilt were present in two-thirds of all conversions, but he suggested that by late adolescence the process was likely to become an extended and gradual progress toward an integrated life rather than a single overwhelming emotional experience. These simplistic findings have been disputed. For instance, F. J. Roberts found that crisis converts had experienced guilt no more often than gradual converts prior to their conversions. His study also showed that those who converted to another faith were no more likely to become neurotic or psychotic.[15] His subjects, however, do not represent a normal cross section of the population since they were made up entirely of seminarians.

Although they attempted to free themselves from traditional religious discourse, the early researchers' own theological categories unduly affected their findings. A step forward was made by E. T. Clark, who characterized three different kinds of conversion experiences among his subjects. He outlined the sudden or crisis awakening in 6.7 percent of his subjects and the gradual conversion experience in 27.2 percent, and he also posited an intermediate position, where a gradual process of religious growth is accelerated by an emotional event that results in sudden religious change (66.1 percent), which he called the emotional stimulus conversion. His classification allows for the distinction between crisis and gradual conversions, but he admits tacitly that the ideal types are rarely evidenced in real life. For Clark, most conversions tended to fall into the intermediary type. Nevertheless, he was able to show that, proportionally, men showed about six times as many definite crisis awakenings as did the women, who evidenced more gradual conversions. The average age for the emotional stimulus convert was twelve to fourteen years. A stern theology was closely associated with the pure type of crisis awakenings, suggesting that fear and anxiety were large components in sudden conversions. Since 41 percent of the emotional stimulus conversion experiences studied by Clark occurred during revivals, which not only were highly emotional settings but opportunities for social control, his improved definition might have left out important social variables. Purely psychological processes were often found to be operant in sudden religious conversions. In his widely cited research, Coe studied two groups of converts. Seventeen persons reported that they expected striking transformations and actually experienced them, whereas twelve who anticipated the same changes did not. As expected, Coe found that emotional factors were dominant in the former group while cognitive factors dominated in the latter group. Persons who experienced the striking transformations were likewise shown to be more susceptible to hypnotic suggestion. Whenever the conversion is sudden, subjects usually report a resulting change in their behavior and mental states.[16] The change in behavior is always toward the moral values that the religious groups espouse, and it is normally understood as repentance. Extramarital sex, alcoholism, profanity, gossip, criticism, and aggression diminish, while positive values, like generosity, charitableness, or the desire and ability to communicate with individuals or to spend time with family and friends all increase.

OTHER DIFFERENCES BETWEEN GRADUAL AND RADICAL CONVERTS

Another recent finding about people who undergo radical emotional experiences is that they evidence a characteristic disharmony in their cognitive evaluation of the new group. Those who undergo long periods of training are more accepting of the beliefs of the new sect, for they have longer periods in which to internalize them. Those who have radical conversions may find that they have as many rational doubts about the doctrine as before their emotional conversion. The process of education or resocialization in the new group has an important effect that is not perceivable when focusing on a single individual's emotional experience. In one group, the devotees distinguished between *verbal converts*, who professed membership on the basis of their emotional experience, and *total converts* who not only made verbal professions of belief but exhibited their commitment through knowledge of the group's values and took an active interest in the group's maintenance.[17] The literature suggests that gradual conversions involve cognitive struggles with issues of meaning and purpose. Strickland observed that sudden conversions are less frequent in a community where gradual conversions are common and especially where they are encouraged through religious education and where conversion is evaluated positively. As such, gradual converts find purpose and meaning through their conversion in a socially approved way. Initial enthusiasm, however, normally wanes, reaching a low but stable level, suggesting that conversion alone cannot explain an individual's commitment to a specific group; rather, conversion is the initial impetus that helps the believer find other sources of commitment.[18] In his early studies Coe said that sudden and gradual conversions should effectively complement each other for a community to function well. Sudden conversion might be good for morale and motivation, but the emotional instability and lack of knowledge of the sudden convert endangers the continuity of a group. Building a stable commitment necessarily involves a strong educational program. Even persons who themselves were sudden converts often attempt to socialize their children via gradual conversion processes.

RECENT STUDIES

The study of conversion was greatly accelerated by a new wave of revivalism in a variety of radical sects among American youth in the 1960s and 1970s. One of the most famous and influential studies is by John Lofland and Rodney Stark, who studied the Unification church of the Reverend Sun Myung Moon.[19] They developed a nonempirical, informal guide for predicting a conversion, based on several interrelated variables—psychological, social, and accidental. They suggest that factors influencing conversion are (1) an experience of tension or dissatisfaction that is (2) interpreted within a religious perspective by (3) persons who perceive themselves as active religious seekers. The person is likely to convert if several environmental factors cooperate: (4) a cult is encountered at a crisis point; (5) a strong affective attachment is established with one or more committed believers; (6) minimal contact is made with nonbelievers; and (7) intensive interaction is made between the subject and the group. This description arises as much from logic and deduction as from the data, though it has been used as an empirical, testable model.[20] Lofland and Stark's model has often been criticized both for its lack of relevance and for its lack of analytic value.[21]

The term *brainwashing* has also been employed to understand conversions. *Brainwashing* was a slang term coined to describe the torture of American servicemen during the Korean War by the communist Chinese and North Koreans for the purposes of gaining their cooperation. The term was used by popular writers to describe the radical personality changes that religious sectarians often underwent, implying that the conversions achieved by the new groups involved an unethical manipulation of their devotee's rationality through mind-altering meditative techniques or coercive persuasion.[22] Recent studies have also noted a similarity to religious conversion in hostages incarcerated by terrorists, as happened most dramatically to Patty Hearst and to a lesser extent to hostages taken in Iran and Beirut.

There is a nagging but incomplete analogy between these two kinds of sudden emotional change. William Sargant noted that these experiences might be stimulated by one of two contrasting techniques, which are used to varying extents in prison camps and religious revivals. The first is sensory deprivation, best illustrated by solitary confinement and sleep deprivation, but similar to the sensory deprivation of contemplation and meditation. The second method is its opposite, overstimulation, as achieved in interrogations with strong lights and loud noises, but also in relatively benign activities such as music making, drumming, and dancing. Mind-altering drugs can function in either or both ways. Sargant also noted that learning acquired under stressful conditions can evince greater strength and retention. He recalled that some of Pavlov's dogs were trapped in their laboratory cages during a flood. After being rescued they were frightened of water, and some lapsed into a state of torpor wherein their previously learned behaviors (conditioned reflexes) were completely wiped out. New behaviors were readily learned in place of the conditioned responses. So, Sargant reasoned, a lifetime of religious ideals might be wiped out and replaced by a new faith acquired under strong emotional duress.

Although there are obvious analogies between the two phenomena, brainwashing is an indefinite and tendentious term. The changes that are evident in concentration camps are stronger and more unstable than religious conversion. Some popular books describing religious conversion as brainwashing evince outright hostility to the whole phenomenon. These books are often based on biased research—reports by hostile observers and no first hand observation of the groups.[23] One can assume that conversions and brainwashing are similar in some respect and that different phenomena are subsumed under each term. It is tempting to say that crisis conversions are affected by emotional conflicts and are less stable than gradual conversions, but there are many exceptions. A significant factor in the outcome of conversion experiences is the nature of the communities that the subject leaves and that he or she enters. Conversion can apply to many different changes—the movement between denominations within the same religion or the movement to an opposing religious philosophy with a radically different life-style.

EMOTIONAL CRISIS IN RADICAL CONVERSIONS

Modern groups accused of brainwashing are often those whose life-style is radically different from the community left behind, even if the highly charged emotions they produce are enticed rather than tortured out of subjects. Highly charged emotional experiences are not unknown in American life. Revival meetings throughout American history have typically had as their main purpose the stimulation of public conversion, with music, sermons, and the related publicity of personal witness all directed toward that end. These revivals have been criticized as insincere Christianity, fakery, and fraud. But since they were dramatic and viewed as Christian mission, as well as improving workers' morals, morale, and efficiency, they are often evaluated as more positive than foreign sects in contemporary media. Religious groups have greatly increased their popularity among the young by developing the manipulation of emotional experience to a science. Some recent studies on cult activities point out that the social dynamic and attitude change effected in conversion events are more reliable measures of the event than the emotion itself, though it is the emotion that is sought after and elicited by the cult leaders.

The meaning of the heightened emotions, whether understood as the infusion of spirit or as internal joy accompanying contemplation as taught by oriental disciplines, appears to be learned in the context of the individual cult. Sometimes even radically differing interpretations of emotional states cannot be distinguished physiologically. Stanley Schachter's attributive theory of emotion bears heavily on the meaning of an intense emotional experience in conversion.[24] Emotions, as opposed to reason, are relatively nonspecific and crude responses to situations. According to Schachter's theory, a subject has a large range of possible interpretations of physical arousal. The subject first feels an undefined physiological state and labels it as a specific emotion depending on the social context. In one situation, a person will interpret a fast pulse as fright, in another as sexual arousal, in a third as physical illness. The emotional system of a human being depends heavily on perception and cognition, as well as on social context for interpretation. Anxiety combined with various deprivation states—lack of sleep, food, or water—and contemplation, meditation, or feelings of happiness in the company of a group of caring friends could bring on ecstasy, and hence it can be interpreted by religious subjects as the activity of the Holy Spirit.[25]

The relevance of these experiments to conversion literature is easy to see: ecstatic states are important cues in some communities for thinking that conversion has taken place, but they are relatively nonspecific emotional states that can be generated by a number of techniques and are not universally necessary for conversion. Emotional states influence learning but apparently influence commitment more. A convert does not cognitively know more about the group after an ecstatic experience than before, though the subject's motivation and attachment might be radically changed. Subjects might continue to question the group's explicit doctrines or outrightly disbelieve them, although they join with and feel happy in the group. As time goes on, however, subjects usually begin to believe more of the doctrine, possibly because they encounter fewer conflicting opinions. But what usually changes in an emotional encounter is primarily the motivation of the believer.

Many social scientists have been misled into thinking that emotional or ecstatic experience is the sine qua non for conversion. It is merely one dimension of the conversion process that can be given special meaning in various conversion communities.[26] Some social science stresses the comparison between conversion and brainwashing, implying that the persuasion is the result of the suggestion that compliance will yield a relief from the brainwashing techniques or the conflict that a person might feel acutely. The conflict in the case of conversion could be rooted in many sources other than incarceration and torture. It could come from doubt, stress, consciousness of incoherent or wrong beliefs, the perception of hypocrisy or contradiction. But this definition depends on considering conversion a rapid phenomenon. Other religious communities, like Judaism for instance, understand conversion entirely on the cognitive level—as a change in ritual and purity status, a decision embarked on after long training.

Anxiety and stress are often products of new social environments. These strong emotions, brought on by the renunciation of a past life, together with the desire for communion with the new group, are always given effective religious meanings by a religious group. Though the image of brainwashing might not be helpful, some unscrupulous religious groups might manipulate the emotions of potential converts deliberately and other sincere religious groups might unintentionally manipulate emotions; except in cases of deliberate fraud, the manipulation might be a strong form of the same kind of manipulation that any society uses to educate its members.

There is an important analogy between brainwashed subjects and converts—namely, value inversion. Brainwashed subjects evince characteristic and radical value changes, for instance, calling something good that they once believed was bad. In concentration camps, inmates often imitate the behavior of their jailors—for instance, pinning on scraps of clothing in imitation of the jailors' symbols of rank. Bettelheim called this phenomenon "identification with the aggressor," seeing it as a "psychotic adjustment" to the stress of incarceration.[27] Given enough time in a new community and enough distance from the original group, such value inversions can be found in converts as well. Although attitude inversions apply to most conversions, changes in moral values must be carefully distinguished from other kinds of value inversions, since returning backsliders can be understood as correcting their behavior to suit values that they have always had but did not act on. There are very strong attitudinal changes in the new religions where the convert comes to do everything that he or she had avoided, but one does not have to posit an unwilling subject and torture to explain the change.[28]

RESOCIALIZATION AND STEREOTYPING IN CONVERSIONS

The fact that brainwashing features resocialization to new and foreign ideologies in countries quite foreign to North American values (or in such deviant, artificial, or total environments as prison camps) underlines the social dimension of conversion phenomena. Along with a new attention to the social side of conversion has come the realization that the focus on psychological and often neurotic aspects of conversion had been skewing results. The early researchers' attention to dramatic crisis conversion was due to a stereotypical understanding of conversion in Christian society, together with a lack of attention to the socially elicited aspects of crisis conversion.[29] It is ironic that we who turn to social science to help solve problems in New Testament historiography must first correct social scientists' stereotypes of Paul's conversion, which have been long since banished from serious New Testament research. George B. Cutten, with a critical judgment that normally comes only with historical distance, noted that psychological investigators had been influenced heavily by Paul's conversion (Acts), hence they took an overly idealized model (Luke) as the pattern for conversion in general and reduced Paul's unique experience to a general formula.[30] Even as early as 1924, Strickland noted that the more typical model of conversion in the New Testament is that of Peter and Andrew on the shore of the Sea of Galilee.[31]

Significant methodological questions arise from the clinical studies of maladjustment in converts; for instance, whose standards of maladjustment are proper for the judging of converts? This is a problem whenever a psychoanalytic study of conversion is attempted. The so-called maladjustments of converts are likely to be typical of all the converts to the same group. Converts subscribe to the norms of their newfound groups, not the group to which the clinical psychologists subscribe. Although a group's converts may contain its share of psychopaths, conversion to extreme groups cannot be adequately explained or predicted by psychopathology. Numerous empirical studies illuminate the positive problem-solving value of conversions on the individual and social level.[32] Psychoanalytic studies of Paul have been more biased than psychoanalytic studies of conversion in general. An exception is Gerd Theissen's *Psychological Aspects of Pauline Theology*.[33] It does a remarkable amount of good exegesis from a psychoanalytic and cognitive point of view. But it suffers from the methodological issue that infects every attempt at psychohistory. The psychoanalytic data—reports from the give and take of analysis—are not available for ancient personalities. Some psychohistory has been relatively successful, such as the psychohistory of Augustine, which is still highly idealized. Paul, by comparison, gives us almost no biographical information, making the best possible psychoanalytic analysis flagrant speculation.

Research in the phenomenon of conversion has been changing from psychological to sociological orientations. In place of a passive subject, converted by external powers over which he or she has no control, as in Luke's description of Paul's conversion, the sociological research stresses the social dimension of the conversion experience and a subject who actively develops a new world of meaning by conversion and entrance into a new community. It also sees that the community itself has an enormous effect on the meaning of a conversion.[34] This perception of the active role of the convert in reforming the world is important to understanding Paul's writing. More important is the effect that Paul's social context has on evaluating the meaning of his letters.

PAUL AND THE MODERN STUDY OF CONVERSION

Some important issues in traditional New Testament scholarship can be clarified by use of modern data. Luke's account of Paul's emotional crisis conversion was probably as much the result of Luke's genius as Paul's reported experience. It has been used for centuries within Western religion as a definition of conversion in general, biasing the scientific literature of the twentieth century, predisposing many researchers to see conversions as isolated, personal, psychological happenings without reference to their social context, and stylizing sudden conversions as the only important kind of conversion. Few early twentieth-century researchers were aware that the Lukan account of Paul was influencing their perceptions, since the phenomenon of sudden conversion is intrinsically interesting. But this ideal type is often the product of ignoring the obvious social dimension, such as the revival setting.

Some data coming from cognitive psychology suggest that the emotional nature of some conversion experiences has more to do with the style of conversion developed by the community than its content. The convert still needs to resocialize to the values of the community, a process that takes a long period of time. Not until that resocialization process is well under way can the convert articulate fully the meaning of his or her conversion. And of course that meaning is largely mediated by the values of the group joined. Even mystical experience contains images and themes that are explicit to a single community and that must be learned.

This is evidently the case with Paul, whose preconversion values were those of Pharisaism: His visions corresponded to the tradition of Jewish mystical apocalypticism with the important difference that the figure on the throne was thought to be Jesus, hence the messiah; yet Paul entered a community largely made up of gentile Christians. This was a virtually unique experience in ancient times. We should be exploiting Paul's memoirs to learn more about these three different types of Judaism.

CONVERSION AS DECISION MAKING

One way to avoid the mire of unevidenced psychoanalytic theorizing about Paul is to stress cognitive psychology.[35] Many studies have shown that both sudden and mixed conversion experiences eventually manifest the same change in attitudes, if enough time has elapsed. This suggests that conversion is a kind of decision, and therefore cognitive descriptions of decision making will be helpful in understanding Paul's attitudes.

One of the most important social psychologists to look at the phenomenon of decision making is Leon Festinger, who was only secondarily interested in the experience of conversion. Festinger looked at how group attitudes influence individual values and behavior. Most scholars of biblical religions have seen the relevance of his book *When Prophecy Fails,*[36] which is a study of the cult mentality. Although the book has been widely overinterpreted, the research is still valuable. It illustrates the immediate gain of looking at individual behavior in a social perspective.

In *When Prophecy Fails* Leon Festinger, Henry Riecken and Stanley Schacter studied a flying saucer cult, showing that when the cult's predicted doomsday did not arrive (called *disconfirmation,* since it appeared to disconfirm the cult's basic beliefs) the reaction of the group was to proselytize. According to the researchers' description, when the predicted apocalyptic event did not happen, the committed cult member sought to proselytize in order to neutralize the perceived disconfirmation. Implicitly, the believer might be saying to himself or herself, "If I can get others to believe this doctrine, then my personal doubts are groundless." This would be a powerful tool for understanding the effectiveness of the Christian mission, if it could be established as valid and reliable. Unfortunately, there are many difficulties with this particular theory, not the least of which is that the findings have been disconfirmed by other studies.[37] Scholars hostile to Festinger's approach, however, in general have gone overboard in their criticism, missing important perceptions about the value of the social context. Though the experimental design of the study itself is open to question, since there was a large percentage of informants in the cult, the fairest criticism, coming from social-psychological research, is not that Festinger's perception about proselytism is wrong, but that there are too many other strategies available to a group facing disconfirmation for anyone to predict the outcome of a disconfirmation crisis. Groups may pick proselytism to avoid disconfirmation, but they may pick a variety of other tactics as well. The tactic that is picked will be defined by a variety of special historical and social factors specific to that group.

An alternative form of avoiding disconfirmation is by a process of hermeneutics—that is, the general group process of the reinterpretation of past tradition to make sense of present realities. A subsequent study of Christian disconfirmation at the Hebrew University by a student heavily influenced by Festinger was sensitive to many other ways of bolstering Christian commitment.[38] This takes the study of Christianity out of the sensationalist realm of famous mistakes and puts it back in the realm of all social groups, which must constantly revalue their assumptions to accommodate new historical events. When other groups experience disconfirmation they do not invariably proselytize. Proselytization is one of a range of possible behaviors open to groups in a crisis of cognitive dissonance.

It is difficult to say whether the experience of Christ's crucifixion can be considered a disconfirmation at all. The Gospels record the disappointment of the small group of Jesus' disciples. But most converts to Christianity entered a post-Easter church, one that proclaimed *both* the crucifixion and the resurrection of Jesus. This kerygma was formulated out of an interaction of Jewish expectations, Jesus' personal history, the experience of the early church, and the early church's use of the Hebrew Bible to understand the Easter experience. The process of reinterpretation of ancient texts in the face of new experience shows cognitive dissonance at work, but it is a process of hermeneutics that is always at work in every scripturally based community.

Though Festinger's theories are directly relevant to Christianity, as they are to all groups, they might be relevant in ways that Festinger himself did not investigate in *When Prophecy Fails;* for instance, Festinger's general theory of cognitive dissonance, rather than *When Prophecy Fails,* is significant for a study of Pauline conversion because it investigates strategies for reducing dissonance. Disconfirmation is but one especially strong variety of cognitive dissonance, which can be reduced by a variety of rational mechanisms of reassessment.[39] Cognitive dissonance describes the state of mind of any subject going through a decision-making process. It is virtually synonymous with the unpleasant anxieties encountered by all of us when we notice inconsistency in our actions. Cognitive dissonance is deliberately left vague in Festinger's writing because he was interested in observable results in social contexts, not in subjective emotional states.

Festinger observed that during a hard decision between two attractive choices, both possibilities initially appear attractive. After a decision, however, people characteristically revalue both the taken and untaken choice so that they no longer appear close. Festinger was able to demonstrate that, in most decisions, the option not taken will recede in importance in the mind of the subject after the decision has been made, reducing dissonance noticeably during the decision-making process. This is an experience almost everyone recognizes. It has been very fully documented by experiment as well, confirming Festinger's theoretical model.

In a classic experiment of the religious value of cognitive dissonance, a number of non-Catholic Yale students were required to write an essay entitled, "Why I Would Like to Become a Catholic." Two experimental conditions were elicited: a weak, low dissonance condition, in which students were paid a (relatively) large sum for their essay; and a strong, high dissonance condition, in which they were paid little. The effect of the remuneration on the experiment is not intuitively obvious. But those who were paid a lot of money apparently reasoned that their difficult task was rewarded by their relatively high reward, thus resulting in relatively low dissonance for agreeing to write the theme. But those paid low wages probably had to deal with their actual religious feelings, which naturally lacked any commitment to Catholicism. As predicted, the high dissonance group became more favorable toward Catholicism after the assignment was over, as measured by an attitude questionnaire. The logic of the theory implies that conversion is likely to be more sincere and committed if it occurs with high dissonance, that is, where there are fewer external pressures for making such a religious change. And this is indeed the perceived result in further experiments.[40]

Dissonance then, though defined in terms of result rather than emotional conflict, is an experience that virtually everyone has noticed. It is a constant part of experience, because few lives are so simple that difficult decisions can be avoided. Whenever ambiguities are involved and hard decisions are necessary, dissonance is created because after the decision, the decision maker will still be aware of the choices refused and the defects in the option exercised. Festinger himself concentrated on the relationship between the predecision and postdecision processes. But later studies showed that in a close decision there can be an interesting secondary effect, a considerable period of reevaluation when subjects regret the option taken and still evince indecision, although the decision has been made, giving a kind of psychological concomitant to the liminal state that Victor Turner defined in rites of passage, in which dissonance is a strong component. Eventually dissonance reduction takes over, increasing the attractiveness in favor of the chosen alternative.[41] Festinger also stressed the role of a peer group in providing a confirmatory environment for the decision. This perception is important for the study of religious communities, which provide a social environment where conversion is rational and sensible, no matter how "insane" it may look to an outside observer. Festinger and his students studied many of the available processes to reduce dissonance.[42] The most commonly used ones have nothing to do with proselytism but are mental processes of rationalization, reinterpretation, or disparagement.[43] First-century Bible interpretation—whether it be midrash, pesher, typology, or allegory—is at once a mechanism for reducing dissonance and a sectarian strategy for constructing a new social world. Paul's exegesis is one of the best examples of this process at work, since it reforms the Pharisaic world into one that is consonant with Christianity. Paul's own exegesis demonstrating the truth of the Christian message would observably serve to reduce his dissonance. To limit the processes of reducing dissonance to proselytism, thus increasing the size of the confirming group, is to miss many of the possibilities of the theory for analyzing religious discourse.

One important aspect of the study of cognitive dissonance is the finding that the strength of the new belief structure will be directly proportional to the difficulty or strength of the conversion experience. The stronger and more difficult the conversion experience, the stronger and more difficult it will be to dissuade the beliefs held.[44] People who are paid a small amount to make a counter-attitudinal statement, for example, will later agree more with the statement than will people paid a larger amount.[45] If a decision produces insufficient rewards, a person might change his or her beliefs so as to make the decision seem more rewarding. "Rats and people come to love the thing for which they have suffered," said Festinger with a healthy degree of cynicism.[46] But insufficient rewards or difficult circumstances can enhance the attractiveness of the choice that led to the suffering, provided that there is an incentive to make the decision. This implies that groups in which conversions are common will have a more committed membership, as well as an incentive to proselytize. It also implies that such a convert as Paul, who goes from one religious community to a radically different one, and who obviously has a strong conversion experience, will have a greater chance of developing a strong commitment to his or her new community and a greater chance of revaluing his or her past than other converts. There are, however, a number of important intervening values in this equation, especially in the role of the community itself in developing commitment (see chapter 3 above).

The most recent data, on religious defection and disaffiliation, shows how complex and individual the process of religious change can be. Four studies in *JSSR* 28 (1989) outline a number of different situations ranging from radical conversion to a new group to slow growth away from an old one into a mainstream group. The most important conclusion from these studies is to note all the kinds of interactions in values between groups that an actively questing subject can provide. Thus, while Paul's conversion brought a high degree of commitment to his Christian group, and a disaffiliation from Pharisaism, he may still have valued his Jewish identity and brought much Pharisaic skill into his new community. But others may have called him an apostate.

Two problematic issues appear to have curtailed recent psychological investigation into conversion.[47] The first is the realization that historical data rarely is appropriate for psychoanalytic or therapeutic discussion, so the most it can do is illustrate some particular facility of the given psychoanalytic notational scheme for describing experience. The second factor is the realization that the term *conversion* is culturally relative. Each group defines what it means by conversion; even ecstatic conversions seem to be behaviors learned within a community, though the content of visions may have individual or unique aspects. As a consequence, a great many contemporary studies of conversion have taken a sociological approach, defining conversion as a change in religious community, as I have done in describing Paul.

ABBREVIATIONS

AJS	*Journal for the Association for Jewish Studies*
ANRW	*Aufstieg und Niedergang der Roemischen Welt*
Antioch	Raymond E. Brown and John Meier, *Antioch and Rome: New Testament Cradles of Catholic Christianity* (New York: Paulist Press, 1983).
Apologetic	Abraham J. Malherbe, "'Not In a Corner': Early Christian Apologetic in Acts 26:26," *Second Century* 5, no. 4 (1985–86): 193–210.
Binitarian	Larry W. Hurtado, "The Binitarian Shape of Early Christian Devotion and Ancient Jewish Monotheism," in *SBL 1985 Seminar Papers* (Atlanta: Scholars Press, 1985), 371–91.
BJS	*British Journal of Sociology*
BZ	*Biblische Zeitschrift*
CBQ	*Catholic Biblical Quarterly*
CJ	*Conservative Judaism*
Conscience	Krister Stendahl, "Paul and the Introspective Conscience of the West," HTR 56 (1963): 199–215. Reprinted in Krister Stendahl, *Paul Among Jews and Gentiles and Other Essays* (Philadelphia: Fortress, 1976).
Conversion	A. D. Nock, *Conversion: The Old and the New in Religion from Alexander the Great to Augustine of Hippo* (Oxford: Oxford University Press, 1933; reprint, Lanham, Md.: University Press of America, 1988).

CSBS	*Canadian Society for Biblical Studies*
Darkness	Beverly Roberts Gaventa, *From Darkness to Light: Aspects of Conversion in the New Testament* (Philadelphia: Fortress, 1986).
dissertation	Carey Newman, "'The Glory of God in the Face of Jesus': A Tradition-Historical Investigation to Paul's Doxa-Christology" (Ph.D. diss., Baylor University, 1989).
EPRO	*Études préliminaires des réligions orientales*
Faces of the Chariot	David Halperin, *The Faces of the Chariot: Early Jewish Responses to Ezekiel's Vision* (Tübingen: Mohr, 1988).
FJB	*Frankfurter Juedische Beitraege*
From Jesus to Christ	Paula Fredricksen, *From Jesus to Christ: The Origins of the New Testament Images of Jesus* (New Haven: Yale University Press, 1988).
Gnostic	Gilles Quispel, *Gnostic Studies* (Istanbul: Netherlands Historisch-Archaeologisch Instituut in het Nubije Osten, 1974).
Heavenly Ascent	Alan F. Segal, "Heavenly Ascent in Hellenistic Judaism, Early Christianity, and Their Environments," *ANRW* II.23:2 (Berlin: de Gruyter, 1980), 1332–94.
Hellenistic Magic	Alan F. Segal, "Hellenistic Magic: Some Questions of Definition," in *Studies,* 349–75.
History	Nils A. Dahl, "History and Eschatology in the Light of the Dead Sea Scrolls," in *The Crucified Messiah* (St. Paul, Minn.: Augsburg, 1974).
HSS	*Harvard Semitic Studies*
HTR	*Harvard Theological Review*
HUCA	*Hebrew Union College Annual*
Introduction	Helmut Koester, *Introduction to the New Testament,* vol. 2, (Berlin: de Gruyter, 1980, trans., Philadelphia: Fortress, 1982).
Jews and God-Fearers	Joyce Reynolds and Robert Tannenbaum, *Jews and God-Fearers at Aphrodisias: Greek Inscriptions with Commentary* (Cambridge: Cambridge Philological Society, 1986).
JBL	*Journal of Biblical Literature*

Jews	R. Mary Smallwood, *The Jews Under Roman Rule* (Leiden: Brill, 1976).
JJS	*Journal of Jewish Studies*
JQR	*Jewish Quarterly Review*
JR	*Journal of Religion*
JSJ	*Journal for the Study of Judaism*
JSNT	*Journal of the Study of the New Testament*
JSSR	*Journal for the Scientific Study of Religion*
JTS	*Journal of Theological Studies*
Kommentar	*Kommentar zum Neuen Testament aus Talmud und Midrasch*
Law	Heikki Raeisaenen, *Paul and the Law* (Philadelphia: Fortress, 1983).
Magical Papyri	Hans Dieter Betz, *The Greek Magical Papyri in Translation* (Chicago: University of Chicago Press, 1986).
Name	Jarl Fossum, *The Name of God and the Angel of the Lord*, WUNT 36 (Tübingen: Mohr, 1985).
NHS	*Nag Hammadi Studies*
NovT	*Novum Testamentum*
NTS	*New Testament Studies*
One God	Larry W. Hurtado, *One God, One Lord: Early Christian Devotion and Ancient Jewish Monotheism* (Philadelphia: Fortress, 1988).
Open Heaven	Christopher Rowland, *The Open Heaven: A Study of Apocalyptic in Judaism and Early Christianity* (New York: Crossroads, 1982).
Opponents	Dieter Georgi, *The Opponents of Paul in Second Corinthians* (Philadelphia: Fortress, 1986).
Origin	John Coolidge Hurd, Jr., *The Origin of 1 Corinthians*, 2d ed. (Macon, Ga.: Mercer University Press, 1983).
Origins	John G. Gager, *The Origins of Anti-Semitism: Attitudes Towards Judaism in Pagan and Christian Antiquity* (New York: Oxford University Press, 1983).
Paul	E. P. Sanders, *Paul, The Law and the Jewish People* (Philadelphia: Fortress, 1983).
Paul's Gospel	Seyoon Kim, *The Origin of Paul's Gospel*,

	WUNT 2/4, 2d ed. (Tübingen: Mohr, 1984).
Pseudepigrapha	James H. Charlesworth, ed., *The Old Testament Pseudepigrapha* (Garden City, N.Y.: Doubleday, 1983–85).
RB	*Revue Biblique*
Rebecca's Children	Alan F. Segal, *Rebecca's Children: Judaism and Christianity in the Roman World* (Cambridge: Harvard University Press, 1986).
Religions	Jacob Neusner, ed., *Religions in Antiquity: Essays in Memory of Erwin Ramsdell Goodenough* (Leiden: Brill, 1968).
RHR	*Revue de l'histoire des religions*
Romans 1–8	James D. G. Dunn, *Romans 1–8*, vol. 38a of *Word Biblical Commentary* (Dallas: Word, 1988).
RRR	*Review of Religious Research*
RSR	*Religious Studies Review*
SBL	*Society of Biblical Literature*
SJT	*Scottish Journal of Theology*
Snow and Machalek	David Snow and Richard Machalek, "The Convert as a Social Type," in *Sociological Theory*, ed. R. Collins (San Francisco: Jossey-Bass, 1983), 259–89.
Spirit	James D. G. Dunn, *Jesus and the Spirit: A Study of the Religious and Charismatic Experience of Jesus and the First Christians as Reflected in the New Testament* (Philadelphia: Westminster Press, 1975).
SR	*Studies in Religion*
ST	*Studia Theologica*
Studies	R. van den Broek and M. J. Vermaseren, eds., *Studies in Gnosticism and Hellenistic Religions Presented to Gilles Quispel on the Occasion of His Sixty-Fifth Birthday* (Leiden: Brill, 1981).
Synopse	Peter Schaefer with Margarete Schlueter and Hans Georg Von Mutius, *Synopse zur Hekhalot-Literature* (Tübingen: Mohr, 1981).
TAPA	*Transactions of the American Philological Association*

TDNT	*Theological Dictionary of the New Testament*
Thessalonians	Abraham J. Malherbe, *Paul and the Thessalonians: The Philosophic Tradition of Pastoral Care* (Philadelphia: Fortress, 1987).
Things Unutterable	James D. Tabor, *Things Unutterable: Paul's Ascent to Paradise in Its Greco-Roman, Judaic, and Early Christian Contexts* (Lanham, Md.: University Press of America, 1986).
Transformation	John Koenig, "The Motif of Transformation in the Pauline Epistles: A History of Religions/Exegetical Study" (Th.D. diss., Union Theological Seminary, 1970).
Two Powers	Alan F. Segal, *Two Powers in Heaven: Rabbinic Reports About Christianity and Gnosticism* (Leiden: Brill, 1977).
Urban	Wayne A. Meeks, *The First Urban Christians: The Social World of the Apostle Paul* (New Haven: Yale University Press, 1983).
VG	*Vigiliae Christianae*
VTSup	*Supplements to Vetus Testamentum*
WUNT	*Wissenschaftliche Untersuchungen zum Neuen Testament*
ZAW	*Zeitschrift fuer die alttestamentliche Wissenschaft*
ZKG	*Zeitschrift fuer Kirchengeschichte*
ZNTW	*Zeitschrift fuer die N.T. Wissenschaft*
ZNW	*Zeitschrift fuer die neutestamentliche Wissenschaft und die Kunde der alteren Kirche*
ZRGG	*Zeitschrift fuer Religions und Geistesgeschichte*

NOTES

INTRODUCTION

1. The second Pharisee to give us his writings is Josephus. But whether Josephus was really a Pharisee is questionable. He seems to have tailored his life to Pharisaism in the course of his public career, but that is not the same as being a· Pharisee. That leaves Paul as the only Pharisee who left us personal observations.

2. Philo may have left us a few murky references at the beginning of *De Specialibus Legibus,* but he relates them as ordinary consciousness.

3. Ironically, we now consider the Gospels ascribed to Jesus' disciples as largely completed by a later generation, hence, not eyewitness accounts either. Thus, Paul today gains a relative authenticity that he sought but did not receive during his own lifetime.

4. For an excellent summary evaluation of what can be known about Paul's life and writings, see *Introduction,* 97–145.

5. The writing of Hyam Maccoby, especially *Revolution in Judea* (London: Ocean Books, 1973) but also *The Mythmaker: Paul and the Invention of Christianity* (New York: Harper and Row, 1986), is a recent example of how dangerously wrong a scholar can go when relying on a romantic, imagined sense of commonality with Paul, without addressing the nature of the historical data. The result in these cases is historically flawed and polemical, apologetic, and tendentious.

6. See the work of Jacob Neusner on this subject. Two works of particular interest in this context (summarizing his form-critical approach) are *The Rabbinic Traditions About the Pharisees before 70,* 3 vols. (Leiden: Brill, 1971) and *Judaism: The Evidence of the Mishnah* (Chicago: University of Chicago Press, 1981).

7. Munich: C. H. Beck'sche Verlagsbuchhandlung, 1928.

8. I have, of course, read a considerable body of Jewish scholarship on Paul. In the twentieth century almost all Jewish evaluations of Paul are heavily influenced by Klausner and Graetz. However, none really matches Klausner's scholarship. All tell us more about the predicament of Jewish existence in the twentieth century than they tell us about Paul, but only Rubenstein's *My Brother Paul* (New York:

Harper and Row, 1972) actually admits that this is so, and this from the Freudian perspective that all scholarship is ultimately a projection of our own personal predicaments.

9. See especially the contribution of J. Christiaan Beker in the first volume of the series of books slated for publication in the next few years as supplements to the new journal *Explorations*. Both the series and the journal are edited by James Charlesworth.

CHAPTER 1. *Paul and Luke*

1. See P. Eduard Pfaff, *Die Bekehrung des H. Paulus in des Exegeses des 20. Jahrhunderts* (Rome: Pontificae Universitatis Gregorianae, 1942); Emil Moske, *Die Bekehrung des Heil. Paulus: Eine exegetisch-kritische Untersuchung* (Münster: Aschendorffschen Buchhandlung, 1907); Ottfried Kietzig, *Die Bekehrung des Paulus: Religionsgeschichtlich und Religionspsychologisch neu Untersucht* (Leipzig: J. C. Hinrichs'sche Buchhandlung, 1932); G. Lohfink, *The Conversion of St. Paul: Narrative and History in Acts* (Chicago: Franciscan Herald Press, 1976), 33–46; U. Wilckens, "Die Bekehrung des Paulus als religionsgeschichtliches Problem," *ZTK* 56 (1959): 273–93; H. J. Schoeps, *Paul* (1959; reprint, Philadelphia: 1961); M. E. Thrall, "The Origins of Pauline Christology," in *Apostolic History and the Gospel*, ed. W. W. Gasque and R. P. Martin (Grand Rapids: Paternoster Press, 1970); H. G. Wood, "The Conversion of Paul: Its Nature, Antecedents, and Consequences," *NTS* 1 (1955): 276–82; J. Dupont, "The Conversion of Paul and Its Influence on His Understanding of Salvation by Faith," in *Apostolic History;* Philippe Menoud, "Revelation and Tradition: The Influence of Paul's Conversion on His Theology," *Interpretation* 7 (1952): 131–41. See H. D. Betz, *Galatians* (Philadelphia: Fortress, 1979), 64, n. 82, for extensive bibliographical information.

2. The discipleship of Peter or Andrew on the Sea of Galilee seems more typical of earliest Christian experience than Paul's sudden dramatic conversion as described by Acts. They are evangelized by Jesus himself. They become his followers as one might adopt a person as a teacher. They might have been converted to their new calling, but the New Testament is silent about their internal feelings and states.

3. See *Introduction*, 97–147. See especially Gerd Luedemann, *Paul the Apostle to the Gentiles: Studies in Chronology* (Philadelphia: Fortress, 1984) from the German *Paulus, der Heidenapostel*, vol. 1 of *Studien zur Chronologie*, FRLANT 123 (Goettingen: Vandenhoeck und Ruprecht, 1980). He takes a strong position separating Luke from Paul and emphasizing that Luke cannot be trusted unless there is evidence in Paul to establish Luke's position. *Antioch* exemplifies the other side of the issue.

4. *Conscience*.

5. These concerns serve as the background for the exegesis of other interpreters of Paul-Lloyd Gaston and John Gager, who concentrate on Paul's views about the salvation of the Jews. See *Origins*, esp. p. 210. John Gager, however, would dissent in seeing Paul's conversion as essential to understanding his thought; see his

"Some Notes on Paul's Conversion," *NTS* 27 (1981): 697–704. Lloyd Gaston's essays, long known by Canadians but less well known in the United States, have been gathered in a handy volume, *Paul and the Torah* (Vancouver: University of British Columbia Press, 1987).

6. See *Snow and Machalek,* 264. See also my appendix for the bibliography on the psychology of conversion.

7. Guenther Bornkamm's suggestion that Paul was called on before his conversion to convert the gentiles is possible too, of course, although there is little evidence for it. See his masterful book *Paul* (New York: Harper and Row, 1971), translated by D. M. G. Stalker from *Paulus* (Stuttgart: W. Kohlhammer, 1969). Paul describes his gentile mission as deriving from a revelation of the Christ.

8. J. Munck, *Paul and the Salvation of Mankind* (Richmond: John Knox, 1959), 24–35; M. Dibelius, *Studies in the Acts of the Apostles* (London: SCM, 1956), 158 n. 47, saw that the prophetic call motif was also part of the literary purpose of Luke. See also E. Haenchen, *The Acts of the Apostles: A Commentary* (Philadelphia: Westminster, 1971), 107–10 and H. J. Cadbury, *The Making of Luke Acts* (London: SPCK, 1968), 213–38.

9. See Kirsopp Lake, "The Conversion of Paul and the Events Immediately Following It," in *The Beginnings of Christianity Part I: The Acts of the Apostles,* ed. F. J. Foakes Jackson and Kirsopp Lake (Grand Rapids, Mich.: Baker Book House, 1966), 5:188–94; Charles W. Hedrick, "Paul's Conversion Call: A Comparative Analysis of the Three Reports in Acts," *JBL* 100, no. 3 (1981): 415–32.

10. It may be more exact to call the conversion a "discourse of heavenly appearance" or *Erscheinungsgespraech,* as does Gerhard Lohfink, "Eine alttestamentliche Darstellungsform fuer Gotteserscheinungen in den Damaskusberichten: Apg. 9; 22; 26," *BZ* 9 (1965): 246–57 and *The Conversion of St. Paul* (Chicago: Franciscan Herald, 1976), 61–85. This perspective has been criticized by O. H. Steck, "Formgeschichtliche Bemerkungen zur Darstellung des Damaskusgeschehens in der Apostelgeschichte," *ZNW* 67 (1976): 20–28 and C. Burchard, *Der dreizehnte Zeuge: Traditions- und kompositionsgeschichtliche Untersuchungen zu Lukas' Darstellung der Fruezeit des Paulus* (Goettingen: Vandenhoeck and Ruprecht, 1970): 54–55. See Hedrick, "Paul's Conversion Call," 416, n. 10, *dissertation,* which traces the biblical roots of the conception of the *Kavod.*

11. See James H. Charlesworth, "The Jewish Roots of Christology: The Discovery of the Hypostatic Voice," *SJT* 39 (1987): 19–41.

12. See Gilles Quispel, "Hermetism and the New Testament, Especially Paul," *ANRW* II.22 (forthcoming).

13. The older methodology of tracing christological titles to the exclusion of exegetical developments is tendentious anyway. See Donald Juel, *Messianic Exegesis* (Philadelphia: Fortress, 1987).

14. Gershom Scholem has asked whether this phrase ought to be identified with the merkabah term *guf hashekhina,* the body of Glory, which we find in merkabah texts. See his *Von der mystischen Gestalt der Gottheit* (Zurich: Rhein-Verlag, 1962), 276, n. 19. But Scholem did not exploit the implications of this perceptive intuition. On the history of the term *Glory,* see *dissertation,* especially chap. 6.

15. See, for example, Bornkamm's opinion (*Paul,* 22f) that Paul's few references to his Damascus Road experience have little to do with the content of his gospel.

16. *Paul's Gospel,* 3–31.

17. The difference between Kim's treatment of the passages and mine is that Kim automatically assumes that this spiritual experience must have come from Paul's Damascus Road experience; I see that experience as unrecoverable but am sure that Paul's spiritual experience continued throughout his career and informed it continuously. In turn, Paul's recollection of these events was influenced by his communal experience.

18. For a recent appraisal of the difficulties involved in reconstructing the conversion account from the memoirs of a convert, see Paula Fredriksen, "Paul and Augustine: Conversion Narratives, Orthodox Traditions, and the Retrospective Self," *Journal of Theological Studies* 37 (1986): 3–34. The consequences of this problem will be discussed below.

19. The new book *Darkness* contains an important argument on this point. Beverly Gaventa suggests that changes in religious status can be subdivided into conversions, alternations, and transformations (12). Paul's experience, she argues, is a transformation, falling midway between the jarring discontinuities of conversion and effortless experience of alternation. I like the term transformation and use it for other reasons. As I try to show, Paul's experience can just as easily be understood as a conversion, since the vocabulary of conversion and transformation is imposed from the outside and the distinction between them is artificial. Nevertheless, I regret that Gaventa's intriguing work did not become available to me earlier. Though I appreciate her work, I fear she underplays the discontinuity between Paul's previous identity as a Pharisee and his Christian commitment. Because of the general scope of her work, she also leaves Paul before she spells out all the implications of his conversion. But her work is a must for any scholar interested in understanding Paul's conversion. From her work, I also found the dissertation *Transformation,* which is a major piece of research on Paul's understanding of Christian conversion.

20. N. Habel, "The Form and Significance of the Call Narratives," ZAW 77 (1965): 297–323.

21. See David. E. Aune, *Prophecy in Early Christianity and the Ancient Mediterranean World* (Grand Rapids: Eerdmans, 1983), 247–62.

22. *Spirit.*

23. Indeed, there are two different ascensions in his history. The gospel implies an ascension with the resurrection, which is fulfilled at the beginning of Acts.

24. Ananias, Peter, and others receive visions *optasiai,* e.g., Acts 2:17; 9:10; 10:3, 17; 11:5. Paul's experience is also a trance, *ekstasei* (22:17).

25. Ioan M. Lewis, *Ecstatic Religion: An Anthropological Study of Spirit Possession and Shamanism* (Baltimore: Penguin, 1971).

26. Of course, one can take the distinction too far, for in 2 Corinthians 12, the same passage that Paul describes a revelation and ascent to the heavens, he argues against other Christians who claim yet more authority for ecstatic experiences. So Paul represents a compromise position between pure periphery and pure centrality

in early Christianity. If he were more characteristic of a peripheral prophet he would not oppose the charismatics so vigorously. He feels, however, that all have a proper place (1 Cor. 12:4–13).

27. There is not sufficient warrant to resume the history of social scientific scholarship on conversion. My appendix contains a discussion of the psychological approach to conversion. But some of the major findings of the modern period can be summarized here.

28. *RSR* 8, no. 2 (1982): 146–59. See also "Conversion," in *The Encyclopedia of Religion* (New York: Macmillan, 1987) 4:73–79.

29. At a recent conference I heard one researcher remark, "Once you've read one Mormon conversion narration, you've read them all." The rather terse remark has nothing to do with Mormon literature, which is neither more nor less stereotypic than other devotional literature. Rather it is a comment about conversion literature in general.

30. See Brian Taylor, "Recollection and Membership: Converts' Talk and the Ratiocination of Commonality," *Sociology* 12 (1978): 316–23; James A. Beckford, "Accounting for Conversion," *British Journal of Sociology* 29, no. 2 (1978): 249–62; *Snow and Machalek;* see also their article "The Sociology of Conversion," *Annual Review of Sociology* 10 (1984): 167–90; Clifford L. Staples and Armand L. Mauss, "Conversion or Commitment? A Reassessment of the Snow and Machalek Approach to the Study of Conversion," *JSSR* 26, no. 2 (1987): 133–47.

31. "'Not in a Corner': Early Christian Apologetic in Acts 26:26," *Second Century* 5, no. 4 (1985–86); 193–210, see 208ff.

32. See Stephen G. Wilson, *Luke and the Pastoral Epistles* (London: SPCK, 1979) for the notion that the pastorals were written by Luke. His discussion of 1 Tim. 1:12–17 appears on p. 109.

33. See *Darkness*, 41–43 for a summary of these passages. My impression of why Paul uses these terms only infrequently differs significantly from Gaventa's.

34. See, for instance, Marvin Harris, *The Rise of Anthropological Theory: A History of Theories of Culture* (New York: Thomas Y. Crowell, 1968), 394, 568–604. See also Sydel Silverman, "Patronage as Myth," in *Patrons and Clients in Mediterranean Societies,* ed. Ernest Gellner and John Waterbury (London: Duckworth, 1977), 7–19, esp. 9–11, 17–19.

35. To review modern scholarship on conversion would take us too far afield here. But the reader is directed to my appendix, which surveys the research done on conversion in the twentieth century.

36. See *Darkness,* 17–52.

37. See, for example André-Jean Festugière, *Personal Religion Among the Greeks* (Berkeley: University of California Press, 1954), 68–84 and especially 76: "One may therefore speak, in a sense, of conversion."

38. The translation is from *Conversion,* 139. For more discussion of the parallel, see my *Heavenly Ascent.* Also my *Hellenistic Magic,* 349–75.

39. See Claude G. Montefiore, who pointed out this problem in his book *Judaism and St. Paul* (London: M. Goshen, 1914). He was followed in turn by James W. Parkes *Jesus, Paul and the Jews* (London: Student Christian Movement

Press, 1936). The doctrines that Montefiore points out that could not have come from Pharisaism may alternatively be part of Paul's own contribution to Christianity.

40. See Rodney Stark and William Sims Bainbridge, *The Future of Religion: Secularization, Revival, and Cult Formation* (Berkeley: University of California Press, 1985); also Rodney Stark, "Jewish Conversion and the Rise of Christianity: Rethinking the Received Wisdom," *SBL Seminar Papers* (Atlanta: Scholars Press, 1986).

41. The situation is similar in our own day, when relatively small religious groups such as secular Jews have contributed an enormous number of children to the ranks of new religions. See Stephen Steinberg, "Reform Judaism: The Origin and Evolution of a 'Church Movement,'" *JSSR* 5 (1965): 117–29; Everett V. Stonequist, *The Marginal Man* (New York: Scribner's, 1937); Rodney Stark, "How New Religions Succeed: A Theoretical Model," in *The Future of New Religious Movements,* ed. David Bromley and Phillip E. Hammond (Berkeley: University of California Press, 1985).

42. See Mishnah Avot 1.1, C. H. Dodd, *The Apostolic Preaching and Its Developments* (Chicago: Willett, Clark, 1937), 7; see also *paralambanō* and *paradidōmi* in *TDNT,* 2, 171; and Delling in *TDNT,* 4, 11–14, with whose conclusions I disagree.

43. *Snow and Machalek.*

44. *JSSR* 26 (1987): 133–47.

45. *JSSR* 26 (1987): 133–47.

46. See Paula Fredriksen Landes, "Paul and Augustine: Conversion Narratives, Orthodox Traditions, and the Retrospective Self," *JTS* 37 (1986): 3–34; "Augustine and His Analysts: The Possibility of a Psychohistory," *Soundings* 61 (1978): 206–27; James E. Dittes, "Continuities Between the Life and Thought of Augustine," *JSSR* 5 (1965): 130–40; see the Symposium on Augustine's *Confessions* in *JSSR* 25, no. 1 (March 1986): 57–115; "Embracing Augustine," *JSSR* 27 no 1 (March 1988).

47. James T. Richardson, "Conflict in Conversion/Recruitment Research," *JSSR* 24, no. 2 (1985): 119–236.

48. For a longer analysis of these broad themes, see my *Rebecca's Children,* 13–67.

49. See Erik Erickson, "The Galilean Sayings and the Sense of 'I,'" *Yale Review* 70 (1981): 321–62.

50. See Peter Berger, *The Sacred Canopy: Elements of a Social Theory of Religion* (Garden City: Anchor Doubleday, 1969). See also Robert N. Bellah, *Beyond Belief: Essays on Religion in a Post-Traditional World* (New York: Harper and Row, 1970).

51. See my *Rebecca's Children,* 68–78.

CHAPTER 2. *Paul's Ecstasy*

1. Albert Schweitzer, *The Mysticism of St. Paul* (London: A. and C. Black, 1931).

2. E.g., 1 Cor. 1:23; 2:1; 2:6–16. See G. Bornkamm, ad loc. TDNT, 4:817–22.

3. See *Things Unutterable*. James Tabor illustrates his contention that this mystical experience is meant to be taken very seriously as a part of Paul's religious life. Although Paul means to criticize those who make claims on the basis of their spiritual gifts, this is not merely a strange corner of Paul's universe, and it is certainly not a parody of an ascent in the tradition of Lucian's *Death of Peregrinus.*

4. Paradise or the Garden of Eden was often conceived as lying in one of the heavens, though the exact location differs from one apocalyptic work to another. See Martha Himmelfarb, *Tours of Hell: The Development and Transmission of an Apocalyptic Form in Jewish and Christian Literature* (Philadelphia: University of Pennsylvania Press, 1984). Second Enoch, for example, locates them in the third heaven. But 2 Enoch may have been influenced by Paul's writings, though the shorter version mentions worship in the Temple in a way that suggests it is still in existence, thus antedating 70 C.E.

5. In different ways, the close relationship between mysticism and apocalypticism has been touched on by several scholars of the past decade, myself included. See my *Two Powers;* Ithamar Gruenwald, *Apocalyptic and Merkabah Mysticism* (Leiden: Brill, 1979); and especially *Open Heaven,* and *Name.* The Pauline passage is also deeply rooted in Jewish and Hellenistic ascension traditions, which imposed a certain structure of ascent on all reports of this period. See also *Heavenly Ascent;* Mary Dean-Otting, *Heavenly Journeys: A Study of the Motif in Hellenistic Jewish Literature* (Frankfurt-New York: Peter Lang, 1984); Ioan Petru Culianu, *Psychoanodia I: A Survey of the Evidence of the Ascension of the Soul and its Relevance* (Leiden: Brill, 1983). Culianu has also published a more general work, *Expériences de l'extase: Extase, ascension et récit visionnaire de l'hellénisme au moyen âge* (Paris: Payot, 1984), with an introduction by Mircea Eliade. The verb *harpazō* in Greek and its Latin equivalent *rapto* is sometimes shared with pagan ascensions (*sol me rapuit,* etc.), but also probably initially denotes both the rapture of vision and the specific heavenly journeys of Enoch (in Hebrew, *laqaḥ;* in Greek, *metethēken*) and Elijah (in Hebrew, *'alah;* in Greek, *anelēphthē*). Similar ascensions can be seen in apocalyptic literature, for instance, 1 Enoch 39.3, 52.1, and 71.1–5, as well as 2 Enoch 3, 7, 8, 11, and 3 Baruch 2. In rabbinic literature, the Aramaic word denoting the journey is often *ithnagid.* Paul's reference to the third heaven confirms the environment of Jewish apocalypticism and mysticism.

6. Whether or not Paul's experiences typified the rabbis has been debated vigorously with acute attention to the implications for rabbinic rationalism. The debate misses the obvious point that the evidence for these experiences occurs all over Judaism in the Hellenistic period and is coterminous with Pharisaic Judaism. If Paul is a mystic, there is a close connection between this apocalypticism and Pharisaic Judaism. The connection still cannot be defined, but Paul gives us interesting hints about it. It is ironic that scholars who accept almost all rabbinic datings at face value seem reluctant to believe these traditions, supposing that all mystical experience is something despicable for the rabbis. Debating the reliability of talmudic reports that the early rabbis engaged in such practices regularly becomes theoretical, as the Mishnah's testimony for the first century is now suspect

on general methodological grounds, according to Jacob Neusner, *The Rabbinic Traditions about the Pharisees Before 70,* 3 vols. (Leiden: Brill, 1971).

7. See William Baird, "Visions, Revelation, and Ministry: Reflections on 2 Cor. 12:1–5 and Gal. 1:11–17," *JBL* 104, no. 4 (1985): 651–62. See also A. Dean Forbes, *NTS* 32 (1986): 1–30. Paul does not say that the man saw nothing, he only mentions what the man heard. On the subject of difficulties, a significant exception to the identification of Paul with the mystic is Morton Smith, *Clement of Alexandria and a Secret Gospel of Mark* (Cambridge: Harvard University Press, 1975); *Jesus the Magician* (New York: Harper and Row, 1978). He has stated that the passage refers to Jesus, although Paul never met the man Jesus. Recently, Smith has been considering favorably the hypothesis that Paul speaks of himself. As we shall see, the passage is probably another record of the kind of experience Paul has in meeting the risen Christ, this time in heaven.

8. Encounters with the divine and heavenly journeys are frought with danger. Jacob was wounded by his wrestling with the angel (Gen. 32:25). Three of the four rabbis who entered paradise suffered injury (b. Ḥagigah 14b). See Baird, "Visions," p. 660 and Johann Maier, "Das Gefaehrdungsmotiv bei der Himmelsreise in der juedischen Apokalyptik und 'Gnosis,'" *Kairos* 5 (1963): 18–40.

9. Some scholars, most recently and vociferously Seyoon Kim in *Paul's Gospel,* maintain that Acts 22:17 recounts the same experience narrated in 2 Corinthians 12; but such a late date would radically alter normal understandings of Pauline chronology, and Luke matter-of-factly reveals the content of the vision without commenting on its secret nature. See Robert Jewett, *A Chronology of Paul's Life* (Philadelphia: Fortress Press, 1979). See also Gerd Luedemann, *Paul, Apostle to the Gentiles: Studies in Chronology* (Philadelphia: Fortress, 1984).

10. See *Things Unutterable; Paul's Gospel* suggests that 2 Corinthians 12 is Paul's conversion experience. Scholarship is divided as to whether or not Galatians 1 and 2 Corinthians 12 can be identified as the same experience. Baird, "Visions," reports that recently most scholars assume a distinction (652 and n. 2). A good example of this position would be *Spirit,* 103: "His Damascus road experience was not simply the first of several or many experiences of the same kind; for Paul it was the last of a number of experiences of a unique kind." While there is no doubt that Paul's conversion experience is unique in some respects, it is inappropriate to deny any relationship to his other ecstatic experiences based on the lack of the term *vision* in Galatians 1. John Knox maintained the identification between the two experiences; see his "'Fourteen Years Later': A Note on the Pauline Chronology," *JR* 16 (1936): 341–49, and "The Pauline Chronology," *JBL* 58 (1939): 15–29. Yet, in a footnote to his *Chapters in a Life of Paul* (Nashville: Abingdon, 1950), 78, he abandoned the notion. See Donald W. Riddle, *Paul: Man of Conflict* (Nashville: Cokesbury, 1940), 63; Charles Buck and Greer Taylor, *Saint Paul: A Study of the Development of His Thought* (New York: Scribner, 1969), 220–26; Morton S. Enslin, *Reapproaching Paul* (Philadelphia: Westminster, 1972), 53–55.

11. See, for instance, *Spirit,* 107–9.

12. See Hekhaloth Rabbati 20, *Wertheimer,* 1:98–99, *Synopse,* 89f, sect. 198f, and L. Schiffman, "The Recall of Neḥuniah ben Hakkanah from Ecstasy," *AJS Review* 1 (1976): 269–81; see also Lieberman's corrections to Schiffman in Gruenwald, *Apocalyptic and Merkabah Mysticism,* p. 241.

13. See *Pseudepigrapha* to see how vast this literature is. But even the two ample volumes edited by Charlesworth could not contain other, separate bodies of apocalyptic and pseudepigraphical literature, such as the Dead Sea Scrolls, the Nag Hammadi library, the Mani Codex and the Hekhaloth Literature.

14. See the interesting theory of Tryggve N. D. Mettinger, *The Dethronement of Sabaoth: Studies in the Shem and Kabod Theologies,* Coniectanea Biblica Old Testament Series 18 (Lund: Gleerup, 1982) for the origin of the *Kavod* idea and its original function in biblical literature.

15. See the recently published work *Faces of the Chariot.*

16. H. Odeberg, *The Hebrew Book of Enoch or Third Enoch,* 2d ed. (New York: Ktav, 1973); Gershom Scholem, *Major Trends in Jewish Mysticism* (New York: Schocken, 1961); *Jewish Gnosticism, Merkabah Mysticism and Talmudic Tradition,* 2d ed. (New York: Jewish Theological Seminary, 1965). See also M. Smith, "Observations on *Hekhaloth Rabbati*," in *Studies and Texts,* ed. A. Altmann, vol. 1 of *Biblical and Other Studies* (Cambridge: Harvard University Press, 1963), and A. Altmann, "Sacred Hymns in Hekhaloth Literature," *Melilah* 2 (1946): 1–24; A. Altmann, "Moses Narboni's 'Epistle on *Shiur Koma,*'" *Jewish Medieval and Renaissance Studies,* ed. A. Altmann (Cambridge: Harvard University Press, 1967), 225.

17. *Two Powers;* David Halperin, *The Merkabah in Rabbinic Literature* (New Haven: American Oriental Society, 1980); Gruenwald, *Apocalyptic and Merkabah Mysticism;* J. Dan, "The Concept of Knowledge in the Shiur Komah," in *Studies in Jewish Intellectual History presented to Alexander Altmann,* ed. S. Stein and R. Loewe (Birmingham: University of Alabama Press, 1979), and "Three Types of Ancient Jewish Mysticism," (Cincinnati: Judaic Studies Program, 1984); Ira Chernus, "Individual and Community in the Redaction of Hekhaloth Literature," *HUCA* 52 (1981): 253–74, "Visions of God in Merkabah Mysticism," *JSJ* 13 (1983): 123–46 and *Mysticism in Rabbinic Judaism: Studies in the History of Midrash* (Berlin: de Gruyter, 1982).

18. *Gnostic; History;* and "Cosmic Dimensions and Religious Knowledge (Eph. 3:18)," in *Jesus und Paulus: Festschrift fuer W. G. Kuemmel,* ed. E. Earle Ellis and E. Graesser (Goettingen: Vandenhoeck und Ruprecht, 1975), 57–75; Wayne A. Meeks, *The Prophet King* (Leiden: Brill, 1967); *Name;* K. Rudolph, "Ein Grundtyp gnostischer Urmensch-Adam-Spekulation," *ZRGG* 9 (1957): 1–20; M. Tardieu, *Trois mythes gnostiques: Adam, Éros et les animaux d'Egypte dans un écrit de Nag Hammadi (II,5)* (Paris: Études Augustiniennes, 1974), 85–139; J. W. Bowker, "'Merkabah' Visions and the Visions of Paul," *JSS* 16 (1971): 157–73; Howard Clark Kee, "The Transfiguration in Mark: Epiphany or Apocalyptic Vision?" *Understanding the Sacred Text: Festschrift for Morton Enslin,* ed. John Reichman (Valley Forge: Judson Press, 1972); André Neher, "Le voyage mystique des quatre," *RHR* 140 (1951): 59–82; Nicholas Séd, "Les traditions secrètes et les disciples de Rabban Yohannan ben Zakkai," *RHR* 184 (1973): 49–66; Peter Schaefer, "New Testament and Hekhalot Literature: The Journey into Heaven in Paul and Merkavah Mysticism," *JJS* 35, no. 1 (1984): 19–35; Peter Schaefer, "Engel und Menschen in der Hekhalot-Literatur," *Kairos* 22 (1980): 201–25; James H. Charlesworth, "The Righteous as an Angel," in *Ideal Figures in Ancient Judaism,* ed. G. W. E. Nickelsburg and John J. Collins (Chico: Scholars

316 Notes to Pages 40–43

Press, 1980); *One God;* H. D. Betz, *Galatians,* Hermeneia (Philadelphia: Fortress, 1979), suggests several relationships between Jewish mysticism and Graeco-Roman magic. See also *Open Heaven.* See the article by Guy Stroumsa, "Form(s) of God: Some Notes on Metatron and Christ," *HTR* 76 no. 3 (1985): 269–88, which summarizes the basic ideas of the *Shiur Koma* and notes their relevance to early Christianity.

19. In *Synopse.*

20. *Shiur Komah,* trans. M. Cohen (Lanham, Md.: University Press of America, 1983); *Hekhaloth Zutartey,* trans. R. Elior, Jerusalem Studies in Jewish Thought (Jerusalem: 1982). For the complete bibliography, see *Faces of the Chariot,* 567–69.

21. See Gilles Quispel, "Hermetism and the New Testament, Especially Paul," *ANRW* II.22, forthcoming.

22. J. Strugnell, "The Angelic Liturgy at Qumran," in *VTSup* 7 (Leiden: Brill, 1960), 318–45.

23. See Carol Newsom, *Songs of the Sabbath Sacrifice: A Critical Edition, HSS* 27 (Atlanta: Scholars Press, 1985), esp. 45–58.

24. See *dissertation* for a sound analysis of the Hebrew Bible references to the *Kavod* or Glory.

25. Matthew Black, "The Throne-Theophany Prophetic Commission and the 'Son of Man': A Study in Tradition-History," in *Jews, Greeks, and Christians: Religious Cultures in Late Antiquity,* ed. Robert Hamerton-Kelly and Robin Scroggs (Leiden: Brill, 1976), 57–73; Christopher Rowland, "The Vision of the Risen Christ in Rev. 1:13ff.: The Debt of an Early Christology to an Aspect of Jewish Angelology," *JTS* 31 (1980): 1–11; and Jarl Fossum, "Jewish Christian Christology and Jewish Mysticism," *VC* 37 (1983): 260–87.

26. See, on a related theme, James H. Charlesworth, "The Jewish Roots of Christology: The Discovery of the Hypostatic Voice," *SJT* 39 (1987): 19–41.

27. See Quispel, "Hermetism and the New Testament," and *Name,* 278.

28. Of course, 3 Enoch must be seen as a late document. See *Binitarian,* 384–85; F. J. Horton, *The Melchizedek Tradition: A Critical Examination of the Sources to the Fifth Century A.D. and in the Epistle to the Hebrews* (Cambridge: Cambridge University Press, 1976); P. J. Kobelski, *Melchizedek and Melchireša* (Washington: Washington Biblical Association, 1981); S. F. Noll, "Angelology in the Qumran Texts," (Ph.D. diss., Manchester University, 1979); Gilles Quispel, "Gnosticism and the New Testament," in *The Bible and Modern Scholarship,* ed. J. P. Hyatt (Nashville: Abingdon, 1965), 252–71; "The Origins of the Gnostic Demiurge," in *Kyriakon: Festschrift Johannes Quasten,* ed. P. Granfield and J. A. Jungman (Münster: Aschendorff, 1970), 1:272–76.

29. See my *Two Powers,* 182–219; Peter Schaefer, *Rivalitaet zwischen Engeln und Menschen: Untersuchungen zur rabbinischen Engelvorstellung* (Berlin: de Gruyter, 1975), 9–74; H. B. Kuhn, "The Angelology of the Non-Canonical Apocalypses," *JBL* 67 (1948): 217–32; F. Stier, *Gott und sein Engel im Alten Testament* (Münster: Aschendorff, 1934).

30. See Saul Lieberman, "Metatron, the Meaning of His Name and His Functions," an appendix in Gruenwald, *Apocalyptic and Merkabah Mysticism,* 235–41, esp. 237–39. Pace Stroumsa.

31. For the growing consensus that apocalypticism implies visionary or mystical experience as well as secret knowledge of the end of time, see *Open Heaven.* See James H. Charlesworth, "The Portrayal of the Righteous as an Angel," *Ideal Figures in Ancient Judaism: Profiles and Paradigms,* ed. George W. E. Nickelsburg and John J. Collins, Septuagint and Cognate Studies 12 (Chico: Scholars Press, 1980); Moshe Idel, *Kabbalah: New Perspectives* (New Haven: Yale University Press, 1988), stresses the theme of transformation but does not consider the Pauline corpus. This is an amazing confirmation of the transformation vocabulary noted in chapter 1 above.

32. Translated by M. Pravednoe, in *Pseudepigrapha,* 1:152.

33. J. Z. Smith, "The Prayer of Joseph," in *Religions,* 253–94. See A.-M. Denis, *Fragmenta Pseudepigraphorum quae Supersunt Graeca Una Cum Historicum et Auctorum Judaeorum Hellenistarum Fragmentis* (Leiden: Brill, 1970), 61–62.

34. E. R. Goodenough, *By Light, Light: The Mystic Gospel of Hellenistic Judaism* (New Haven: Yale University Press, 1935), 199–234; Wayne A. Meeks, *The Prophet-King;* "Moses as God and King," in *Religions,* 354–71; "The Divine Agent and His Counterfeit in Philo and the Fourth Gospel," in *Aspects of Religious Propaganda in Judaism and Early Christianity,* ed. E. S. Fiorenza (Notre Dame: Notre Dame University Press, 1976), 43–67; C. R. Holladay, *Theios Anēr in Hellenistic Judaism,* SBL Dissertation Series 40 (Missoula: Scholars Press, 1977), 103–69.

35. "The Divine Agent," 45; see also Larry W. Hurtado, "Exalted Patriarchs," in *One God.*

36. See Gilles Quispel, "Ezekiel 1:26 in Jewish Mysticism and Gnosis," *VC* 34 (1980): 1–10; Review of J. Frickel, *Hellenistische Erloesung in christlicher Deutung,* vol. 19 of *Nag Hammadi Studies* (Leiden: Brill, 1984), in *VC* 39 (1985): 196–99; also his "Gnosis," *Die orientalischen Religionen im Roemerreich,* ed. M. J. Vermaseren (Leiden: Brill, 1981), 413–35; see also C. R. Holladay, "The Portrait of Moses in Ezekiel the Tragedian," *SBL Seminar Papers 1976* (Missoula: Scholars Press, 1976), 447–52; H. Jacobson, "Mysticism and Apocalyptic in Ezekiel's Exagoge," *Illinois Classical Studies* 6 (1981): 272–93; P. van der Horst, "Moses' Throne Vision in Ezekiel the Dramatist," *JJS* 34 (1983): 21–29 and "Some Notes on the *Exagoge* of Ezekiel," *Mnemosyne* 37 (1984): 354–75.

37. See *The Exagoge of Ezekiel,* ed. Howard Jacobson (Cambridge: Cambridge University Press, 1983), 54–55, ll. 68–89. Jacobson denies that there is any mystical content to the book. But this is not the best conclusion from these traditions. For one thing, those scholars who most vociferously deny the mystical content of these traditions seem to have no idea what mysticism meant in the first century, importing instead some anachronistic twentieth-century definition of mystical experience. R. G. Robertson has pointed out, if only in passing, the relevance of this passage to the son of man figure in his translation of Ezekiel the Tragedian for *Pseudepigrapha,* 2:812, see n. b2.

38. See my *Two Powers;* see also *Gnostic* and *History,* and especially Jarl Fossum, who has reviewed all the known evidence in a most complete and scholarly fashion in his book *Name;* and see *One God.*

39. See *Two Powers,* 159–82, and *Name,* 268ff. For the whole picture of

Philo's allegory on this topic, see Lala K. K. Dey, *The Intermediary World and Patterns of Perfection in Philo and Hebrews,* SBL Dissertation Series 25 (Missoula: Scholars Press, 1975); see especially *One God.*

40. See for example, T. Sim. 5.4; T. Levi 10.5; 14.1; T. Judah 18.1; T. Zeb. 3.4; T. Dan 5.6; T. Naph. 4.1; T. Benj. 9.1. See L. Hurtado, "Exalted Patriarchs," in *One God.*

41. See *Two Powers,* 182–220, 244–360.

42. *Two Powers,* 33–147.

43. *Name,* 76–95.

44. The Enoch literature is possibly as old or older than the Daniel son of man traditions in which it participates. See M. A. Knibb, *The Ethiopic Book of Enoch* (Oxford: Oxford University Press, 1978).

45. Charles has *bull,* E. Isaac, in *Pseudepigrapha,* 1:71 has *cow.*

46. This is now reconfirmed by James VanderKam's essay in *The Messiah,* ed. James H. Charlesworth with James Brownson, Steven Kraftchik, and Alan F. Segal (forthcoming). See also George Nickelsburg's ("Salvation Without and with a Messiah: Developing Beliefs in Writings Ascribed to Enoch," 49–68), Howard Kee's ("Christology in Mark's Gospel," 187–208), and James Charlesworth's ("From Jewish Messianology to Christian Christology: Some Caveats and Perspectives," 225–64) contributions to *Judaisms and Their Messiahs at the Turn of the Christian Era,* ed. Jacob Neusner, William S. Green, and Ernest Frerichs (Cambridge: Cambridge University Press, 1987).

47. Translated by E. Isaac in *Pseudepigrapha,* 1:50.

48. Another unemphasized aspect of the journey motif is that it is a kind of travel narrative, purporting to be the actual experience of a trustworthy patriarch of the profoundly moral structure of the cosmos confirming the biblical account, which reassures the righteous of their final reward.

49. See Quispel, "Hermetism and the New Testament," and *Name,* 278.

50. See M. A. Knibb, "The Date of the Parables of Enoch: A Critical Review," *NTS* 25 (1979): 345–59; also J. T. Milik with M. Black, *The Books of Enoch: Aramaic Fragments of Qumran Cave 4* (Oxford: Oxford University Press, 1976). Though Milik and Black's dating of Hekhaloth literature has been criticized, the book does contain a good summary of the scholarship on the problem. (See also E. Isaac in *Pseudepigrapha,* 1:6–7, who dates the Parables to the late first century. Hence, he believes that the parables may be post-Christian.) According to James Charlesworth, the SNTS Pseudepigrapha session in Paris almost unanimously agreed, including Matthew Black but still excluding Milik, that the Parables are very early. I realize that I am dating the Parables later than most scholars, but I think that this conservative dating is necessary on account of the lack of any fragments from the parables in the Dead Sea Scrolls, in spite of Qumranic appreciation for Enochian literature. Therefore, although Milik's late dating of the Parables may be too extreme, a post-Christian date seems prudent, as a methodological necessity, until some new positive evidence for the early date of the Parables appears. For scholarly opinion in print, see Knibb's review of Milik in *NTS* 1979 and M. E. Stone, "The Book of Enoch and Judaism in the Third Century B.C.E.," *CBQ* 40 (1978): 479–92; G. W. E. Nickelsburg, "Enoch, Levi, and Peter: Recipients of Revelation in Upper Galilee," *JBL* 100 (1981): 575–600. Of course, if the

Parables are pre-Christian, as many scholars now believe, my case is measurably stronger. I am only dating these texts late as a control on my own enthusiasm. The evidence from Paul satisfies me that the transformation motif originates before the first century within Judaism. At the NYU conference on the Dead Sea Scrolls, and in private consultation, Morton Smith informs me that he has found a text that will firmly anchor these experiences to the first century and to Qumran, thus necessarily with a long prehistory. In 4QMᵃ of the Dead Sea Scrolls found at Qumran, Morton Smith sees evidence to translate a passage:

> [El Elyon gave me a seat among] those perfect forever,
> a mighty throne in the congregation of the gods.
> None of the kings of the east shall sit in it
> and their nobles shall not [come near it.]
> No Edomite shall be like me in glory.
> And none shall be exalted save me, nor shall come against me.
> For I have taken my seat in the [congregation] in the heavens,
> and none [find fault with me.]
> I shall be reckoned with gods
> and established in the holy congregation.

Prudent judgment will await the publication of the text. But Smith's translations appear careful and his reconstructions conservative. If they are correct, there is evidence that the mystics at the Dead Sea understood that they were one company with the angels, whom they call the *bnei Elohim,* and which they must have achieved through some rite of translation and transmutation. If that is so, we could count the *Wisdom of Solomon* 5.5–8 as a similar passage. Smith's translation parallels other hints of ascension in the Qumran texts. See, for example, 4QAgesCreat, 2; 4QpIsa 11.1–4; 1QSb C; 1QH 3.3, 3.19, 6.12, 7.22, 18.16, and fragment 2. These passages are discussed in Allan J. Pantuck's "Paul and the Dead Sea Scrolls: Ascent and Angelification in First Century Judaism," (unpublished).

51. Paul's experience in the third heaven might have transformed him proleptically into an angelic creature, as Enoch was transformed in his heavenly journey. Paul may thus attain to the title *apostle,* in the same way as many other angelic figures did, by literally becoming God's—or, in this case, Christ's—messenger on earth.

52. See *Things Unutterable,* 84–85. See also James D. Tabor, "'Returning to Divinity': Josephus's Portrayal of the Disappearances of Enoch, Elijah, and Moses," *JBL* 108 (1989): 225–38.

53. *Things Unutterable,* 85–86.

54. Translation by A. F. J. Klijn, in *Pseudepigrapha,* 1:638.

55. Bruce Lincoln, *Myth, Cosmos, and Society: Indo-European Themes of Creation and Destruction* (Cambridge: Harvard University Press, 1986).

56. R. van den Broek, "The Sarapis Oracle in Macrobius Sat. i, 20, 16–17," in *Hommages à Maarten J. Vermaseren,* ed. M. B. de Boer and T. A. Eldredge, EPRO 68 (Leiden: Brill, 1978) 1, 123–41; R. van den Broek, "The Creation of Adam's Psychic Body in the Apocryphon of John," in *Studies,* 38–57; A. J. Festugière, *Corpus Hermeticum,* tome. I (Paris: Société d'Edition "Les Belles Lettres", 1972), 137–38.

57. See my *Heavenly Ascent*, 1368, and *Rebecca's Children*, 87–90.

58. See my *Two Powers*, 244–59; *Name*, 257–332. See also W. Schoedel, "Topological Theology and Some Monistic Tendencies in Gnosticism," in *Essays on the Nag Hammadi Texts in Honour of Alexander Boehlig*, ed. M. Krause, NHS 3 (Leiden: Brill, 1972), 107.

59. For further information on the church fathers, see my *Two Powers*, 220–34 and G. Stroumsa, "Polymorphie divine et transformations d'un mythologeme: L' 'Apocryphon de Jean' et ses sources," *VC* 35 (1981): 412–34; "The Hidden Closeness: on the Church Fathers and Judaism," in *Essays from Jerusalem on Jewish Thought* 2 (1982): 170–75 (in Hebrew); and "The Incorporeality of God: Context and Implications of Origen's Position," *Religion* 13 (1983): 345–58.

60. Josephus reports that the Essenes know the correct names of all the angels.

61. P. W. van der Horst, "Moses' Throne Vision in Ezekiel the Dramatist," *JJS* 34 (1983): 24–25.

62. See P. S. Alexander, "The Historical Setting of the Hebrew Book of Enoch," *JJS* 28 (1977): 156–80. He dates the material to the fourth century but suggests that these chapters are much earlier. He may be right, but because it is uncertain, Paul still remains the earliest sure witness to this material.

63. See *dissertation*, esp. chap. 6.

64. Whether Paul identifies the figure purely on the basis of his vision or because of previous instruction in mystical and apocalyptic Judaism, either as a Pharisee or a Hellenistic Jew, or because he has been taught to do so by another Christian in his community, is a question that admits of no practical solution. But the question does not demand a specific solution, since we know how closely individual mystic experience adheres to communal rules. Paul's visions make most sense as a new Christian development within an established Jewish apocalyptic and mystical tradition. Paul or his close contemporary no doubt learned some of it and likely had experiences in a Christian community that confirmed, indeed educated, his visionary experience that Christ was the figure on the throne. This is altogether natural; it is impossible to separate the traditional parts from the parts that are his own revelation, for the elements of apocalyptic and mystical revelation, as we have seen, are traditional in many respects. Only the identification of the Christ as the figure on the throne was novel by most Jewish standards, yet this would have been normative in Christian community. Each Jewish sect had its distinctive beliefs and Christianity is no exception. Paul's experiences are, when seen in this light, not unique so much as characteristic of Jewish mystical thought; indeed, they give us good evidence that the mystical ascent of adepts to heaven was known in the first century.

65. Robert R. Wilson, *Prophecy and Society in Ancient Israel* (Philadelphia: Fortress, 1980).

66. For an alternative explanation and more detail, see *Faces of the Chariot*, 38–48.

67. It may be that this scene is heavily influenced by similar throne-room scenes of Baal and El in Canaanite literature. If so, knowledge of the original Canaanite source, which would have been odious to the author, must have long since disappeared.

68. Scholars who question the mystical content of these legends include E. E. Urbach, "The Tannaitic Traditions of Esoteric Lore" (in Hebrew), *Studies in Kabbalah and the History of Religions Presented to Gershom Scholem* (Jerusalem: Magnes Press, 1968), 1–28, though he mentions an "ascetic ecstasy" that he claims is not mystical, which impresses me as playing with words; Halperin, *The Merkabah in Rabbinic Literature,* and the equally excellent *Faces on the Chariot,* where the mystical nature of the earliest traditions is disputed; Martha Himmelfarb, "Heavenly Ascent and the Relationship of the Apocalypses and the Hekhaloth Literature," *Jewish Spirituality,* vol. 2 ed. Arthur Green (forthcoming); Martha Himmelfarb, "The Experience of the Visionary and the Genre in the Ascension of Isaiah 6–11 and the Apocalypse of Paul," *Semeia* 36 (1986): 97–111; Philip Alexander, "The Historical Setting of the Hebrew Book of Enoch," *JJS* 28 (1977): 173–80; Peter Schaefer, "Prolegomena zu einer kritischen Edition und analyse der Merkava Rabba," *FJB* 5 (1977): 65–99; "Die Beschwoerung des sar ha-panim, Kritische Edition und Uebersetzung," *FJB* 6 (1978): 107–45; "Aufbau und redaktionelle Identitaet der Hekhalot Zutrati," *JJS* 33 (1982): 569–82; "Tradition and Redaction in Hekhaloth Literature," *JSJ* 14 (1983): 172–81.

69. This should function as a caution to those who insist that there is no ecstatic experience in the Mishnah. One could never be sure that the rabbis attended a wedding from the mishnaic evidence either, because of the nature of their reports. The visionary setting of these theophanies is both clear from the original biblical context and, more important, from the description of the theophany in apocryphal and pseudepigraphical literature. The important point is that rabbinic literature is not confessional literature; religious experience is almost never directly discussed. What is of interest to the rabbis in their writings is the implications of a particular event or experience for legal and exegetical analysis. That is the rabbinic enterprise. But Judaism, even rabbinic Judaism, never ceased to explore other genres of religious expression. This is particularly obvious in later periods when Jewish mysticism develops its own peculiar methods of expression. Paul himself, as we shall see, gives us certain testimony that such mysticism already existed in the first century. Whether the leading rabbis of the day also sought out such visions, as the talmud seems to imply, is a moot point. But the rabbis were clearly not the kind of rationalists that later generations of apologists have styled them.

70. See Benjamin Kilborne's article, "Dreams," in the *Encyclopedia of Religion* and John S. Hanson, "Dreams and Visions in the Graeco-Roman World and Early Christianity," *ANRW* II.23:2 (1981): 1395–427. He shows that such Hellenistic conventions influenced Luke's descriptions in Acts, especially 16:6–12. For a discussion of the shamanic techniques in healing, see especially Culianu, *Psychanodia I,* 35–41.

71. See Helmut Saake, "Paulus als Ekstatiker: pneumatologische Beobachtung zu 2 Cor. xii 1–10," *Nov T* 15 (1973): 152–60: Ernst Benz, *Paulus als Visionaer,* Akademie der Wissenschaften und der Literatur (Weisbaden: Steiner, 1952).

72. *Paul's Gospel,* 214.

73. See Robert Alan Segal, *The Myth of the Poimandres* (Paris: Mouton, 1986).

74. Much gnostic and apocalyptic material is, like the *Poimandres,* second

century and later, and therefore no direct influence on Paul. Yet the origin of gnostic and apocalyptic traditions is obviously earlier; how much earlier is unknown. And our first-century historical evidence is incomplete. Thus, though not directly relevant, later material is still significant for suggesting several thought worlds in which Paul may have participated and for guiding inquiry into Paul's writing. In the case of the *Poimandres,* for instance, the Hellenistic Jewish atmosphere of Alexandria that may be presumed to exist in the first century is significant for understanding Paul's thought.

75. Hans Lewy, *Sobria Ebrietas: Untersuchungen zur Geschichte der antiken Mystik* (Giessen: Topelmann, 1929).

76. See Gruenwald, *Apocalyptic and Merkabah Mysticism,* 156, 193 n. 4.

77. The term often used to describe merkabah mystics, "the descenders into the chariot" (*yordei merkabah*), seems to me best understood as referring to this position, (pace Gruenwald).

78. See *Otsar Ha-Geonim,* ed. Benjamin Lewin, *Hagigah* (Jerusalem: 1931), *Teshuvoth,* 14–15.

79. I cannot agree with Halperin, *The Merkabah in Rabbinic Literature,* that the Gaon totally misunderstands the Ezekiel traditions on the basis of the mysticism of his own day. Apocalypticism is well known to be a highly exegetical enterprise, as Lars Hartman pointed out in his *Prophecy Interpreted: The Formation of Some Jewish Apocalyptic Texts and of the Eschatological Discourse Mark 13 par.* (Lund: Gleerup, 1966). Halperin's distinction between the exegetical character of rabbinic comment on Ezek. 1 and the apocalyptic-mystical does not hold. Both groups use the themes exegetically; both may have understood them mystically and have sought to reproduce the experience.

80. Scholem, *Major Trends in Jewish Mysticism,* and Morton Smith, "Some Observations on Hekhaloth Rabbati," in *Studies and Texts,* ed. A. Altmann, vol. 1 of *Biblical and Other Studies.* Also see the Jewish Christian evidence, for instance, Ps.-Clem. Hom. 17.16. See *Name,* 214ff.

81. See the summary article of Morton Smith, "Ascent to the Heavens and the Beginnings of Christianity," *Eranos Jahrbuch* 50 (1981): 403–29, as well as the work of Odeberg, Meeks, and Dahl.

82. See my *Two Powers,* 205–19; also *Binitarian.*

83. This was one of the consensual statements of the NEH Conference on first-century Jewish messianism. The papers and agreements of the conference will be published in *The Messiah,* ed. James H. Charlesworth with James Brownson, Steven Kraftchik, and Alan F. Segal (forthcoming).

84. See my *Rebecca's Children,* 60–67, 78–95 for a thumbnail sketch of this development.

85. A plausible history of tradition, locating the connection between Dan. 7:13 and Jesus in the interpretation of the early church, has been suggested by Donald Juel, *Messianic Exegesis* (Philadelphia: Fortress, 1987).

86. J. J. Collins, "Apocalyptic Eschatology as the Transcendence of Death," *CBQ* 36 (1984): 21–43. See also *Heavenly Ascent;* and Alan F. Segal, "'He Who Did not Spare his Own Son . . .': Jesus, Paul and the Akedah," in *From Jesus to Paul: Studies in Honour of Francis Wright Beare,* ed. Peter Richardson and John C. Hurd (Waterloo, Ont.: Wilfred Laurier University Press, 1984), 169–84.

87. As a summary, see Christopher Rowland, *Christian Origins: From Messianic Movement to Christian Religion* (Minneapolis: Augsburg, 1985); *The Influence of the First Chapter of Ezekiel on Jewish and Early Christian Literature* (Ph.D. diss., Cambridge University, 1974); "The Vision of the Risen Christ in Rev. 1:13ff: The Debt of an Early Christology to an Aspect of Jewish Angelology," *JTS* 31 (1980): 1–11 and *JSNT* 24 (1985); Matthew Black, "The Throne-Theophany, Prophetic Commission, and the 'Son of Man': A Study in Tradition-History," *Jews, Greeks and Christians: Festschrift for W. D. Davies* (Oxford: Oxford University Press, 1976); Seyoon Kim, *The Son of Man as the Son of God* (Tübingen: Mohr, 1983); *Name; Two Powers,* 182–219; in *Binitarian,* Hurtado agrees with my view of the novelty of the Christian interpretation within a general context in which such identifications were possible. In *One God* he takes the claim of the uniqueness of worshiping the second power much further than I. While Hurtado may have overlooked the occasional example of angelolatry in sectarian Judaism, his point is well-taken. The worship of Christ as a god was characteristic of early Christianity, even in the eyes of its detractors, while other groups with angelic heroes seem more circumspect about offering prayer to it.

88. See Juel, *Messianic Exegesis.*

89. Terrance Callan, "Prophecy and Ecstasy in Greco-Roman Religion and in 1 Corinthians," *NovT* 27 (1985): 125–40. Callan shows how Paul wished to limit the term ecstasy. Prophecy for Paul is not ecstatic, in that it need not be accompanied by trance. Therefore, our use of it, though proper, also remains an *etic* term.

90. Neher, "Le voyage," and Séd, "Les traditions."

91. The most recent good analysis of pseudepigraphical writing is David G. Meade, *Pseudonymity and Canon: An Investigation into the Relationship of Authorship and Authority in Jewish and Earliest Christian Tradition* (Tübingen: Mohr [Siebeck], 1986). Mystical notions are not even mentioned.

92. In this section, I am particularly indebted to Gilles Quispel, "Hermetism and the New Testament, Especially Paul," *ANRW* II.22 (forthcoming).

93. The polemical context of this passage (2 Cor 3:1–17) should be noted but I cannot deal with it until chapter 5. For the issue of the imagery of darkness and light, see *Darkness,* 45–48.

94. The use of the mirror here is also a magicomystical theme, which can be traced to the word *'eyyin* occurring in Ezekiel 1. Although it is sometimes translated otherwise, *'eyyin* probably refers to a mirror even there, and possibly refers to some unexplained technique for achieving ecstasy. The mystic bowls of the magical papyri and the talmudic era were filled with water and oil to reflect light and stimulate trance. The magical papyri describe spells that use a small bowl that serves as the medium for the appearance of a god for divination: e.g., PGM IV, 154–285 (*Magical Papyri,* 40–43), PDM 14.1–92, 295–308, 395–427, 528–53, 627–35, 805–40, 841–50, 851–55 (*Magical Papyri,* 195–200, 213, 218–19, 225–26, 229, 236–39). The participant concentrates on the reflection in the water's surface, often with oil added to the mixture, sometimes with the light of a lamp nearby. Lamps and charms are also used to produce divinations, presumably because they can stimulate trance under the proper conditions. The *Reuyoth Yehezkel,* for instance, mention that Ezekiel's mystical vision was stimulated by

looking into the waters of the River Chebar. It seems to me that Philo appropriates the mystic imagery of the mirror to discuss the allegorical exposition of Scripture. See *The Contemplative Life*, 78, and Dieter Georgi, *Die Gegner des Paulus im 2. Korintherbrief*, 272–3. Also Schulz, ZNTW 49 (1958): 1–30. Paul's opponents then look into the mirror and see only the text. But because Paul and those truly in Christ actually behold the Glory of the Lord, they have a clearer vision of the truth. See chap. 6 below for further discussion of Paul's opponents in Corinthians. My thanks to David Balch for insisting that I deal with these issues, though he will no doubt dissent from my opinion.

95. The romance of exaltation to immortality was hardly a unique Jewish motif; rather, it was characteristic of all higher spirituality of later Hellenism—witness the Hermetic literature. Even in a relatively unsophisticated text like the magical *Recipe for Immortality* (the so-called Mithras Liturgy) of third-century Egypt, the adept gains a measure of immortality by gazing directly on the god and breathing in some of his essence.

96. See Carol Newsom, *Songs of the Sabbath Sacrifice: A Critical Edition*, HSS 27 (Atlanta: Scholars Press, 1985).

97. Jakob Jervell, *Imago Dei* (Goettingen: Vandenhoeck und Ruprecht, 1960), 196, 209.

98. Ralph P. Martin, *Carmen Christi: Philippians 2:5–11 in Recent Interpretation and in the Setting of Early Christian Worship*, rev. ed. (Grand Rapids: Eerdmans, 1983), from the 1967 Cambridge University Press edition. See also James Sanders, "Dissenting Deities and Phil. 2:1–11," *JBL* 88 (1969), 279–90.

99. The other candidate, Peter's Pentecost Discourse, in Acts 3 seems to me to have undergone much more editing before reaching written form. See J. A. T. Robinson, "The Most Primitive Christology of All," *Twelve New Testament Studies* (London: SCM Press, 1962), reprinted from JTS 7 (1956):177–89.

100. The bibliography on the Pauline and post-Pauline hymns in Phil. 2:6–11 and Col. 1:15–20 appears endless. See E. Schillebeeckx, *Jesus: An Experiment in Christology* (New York: Seabury, 1979); M. Hengel, "Hymn and Christology," in *Between Jesus and Paul*, 78–96; J. Murphy O'Connor, "Christological Anthropology in Phil. 2:6–11," *RB* 83 (1976): 25–50, and D. Georgi, "Der vorpaulinische Hymnus Phil. 2:6–11," in *Zeit und Geschichte, Dankesgabe an Rudolf Bultmann*, ed. E. Dinkler (Tübingen: Mohr, 1964), 263–93, esp. 291 for bibliography. As Balch reminds me, Kaesemann emphasizes that Paul's metaphoric use of the body and its separate parts is characteristic of paraenetic sections, emphasizing the relationship between the believer and the risen Lord. See Schweitzer, *TDNT* 7, 1073. For a discussion of the hymn and the unlikelihood of an interpolation, see Ralph P. Martin, *Carmen Christi: Philippians 2:5–11 in Recent Interpretation and in the Setting of Early Christian Worship*, rev. ed. (Grand Rapids: Eerdmans, 1983), 199–228.

101. See my *Two Powers*, 33–158, esp. 68–73; and *Binitarian*, 377–91.

102. Scholars like Kim who want to ground all of Paul's thought in a single ecstatic conversion experience, which they identify with Luke's accounts of Paul's conversion, are reticent to accept this passage as a fragment from Christian liturgy, because to do so would destroy its value as Paul's personal revelatory experience. But there is no need to decide whether the passage is originally Paul's (hence

received directly through the Damascus revelation) since ecstatic language normally is derived from traditions current within the religious group. Christian mystics use Christian language, Muslim mystics use the languages developed for mysticism in Islam, and no mystic is ever confused by another religion's mysticism unless it is the conscious and explicit intent of the mystic's vision to do so. See R. C. Zaehner, *Hinduism and Muslim Mysticism* (New York: Schocken, 1969); Steven Katz, "Language, Epistemology, and Mysticism," and *Mysticism and Philosophical Analysis*, ed. Steven Katz (New York: Oxford University Press, 1978). In this case the language is not even primarily Christian. The basic language is from Jewish mysticism, though the subsequent exegesis about the identification of Christ with the figure on the throne is Christian; the vision of God enthroned is the goal of Jewish mystical speculation.

103. Robin Scroggs, *The Last Adam: A Study in Pauline Anthropology* (Philadelphia: Fortress, 1966), 75–114.

104. See *Spirit*, 322.

105. J. Louis Martyn in W. R. Farmer et al., *Christian History and Interpretation* (Cambridge: Cambridge University Press, 1967), 269–87, esp. 274.

106. *Spirit*, 327.

107. See Segal, *The Myth of Poimandres*.

108. See the "Recipe for Immortality" from the Paris Magical Papyrus, also known as the Mithras Liturgy. See Jonathan Z. Smith, "The Temple and the Magician," *God's Christ and His People: Studies in Honour of Nils Alstrup Dahl* (Oslo: Universitetsforlaget, 1977), 233–47. See A. D. Nock, "Paul and the Magus," in *The Beginnings of Christianity*, ed. F. J. Foakes Jackson and Kirsopp Lake (Grand Rapids: Baker, 1966), 5:164–87.

109. Fred O. Francis, "Humility and Angelic Worship in Col. 2:18," *ST* 16 (1962): 109–34; Fred O. Francis and Wayne A. Meeks, *Conflict at Colossae: A Problem in the Interpretation of Early Christianity Illustrated by Selected Modern Studies*, rev. ed., Sources for Biblical Study 4 (Missoula: Scholars Press, 1975); W. Carr, *Angels and Principalities: The Background, Meaning and Development of the Pauline Phrase: hai archai kai hai exousiai* (Cambridge: Cambridge University Press, 1981); C. A. Evans, "The Colossian Mystics," *Biblica* 63 (1982): 188–205.

110. Of course, *apostle* was a frequent title for an angelic messenger as well. It is possible that some apostles thought of themselves as already divinized.

111. George Nickelsburg, "An Ektroma, Though Appointed from the Womb: Paul's Apostolic Self-Description in 1 Corinthians 15 and Galatians 1," *HTR* 79, nos. 1–3 (1986), 198–205.

112. See Ioan M. Lewis, *Ecstatic Religion: An Anthropological Study of Spirit Possession and Shamanism* (Baltimore: Penguin, 1971); see also Elaine Pagels, *The Gnostic Gospels* (New York: Random House, 1979), esp. chaps. 1 and 2.

CHAPTER 3. *Conversion in Paul's Society*

1. *Conversion.*

2. See Ramsey MacMullen, *Christianizing the Roman Empire, A.D. 100–400* (New Haven: Yale University Press, 1984); see also his *Paganism in the Roman Empire* (New Haven: Yale University Press, 1981), 94–137, for issues

regarding conversion in paganism, dynamic religions, and the decline of paganism. See Robin Lane Fox, *Pagans and Christians: Religion and the Religious Life from the Second to the Fourth Century A.D. when the Gods of Olympus Lost Their Dominion and Christianity, with the Conversion of Constantine, Triumphed in the Mediterranean World* (New York: Knopf, 1986). For a good summary of the social structure of pagan society, see David Balch and John E. Stambaugh, *The New Testament in its Social Environment* (Philadelphia: Westminster Press, 1986). For a good summary of Nock's contentions that the philosophical schools also developed special definitions of conversion, see *Apologetic* and *Thessalonians.*

3. See D. Macdonald, *The Legend and the Apostle* (Philadelphia: Westminster, 1983), and Elizabeth Fiorenza, *In Memory of Her: A Feminist Theological Reconstruction of Christian Origins* (New York: Crossroad, 1983).

4. Peter Berger and Thomas Luckmann, *The Social Construction of Reality: A Treatise in the Sociology of Knowledge* (Garden City, N.Y.: Doubleday, Anchor Books, 1967), 15; Robert N. Bellah, *Beyond Belief: Essays On Religion in a Post-Traditional World* (New York: Harper and Row, 1970).

5. See Harold Remus, "Sociology of Knowledge and the Study of Early Christianity," *SR* 11, no. 1 (1982): 47f.

6. There is no need to document this in detail. But a recent survey by the American Jewish Committee in New York has demonstrated it again. Egon Mayer and Amy Avgar interviewed partners of 309 intermarried couples. About a third of the couples identified included a partner who had converted to Judaism. The overwhelming majority of partners converted to Judaism were women. They reported that the children of these couples are raised as Jews and the spouses were highly identified with the synagogue and the Jewish community (*New York Times,* June 22, 1987, B 9).

7. *Commitment and Community* (Cambridge: Harvard University Press, 1972), 64.

8. Kanter, *Commitment and Community,* 61–74. Though Kanter does not discuss the issue, her typology allows for a neat distinction between the two types of conversions that were isolated by psychologists: Sudden conversions would necessarily begin with a high degree of affective commitment, while gradual conversions work explicitly to develop high dimensions of moral and instrumental commitment as well.

9. D. G. Bromley and A. D. Shupe, Jr., *Moonies in America: Cult, Church, and Crusade* (Beverly Hills: Sage, 1979), 172.

10. Gerhard Lenski, *The Religious Factor,* rev. ed. (Garden City, N.Y.: Doubleday, 1963).

11. Dean Kelley, *Why Conservative Churches are Growing* (New York: Harper and Row, 1972).

12. *Snow and Machalek,* and "The Sociology of Conversion," *Annual Review of Sociology* 10 (1984): 167–90.

13. See *Snow and Machalek,* chap. 1 n. 6, app. Also see Snow and Machalek, "The Sociology of Conversion."

14. Clifford L. Staples and Armand L. Mauss, "Conversion or Commitment? A Reassessment of the Snow and Machalek approach to the Study of Conversion,"

JSSR 26 (1987): 133–47. Staples and Mauss were specifically trying to see if the criteria deduced by Snow and Machalek from an Eastern sect would hold true for a sect of born-again Christians. The answer was positive, but, as they say, only one of the criteria is specific to conversion.

15. J. Munck, *Paul and the Salvation of Mankind* (Richmond: John Knox, 1959), 264–65; S. Aalen, *Die Begriffe "Licht" and "Finsternis" im Alten Testament, im Spaetjudentum und im Rabbinismus* (Oslo: Gleerup, 1959); H. J. Schoeps, *The Jewish Christian Argument,* trans. D. E. Green (New York: Holt, Rinehart, and Winston, 1963), 12; *Conversion to Judaism: A History and Analysis,* ed. D. M. Eichhorn (New York: Ktav, 1965); B. J. Bamberger, *Proselytism in the Talmudic Period* (New York: Ktav, 1968), 24; James Parkes, *The Conflict Between Church and Synagogue* (New York: Atheneum, 1969), 23; William G. Braude, *Jewish Proselytizing in the First Five Centuries of the Common Era* (Providence: Brown University Press, 1940); R. R. de Ridder, *The Dispersion of the People of God: The Covenantal Basis of Matthew 28:18–20 Against the Background of Jewish, Pre-Christian Proselytizing and Diaspora, and the Apostleship of Jesus Christ* (Kampen: J. H. Kok, 1971); J. N. Sevenster, *The Roots of Pagan Anti-Semitism in the Ancient World* (Leiden: Brill, 1975), 202–3; S. B. Hoenig, "Conversion During the Talmudic Period," in *Conversion to Judaism,* 210; J. C. Meagher, "As the Twig was Bent: Anti-Semitism in the Greco-Roman and the Earliest Christian Times," in *Anti-Semitism and the Foundations of Christianity,* ed. A. Davies (New York: Paulist Press, 1979); Schuyler Brown "The Matthean Community and the Gentile Mission," *NovT* 22 (1980): 193–221; John Peterson, *Missionary Motives in the Old Testament and Their Gradual Development* (Chicago: University of Chicago Press, 1946); A. S. Goldstein, "Conversion to Judaism in Bible Times," in *Conversion to Judaism;* Frederick Milton Derwacter, *Preparing the Way for Paul: The Proselyte Movement in Later Judaism* (New York: Macmillan, 1930); M. H. Hengel, *Judaism and Hellenism* (Philadelphia: Fortress, 1974), 131–53; G. Alon, *Jews, Judaism, and the Classical World,* trans. Israel Abrahams (Jerusalem: Magnes Press, 1977); *Jews;* M. Simon, *Verus Israel: Etudes sur les relations entre chrétiens et juifs dans l'Empire roman* (Paris: E. de Boccard, 1948); J. Leon, *The Jews of Ancient Rome* (Philadelphia: Jewish Publication Society, 1960), 75–126. Recently Shaye Cohen has been writing a series of detailed articles on conversion and intermarriage in antiquity, which I assume will be collected into a fine book. On the whole, they reach the conclusion that the definition of conversion would depend on the various authorities asked, which is in line with my contention that different groups had different interests and definitions of conversion. Nevertheless, realizing the local character of the issues, I feel a certain number of generalizations can be framed, provided it is always possible to refine them in the presence of each complex and varied situation. Louis Feldman has recently completed a typescript of his excellent survey of the discussions of Jewish proselytism in the ancient world.

16. See my *Rebecca's Children,* 22–28, 58–60. Also T. Mommsen, *The Provinces of the Roman Empire,* trans. W. P. Dickson (New York: 1899), 2:177, and S. N. Eisenstadt and L. Roniger, *Patrons, Clients and Friends: Interpersonal Relations and the Structure of Trust in Society* (Cambridge: Cambridge University Press, 1984).

17. Josephus, *The Life,* trans. H. St. J. Thackeray, Loeb Classical Library (Cambridge: Harvard University Press, 1926), 5–7. The translation must be used with great care.

18. See the dissertation of Leonard Gordon, Columbia University, in progress.

19. See Justin Martyr, 1; *Dial.* Dio Chrysostom; and St. Augustine. See Heydahl, *Philosophie und Christentum,* 1966.

20. See Alan Mason, "Was Josephus a Pharisee? A Re-Examination of the *Life* 10–12," *JJS* 40 (1989): 31–45.

21. See Lawrence Schiffman, *Sectarian Law in the Dead Sea Scrolls: Courts, Testimony and the Penal Code* (Atlanta: Scholars Press, 1983), 155–74.

22. See appendix for more information.

23. See *Thessalonians,* 21–27, relying on the past work of Festugière and Nock, supplemented by Malherbe's own research on the Cynic movement.

24. Musonius Rufus, *Fragment* 49, quoted in *Thessalonians,* 25 and n. 81.

25. *Thessalonians,* 26.

26. See the splendid discussion of Dieter Georgi in *Die Gegner des Paulus im 2. Korintherbrief: Studien zur Religioesen Propaganda in der Spaetantike* (Neukirchen-Vluyn: Neukirchener Verlag, 1964), which has now been translated into English as *Opponents.* The new epilogue brings the book up to date bibliographically and records the author's evolving opinions on these important issues.

27. Peder Borgen, "Debates on Circumcision in Paul and Philo," in *Philo, John and Paul: New Perspectives on Judaism and Early Christianity* (Atlanta: Scholars Press, 1987), 233–55; also *Paul Preaches Circumcision and Pleases Men and Other Essays on Christian Origins* (Trondheim: Tapir, 1983). Borgen portrays Philo correctly as demanding literal circumcision, as well as an ethical circumcision. He seems mistaken, however, in maintaining that Paul conversely was misunderstood by his followers to have advocated literal circumcision when he merely used the same figure of speech of ethical circumcision that Philo did.

28. See Abraham J. Malherbe, *The Social Aspects of Early Christianity,* 2d ed., enlarged (Philadelphia: Fortress, 1983), 51–52. Ellen Birnbaum is currently working on a dissertation at Columbia, which will try to unpack Philo's ambivalent and conflicting perspectives on the issue.

29. Ptolemy the Historian, from Josephus, *Ant.* 13.257, 318. Horace refers to the Jews' desire for non-Jews to join their group: "in hanc concedere turbam." Also Seneca, *De Superstitione.* See Menahem Stern, *Greek and Latin Authors on Jews and Judaism,* 2 vols. (Jerusalem: Israel Academy of Sciences, 1974, 1980), nos. 127, 146, 147, 365. See also Valerius Maximus, *Facta et Dicta Memorabilia* 1.3.3; Horace, *Sermones* 1.4.142–43; Augustine, *De Civitate Dei* 6.11 and *Epistolae Morales* 108.22; Martial, *Epigrammata* 7.30.5–8, 35.3–4, 82.5–6, 9.94.1–8; Petronius, *Satyricon* 68.8; Dio Cassius, *Hist. Rom.* 67.14.1–3. See also *Jews,* 379 and n. 82. See also Shaye J. D. Cohen, "Conversion to Judaism in Historical Perspective: From Biblical Israel to Postbiblical Judaism," *CJ* (Summer 1983): n. 15; and Henry Green, *The Economic and Social Origins of Gnosticism,* SBL Dissertation Series 77 (Atlanta: Scholars Press, 1985), 89f; also "Interpersonal Relations, Ethnic Structure and Economy—A Sociological Reading of Jewish Identification in Roman Egypt," *Proceedings of the Ninth World Congress of Jewish Studies,* Division B (Jerusalem: World Union of Jewish Studies, 1986) 1:15–22.

30. Philo, *Hypothetica*, see Eusebius, *Praeparatio* 8.6–7, 355c-361b; Josephus, *Against Apion* 2.190.

31. See *Jews*, 128–42, 174–80, 202–45.

32. See Bamberger, *Proselytism in the Talmudic Period;* Salo Baron, *A Social and Religious History of the Jews* (New York: JPS, 1952), 1:174f; Hengel, *Judaism and Hellenism*, 1:307; S. Zeitlin, *The Rise and Fall of the Judean State*, 3:326; S. Applebaum, "The Social and Economic Status of the Jews in the Diaspora," in *The Jewish People in the First Century*, ed. S. Safrai and M. Stern (Philadelphia: Fortress, 1976), 2:622f; J. R. Rosenbloom, *Conversion to Judaism* (Cincinnati: Hebrew Union College Press, 1978); J. Z. Smith, "Fences and Neighbors: Some Contours of Early Judaism," *Imagining Religion: From Babylon to Jonestown* (Chicago: University of Chicago Press, 1982), 1–19; H. A. Green, "Jewish Identification and Assimilation: Continuities and Discontinuities in Roman Egypt," *SBL 1985 Seminar Papers*, ed. Kent Harold Richards (Atlanta: Scholars Press, 1985), 505–13.

33. Everett V. Stonequist, *The Marginal Man* (New York: Scribner's, 1937). In the latter case, secularized Jews themselves might be tempted to convert to other groups.

34. See 1 Macc. 1:11–15; 3 Macc. 2:31 and 7:10; also Philo, *Vita Mosis* 1.130 and *De Virt.* 182.

35. See John J. Collins, "A Symbol of Otherness: Circumcision and Salvation in the First Century," Brown Conference, August 1984, in *To See Ourselves as Others See Us* (Atlanta: Scholars Press, 1986), 163–86, esp. 171–72.

36. Aryeh Kasher, *The Jews in Hellenistic and Roman Egypt: The Struggle for Equal Rights* (Tübingen: Mohr, 1985).

37. George la Piana, "Foreign Groups in Rome During the First Centuries of the Empire," *HTR* 20 (1927); 183–403; Pauly-Wissova, *Collegium*, 4, cols. 380–480; *Jews*, 133f; J. N. Sevenster, *The Roots of Pagan Anti-Semitism in the Ancient World* (Leiden: Brill, 1975), 148–58; W. Ruppel, "Politeuma," *Philologus* 82 (1927): 268–312, 433–54.

38. Plutarch, *Theseus* 33.2; G. E. Mylonas, *Eleusis and the Eleusinian Mysteries* (Princeton: Princeton University Press, n.d.), 77. My thanks to Holland Hendrix for this idea and reference.

39. See *Jews and God-Fearers*, 66–67.

40. See *Transformation*, 73–85, on which this discussion depends.

41. G. Staehlin, "Fortschritt und Wachtum," in *Festgabe, Joseph Lortz*, vol. 2 of *Glaube und Geschichte*, ed. E. Iserloh and P. Manns (Baden-Baden: Bruno Grim, 1957), 18.

42. John J. Collins, "Symbol of Otherness," n. 47.

43. Italics mine. See Mishnah Avodah Zarah 2.3 and chapter 7, p. 232 above.

44. Moses Hadas, *Aristeas to Philocrates* (New York: Harper and Row, 1951), 62.

45. *Joseph and Asenath* may have some Jewish Christian influence as the bread is marked with a sign that looks like the cross.

46. J. B. Frey, *Corpus Inscriptionum Ioudaicarum* II (Rome: Pontificcio instituto di archeologia cristiana, 1936), 766. The literature on this group is large. But see L. Feldman, "Jewish 'Sympathizers' in Classical Literature and Inscrip-

tions," *TAPA* 81 (1950): 200 and his more recent unpublished paper called "Jewish Proselytism," which he has been kind enough to share with me; and Leon, *Jews of Ancient Rome*, 247, 251. See also Kirsopp Lake, "Proselytes and God-Fearers," *The Beginnings of Christianity: Part I, The Acts of the Apostles*, ed. F. J. Foakes Jackson and Kirsopp Lake, vol. 5 of *Additional Notes to the Commentary* (Grand Rapids: Baker, 1966), 74–95. The arguments are clearly reviewed and critiqued in greater detail by John G. Gager, "Jews, Gentiles and Synagogues in the Book of Acts," in *Christians Among Jews and Gentiles: Essays in Honor of Krister Stendahl on His Sixty-Fifth Birthday*, ed. George W. E. Nickelsburg with George W. MacRae, S. J. (Philadelphia: Fortress, 1986), 91–99. See also J. Andrew Overman,"The God-fearers: Some Neglected Features," *JSNT* 32 (1988): 17–26.

47. A. T. Kraabel, "The Disappearance of the 'God-Fearers,'" *Numen* 28 (1981): 113–26; see also "The Roman Diaspora: Six Questionable Assumptions," *JJS* 33 (1982): 445–64. Shaye Cohen, "Crossing the Boundary" (Paper delivered at SBL Conference, Boston, 1987), equally expresses reservations: "A modern scholar does not say anything substantive by calling someone in antiquity a judaizer or a God-fearer. These terms are vague and require explication." As will be clear, I think Cohen and Kraabel are exaggerating our lack of knowledge. It is one thing to say that the term requires explication. It is quite another to say that it says nothing substantive.

48. A. T. Kraabel, "Sardis from Prehistoric to Roman Times," *Results of the Archeological Exploration of Sardis, 1958–1975* (Cambridge: Harvard University Press, 1983), 184, quoted from Gager, "Jews, Gentiles, and Synagogues," 91–99.

49. See Gager, "Jews, Gentiles, and Synagogues," n. 48, who cites his indebtedness to Joyce Reynolds and Robert Tannenbaum, the editors of the Aphrodisias Synagogue Inscriptions, and to G. W. Bowersock, for his public lecture discussing the inscriptions. Joyce Reynolds and Robert Tannenbaum have now published their research in *Jews and God-Fearers*.

50. *Opponents*, 97.

51. Jacob Neusner, *From Politics to Piety* (Englewood Cliffs: Prentice Hall, 1973). Even so, the *havuroth* and the Pharisees are probably not identical. See E. P. Sanders, *Jesus and Judaism* (Philadelphia: Fortress, 1985), 187–88, 388–89.

52. For fuller discussion of Jewish rules of conversion, see Lawrence H. Schiffmann, "At the Crossroads: Tannaitic Perspectives on the Jewish-Christian Schism," *Jewish and Christian Self-Definition*, vol. 2 of *Aspects of Judaism in the Hellenistic World*, ed. E. P. Sanders with A. I. Baumgarten and Alan Mendelson (Philadelphia: Fortress Press, 1981), 122–56. Schiffman has expanded these thoughts into a book: *Who Was a Jew: Rabbinic and Halakhic Perspectives on the Jewish-Christian Schism* (Hoboken, N.J.: Ktav, 1985), where the rabbinic rules are fully spelled out in convenient form but no serious questions about their historical validity for the first century have been asked. See also Shaye J. D. Cohen, "Conversion to Judaism in Historical Perspective: From Biblical Israel to Postbiblical Judaism," *CJ* (Summer 1983).

53. For a recent treatment of the topic see Lawrence H. Schiffman, "The Conversion of the Royal House of Adiabene in Josephus and Rabbinic Sources," in *Josephus, Judaism, and Christianity*, ed. Louis H. Feldman and Gohei Hata (De-

troit: Wayne State University Press, 1987), 293–312. Schiffman concentrates on very different issues than are discussed here. *Jews and God-Fearers,* 46–67, published while this book was being drafted, concurs with my analysis and adds many important pieces of evidence from inscriptions and reports to buttress the argument.

54. *Joseph et Asenath. Introduction texte critique traduction et notes,* ed. M. Philonenko, (Leiden: Brill, 1968). See the new English translation by C. Burchard, in *Pseudepigrapha,* 2.

55. Alfredo Mordechai Rabello, "The Legal Condition of the Jews in the Roman Empire," *ANRW* II.13, ed. Hildegard Temporini and Wolfgang Haase (Berlin: de Gruyter, 1980), 665–762.

56. Many Jewish and New Testament scholars have investigated this issue. See my book *Rebecca's Children,* 70–95, for a review of the literature.

57. The major voices in this new scholarly approach are Balch, Gager, Meeks, Malherbe, Hock, Pagels, Holmberg, Kee, Brown, Schuetz, and Theissen. See *Rebecca's Children,* 96–116, and *Urban,* 1–8, for a discussion of the major voices in the scholarly enterprise.

58. R. Horton, "On the Rationality of Conversion," *Africa* 34 (1975), pt. 1, 219–35 and pt. 2, 373–98. See also his "African Conversion," *Africa* 41 (1971): 85–107. Against Horton, see Humphrey J. Fisher "Conversion Reconsidered: Some Historical Aspects of Religious Conversion in Black Africa," *Africa* 43 (1973): 27–40; Robert Baum, "Rational Conversion and the Diola-Esulalu Religious Experience," *Proceedings of the African Studies Association* (Boston, 1976); Richard Bruce, "Conversion Among the Pyem," Department of Sociology, Zaria.

59. Other religions providing similar sources of meaning would have included education in a philosophical school, which was organized as a club, and initiation into one of the mystery religions. Each of these groups would have attracted different clienteles, just as each of the different sects in Judea attracted different clienteles with similar motivations. For instance, the Mysteries of Mithras seem to have appeared most attractive to the army, since the underground caverns of this mystery cult are found everywhere in the Roman Empire but especially frequently near the borders and at army camps. Though synagogues were sometimes supported by local Roman rulers, Judaism never had the access to power that Mithraism had.

60. See my *Hellenistic Magic* for the full bibliography. See also Jack N. Lightstone, *The Commerce of the Sacred: Mediation of the Divine Among Jews in the Graeco-Roman Diaspora,* BJS 59 (Atlanta: Scholars Press, 1984); Jonathan Z. Smith, "The Temple and the Magician," *Map Is Not Territory* (Leiden: Brill, 1978), and "Toward Interpreting Demonic Powers in Hellenistic and Roman Antiquity," *ANRW* II.16:1 (Berlin: de Gruyter, 1978), 425–39.

61. See E. R. Dodds, *Pagan and Christian in an Age of Anxiety* (Cambridge: Cambridge University Press, 1965).

62. See *Transformation,* 55–64.

63. It does not necessarily entail their becoming Jews, only their coming to worship God. Circumcision and kashrut are not mentioned.

64. See Isaac in *Pseudepigrapha,* 1:71.

65. See *Transformation*, 61–64.

66. See Richard A. Horsley, *Jesus and the Spiral of Violence: Popular Jewish Resistance in Roman Palestine* (San Francisco: Harper and Row, 1987).

67. See *Rebecca's Children*, 80–88.

68. James H. Charlesworth, *Jesus within Judaism: Jesus in Light of Exciting Archaeological Discoveries* (New York: Doubleday, 1988), 36.

CHAPTER 4. *The Consequences of Conversion: Paul's Exegesis*

1. In a recent seminar paper ("Preaching Circumcision, Galatians 5:11 and the Origin of Paul's Gentile Mission") for the Canadian Society of Biblical Studies 1988 Conference in Windsor, Ontario, and in private correspondence, Terrence Donaldson suggests that Paul's theology can be understood as a paradigm shift, brought on by a strong conversion experience. I heartily agree and look forward to the book of which the seminar paper is part. It is possible, however, as we have seen, that the conversion can be gradual, and also that Paul's *eti* (Gal. 5:11) can apply to a period after his conversion but before the mature position he outlines in his writing. See chapter 7 below.

2. *Pauline Autobiography: Towards a New Understanding*, SBL Dissertation Series 73 (Atlanta: Scholars Press, 1985), 146–52.

3. Martin Dibelius and Hans Conzelmann, *The Pastoral Epistles*, trans. Philip Buttolph and Adela Yarbro (Philadelphia: Fortress, 1972); *Hermeneia*, ed. Helmut Koester (Philadelphia: Fortress Press, 1972), 28. See also Martinus C. de Boer, "Images of Paul in the Post-Apostolic Period," *CBQ* 42 (1980): 374–75 and n. 58.

4. See Clifford L. Staples and Armand L. Mauss, "Conversion or Commitment? A Reassessment of the Snow and Machalek Approach to the Study of Conversion," *JSSR* 26 (1987): 133–47.

5. Lev. 18:5; Deut. 6:24; Prov. 6:23; Sir. 17:11; 45:5; Bar. 3:9; Ps. Sol 14:2; 4 Ezra 14:30; Avot 2.7. See Strack-Billerbeck 3.237, 238. According to Exodus Rabba 5 (17a) the Torah is life to the Israelites but death to the gentiles because they do not accept it. See *Romans 1–8*, 384. But, of course, this midrash may more easily be understood as a direct response to Christianity rather than as a predecessor to it.

6. See *Paul*, 23–26. To counter A. E. Harvey, who says that the law is now wrong because it cursed Christ, Sanders states that the argument based on the curse of the law argument is subsidiary. Harvey has overinterpreted, for reasons that Sanders states—namely, that the purpose of the passage is not to prove that the law is wrong but that circumcision is unnecessary for the gentiles. Sanders and Harvey, however, should remember that the content of Torah depended heavily on the perspective of the individual Jew in the first century. Pharisees had an inclusive understanding of the number of ordinances that God required. The chiastic argument of turning the curse into a blessing has more centrality to Paul's argument and experience than Sanders admits. Except for this, Sanders and I clearly come to similar conclusions from very different perspectives. Neither Sanders nor Harvey, however, points up the irony of Paul's previous piety as sharply as I would. Further, neither emphasizes the sociological implications of this decision. Paul is not analyz-

ing Torah in general. He is talking about its use for defining the believing community.

7. See Sifra Kedoshim 8, b. Shabbath 31a, and chapter 3 above.

8. Converts receive the new family name *ben Avraham* in Jewish tradition. The later rabbinic stories of Abraham emphasize that he observed all the commandments (Yoma 28b, Kid. 4.14) in seeming polemic with the Christian view of the Abraham of faith. For the use of Abraham in Christian tradition, see Jeffrey S. Siker, "The Making of Orphans: The Use of Abraham in Early Christian Controversy with Judaism from Paul through Justin Martyr" (Ph.D. diss., Princeton Theological Seminary, 1988), and Bruce Schein, "Our Father Abraham" (Ph.D. diss., Yale University, 1972). See also J. Louis Martyn, "A Law-Observant Mission to Gentiles: The Background of Galatians," *Michigan Quarterly Review* 22 (1983):221–36, repr. in *Scottish Journal of Theology* 38 (1985): 307–24; Halvor Moxnes, *Theology in Conflict: Studies in Paul's Understanding of God in Romans, Supplements to NovT* 7 (Leiden: Brill, 1980), 132–63.

9. See for example A. E. Harvey, *Jesus and the Constraints of History* (Philadelphia: Westminster Press, 1982).

10. Nils A. Dahl, "Widersprueche in der Bibel, ein altes hermeneutisches Problem," *ST* 25 (1971): 1–19, translated and reprinted in *Studies in Paul* (Minneapolis: Augsburg, 1977), 159–77.

11. As Harvey maintains in *Jesus and the Constraints of History,* n. 47.

12. Marcus Barth, *Ephesians* (Garden City, N.Y.: Doubleday, 1977), 246. See Gager, *Origins,* 233. *Nomos* appears to refer to Jewish law in Rom. 7:8, and 2:21–22, with "works of law" nearby in 2:15 and further away in 3:20, 13:9. This is crucial to understanding what Paul was saying to his own generation. In fact, I should like to strengthen Gager's observation about this term.

13. James D. G. Dunn, "Works of the Law and the Curse of the Law (Galatians 3:10–14)," *NTS* 31 (1985): 523–42. He explicitly translates the term *erga nomou* as "service of the law." I think he could have paraphrased it as observance of the ceremonial laws, which is what Dunn actually means. Dunn's translation is justifiable because it is the context of the discussion rather than the word itself that gives this meaning. Paul is talking to a gentile community about the ceremonial requirements for entrance into Judaism and Jewish Christianity, arguing away the gentile doubt that they are necessary for full membership in their new order. Dunn is supported in his fortunate translation by the work of E. Lohmeyer's translation *Dienst des Gesetzes,* in *Probleme paulinischer Theologie* (Stuttgart: Kohlhammer, n.d.), 33–74, 67, and J. B. Tyson, "'Works of Law' in Galatians," *JBL* 92 (1973): 423–31, 424–25.

14. See Dunn, "Works of the Law," 529.

15. E. P. Sanders, *Paul and Palestinian Judaism: A Comparison of Patterns of Religion* (Philadelphia: Fortress Press, 1977), 442f.

16. See John G. Gager, "Some Notes on Paul's Conversion," *NTS* 27 (1981): 697–704, who points out the importance of Paul's conversion for the structure of his thought.

17. See Gager, "Some Notes on Paul's Conversion," and in private correspondence, Paula Fredriksen Landes, "Paul and Augustine: Conversion Narratives, Orthodox Traditions and the Retrospective Self," *JTS* 37 (1986): 3–34;

"Augustine and His Analysts: The Possibility of a Psychohistory," *Soundings* 61 (1978): 206–27; James E. Dittes, "Continuities Between the Life and Thought of Augustine," *JSSR* 5 (1965): 130–40; see also the Symposium on Augustine in *JSSR* 25:1 (1986): 57–115 with papers by Dittes, Gay, Fenn, Teselle, and Kleiver.

18. L. Festinger, H. W. Riecken, and S. Schachter, *When Prophecy Fails: A Social and Psychological Study of a Modern Group that Predicted the Destruction of the World* (New York: Harper and Row, 1956), 28.

19. Hans Huebner, *Law in Paul's Thought* (Edinburgh: T and T Clark, 1984), translated by James C. G. Grieg from the German ed. (Goettingen: Vandenhoek und Ruprecht, 1978), in his introduction, would have had a simpler time, had he understood that *some* Torah is incumbent on gentiles as well, according to rabbinic thought.

20. See *Origins*. The relevant articles of Gaston and Stendahl are cited there.

21. See chapter 7.

22. See chapter 6.

23. See Huebner, *Law in Paul's Thought*, 1, for a succinct discussion of the strength of this statement in Galatians. Like Huebner, Raeisaenen, and Sanders, I try to show that Paul's view changes, but because my understanding of the dialectic differs, I see Paul as speaking about communal groups, not about an abstract analysis of the value of moral action from the point of view of God's plan.

24. See Gaston, *Paul and the Torah; Law*, 18–23; Huebner, *Law in Paul's Thought*, 151–54.

25. A number of passages have been seen by scholars as intimating that the law has been abolished: Rom. 7:1–10, Gal. 2:19, 2 Cor. 3:4–17, and Eph. 2:14–16. There are, however, a number of passages that contradict the assumption: Rom. 7:6, 3:31, 7:22, and 13:8–10. The way to understand the seeming contradiction is to look at the limitations that he defines in each context.

26. See Lloyd Gaston, "Paul and the Torah," in his *Paul and the Torah*, and *Origins*, 233.

27. As a Jew, I would like very much to agree with Stendahl, Gager, and Gaston that Paul never denies that salvation comes from the law, however I cannot do so on the basis of this passage. I would love to find a way to say that Paul recognized the validity of Judaism, therefore so should Christianity. But this is the wrong tack. Paul was not criticizing Judaism but the use of Jewish ritual to define Christian group membership. The strong form of the Stendahl-Gager-Gaston hypothesis is overstated. Paul does not here allow two paths for salvation. Romans is a slightly different case. In Romans he does retreat a bit, but it is a strategic retreat, for the purposes of compromise, not an ideological change. And his retreat is not to allow for two paths to salvation, rather to prevent two differing definitions of what Christianity is, as I show in chapters 5, 7, and 8.

28. See *Opponents*.

29. Sanhedrin 10 and the Babylonian Talmud ad loc. He who denies that the Torah is from heaven has no place in the world to come.

30. There is something extremely strange to Jewish ears about considering sin as a state rather than an action. Paul's concept of sin goes beyond the borders

of this study. The issue of proselyte baptism in Judaism is, however, very cogent. Many scholars have noted the lack of any first-century evidence for proselyte baptism in Judaism. See G. R. Beasley-Murray, *Baptism in the New Testament* (Grand Rapids: Eerdmans, 1962), 18–31, for a review of twentieth-century scholarship on the issue. But this lack of evidence has been overplayed to under-line falsely the uniqueness of the Christian rite. While it is true that no first-century Jewish source mentions baptism in the context of proselytism, it is not necessarily true that baptism did not accompany proselytism. It was a widely practiced rite among Jews. Anyone wishing to join the Jewish band would need to come to terms with it. The rabbis discuss baptism in later centuries as a border to the state of proselyte. It seems that it was necessary to practice the Jewish rite when one took on the rites of Judaism but that its special status only gradually evolved in the first two centuries. To the historian, the importance of baptism in Qumran and Christianity in the first century only points out its necessary impor-tance within the Jewish community, hence its necessity for anyone entering it. The interesting part of its history is its placement in an eschatological framework by Qumran, John the Baptist, and Christianity. Again, Christian evidence helps us understand Jewish history.

31. See introduction and chapter 1 above, also my *Heavenly Ascent* and my *Hellenistic Magic*. See also A.J.M. Widderburn, *Baptism and Resurrection: Stud-ies in Pauline Theology against its Graeco-Roman Background*, WUNT 44 (Tu-bingen: Mohr, 1987).

32. See the experience of ben Zoma and ben Azzai (b. Hag. 14bf). In Jewish mysticism there is a close connection between ascent to heaven and baptism as well.

33. See *Darkness*.

34. *Urban*, 23–25, see also Wayne A. Meeks, "Image of the Androgyne: Some Uses of a Symbol in Early Christianity," *HR* 13 (1974): 165–208; Dennis Ronald MacDonald, *There is No Male and Female: The Fate of a Dominical Saying in Paul and Gnosticism* (Atlanta: Scholars Press, 1987).

35. *Urban*, 155.

36. *Urban*, 87.

37. See my *Rebecca's Children*, 96–116, for more detail.

38. G. Bornkamm, "Baptism," in *Early Christian Experience* (New York: Harper and Row, 1969), 71–86, esp. 76–77; R. Tannehill, *Dying and Rising with Christ* (Berlin: de Gruyter, 1967), 10–12, 21, 32, 38, 81. In Rom. 6:5, Paul insists that resurrection is future; contrast the baptismal formula in Col. 2:12 and Eph. 2:6 that speaks of resurrection as a past—i.e., a baptismal—event.

39. This has been suggested by James A. Sanders, "Torah and Paul," in *God's Christ and His People: Festschrift for N. A. Dahl*, ed. Jacob Jervell and Wayne A. Meeks (Oslo: Universitetsforlaget, 1977), 132–41 and supported forcefully by David Balch, in private correspondence to me. This suggestion cor-relates nicely with the work of Michael Goulder, who, in an unpublished paper supplied by private correspondence, suggests that *to me huper ha gegraptai* (1 Cor. 4:6) means that Paul wishes his opponents not to go beyond the dictates of the written law. Goulder's suggestion in regard to 1 Cor. 4:6 seems inappropriate

to the context but his observations on the diplomatic way by which Paul adjudicates between the Jewish and Christian factions of the community seems exactly right.

40. See *From Jesus to Christ*, 149–176. Also see Michael Wyschogrod, "The Law, Jews, and Gentiles—A Jewish Perspective," *Lutheran Quarterly* 21 (1969): 405–15. Unfortunately, Wyschogrod assumes that Paul remains a Torah-true Pharisee his entire life, which seems quite impossible to me. See chapters 6 and 7.

41. See H. Koester, "The Purpose of the Polemic of a Pauline Fragment," *NTS* 8 (1962): 317–32.

42. See *Transformation*, 180.

43. *Romans 1–8*, 301–57 and Abraham J. Malherbe, "*Me Genoito* in the Diatribe and Paul," *HTR* 73 (1983): 231–40.

44. There are, of course, exceptions. The rabbis appear to have objected to Christianity as having violated monotheism. See my *Two Powers*. But the organized opposition would have been later than Paul.

45. Chapters 6 and 7 address these complex issues as they arise.

46. Nils A. Dahl, "The Purpose of Luke Acts," in *Jesus in the Memory of the Early Church* (Minneapolis: Augsburg, 1976), 87–98; Jacob Jervell, "The Law in Luke-Acts," *Luke and The People of God: A New Look at Luke-Acts* (Minneapolis: Augsburg, 1972), esp. 141–47; Robert Brawley, *Luke-Acts and the Jews: Conflict, Apology, and Conciliation*, SBL Monograph Series (Atlanta: Scholars Press, 1988).

CHAPTER 5. *Paul's New Conversion Community Among the Gentiles*

1. See Wayne A. Meeks, *The Moral World of the First Christians* (Philadelphia: Westminster, 1986), for an extended discussion of the social sources and functions of Pauline morality. An explicitly ethical analysis of Pauline community is undertaken by Sally Barker Purvis, "Problems and Possibilities in Paul's Ethics of Community" (Ph.D. diss., Yale University, 1987).

2. See *Transformation*, 114–19.

3. Judaism, if not all Jews, understood that God's law was to be tempered by mercy, while careful consideration of intention was one of the hallmarks of the rabbinic movement. Paul obviously knew all this and would have agreed with it. But his Corinthian audience is not composed of Jews, rather they are similar to the Galatian community: those Christians who were evangelized into his movement and then have come into contact with a more traditionally Jewish form of Christianity. Because of the contrast between the two communities, they have become perplexed by their anomalous status in lacking full membership in Judaism. Perhaps they have heard from Jews or a more traditionally Jewish form of Christianity, since there would not have been a clear distinction between Jews and Christians at the time.

4. See for example, S. Schulz, "Die Decke des Moses: Untersuchungen zu einer vorpaulinischen Ueberlieferung in II Kor. 3, 7–8," *ZNW* 49 (1958): 1–30, and *Opponents*. See also *Transformation*, 119–65, which is based on Georgi and Schulz's interpretation. Koenig gives an extremely helpful evaluation of their ar-

guments there. On the issue of veiling, see Dennis Ronald MacDonald, *There is No Male and Female: The Fate of a Dominical Saying in Paul and Gnosticism* (Atlanta: Scholars Press, 1987), 65–112, though he scarcely mentions the issue of men being veiled. If I am correct that the primary referent here is the practice of veiling one's face in various parts of the service, as I explain below, Paul's opponents are surely Jewish Christians or Jews (if one can distinguish) rather than gnostics. This is not the place to enter into a detailed consideration of the many fine points of their arguments. For a summary of the entire field of scholarship on the matter, see *Origin*, 96–108.

5. Gen. R. 17 (12a), *Kommentar*, 3:423–6.

6. See Abraham Millgrom, *Jewish Worship* (Philadelphia: JPS, 1971).

7. They, as Georgi pointed out, may have ascribed to Moses a supernatural perfection, as Philo himself wrote. Paul's point is primarily that the Christ is even more divine than Moses, with all the implications attendant on that claim.

8. See Mary Douglas, *Natural Symbols: Explorations in Cosmology*, 2d ed. (London: Barrie and Jenkins, 1973).

9. See *Transformation*, 125. The contrast between Paul's style of argument and mature, nonapocalyptic rabbinic Judaism is striking, for, as we shall see, the rabbis granted salvation to others for their moral actions, with few exceptions, not for assent to explicit Pharisaic customs. In rabbinic Judaism, an angelic figure called the Lord of the World sometimes makes a brief appearance, but the title refers to the good angel Metatron, who is enthroned in heaven, having as Lord of the World the job of singing nature's praise of God. In sectarian Jewish life, the world is hostile, therefore its angelic leader is hostile. In rabbinic Judaism, in spite of the opposition of worldly authorities, the world remains friendly. For more detail, see my "Ruler of this World: Attitudes About Mediator Figures and the Importance of Sociology for Self-definition," in *Jewish and Christian Self-Definition: Volume 2, Aspects of Judaism in the Greco-Roman Period*, ed. E. P. Sanders with A. I. Baumgarten and Alan Mendelson (Philadelphia: Fortress, 1981), 245–68, 403–13, reprinted in *The Other Judaisms of Late Antiquity* (Atlanta: Scholars Press, 1987). This demonization of the secular world is characteristic of a sect with apocalyptic feelings or a pariah status.

10. This involves reading *phoresomen* as a future rather than a jussive, but the context itself makes this clear.

11. See *Transformation*, 147–59. Koenig, in presupposing the analysis of Schulz and Georgi, must account for several differences between the presupposed Jewish Christian polemic and the Pauline response. What Koenig, Schulz, and Georgi attribute to Paul's opponents seems likely to be Paul's own argument. But Koenig's solution to the issue of present and future transformation is ingenious.

12. This is Isaac's translation in *Pseudepigrapha*, 1:89. Charles's translation uses *transform* in place of change.

13. As we have seen in chapter 2 above, when discussing Paul's mystical notion of transformation, Paul uses this puzzling language to express the continuity between believers' present existence and their eternal reward in the same way that the Platonic notion of the soul will express continuity between mortality and immortality in later Christianity. Paul, however, uses *soul* in its strictly

Hebrew sense. He only uses the word thirteen times, making it a rather rare word for Paul. When he uses it, it is with the sense of life or personality. See Kittel, *TDNT*, 9.648.

14. J. A. T. Robinson, *The Body: A Study of Pauline Theology* (London: SCM Press, 1952).

15. *Urban*, 183–192.

16. See Nils A. Dahl, "Wiedersprueche in der Bibel," and "Paul's Letter to the Galatians" (Paper presented at the annual meeting of the Society of Biblical Literature, Chicago, 1973).

17. See my book *Rebecca's Children*, 69–80. See also Yonina Talmon, "Pursuit of the Millennium: The Relationship Between Religions and Social Change," in *Reader in Comparative Religion: An Anthropological Approach*, 2d ed., ed. W. Lessa and E. Vogt (New York: Harper and Row, 1965), 522–37; Bernard Barber, "Acculturation and Messianic Movements," in *Reader in Comparative Religion: An Anthropological Approach*, 3d ed., ed. W. Lessa and E. Vogt (New York: Harper and Row, 1972), 512–16; Ralph Linton, Anthony F. C. Wallace, W. W. Hill, J. S. Slotkin, Cyril S. Welshaw, David Aberle and Clifford Geertz, "Dynamics in Religion," in *Reader*, 3d ed., 496–543; Robert Bellah and E. J. Hobsbawm, *Primitive Rebels: Studies in Archaic Forms of Social Movement in the Nineteenth and Twentieth Centuries* (Manchester: Manchester University Press, 1971); Stephen Sharot, *Messianism, Mysticism, and Magic: A Sociological Analysis of Jewish Religious Movements* (Chapel Hill: University of North Carolina Press, 1982); Peter Worsley, *The Trumpet Shall Sound: A Study of "Cargo" Cults in Melanesia* (London: Macbivvon and Lee, 1957), 225–27; Vittorio Lanternari, *The Religions of the Oppressed: A Study of Modern Messianic Cults*, trans. L. Sergio (New York: Mentor, 1965); Anthony F. C. Wallace, "Revitalization Movements," *American Anthropologist* 58 (1956): 264–81. John G. Gager, *Kingdom and Community: The Social World of Early Christianity* (Englewood Cliffs: Prentice-Hall, 1975); Sheldon Isenberg, "Millennarianism in Greco-Roman Palestine," *Religion* 4 (1974): 32. Also see the proceedings of the interesting colloquium on apocalypticism in Uppsala, 12–17 August 1979, *Apocalypticism in the Mediterranean World and the Near East*, ed. David Hellholm (Tübingen: Mohr, 1983).

18. For the date of the Thessalonian correspondence and its relationship to the letters to Corinth, see *Origin*, 232–33.

19. Meeks, *Moral World of the First Christians*, 126.

20. Wayne A. Meeks, "Social Functions of Apocalyptic Language," *Apocalypticism in the Mediterranean World and the Near East* (Tübingen: Mohr, 1983), 687–705; David Balch, *"Let Wives be Submissive . . .": The Origin, Form and Apologetic Function of the Household Duty Code (Haustafel) in 1 Peter* (Chico: Scholars Press, 1984); Malherbe, *Social Aspects of Christianity*.

21. Meeks, Malherbe, and Balch show that the problem is evidenced only in some places, perhaps in those places where Christianity was evangelizing most successfully. There are also places where Christian converts were not socially exclusive, even when they were religiously exclusive. First Cor. 5:10, 10:27, and 29 seem to presuppose that some Christians were not socially exclusive. Balch reminds me that Barrett has argued (see below) that Christians did not withdraw

into a ghetto. He asks: "Would not Erastus (Rom. 16:23) have participated in civic rites in Corinth?" Possibly he did, though it is not clear exactly how. With the proviso that not every Christian community was apocalyptic—Corinthian and Thessalonian communities seem to differ strongly in this respect—apocalypticism was something that Paul could stress to build commitment. The forces at work in different Christian communities were quite complex, as Paul's varied methods of arguments against his opponents makes clear.

22. For a discussion of Christian apocalypticism and the relevant bibliography, see my *Rebecca's Children*, esp. chap. 4, 96–116.

23. See R. Jewett, *The Shaken Millennium: The Audience and Rhetoric of the Thessalonian Correspondence* (Philadelphia: Fortress, 1987). His reconstruction of the millennial movement depends rather heavily on a similar movement within the Cabirus cult, which cannot be established. But the millennialism of 2 Thessalonians seems unmistakable, regardless of the author or intended audience.

24. See, for example, Joerg Baumgarten, *Paulus und die Apocalyptik* (Neukirchen-Vluyn: Neukirchener Verlag, 1975); Christiaan Beker, *Paul The Apostle: The Triumph of God in Life and Thought* (Philadelphia: Fortress, 1980); and *Paul's Apocalyptic Gospel* (Philadelphia: Fortress, 1982). See Purvis, *Problems and Possibilities in Paul's Ethics of Community* for an excellent discussion of the conflicts and continuities between ethics and apocalypticism.

25. The most succinct study of apocalypticism as centered on mystical knowledge is *Open Heaven*. Rowland's work, in turn, relies on the work of several scholars who had previously seen the relevance of Jewish mysticism to New Testament writings. See Gershom Scholem, *Major Trends in Jewish Mysticism; Merkabah Mysticism, Jewish Gnosticism and Talmudic Tradition* (New York: JTS, 1965). See also *History;* Gilles Quispel, especially in "Hermetism and the New Testament, Especially Paul," *ANRW* II.22 (forthcoming); my *Two Powers;* and Ithamar Gruenwald, *Apocalyptic and Merkabah Mysticism* (Leiden: Brill, 1980).

26. Meeks, "Social Functions of Apocalyptic Language."

27. *Origin*, 236–37.

28. See J. Gnilka, "2 Cor. 6:14–7:1 in the Light of the Qumran Texts and The Testaments of the Twelve Patriarchs," reprint and translation in *Paul and Qumran*, ed. J. Murphy O'Connor (Chicago: Priory Press, 1968), 46–68; J. A. Fitzmyer, "Qumran and the Interpolated Paragraph in 2 Cor. 6:14--7:1," *CBQ* 23 (1961): 271–80. N. A. Dahl, "A Fragment and its Context: 2 Corinthians 6:14–7:1," in *Studies in Paul: Theology for the Early Christian Mission* (Minneapolis: Augsburg, 1977), suggests that Jub. 1.15–26, 2.19–22, 22.14–24, 30.11, 33.11–20 may be even closer parallels than Qumran; David Rensberger, "2 Corinthians 6:14–7:1—A Fresh Examination," *Studia Biblica et Theologica* 82 (1978): 25–49; N. A. Dahl, "Der Epheserbrief und der vorlorene erste Brief des Paulus an die Korinther," in *Abraham unser Vater, Festschrift fuer Otto Michel* (Leiden: Brill, 1963), 65–77.

29. See Dahl, "Der Epheserbrief," 65–77.

30. *Paul*, 84, 113.

31. See Michael Newton, *The Concept of Purity at Qumran and in the Letters of Paul* (Cambridge: Cambridge University Press, 1985).

32. Newton, *Concept of Purity,* 86–87.

33. Newton, *Concept of Purity,* 60–61: This priestly avocation would contrast with Paul's previous life as a Pharisee, where he was to make the Torah available without charge.

34. Newton, *Concept of Purity,* 70–71.

35. See Elisabeth Schuessler-Fiorenza, "'Neither Male Nor Female': *Galatians* 3:28—Alternative Vision and Pauline Modification," in *In Memory of Her: A Feminist Theological Reconstruction of Christian Origins* (New York: Crossroads, 1983), 205–41; Robin Scroggs, "Paul and the Eschatological Woman," *JAAR* 40 (1972): 283–303; Wayne A. Meeks, "The Image of the Androgyne: Some Uses of a Symbol in Earliest Christianity," HR 13 (1974): 165–208; Robert Jewett, "The Sexual Liberation of the Apostle Paul," *JAAR Supplements* 47, no. 1 (1979): 55–87; S. B. Clark, *Man and Woman in Christ: An Examination of the Roles of Men and Women in Light of Scriptures and the Social Sciences* (Ann Arbor: Servant Books, 1980); Krister Stendahl, *The Bible and the Role of Women* (Philadelphia: Fortress, 1966); Elaine Pagels, *Adam, Eve, and the Serpent* (New York: Random House, 1988). For an exciting new interpretation of Philemon, see Sara C. Winter "Paul's Letter to Philemon," *NTS* 33 (1987) 1–15.

36. Victor Turner, *The Ritual Process: Structure and Anti-Structure* (Ithaca: Cornell University Press, 1969). See *Urban,* 74–111.

37. Douglas, *Natural Symbols.*

38. See Sally Barker Purvis, "Problems and Possibilities in Paul's Ethics of Community" (Ph.D. diss, Yale University, 1987).

39. See Dennis Smith, "Social Obligations in the Context of Communal Meals: A Study of the Christian Meal in 1 Corinthians in Comparison with Graeco-Roman Communal Meals" (Th.D. diss., Harvard University, 1980) and Peter Gooch, "Food and the Limits of Community: 1 Corinthians 8 to 10" (Ph.D. diss., University of Toronto, 1988). See also Baruch Bokser, *The Origins of the Seder* (Berkeley: University of California Press, 1984). Bokser makes the point that the rabbis' liturgy of the seder was very different than the kinds of ribaldry that went on at Greek dinner parties. This is true, but when one notes the appropriation of the formal characteristics of Greek dining in the seder, one must conclude that the influence was present as well. By cleansing it of idolatry and ribaldry, the rabbis turned a secular, and from their perspective, disreputable practice into a liturgical form. This would correspond to a deeper blending of Hellenistic and Jewish custom than is evident in the earlier Hellenistic period. In *Rebecca's Children,* I distinguish between primary Hellenization, in which names and styles are learned in the earliest cultural contacts, and a more significant, secondary Hellenization, which often is ostensibly a rejection of Hellenistic life but is actually in a deeper way an appropriation of Hellenistic cultural forms reinterpreted for Jewish use.

40. "Anamnesis: Memory and Commemoration in Early Christianity," *Jesus in the Memory of the Early Church: Essays by Nils Alstrup Dahl* (Minneapolis: Augsburg, 1976).

41. *Urban,* 158. Another thought, which is relevant below, is that these remembrances of Jesus incorporated in the meal could have been easily confused by Jews with pagan worship of the dead, which was forbidden in Jewish law. See chapter 7 below.

42. See the recent article by Charles H. Cosgrove, "Justification in Paul: A Linguistic and Theological Reflection," *JBL* 106, no. 4 (1987): 653–70, for a summary discussion and some interesting suggestions.

43. For an interesting discussion about the various possibilities inherent in Paul's language, see *From Jesus to Christ*.

44. Fitzmyer, *The Dead Sea Scrolls and the New Testament* (Missoula: Scholars Press, 1975).

45. See Nils A. Dahl, "The Doctrine of Justification: Its Social Function and Implications," in *Studies in Paul: Theology for the Early Christian Mission* (Minneapolis: Augsburg, 1977), 95–120, originally appearing in the *Norsk teologisk tidsskrift* 65 (1964). See also E. P. Sanders, *Paul and Palestinian Judaism: A Comparison of Patterns of Religion* (Philadelphia: Fortress, 1977), 238–328, 523–42.

46. Gerd Theissen, *Psychological Aspects of Pauline Theology* (Philadelphia: Fortress, 1983) 81–107.

47. For instance see G. E. W. Scobie, "Types of Religious Conversion," *Journal of Behavioral Science* 1 (1973): 265–71, and the discussion in chapter 4 above.

48. R. F. Paloutzian, "Purpose in Life and Value Changes Following Conversion," *Journal of Personality and Social Psychology* 41 (1981), 1153–60.

49. See Dahl, "The Doctrine of Justification," 100; also D. Flusser, "The Dead Sea Sect and Pre-Pauline Christianity," *Scripta Hierosolymitana* 4 (1958): 215–66.

50. Dahl, "The Doctrine of Justification," 104–6.

51. See chapter 3 above.

52. See, for example, the perceptive work of Johannes Munck, *Paul and the Salvation of Mankind* (Richmond: John Knox, 1959).

53. Steven M. Tipton, *Getting Saved from the Sixties: Moral Meaning in Conversion and Cultural Change* (Berkeley: University of California Press, 1982), 232–33.

CHAPTER 6. *Circumcision and the Noahide Laws*

1. See Ken Pomykala (Unpublished graduate paper on the Apostolic decree and the Jerusalem conference, Claremont).

2. See *From Jesus to Christ*.

3. J. Paul Sampley, *Pauline Partnership in Christ: Christian Community and Commitment in Light of Roman Law* (Philadelphia: Fortress, 1980).

4. An excellent summary of the many possible ways of rectifying the seeming contradictions between Paul's own writing and the conference is to be found in *Origin*, 246–70. On the issue of the council in relationship to Galatians 2, Hurd says, "To quote this passage is to open Pandora's box, for a library could be filled with what has been written concerning this account. To deal with the problems of Galatians in any systematic way would require another book" (266). After such a warning, I have tried to stay away from any unnecessary positive conclusion about the relationship between the conference and Paul's Galatians opinions. A number of different solutions to the problem, including Hurd's own very persuasive one,

would harmonize with my analysis. Since I do not have to settle the issue, I do not attempt it.

5. See *Origin*, 273–96.

6. For a more detailed proposal on the relationship between the two documents see James D. G. Dunn, "The Incident at Antioch (Gal. 2:11–18)," *JSNT* 18 (1983): 3–57; "The Relationship Between Paul and Jerusalem According to Galatians 1 and 2," *NTS* 28 (1982): 461–78. See also Peter Richardson, *Israel in the Apostolic Church* (Cambridge: Cambridge University Press, 1969), 84–97.

7. Mishnah Sanhedrin 10, Tosefta Sanhedrin 13.2, Sanhedrin 105a, Sifra 86b, b. Baba Kamma 38a. But these discussions are certainly not *ipsissima verba* of the rabbis and may not be historically accurate in any way. So the issue must be tested against the Christian record. See *Rebecca's Children*, 166–8.

8. See Peter Richardson, *Israel in the Apostolic Church* (Cambridge: Cambridge University Press, 1969), 70–159, for a discussion of the various possibilities, as well as the argument that Galatians can be earlier than the conference.

9. See David Novak, *The Image of the Non-Jew in Judaism: An Historical and Constructive Study of the Noahide Laws* (Toronto: Edwin Mellen Press, 1983), 3–35. Novak discounts the witness of Jubilees. But his main emphasis is on the later discussion of these rules in talmudic and post-talmudic times, which is more convincing.

10. Notice that like Paul and other apocalyptic groups especially, but in line with Judaism generally, pollution can be used as a metaphor for unrighteousness.

11. So translates O. S. Wintermute in *Pseudepigrapha*, 2: 87.

12. See, for example, H. Waitz, "Das Problem des sog. Aposteldecrets," *ZKG* (1936): 227.

13. Traces of the decree appear in Rev. 2:14, 20, 24, *Didache* 6.3, Justin, *Dial.* 34–35, Tertullian, *Apol.*, Eusebius, *H. E.* 5.1.26 in a letter dated 177 C.E. from Lyons, Minucius Felix, *Octavius* 30, Sibylline Oracles 2.93, *Pseudo-Clementine Homily* 7.8.1.

14. See *Origin*, 250–53, for the basic bibliography.

15. See *Rebecca's Children*, 165–181, for a fuller discussion.

16. Here the work of David Novack, *The Image of the Non-Jew in Judaism*, is right on the mark. But Christian scholarship has preceded him. See Dunn, Wilson, Hurd, and Richardson, as cited above, for the history of scholarship on this point.

17. See Steven Wilson, *The Gentiles and the Gentile Mission* (Cambridge: Cambridge University Press, 1974). My interpretation softens Wilson's arguments a bit.

18. See the helpful article of Kirsopp Lake, "The Apostolic Council of Jerusalem," and "Paul's Controversies," in *The Beginnings of Christianity: The Acts of the Apostles,* vol. 5 of *Additional Notes* (Grand Rapids: Baker, 1966), 195–211 and 212–23.

19. *Law*, 36, 38.

20. *Law*, 20.

21. Pace *Law*, 21. Raeisaenen and some Christian exegetes are misled by this statement into thinking that gentiles are subject to the Torah but can never adequately practice it (see *Law*, 26). This is an uncharitable reading of rabbinic (and other Jewish) literature.

22. Of course, why Paul should here maintain that justification is by works rather than faith, even to condemn his opponents, is a long story. See chapter 8 below for more on this passage. To understand this passage one has to give up the theological principle that Paul taught an end to righteousness based on works.

23. See Gaston's discussion of "Paul and the Law in Galatians Two and Three," in *Anti-Judaism in Early Christianity*, ed. G. Peter Richardson (Waterloo, Ont.: Wilfred Laurier University Press, 1986) and *Origins*, 233. Gaston's translation of *parabatēn* as apostate is tendentious, even though pretty much the same sense can be rendered from the passage by translating it simply as transgressor.

24. See *From Jesus to Christ*, 161–76.

25. See *Jews and God-fearers*, 85, which agrees with my contention that the principate's laws tended to make God-fearing rather than conversion a more attractive choice. Once the empire became Christian, some pagans may have chosen to Judaize rather than subject themselves to Christianity.

26. See *Urban*, 116.

27. See *Antioch* for more detail on the variety of Christian opinions with respect to Torah.

28. In suggesting that Paul purposely accommodated his thinking, I am in general agreement with Hans Huebner, *Law in Paul's Thought* (Edinburgh: T. and T. Clark, 1984), 62–65. Whereas Huebner states that James must have caused him to reconsider (63), I am less confident of the circumstances. *Origins* also implies that it was the church conference that made Paul reconsider his actions and try to moderate the practice of the churches he founded, using the Corinthian correspondence as demonstration. All we know for sure is that *if* Luke is correct, Paul must have sought a more conciliatory position. The circumstances might be different from Luke's portrayal.

29. As to the problems and chronology of the councils, it is not necessary to solve that vexed issue. But see Kirsopp Lake, "Paul's Controversies," 195–222 for the idea that Acts actually unwittingly includes two different accounts of the same conference, told from different perspectives. See Paul Achtemeier, *The Quest for Unity in the New Testament Church* (Philadelphia: Fortress, 1987).

30. See Robin Scroggs, "Paul and the Eschatological Woman," 293; *In Memory of Her: A Feminist Theological Reconstruction of Christian Origins* (New York: Crossroads, 1983), 205–41.

31. This is discussed in more detail in chapter 7 below.

32. Terence Callan, "Pauline Midrash: The Exegetical Background of Gal. 3:19b," *JBL* 99 (1980): 549–67.

33. U. Wilckens, *Rechtfertigung als Freiheit: Paulusstudien* (Neukirchen: 1974). I agree.

34. It has therefore been written about many times, recently by my colleague Shaye J. D. Cohen. His interpretation is that Timothy was a gentile. Since Paul was both converting Timothy to Christianity and circumcising him, he was thus accepting the opposition's view of conversion. This argument is governed by the contemporary Jewish issue of the status of children in mixed marriages. Cohen is using the New Testament as a historical source to set up standards for contemporary Conservative Judaism, which was discussing the issue of the patrilinal principle in Judaism when he wrote. For Cohen, the events are not only historically important

but actual evidence for setting contemporary Jewish practice. In the Reform movement and the Orthodox movement, there are fewer problems with the issue of the offspring of intermarriages because the contemporary Reform movement's methods of defining personal status are more liberal, while Orthodox arguments allow no new principles. The Reform movement accepts rabbinic halakha only as one guide among many for individual conscience in contemporary ethical decisions, while the Orthodox movement has invalidated any change in the halakha at all. The Conservative movement takes an intermediate position, judging the validity of a tradition on the basis of antiquity. Thus, the later Cohen can date the halakhic definition of a Jew as the child of a Jewish mother, the more lattitude available to Conservative Judaism's practice. This is an outcome that I personally applaud. For Cohen the story becomes a precedent for contemporary Jewish practice, because it proves that the well-established definition of a Jew as the offspring of a Jewish mother did not yet exist, thus the principle becomes something that Conservative Judaism can discard. This is a decision that Cohen may have desired because it has uniquely liberalizing implications for the definition of a Jew in the Conservative movement today. (In the meantime, Conservative Judaism has reached the conclusion that only the matrilineal principle is valid in Judaism, largely to assuage those Conservative Jews who were offended by the decision to allow women in the rabbinate.) Unfortunately, I have to show that the New Testament text will not easily allow this interpretation.

35. In the book he wrote together with John P. Meier (*Antioch*, 5).

CHAPTER 7. *Romans 7 and Jewish Dietary Laws*

1. For a review of the literature on this problem see Anders Nygren, *Commentary on Romans* (Philadelphia: Fortress, 1949), 284–85. Also see O. Kuss, *Der Roemerbrief*, 2d ed. (Regensburg: F. Pustet, 1963), 479.

2. E.g., 1QH 3.23ff, 4.29ff. See W. Wrede, *Paulus*, reissued in *Das Paulusbild*, ed. R. Rengstorf (Darmstadt: Wissenschaftliche Buchsgesellschaft, 1907), 1–97; W. G. Kuemmel, *Roemer 7 und die Bekehrung des Paulus* (Leipzig: Hinrichs, 1929); and especially O. Michel, *Roemerbrief*, 14th ed. Meyer Commentary (Goettingen: Vandenhoeck und Ruprecht, 1977), ad loc.

3. "I" is found 845 times in the letters of Paul and 180 times in Romans. "We" is found 637 times in the Letters of Paul and 141 in Romans. E. Stauffer, "Ego," TDNT, 2:356–62, and bibliography there. See especially E. Dobschuetz, "Wir und Ich bei Paulus," *Zeitschrift fuer systematische Theologie* 10 (1932): 251–77, and J. M. E. Cruvellier, *L'exégèse de Romains 7 et le mouvement de Keswick* (Amsterdam: Academisch Proefschrift, Universiteit te Amsterdam, 1961), 131.

4. Erhard S. Gerstenberger, "Jeremiah's Complaints: Observations on Jer. 15:10–21," *JBL* 82 (1963): 393–408.

5. Other recent studies agreeing with me are: J. Christiaan Beker, *Paul the Apostle: The Triumph of God in Life and Thought* (Philadelphia: Fortress, 1980), 236–43, although Beker sees Paul as evincing a heretofore secret dissatisfaction with the law; also Paul Meyer, "Romans 10:4 and the End of the Law," in *The Divine Helmsman* (New York: Ktav, 1980), 67, although Meyer sees an existential reason behind the rejection of righteousness in the law. See *Paul*, 76–77, 88–91.

6. W. D. Davies, *Paul and Rabbinic Judaism* (London: S.P.C.K., 1948), 321.

7. See, for example, E. Gaugler, *Der Brief an die Roemer* (Zurich: Zwingli-Verlag, 1945), 233; F. J. Leenhardt, *L'épitre de St. Paul aux Romains* (Paris: Delachaux et Niestle, 1957), 106; P. Althaus, *Der Brief an die Roemer* (Goettingen: Die Neue Testament Deutsche 6, 1953), 65, 221; Francis Watson, *Paul, Judaism and the Gentiles: A Sociological Approach* (Cambridge: Cambridge University Press, 1986), 151–58. *Romans 1–8,* 375–412, assembles a very complete list of past commentators and favors this hypothesis but maintains also that Paul speaks with a personal "I."

8. This suggestion has been often made. See, for example, O. Michel, *Roemerbrief* (see n. 2 above).

9. Claude G. Montefiore, *Judaism and St. Paul* (London: Goschen, 1914). See also James W. Parkes, *Judaism and Christianity* (Chicago: University of Chicago Press, 1948); *Jesus, Paul, and the Jews* (London: SCM Press, 1936). Hyam Maccoby, *The Mythmaker: Paul and the Invention of Christianity,* uses the Ebionite tradition about Paul and the pseudo-Clementine correspondence to suggest that Paul never was a Pharisee. This suggestion, which uses late, unreliable, and wildly biased documents as historical data, while propounding that everything Paul himself said is a lie, seems to grow naturally out of the author's too obvious polemical and apologetic motives.

10. *Conscience.* While I would maintain that understanding the psychological concomitants of Paul's conversion is crucial to understanding Paul, Stendahl's observations about psychoanalytic and existential positions are well founded. Other aspects of contemporary psychology are far more helpful than psychoanalysis in understanding Paul. See my *Rebecca's Children,* 96–116.

11. According to *Romans 1–8,* 383, this position is also maintained by Maillot, C. L. Mitton, "Romans 7 Reconsidered," *Expository Times* 65 (1953–54): 78–81, 99–103, 132–35, and R. Y. K. Fung, "The Impotence of the Laws: Towards a Fresh Understanding of Romans 7:14–25," in *Scripture, Tradition and Interpretation: Festschrift for E. F. Harrison,* ed. W. W. Gasque and W. S. La Sor (Grand Rapids: Eerdmans, 1978), 34–48. Dunn's critique that this would imply a second, unattested conversion is not convincing, because Paul himself admits to alternation between observance and nonobservance in 1 Cor. 9:20–22. It is certainly conceivable for a convert to feel anguish over some aspects of behavior after conversion, trying to work out the proper consequences of that conversion.

12. Furthermore, as Hurd's *Origin* has pointed out so clearly, the entire passage must be part of one letter, not several letter fragments. But are the opponents Jews or Jewish Christians or both?

13. The opponents of Paul and his gentile Christians in Corinth are also likely to be Jewish Christians rather than Jews because, as Peter Richardson has pointed out, there is little explicitly "Anti-Judaistic" language in 1 Corinthians, especially by comparison with Galatians, for instance. See "On the Absence of 'Anti-Judaism' in 1 Corinthians," in *Anti-Judaism in Early Christianity* (Waterloo: Wilfred Laurier University Press, 1986), 1:59–74. Also see H. Koester, "The Purpose of the Polemic of a Pauline Fragment," *NTS* 8 (1962): 317–32.

14. Such is the case even today when Jews eat with knowledgeable New Testament scholars.

15. See the new discussion of food laws in regard to Jesus in E. P. Sanders, *Jesus and Judaism* (Philadelphia: Fortress Press, 1985), 175–221.

16. For a review of pagan dinner customs see Dennis Smith, "Table Fellowship as a Literary Motif in the Gospel of Luke," *JBL* 106 (1987), 613–38; and "Social Obligation in the Context of Communal Meals: A Study of the Christian Meal in 1 Corinthians in Comparison with Graeco-Roman Communal Meals" (Th.D. diss., Harvard University, 1980); Peter Gooch, "Food and the Limits of Community: 1 Corinthians 8 to 10" (Ph.D. diss., University of Toronto, 1988). Also see Werner Jaeger, *Paedeia: The Ideals of Greek Culture,* 3 vols. (New York: Oxford University Press, 1939–44), 2:174–97. The suggestion that the rabbis may have been bothered by the Lord's Supper itself is my own.

17. Paul Minear, *The Obedience of Faith: The Purposes of Paul in the Epistle to the Romans* (Napierville, Ill.: Alec Allenson, 1971), has suggested the relevance of these passages to Jewish food laws, but he does not sufficiently recognize that the basic issue is the rules about idolatry. Gerd Theissen, "The Strong and the Weak in Corinth," in *The Social Setting of Pauline Christianity: Essays on Corinth* (Philadelphia: Fortress Press, 1982), translated by John Bowden from the 1974 German article, has made very interesting suggestions about the gentile sociological situation in Corinth and has specially noted the generality of Paul's statements, but he has failed to unpack the basic Jewish custom underlying the controversies at Corinth and Rome.

18. See *Antioch* for a discussion of the broad spectrum of Christian opinion on Jewish law. For an appealing reconstruction of the Antioch incident see James D. G. Dunn, "The Incident At Antioch (Gal. 2:11–18)," *JSNT* 18 (1983): 3–57, esp. 36f. See also the following article "A Response to James D. G. Dunn," 58–67. *Origin,* 240–70, also makes significant points in this regard. It may be, as Dunn says, that the conflict is caused by Paul's agreement to abide by the Apostolic Decree, which is John Hurd's opinion as well.

19. H. Lietzmann, *The Beginnings of the Christian Church* (London: Lutterworth, 1937), 199. And Hurd's *Origin* maintains that the controversy is caused precisely by Paul's acquiescence to the decree.

20. See the extremely helpful article C. K. Barrett, "Things Sacrificed to Idols," *Essays on Paul* (Philadelphia: Westminster, 1982), 40–59. See also Justin, *Dialogue* 34; Ireneus, *Against Heresies* 1.6.3; Clement, *Stromata* 4.15; Novatian, *On Jewish Meats* 7.

21. It is an oath rather than a vow, for it is a promise assumed by the person. See Mishnah Shavuoth 3 and 4. The rabbinic desire to limit oaths and vows to those that can be taken seriously has been discussed by Saul Lieberman, "Oaths and Vows (in Ordinary Speech)," *Greek in Jewish Palestine: Studies in the Life and Manners of Jewish Palestine in the II–IV Centuries C.E.* (New York: Feldheim, 1965), 115–43.

22. *Origin,* 273–96.

23. There are many difficulties with this passage. Cutting one's hair so far from Jerusalem presents a kind of problem, since there is no other example of the ritual being performed outside of Jerusalem. As stated above, the grammar of the passage is so loose as to allow the subject of the shearing to be Aquila rather than Paul. This seems rather farfetched given the subsequent narration, so, for the sake

of argument, Paul's participation (which is the usual interpretation) is assumed. But, as above, Acts' witness is used as support but nothing definitive is concluded from Acts' narrative itself. See Ernst Haenchen, *Die Apostelgeschichte* (Goettingen: 1955), 483 and Robert Jewett, *A Chronology of Paul's Life* (Philadelphia: Fortress, 1979), 18.

24. See especially chap. 1 of Mishnah Nazir and David Weiss-Halivni, "On the Supposed Anti-Asceticism or Anti-Naziritism of Simon the Just," *JQR* 58 (1968): 243–52.

25. See *Origin*. For a different but related interpretation of this passage, see Lloyd Gaston, "Paul and the Law in Galatians Two and Three," in *Anti-Judaism in Early Christianity,* ed. P. Richardson, and *Origins,* 233.

26. Ironically, Paul appears to have subtly changed his earlier dualism, in which he was willing to equate law in its soteriological function with death, though he sometimes affirms its value as a standard of righteousness even for Christians (see the puzzling passages 1 Cor. 7:19, Rom. 13:9).

27. See *Paul,* 70–80, for the idea that Paul is pulling back from his earlier positions. See also *Origin*.

28. The relationship between idolatry and desire is mentioned by Wendell Lee Willis, *Idol Meat in Corinth: The Pauline Argument in 1 Corinthians 8 and 10* (Chicago: Scholars Press, 1985), 144–53, though we obviously differ significantly on other issues.

29. See Lawrence Patrick Jones, "Religious Responses to Slavery in the Second Century CE: A Case Study in 'Gnosticism'" (Ph.D. diss., Columbia University, 1988). Although the purpose of surveying Roman slavery is to make some astute observations about the appeal and message of Gnosticism, Jones's study of slavery also points up Paul's metaphor of adoption (see esp. 1–77).

30. He addresses them specifically in Rom. 1:5f, 1:13, 11:13, 15:15, and probably also in 9:3f, 10:1f, 11:23, 28.

31. See Bartsch, "Die historische Situation des Roemerbriefes," *Communio Viatorum* 8 (1965): 200; R. Fuller, *A Critical Introduction to the New Testament* (Naperville, Ill.: Alec Allenson, 1966), 53; and Willi Marxsen, *Introduction to the New Testament: An Approach to its Problems* (Oxford: Blackwell, 1968), 103. See *Transformation,* 161 ff.

CHAPTER 8. *The Salvation of Israel*

1. Robert L. Wilken, *John Crysostom and the Jews* (Berkeley: University of California Press, 1983).

2. See Hans Huebner, *Law in Paul's Thought* (Edinburgh: T. and T. Clark, 1984), 66.

3. See John T. Fitzgerald, *Cracks in an Earthen Vessel: An Examination of the Catalogues of Hardships in the Corinthian Correspondence,* SBL Dissertation Series (Atlanta: Scholars Press, 1988).

4. See also Gal. 2:15–21, and p. 201 above.

5. There are, of course, many detailed discussions of this and the following passages in Romans. None of them in my mind surpasses the new commentary *Romans 1–8* as a resource for scholarship. Though I demur from some of its

conclusions, the commentary is up-to-date and fairly represents the positions of the other major scholars.

6. *Paul,* 123.

7. See *Romans 1–8,* 89.

8. See, for instance, Samuel Sandmel, *The Genius of Paul* (New York: Farrar, Straus and Cudahy, 1958); Samuel Belkin, *Philo and the Oral Law* (Cambridge: Harvard University Press, 1940); and C. H. Dodd, *The Bible and the Greeks* (London: Hodder and Stoughton, 1935), 33–34. Against this position see Alan F. Segal, "Torah and *Nomos* in Recent Scholarly Discussion," *SR* 13:1 (1984): 19–27 and Stephen Westerholm, "*Torah, Nomos,* and Law: A Question of Meaning," *Studies in Religion/Sciences Religieuses* 15, no. 3 (1986): 327.

9. See, for instance, Mary Lefkowitz, *Women in Greek Myth* (London: Duckworth, 1986), 69, quoting and translating F. H. Sandbach, *Menandri Reliquiae Selectae* (Oxford: 1972), 328–30 or *WLGR* 38: "There is a covenant (*nomos*) between man and wife."

10. See Nils A. Dahl, *Das Volk Gottes: Eine Untersuchung zum Kirchenbewusstsein des Urchristentums* (Darmstadt: wissenschaftliche Buchgesellschaft, 1963), reprint of the 1947 Oslo edition, and Peter Richardson, *Israel in the Apostolic Church* (Cambridge: Cambridge University Press, 1969).

11. *Paul,* 173–76.

12. Peter Richardson, *Israel in the Apostolic Church* (Cambridge: Cambridge University Press, 1969), 74–84, versus Dahl, *Das Volk Gottes,* 212.

13. See from another perspective *Paul,* 171–78. See also Francis Watson, *Paul, Judaism, and the Gentiles: A Sociological Approach* (Cambridge: Cambridge University Press, 1986), 38–48, who feels that Paul's actions and thought changed Christianity from a reform movement to a sect. I admire this work a great deal, especially for its distinction between the theological and social approaches to Paul. But for me Paul's writing reflects that the change has occurred in Christianity before Paul and that Paul fought unsuccessfully against it, although he would not give up his prior commitment to the validity of the gentile movement. Watson has certainly outlined a provocative analysis of the issues from a sociological perspective.

14. Elaine Pagels, *The Gnostic Paul* (Philadelphia: Fortress, 1975); also Henry Green, "Power and Knowledge: A Study of the Social Development of Early Christianity" (Paper presented to AAR/SBL Southeast Regional Meeting in Williamsburg, Virginia, 23 March 1984).

15. For both sides of this question see *The Writings of St. Paul,* ed. Wayne A. Meeks (New York: W. W. Norton, 1972), pt. 3, sec. 5, 277–319.

16. See *Urban,* 52; Gerd Theissen, "Soziale Integration und sakramentales Handeln: Eine Analyse von 1 Cor. XI 17–34," *NovT* 24 (1979): 290–317; Abraham J. Malherbe, *Social Aspects of Early Christianity* (Baton Rouge: Louisiana State University Press, 1977), 29–59.

17. See Ramsey MacMullen, *Christianizing the Roman Empire A. D. 100–400* (New Haven: Yale University Press, 1984).

18. See my *Two Powers.*

19. See *One God.*

20. See *Rebecca's Children,* chap. 8, 171–81.

21. See my *Two Powers; Name.*

22. See, for instance, Donald Juel, *Luke-Acts: The Promise of History* (Atlanta: John Knox Press, 1983), 103–5. See also Jacob Jervell, *Luke and the People of God: A New Look at Luke-Acts* (Minneapolis: Augsburg, 1972). Also see Robert Brawley, *Luke-Acts and the Jews: Conflict, Apology, and Conciliation,* SBL Monograph Series (Atlanta: Scholars Press, 1988).

23. One of the only scholars to point this out is Nils A. Dahl, "The Future of Israel," *Studies in Paul: Theology for the Early Christian Mission* (Minneapolis: Augsburg, 1977), who has influenced my thought significantly in this section.

24. Dahl, "Future of Israel," 142–143.

25. Here again Paul's witness shows that rabbinic traditions, in this case, the method of reconciling Scripture, can be traced to the first century, when Jewish literature will not allow us to make such confident guesses about dates.

26. See Gager, Stendahl, Gaston.

APPENDIX. *Paul's Conversion: Psychological Study*

1. *Varieties of Religious Experience* (New York: Longmans, Green, 1902).

2. *Adolescence,* 2 vols. (New York: Appleton, 1904).

3. *A Psychological Study of Religion* (New York: Macmillan, 1912).

4. *The Psychology of Religion* (New York: Scribner's, 1899).

5. "Conversion," *Pastoral Psychology* 10 (1959): 51–56, and *The Psychology of Religion* (New York: Abingdon, 1959). For more detail, see Bernard Spilka, Ralph W. Hood, Jr. and Richard L. Gorsuch, *The Psychology of Religion: An Empirical Approach* (Englewood Cliffs: Prentice-Hall, 1985), esp. 203.

6. *The Spiritual Life* (New York: Eaton and Mains, 1900).

7. *The Psychology of Religious Awakening* (New York: MacMillan, 1929).

8. G. E. W. Scobie, "Types of Christian Conversion," *Journal of Behavioral Science* 1 (1973): 265–271.

9. J. W. Drakeford, *Psychology in Search of a Soul* (Nashville: Broadman, 1964). R. C. Ferm, *The Psychology of Christian Conversion* (Old Tappan, N.J.: Fleming H. Revell, 1959).

10. *Religion in America 1979–1980* (Princeton, N.J.: Princeton Religion Research Center, 1979).

11. *The Spiritual Life,* 152.

12. R. A. Strauss, "Religious Conversion as a Personal and Collective Accomplishment," *Sociological Analysis* 40 (1979): 158–65.

13. *The Psychology of Religious Experience* (Boston: Houghton Mifflin, 1910).

14. *The Psychology of Religion* (Chicago: University of Chicago Press, 1916).

15. F. J. Roberts "Some Psychological Factors in Religious Conversion," *British Journal of Social and Clinical Psychology* 4 (1965): 185–87.

16. See, for example, W. P. Wilson, "Mental Health Benefits of Religious Conversion," *Diseases of the Nervous System* 33 (1972): 382–86.

17. J. Lofland and R. Stark, "Becoming a World-Saver: A Theory of Conversion to a Deviant Perspective," *American Sociological Review* 30 (1965): 864.

18. R. F. Paloutzian, "Purpose in Life and Value Changes Following Conversion," *Journal of Personality and Social Psychology* 41 (1981): 1153–60.

19. Lofland and Stark, "Becoming a World-Saver," 862–74; J. Lofland, *Doomsday Cult* (Englewood Cliffs: Prentice-Hall, 1966); N. Skonoud, "Conversion Motifs," *JSSR* 20 (1981): 373–85. Most recently, studies of religious defection and disaffiliation have begun to appear in journals. See, for example, E. Burke Rochford, Jr., "Factionalism, Group Defection, and Schism in the Hare Krishna Movement," Howard M. Barr and Stan L. Albrecht, "Strangers Once More: Patterns of Disaffiliation from Mormonism," C. Kirk Hadaway, "Identifying American Apostates: A Cluster Analysis," Joseph B. Tamney, Shawn Powell, and Stephen Johnson, "Innovation Theory and Religious Nones," all in *JSSR* 28 (1989), 162–79, 180–200, 201–15, 216–29.

20. H. A. Baer, "The Levites of Utah," *RRR* 19 (1978): 279–84.

21. J. Seggar and P. Kunz, "Conversion: Evaluation of a Step-like Process for Problemsolving," *RRR* 13 (1972): 178–84.

22. R. J. Lifton, *Thought Reform and the Psychology of Totalism* (New York: Norton, 1961); E. Schein, *Coercive Persuasion* (New York: Norton, 1971); W. Sargant, *Battle for the Mind* (New York: Harper and Row, 1959).

23. Flo Conway and Jim Siegelman, *Snapping: America's Epidemic of Sudden Personality Change* (Philadelphia: J. B. Lippincott, 1978). Also *Holy Terror: The Fundamentalist War on America's Freedoms in Religion, Politics and Our Private Lives* (New York: Delta, 1982).

24. See *Emotion, Obesity, and Crime* (New York: Academic Press, 1971).

25. See also Stanley Schachter and Jerome Singer, "Cognitive, Social and Psychological Determinants of Emotional States," *Psychological Review* 69 (1969): 379–99; Walter B. Cannon, *Bodily Changes in Pain, Hunger, Fear and Rage,* 2d ed. (New York: Appleton, 1929); G. Maranon, "Contribution à l'étude de l'action émotive de l'adrenaline," *Revue française de l'endrochronologie* 2 (1924): 301–25. For a review of the relevance of attribution theory to the study of conversion and other religious phenomena, see Wayne Proudfoot and Phillip Shaver, "Attribution Theory and the Psychology of Religion," *JSSR* 14, no. 4 (1975): 317–30; also Wayne Proudfoot, "Religious Experience, Emotion and Belief," *HTR* 70 (1977): 343–67; more recently, Wayne Proudfoot, *Religious Experience* (Berkeley: University of California Press, 1985).

26. The best example of this thinking comes again from Sargant who says that religious conversion is the result of an (ab)reaction in which the mind is simply overloaded with emotion. This use of abreaction is eccentric psychoanalytically, for a Freudian would demand that it be a resummoning of an experience of unconscious processes.

27. Of course, since we are dealing with the attitudinal aspect as well as the affective one in considering this behavior, an alternative explanation would be that this behavior is an extreme and artificially induced form of cognitive dissonance.

28. See Lofland and Stark, "Becoming a World-Saver," 862–75. Also "Becoming a World-Saver Revisited," in *Conversion Careers: In and Out of the New Religions,* ed. J. T. Richardson (Beverly Hills, Calif.: Sage, 1977).

29. See J. B. Pratt, *The Religious Consciousness* (New York: Macmillan, 1920). See also Bernard Spilka, Ralph Hood, and Richard Gorsuch, *The Psychol-*

ogy of Religion: An Empirical Approach (Englewood Cliffs: Prentice-Hall, 1985), which contains a succinct summary of the research on conversion with sober judgments about its limitations.

30. *The Psychological Phenomena of Christianity* (New York: Scribner's, 1908); *Speaking with Tongues* (New Haven: Yale University Press, 1927).

31. L. Strickland, *The Psychology of Religious Experience* (New York: Abingdon, 1924).

32. M. I. Harrison, "Sources of Recruitment to Catholic Pentacostalism," *JSSR* 13 (1974): 49–64. M. B. McGuire, "Towards a Sociological Interpretation of the Catholic Pentacostal Movement," *RRR* 16 (1975): 94–104.

33. John P. Gavin's translation of *Psychologische Aspekte paulinischer Theologie,* FRLANT 131 (Goettingen: Vandenhoeck und Ruprecht, 1983; trans., Philadelphia: Fortress, 1987).

34. James T. Richardson, "Conflict in Conversion/Recruitment Research," *JSSR* 24, no. 2 (1985): 119–236.

35. Theissen, in *Psychological Aspects of Pauline Theology,* supplements depth psychology with various cognitive systems to emphasize his point.

36. Leon Festinger, Henry W. Riecken, and Stanley Schacter, *When Prophecy Fails: A Social and Psychological Study of a Modern Group that Predicted the Destruction of the World* (New York: Harper and Row, 1956).

37. Jane Allyn Hardwyck and Marcia Braden, "Prophecy Fails Again: A Report of a Failure to Replicate," *Journal of Abnormal and Social Psychology* 65 (1962): 136–41.

38. U. Wernik, "Cognitive Dissonance and its Solution: The Application of a Psychological Model to the Status of Christology in New Testament Scripture" [in Hebrew] (M. S. thesis, Hebrew University, 1972).

39. Leon Festinger, Stanley Schachter, and Kurt Bach, *Social Pressures in Informal Groups: A Study of Human Factors in Housing* (Palo Alto: Stanford University Press, 1950); Leon Festinger, *A Theory of Cognitive Dissonance* (Evanston: Row Peterson, 1957). For a general review of the literature see Robert B. Zajonc, "The Concepts of Balance, Congruity and Dissonance," *Public Opinion Quarterly* 24 (1960): 280–96.

40. For example, T. C. Brock, "Implications of Conversion and Magnitude of Cognitive Dissonance," *JSSR* 1 (1962): 198–203.

41. Robert A. Wicklund and Jack W. Brehm, *Perspectives on Cognitive Dissonance* (Hillsdale, N.J.: Lawrence Erlbaum Associates, 1976), 98–124.

42. Leon Festinger, with the collaboration of Vernon Allen, Marcia Braden, Lance Kirkpatrick Canon, Jon R. Davidson, Jon D. Jecker, Sara B. Kiesler, and Elaine Walster, *Conflict, Decision and Dissonance* (Stanford: Stanford University Press, 1964).

43. Robert P. Carroll, in *When Prophecy Fails: Cognitive Dissonance in the Prophetic Traditions of the Old Testament* (New York: Seabury Press, 1979), 87–88, agrees with me that hermeneutical activity has the effect of reducing dissonance. He applies this perception to Old Testament prophecy.

44. See, for example, "Commitment and the Internal Organization of Millennial Movements," *American Behavioral Scientist* 16, no. 2 (December 1972): 143–219. See also Leon Festinger, "The Psychological Effects of Insufficient Re-

ward," *American Psychologist* 16 (1961): 1–11; also *Conflict, Decision, and Dissonance.*

45. See Leon Festinger and J. M. Carlsmith, "Cognitive Consequences of Forced Compliance," *Journal of Abnormal and Social Psychology* 58 (1959): 203–10. Later Bem, "Self-Perception Theory," *Advances in Experimental Social Psychology* (New York: Academic Press, 1972), 6: 1–62, noted that this might be due to an inference made by the experimental subjects of the basis of observing their own behavior. They would have thought, "I must have believed the statement I made if I was willing to make it for such a small fee," or "I must really not have believed the statement if they had to pay me so much to make it."

46. Festinger and Carlsmith, "Cognitive Consequences of Forced Compliance," 205.

47. See, for example, L. Rambo's analytical article in the *Encyclopedia of Religion.*

For references to other ancient literatures, see the General Index.

OTHER HEBREW LITERATURE

GENERAL INDEX

Abraham, 120–21, 123, 181, 195, 213,263
Adam, 41, 42, 43, 65–66, 68, 152, 183
Adoption metaphor, 249–50, 347n29
Ananias, 8, 310n24
Ancient of days, 41, 57
Angelic transformation, 46–47
Anthropology, vocabulary of ethnography, 20–21
Anthrōpos, 65–66, 132
Antinomianism, 117, 144–45
Antioch, 26, 187–90, 201, 213, 217
Antiochus IV, 107, 222
Apocalypse of Abraham, 42
Apocalypse of Zephaniah, 42
Apocalypse: sociology of, 158–59, 165; ties to mysticism, 317n31, 339n25
Apokalypsis (revelation), 13
Apostolic council, 238–41
Apostolic Decree, 189, 197, 199, 236, 342n13, 346n18
Apuleius, *The Golden Ass*, 23–24, 54, 311n37, 311n38
Aquila, 222, 238, 346n23
Aristeas, 199
Ascension of Isaiah, 42, 49
Astral transformation, 24–25, 50
Augustine, 3, 227, 287, 294
ben Azzai, 335n32

Babylonian exile, 31, 52, 280
Baptism, 23, 27, 61–62, 63–64, 69, 134–38, 334n30
Belial, 167
Biography, xi; romantic, xiii, 307n5; in ancient world, 3–4

Caesar, transformation of, 24–25
Canaan, 30; influence on Daniel, 320n67

Castration, 206, 208, 209
Christ. *See* Jesus
Christianity: modern internal conversion, 6, 38, 287; Lutheran, 5, 287; roots in Jewish apocalyptic mysticism, 7, 16, 37, 41, 149, 168, 320n64; born-again, 21, 326n14; disunified beginnings, 26, 216–17; Jesus Freaks, 28; Pentacostal, 38; concept of immortal soul, 47; Ethiopic, 47; church fathers on angelic mediator, 51, 320n59; modern unfamiliarity with ecstasy, 61; and baptism, 63–64, 137, 158, 179; Pauline political threat, 70, 266; God-fearers attracted to, 93–95, 105, 114, 222, 265, 272; attracted to Judaism, 124, 141, 151, 210, 255; Hellenistic mystery religion, 136, 137, 149; isolation of gentile churches, 142, 155, 222, 268; history of Jewish Christianity, 146, 150, 256, 271, 272–73, 275; success of Pauline gentile church, 147, 267–68, 272–73; apocalypticism of, 159–60, 165, 271–72, 273; and pagan civic cults, 164, 338n21; as threat to civil order, 164–65; persecutions of, 165, 252; ideal Pauline community, 172; church as body of Christ, 172–73; development of Eucharist and Lord's Supper rituals, 173–74; similarity to Essenism, 178–80; taking advantage of persecution of Judaism, 206–07; cognitive dissonance in early church, 206, 265, 267, 268; Pharisaic, 71, 214; non-Pauline dietary rules in early church, 236; attractiveness to women, 270; Catholic, 287; Unification Church, 289; Mormon, 311n29; and *Shiur Koma*, 316n18; influence in *Joseph and*

362